36⁶⁰

BARUCH LEVINE
University of Illinois at Chicago Circle

Group
Psychotherapy

Practice and Development

PRENTICE-HALL, INC., *Englewood Cliffs, N.J. 07632*

Library of Congress Cataloging in Publication Data

Levine, Baruch.
    Group psychotherapy.

    Bibliography: p.
    Includes index.
    1. Group psychotherapy. I. Title.
RC488.L48   616.8'915   78-11392
ISBN 0-13-365296-3

©1979 by Prentice-Hall, Inc., Englewood Cliffs, N.J. 07632

Printed in the United States of America

10   9   8   7   6

Editorial/production supervision and interior design by Scott Amerman
Cover design by Jorge Hernandez
Manufacturing buyer: Nancy Myers

PRENTICE-HALL INTERNATIONAL, INC., *London*
PRENTICE-HALL OF AUSTRALIA, PTY. LIMITED, *Sydney*
PRENTICE-HALL OF CANADA, LTD., *Toronto*
PRENTICE-HALL OF INDIA PRIVATE LIMITED, *New Delhi*
PRENTICE-HALL OF JAPAN, INC., *Tokyo*
PRENTICE-HALL OF SOUTHEAST ASIA PTE LTD., *Singapore*
WHITEHALL BOOKS LIMITED, *Wellington, New Zealand*

This book is dedicated to Ginger (Virginia Gallogly)
for her inspiration and help
through her roles as my co-therapist,
co-author, colleague, and wife.

Contents

Foreword

The use of group approaches in helping to alleviate personal anguish, inner turmoil and to help individuals cope more effectively with the problems of daily living is indeed widespread. Group modalities are utilized in prisons, in-patient psychiatric facilities, mental health clinics, family service agencies, hospitals, and in the private practice of psychotherapy and counseling. Groups are sometimes organized for specific patient populations: alcoholics, drug abusers, epileptics, asthmatics, schizophrenics, neurotics, character disorders, sex offenders, parents, teenagers, the aged, and relatives of the terminally ill to name just a few.

The level and depth at which such groups will be conducted depend on several factors: the function of the agency or institution; the purpose(s) of organizing the group; the nature of the problems for which the members are seeking help; and the experience and training of the leader.

Some groups will have a more educational emphasis, others will have more of a supportive function, while others will be directed more to the uncovering and the working through of intra- and inter-personal conflicts.

Regardless, however, of the primary emphasis, the leader must have a basic understanding of individual, inter-personal, and group dynamics if he is to comprehend and utilize the therapeutic and educational potential of the group process.

A group is not inherently therapeutic. When people are brought together in a small group various forces are generated that can be harnessed for therapeutic and educational influence, while others must be mediated or blocked since they can impede the development of the therapeutic alliance and be destructive to individual members.

The lack of successful outcome or the occasional casualty is often the result of improper selection and balancing of the group or the failure on the part of the therapist to sufficiently comprehend the individual, interpersonal, or the group dynamic elements.

Baruch Levine's book makes a significant contribution to the theory and practice of group psychotherapy. He has analyzed in a rather clear, organized manner the dynamics of group formation and development and its impact on the individual members and the group therapist. He clearly presents the individual, the sub-group, and the group-as-a-whole issues that characterize each stage of the therapeutic process. In presenting these issues he offers valuable suggestions and guides for therapeutic interventions which never lose sight of the individual member's needs, conflicts, and aspirations. In contrast, other books on group therapy seem to focus on a single aspect: either the group issues or the individual issues.

Despite my excellent training and my many years as a practitioner and teacher, I must admit that a number of Levine's formulations and concepts are intriguing, have given me much food for thought, and have added a new dimension to my theoretical understanding and to my practice of group therapy. This book will be valuable to the experienced clinician whether he be a psychiatrist, a psychologist, or a social worker.

Educators, supervisors and trainers too will find this book a valuable compliment to Slavson's *Textbook on Analytic Group Psychotherapy* and Yalom's *Theory and Practice of Group Psychotherapy.*

Emanuel Hallowitz,
Professor, University of Chicago

Preface

In my twenty-five years of clinical group leadership, I have had many opportunities to formulate, test, and reformulate my own and other peoples' theories. For the past eighteen of those twenty-five years, my students, consultees, and supervisees have served as sounding boards and reliability checks in their reactions to the use of my theories in their practice. This book is the product of the studying, practicing, teaching, and theorizing of group psychotherapy through my professional life.

Four major areas have been the object of my thinking: 1. pre-group planning and preparation, 2. group development, 3. emotional dynamics, and, 4. leadership modes and styles.

In Part 1, Chapter 1, purpose, grouping, and structure are posed as the basic elements of pre-group planning. The three elements are interrelated in that any variation in one necessitates variations in the other two (for instance, closed-ended group with a short-term structure needs a more delimited purpose and more homogeneous membership than a long-term, open-ended group). The juxtaposition of purpose, grouping, and structure represents a new way of thinking about the problem of organizing groups for the myriad of therapeutic purposes prevalent today. While many variations and examples are discussed in the chapter, the intent is to provide a way to think about the organization of group services, rather than to provide a gospel about which services should be rendered and how.

Chapters 2 and 3 of Part 1 deal with preparing the client and preparing the therapist respectively. While these chapters are by no means profound in their theory, they are intended to help with some of the basics of preparation for service.

Part II represents the major theoretical contribution of the book. In the theory of therapy group development summarized in Chapter 1 and elaborated through the next seven chapters, there are several major theoretical objectives. The first objective is to discover the parallels between individual development and the individual's experience in the course of group development. These parallels have implications both for the parameters of the group and for potentials for treatment of the individual through the group. For example, groups of children or adults who are chronic schizophrenic cannot be expected to develop very far, but can be expected to gain a deal from a protracted period of low-level group development.

A second objective is to synthesize the sequential and recurrent theories of group development. In my practice with groups, I have found that some phenomena occur in sequence while other phenomena recur over and over in a spiral. While adhering to sequential theories, I have had to explain recurrent phenomena in terms of regression. While adhering to recurrent theory, I have found it difficult to account for growth and change except through the improved coping with the recurrent phenomena. The theory of group development presented in Part II attempts to identify group phenomena which are sequential and subsume those under four developmental phases: parallel, inclusion, mutuality, and termination. Recurrent group phenomena are collected into recurrent crisis concepts: authority, intimacy, and separation. The interaction of the phases and crises is described in Part II, Chapter 1 and represents a synthesis of the recurrent and sequential schools of therapy group development.

There are many possible variations for a group on its unique developmental path. A group may become fixated at an early phase of development and/or may not resolve any of its recurrent crises. For example, a group of adults who are chronic schizophrenics may remain in the parallel phase for several months to several years. Another possibility is that a group will move from one phase to the next without sufficiently resolving earlier phase issues, or a group may move on to the next phase but demonstrate rather constricted or limited versions of that advanced phase. For example, a group of children may resolve their parallel and inclusion phase phenomena, but they may have a rather narrow version of mutuality as compared to a group of normal or neurotic adults.

In the use of this theory over the past several years, I have often run into a student or consultee who says that the theory simply doesn't apply to his or her group. When we look into the matter in more detail, we usually find that the group is hung up in an early phase of development. It isn't that the theory doesn't apply as much as the group didn't develop beyond the parallel or inclusion phase. Usually, when the student and I have taken a closer look we begin to see not only that the group is located in the developmental theory, but we can also see why it is still there.

The third major objective in the theory of group development is to make connections between individual and group dynamics that can facilitate a dual focus: individual and group. Many group therapists simply decide that either the individual or the group is more important and give little throught to the other. Other therapists attempt to keep the dual focus on individuals and on groups in balance but find themselves most often lapsing into one or the other. The notions of differentiation and emotional dilemmas, in particular, help to bring out the simultaneous issues for individuals and group dynamics as they interact in the developing group.

Part III is a potpourri of other important group theories. Chapter 1 brings together a presentation and discussion of the major emotional dynamics in therapy groups. These emotional dynamics are discussed from the standpoint of how they function within and between members. It has always intrigued me to consider how little theory has been developed on a subject as important as emotional dynamics in therapy groups. Anxiety, hostility, identification, empathy, transference, and conflict are the major emotional dynamics discussed in Chapter 1, Part III.

Chapter 2 of Part III discusses the therapist's role in the course of group development and the differential use of time sphere (here and now or there and then) foci at different points in the developmental life of the group. The chapter cites the necessity for variable roles in relation to different groups and the need for different roles at various points in group development. There is nothing more controversial in group therapy than the use of time sphere focus. In Chapter 2, I make a case for selective use of here and now and there and then and attempt to discuss the merits and need for both.

Part III, Chapter 3—co-leadership—has truly been coauthored. The reader can readily see how the writing style in Chapter 3 differs from the rest of the book. Collaboration in writing came easily to Virginia Gallogly and I since we have had much practice in collaborating as cotherapists of several long-term therapy groups and as coleaders of various training workshops and consultative ventures. However, the relative ease of collaboration on Chapter 3 is the product of much working out of our co-therapy relationship. Many of the considerations for cotherapists have come from our own experiences as well as experiences of cotherapists we have supervised.

This book has been designed to be used as both a text and a reference. Consequently, there may be repetition particularly in the discussion of group development. Part II is designed to be used in many different ways. Chapter 1 of that section provides the overview of group development and can be used in a basic course in group therapy. The introduction in Chapters 2 through 8 can serve for a little more elaboration on group developmental theory. However, the remainder of the chapters on each phase and crisis are best used as a reference for a therapist as he works with a group and the group is in or near that phase or crisis. Continuous reading of Part II without application to an existing group might prove rather cumbersome. However, reading about a particular phase or crisis in detail while the reader is faced with the situation in a therapy group can prove quite useful.

There are a number of people to whom I am deeply indebted for their help in the development of the theory and the preparation of this document.

Foremost among these people is Virginia Gallogly who served as coordinator of research for the book and co-author of the last chapter.

I would also like to thank my daughter, Shauna Levine, for her help in the research.

Thank you to all the students and mental health professionals who provided the necessary audience, support, and challenge to my theories during my years of teaching and consultation. Special thanks to the students in my advanced group therapy seminar for their collaboration in the work of contrasting group theories: Sister Mirada Corde, Kevin Dubrow, Barbara Farnum, Susan Hartman, John Mazurek, John Rowe, Cache Seitz, and Susan Turner.

Last but not least, thanks to the several thousands of clients in several hundreds of groups that I have led, supervised, or consulted upon.

Baruch Levine

PART ONE

1

Preparing the Group

PURPOSES, GROUPING, AND STRUCTURE

Much of the therapist's influence on group development begins before the group meets. More can be done about the nature and direction of a therapy group during the organizational process than after the meetings start. Once group membership has been established, the combination of people with their individual characteristics, capacities, and aspirations in large part determines the limitations and potentials of the group's development. Although the group can grow significantly with the help of the therapist, the parameters of group growth and function are built in from the outset. (Slavson, 1964:198-99; Redl, 1966: 236-53; Bernstein, 1951).

Three major considerations in organizing therapy groups are: (1) group purpose, (2) group structure, and (3) group membership. Group purposes encompass the reasons why the group was organized and why each member attends. As the group develops, the therapist and group members negotiate, directly and indirectly, the purposes for the group during the process of group formation. Before the energies of any group can be mobilized for work, members and therapist must agree on the group's purposes or they must develop agreements in which the differing goals of all can be achieved (Cartwright and Zander, 1968:401-17). The purposes of the therapist and the members may be overt (consciously manifest in words and actions) or covert (unexpressed or unconscious). In therapy groups, the covert purposes of the therapist and the members most often need to be unearthed and reconciled if the group is not to be hampered in its work and development.

Group structure is the formal and informal parameters and patterns governing the organization and relationships among members and between the therapist and the members. Structural elements may be predetermined by the therapist or developed through the normative processes of the group. Whether or not the therapist predetermines structure, each group carves out its characteristic modes of operation through its interactive processes.

Grouping refers to the selecting and matching of members to participate in the group. Members are most often selected by the therapist, usually based on the therapist's ideas about which members will fit the kind of group contemplated or share the goals of the therapist and the other members.

Purpose, structure, and grouping, while discrete organizing entities of therapy groups, are interrelated and interdependent. A particular group may be conceived around any of the three organizing entities, but consideration of the other two must follow. Establishment of a purpose for a group immediately includes those people who are in need of this purpose and excludes those who are not. The structure considered for the group must be related to how the therapist thinks the purpose may be achieved for the kinds and combination of people to be involved in the group.

Purposes for Therapy Groups

Purpose is the core of group function. Therapy groups can be formed for an infinite variety of purposes. In general, the shorter the term of the group, the more the group needs a definitive purpose. Although long-term groups (more than 24 weekly sessions) can have a definitive purpose, the longer the term the more purpose can be a matter of group development. Longer-term groups can take a wider variety of purposes because the purposes undergo a negotiation process and the members can better accept diverse purposes. In addition, long-term groups have time to reconcile the differences among the members' purposes; short-term groups (fewer than 24 weekly sessions) have insufficient time to pursue many divergent purposes.

In short-term groups, commonality of purposes is essential; the common purpose reduces the time and energy needed to reconcile divergent purposes, a necessary step for a group to develop and work. Long-term groups develop basic affective bonds rather than common purposes and consequently can tolerate and support a wider array of purposes.

Another major dimension of group purposes established by the therapist arises from the intended treatment objectives for the members. Treatment objectives can be divided into three categories: supportive, interpersonal insight development, and intrapsychic insight development. The three major categories of treatment objectives are, by no means, mutually exclusive. Depending on their orientation and the assessed needs and capacities of their group members, group practitioners may incorporate any or all of these objectives, perhaps giving major thrust toward the objective they deem most appropriate.

Supportive treatment generally involves the restoration, enhancement, or maintenance of the person's levels and modes of function or problem solving or both. Authors dealing with supportive group treatment services are primarily concerned with purposes of therapists, members, and ultimately the group. (See, for example: Northen, 1969:86-115; Konopka, 1963:79-105; Hartford, 1971: 98; Levine, 1967:4-11.)

Authors concerned with interpersonal growth (for example: Yalom, 1975: 303; Whitaker and Lieberman, 1964:204-15; Bion, 1861:187-90) are concerned less about the individual reasons for each member coming for treatment and assume that, for those people capable of participation in groups, help will be provided through all members gaining insight, growth, and change in their relationships.

Authors concerned with intrapsychic insight development (for example: Slavson, 1964:107; Durkin, 1964:341-52) are also less concerned about individual reasons for prospective members coming for therapy and assume that the intrapsychic insight derived from the group will facilitate growth and change. These authors, of course, would not include in a group a member deemed incapable or inadvisable for insight development. Interpersonal and insight development group therapies are, in a sense, each singular in purpose. Their purposes are depth of interpersonal and/or intrapsychic insight and change. Thus, the specific reasons and purposes for each member are of less consequence than the various purposes that are achievable through interpersonal growth and insight development.

Supportive treatment services can be long or short-term and can address themselves to a wide array of objectives, such as socialization, crisis, transitional state, emotional relief, problem solving, and preparation for handling a wide variety of situations. While developing interpersonal growth and insight may be part of the objective in a supportive group, depending upon the particular purposes and members, more important is the need to consider the specific purposes for each member and the group and attempt to match the members accordingly.

Since many groups brought together by mental health professionals are composed of people not directly amenable to long-term depth of interpersonal and/or insight development, it is important that therapists contemplating more supportive groups not attempt to dilute the kinds of structures, principles, and practices appropriate to long-term groups but rather that they more positively consider principles and practices suited to the purposes, structures, and memberships that they must treat (Levinson, 1973:66-73). For example, most schizophrenics are not amenable to the depth of interpersonal growth and interaction aimed for by Yalom, Whitaker and Lieberman, Slavson, or Foulkes (1965). Chronic schizophrenics respond more effectively to groups with a clear delineation of the purposes and expectations, which one would hope are tailored to the realistic capacities and potentials of the members (for example, groups to help with preparing to leave the hospital, responding to post-hospital adjustment, learning to communicate and interact with other people). On the other hand, for those outpatient neurotics that are amenable to depth of interpersonal growth and/or insight development, the interpersonal and insight authors have much to contribute. The goal in these instances is fixed and consideration must then be given to the kind of members amenable to these goals and the kinds of structure that can help the members achieve these goals. Members may have individual goals within the larger context of interpersonal growth or insight development, but they converge on the purpose of the group set forth by the therapist. Members who are not amenable or do not for any reason want this growth should not be placed in such groups.

In sum, short-term groups and long-term groups aimed at supportive treatment should have purposes that are clear and common to all the members. Long-term groups aimed at interpersonal growth and/or insight development can and should have members with very divergent purposes within the rubric of interpersonal growth or insight development.

Structure of Therapy Groups

Group structure is the when, where, and how of therapy groups. Structure can facilitate or inhibit group development and the accomplishment of group purposes. Some aspects of structure must be determined by the therapist before the group meets; other aspects are best left for the group to determine and develop. Aspects of structure that the therapist must decide upon before the group meets are: (1) number of meetings the group will have; (2) how often the group will meet; (3) how long each meeting will last; (4) where the group will meet; (5) whether the group will be open-ended or closed; (6) what degree of political control will be retained by the therapist; (7) format meetings will have— for example, predetermined versus spontaneous. (For more discussion of structure see supportive groups: Hartford, 1971:159-91; Northen, 1969:86-115; Konopka, 1963:52-55; interpersonal and analytic groups: Yalom, 1975:276-99; Kadis et al., 1974:33-45; Whitaker and Lieberman, 1964:3-11.)

Time and Place. The number of meetings or length of time the group will meet should be related to the group's purposes and the members with whom these purposes are to be accomplished. Very often, the number of meetings is dictated by such external realities as the individual member's stay in the agency or hospital, or the length of the school year. When externalities dictate the number of meetings, the purposes and grouping must be oriented to those realities. Otherwise, the number of meetings should be related to the purposes to be accomplished.

Most groups meet once a week. Generally such scheduling fits most people's inner time clocks and allows sufficient continuity from week to week for groups to develop. Meeting twice a week on a protracted basis, although it will not double the rate at which the group develops, will allow somewhat faster development; how much faster will be dependent on who is in the group. Groups meeting less than once a week will be somewhat hampered in development since some of the continuity in development and impact tends to be lost between meetings. Biweekly or monthly meetings may suffice for many supportive or educational groups not requiring group development for goal achievement.

The one to one-and-one-half hour group meeting has become standard in therapy groups, although there is no logical reason for this. Ideally the duration of meetings should be related to the nature of the members in the group, the purposes for which the group meets, and the format of the meetings. In general, the duration of the group meetings must be related to the capacities of the members to handle the time span. Meetings that are too long for the capacities of the members may create undue anxiety and result in defensive superficiality, if not outright resistance in the form of nonparticipation, lateness, and absences. Duration can be increased as the group becomes able to handle more time. It is usually better to start with shorter meetings and increase the time as the members appear able to handle more time. It is also generally better to start with a short but definite time span, rather than to have a longer official time, then end the meeting when it stops being productive. The variable ending begins to be seen by the members as a judgment on whether the group has been productive. When this occurs, it can seriously interfere with the progress of the group by creating guilt about inevitable regressions or overexpectations after particularly productive meetings. The range of time for meetings can vary from ten minutes to several hours. In some groups, shorter, more frequent meetings are better (for example, with children, inpatients, withdrawn groups). Where the structure of the host agency or other practical realities dictate the time span, the format of meetings should be varied in ways that will help delimit the time for intensive interaction.

The room where the group meets and its set-up can greatly enhance or distract from the group's development. In general, the room should be the right size for the group (Winick and Holt, 1961:56-62). Too large a room can detract from feelings of intimacy. Too small a room can frighten members if they are prematurely forced into intimate contact because their sense of personal space is violated. For some groups it is good to have a meeting place that allows members to come in and out easily or that makes it easy for members or potential members to hang around near the group; this pertains primarily to inpatient groups. In many inner-city project groups, insufficient attention is given to where the members must come and what realistic or imagined dangers they must face to get to meetings. For children's groups, potential distractions in the room must be considered; telephones, property belonging to other people, and chairs with wheels are possible distractions that children could use for acting out, requiring an unnecessary degree of limit-setting. In general, a room for children's groups should be as free as possible of potential distractions and needs for limits. Although a few limits are essential for children's groups, every effort should be made to reduce the number of potential sources of distraction and acting out that result in a need for setting too many limits.

The traditional circle is the optimum seating arrangement for group meetings. When a circle is not possible, it is important to avoid having too many people in a straight line. Seating three or more people in a row along one side of a room makes it difficult and often impossible for the members on each end to communicate directly with each other. Although the proper room arrangement is often impossible, the potential effects of improper seating should be reduced as much as possible (Phillips, 1966:42; Steinzor, 1950:552-55).

Many groups meet in an open circle with nothing but a low coffee table in the middle, an arrangement in which the furniture doesn't give a sense of separation. However, meeting around a table can be useful for many groups. In groups of acting-out children a table may reduce the opportunities for physical combat. Children generally sit next to their friends, with their enemies across the table. Because the child must make a special effort to reach someone on the other side of the table, the impulsive hitting or kicking may be reduced. Tables may also prove useful in groups where members are working on some non-verbal project during meetings. Thus, the members can feel that they are part of a larger structure while they are each working, even though each may be doing something as an individual. For some groups, the table helps to give further support to the group concept and serves as a link for all the members. In many adolescent, withdrawn, and combative groups where some members are ambivalent or very hostile to being in the group, the table delineates the group, and ambivalent or hostile members can express their wishes to not be in the group by sitting away from the table, yet remaining in the room. Finally, in groups where members are extremely self-conscious and need to feel less conspicuous by staying in the room, the table provides partial protection from the full physical exposure to others. Any members who for physical or emotional reasons need partial seclusion from others may find it easier to sit around a table.

Open-ended vs Closed.   The choice of an open-ended structure or a closed structure (Kadis et al., 1968:101-104) for groups is very often related to exigencies of the agency or therapists. Closed groups, that is, groups in which everyone starts and finishes together, are generally suited to situations where outside realities dictate how long the members can remain in the group—for example, the school year in school groups—or where the task is defined well enough to be accomplished by most or all the members in a specified period of time. The number of meetings for closed groups is usually limited, since closed group structure is most often chosen because of time limitations. The major problem with closed group structure is the assumption that, from either a long-term or a short-term standpoint, everyone in the group can accomplish his or her purpose in the same or a similar period of time. Even for a clearly defined short-term process, there can be no guarantees that all the members will arrive at the same place at the same or similar times. Longer-term closed groups often have the problem of people dropping out either prematurely or because they have accomplished their goals for group participation.

Many therapists equate the use of the closed group structure with short-term groups. Yet, short-term groups can have an open-ended structure if they have a sufficient supply of new members to sustain the group as those who achieve their goals stop participating. Examples of this are crises and transitional states. However, if the reason for forming the group is a need that does not frequently recur or if there are insufficient new prospects for membership, the closed group can be used to meet these needs.

Control and Authority. A major aspect of group structure is the political climate of the group and the relative balance of political control between the therapist and the members. Some forms of group therapy require a high degree of control by the therapist, others, a low degree. Sound group development requires sufficient levels of control—in relation to who is in the group—to help the group get started, then the progressive transfer of the political power to the group as the group is ready to assume that power (see Chapter 1, Part 3). In general, the younger the group and/or the lower the social-emotional capacity of the members, the more political control by the therapist will be essential. If and as the group develops, more political control can be vested in the group (see authority crises, Chapter 3, Part 2). The initial structural determination for the therapist is how much and what kinds of controls the group will need at the outset, then the appropriate timing of the transfer of this power.

Format for Meetings. Format of the meetings refers to the nature of the group activity when it is together and the person who determines those activities. Most often when therapists speak of group structure they are really talking about the format for meetings. Dimensions for format range from verbal to non-verbal forms of interaction and from preplanned or programmed experiences to spontaneous experiences. Different schools of group therapy vary in accordance with their position on the verbal-nonverbal and predetermined-spontaneous continua. The wide range in structural format for group psychotherapy, particularly in children's groups can be seen in the nondirective approach of Slavson (1950:124-37) as compared to the more directive approach of Churchill and Ganter et al. (1967:47-52).

Aside from the philosophical stance of the therapist with respect to how group therapy is accomplished, the determination of format should be related to the intended goals for the group, the nature of the members, and the number, frequency, and duration of meetings. Most groups of latency-aged children are not capable of sitting and talking for long periods of time. If the duration of children's meetings will, of necessity, exceed their capacity for talking, then non-verbal activities are essential. If group members, because of age or unwillingness are unable to participate in verbal interaction, then nonverbal techniques can be more fruitfully employed. In some groups, verbal techniques that do not focus directly on treatment issues are at times essential. In most adolescent groups, early meetings often are more profitably spent in building relationships through whatever topics arise than in forcing discussion of more crucial therapeutic issues. In groups of schizophrenics, gaining experiences in verbal interactions around either spontaneous topics or preplanned but safe and less revealing subjects is often more crucial for social-emotional growth than direct discussion of problems. In other words, it is often important that the format allow for or support development of communication and relationships before that network of communication and relationships can be employed more directly for therapeutic benefit. The therapy in such groups lies in the development of communication and relationships more than in focusing on the problem. Thus, the first decision in format is based on what the members need because of their capacities or incapacities for interaction.

The problem of predetermination of subject matter for discussion or non-verbal activities is related to the capacities of the members, the purposes for which the group is formed, and the number of meetings intended for the group. If a very short-term process is proposed for a closed group, then a preplanned curriculum of subjects or activities might serve well. Without sufficient time for the group to develop, the group's dependency on the therapist for structural format might as well be accepted. Certainly, if the group is to meet for fewer than eight meetings, a prestructured program would serve the group better than an attempt to help the group develop. An outpatient adult group can barely resolve their inclusion struggles in fewer than eight meetings. The danger in having an unstructured closed group come together for four to six meetings is that the group will more than likely terminate with a great many stirred up but unresolved authority and inclusion-feeling issues, which will more than likely leave the group angry. Thus, a highly structured format leaving less room for deeper group development might better serve to get across an intended, and, one would hope, clear and delimited purpose. At the same time, such a format would run less risk of members leaving with unrequited anger about the group (MacLennan and Felsenfeld, 1968:74-76).

Most outpatient adult groups of neurotics and people with stronger social and emotional capacities (either open or closed groups that meet more than twelve times) can and do develop their own formats in the process of norm development. Whitaker and Lieberman (1964), more than most writers on group psychotherapy, bring out the normative processes and their role in development of group structure and culture in long-term group psychotherapy aimed at inter-personal growth. Groups of lesser capacity that don't meet often may need a more preconceived structural format. Groups of lesser capacity that meet for more than twelve meetings can, if and as they become able, take increasing responsibility for their format, verbal content, and/or activities. The process involves the therapist taking increasing cognizance of the members' expressed or implied wishes for the group and increasingly helping the group to either more directly express and negotiate their wishes for format, content, and activities or develop norms toward increasing spontaneity.

Group, Family or Individual Therapy. Prior to any discussion of selection and matching of persons to be included in groups, some consideration must be given to whether group, family, or individual therapy is most appropriate for a particular individual. The problems of selecting one of these treatment modalities stem more from their overlapping in potentials for help rather than in their mutually exclusive possibilities. As the author's bias toward groups would lead him to more decisions in favor of group therapy, others with a bias toward individual and family modes of treatment would tend toward more decisions for individual or family treatment.

For the author, the decision between family and other modalities is more critical than the decision between individual and group modalities. Where potential for helping exists in face-to-face interaction among those who are most significant to the person deemed to be in difficulty, the possibilities of family or couple treatment must be given first consideration. The question of how to determine which problems are intrapersonal and which are interpersonal (or how much of each) and the question of how to determine which problems are reactive and which are or have become primary to the individual are too large for the scope of this book. Suffice to say that the dilemma between family and other modes of treatment will need further coexistence in the therapy field to truly determine and differentiate their respective efficacies beyond the protestations of the indoctrinated.

Group therapy can help with most anything that individual therapy can, providing an appropriate group is available and the individual will accept the group as the mode of treatment. If the individual will not accept group therapy or if an appropriate group is not available, then, of necessity, individual or family therapy is the answer. However, for a number of people, group therapy is contraindicated. The characteristic these people have in common is their imperviousness to other people (Neighbor et al., 1963:419). Highly structured paranoid personalities and people in a manic phase are not amenable to group therapy. Most people with paranoid tendencies or people with paranoid schizophrenia are amenable to groups of the appropriate composition—that is, groups composed of other people at a similar social-emotional level. Paranoid people who tighten their projective defenses *every* time they interact with others should not be in group therapy. People who are in a manic state or who perenially function at a hypomanic level whenever in contact with others are too unproductively stimulated by group situations.

A person in a manic phase is not reachable by group therapy, but may be reachable after the descent from the mania. People with hypomanic personalities may never be reachable through group therapy if they cannot ever alight in interpersonal situations.

While the question of the appropriate group is important for all potential members, for a few kinds of people the availability of an appropriate group is crucial. People who are in a crisis or anxiety state before they enter a group must get over the crisis or reduce their anxiety before they join. However, if in the unlikely event that a group exists with everyone facing the same or similar crisis, then these people can be served.

People with character disorders, addictions, and narcissistic personalities must be able to tolerate some anxiety if they are to be placed in heterogenous groups with others who can tolerate some degree of anxiety. If a person with a character disorder, addiction, or primary narcissism cannot tolerate much or any anxiety, then he or she can be placed either in a group of similar people which is structured to their needs and capacities or helped in some way other than group therapy in a heterogenous group. These people will tend to hold back the process of heterogenous groups or persist in seeking a primary dependence on the therapist to the exclusion of others in the group.

Severely depressed people are also impervious to others. People who enter a group while in a state of severe depression tend to usurp a great deal of time and energy while fending off any help or empathy that the others might provide. The depression and the fending off tend to depress and/or anger the other members to the point of futility and can be disruptive, if not lethal, to the group. It is usually better to help the severely depressed person individually until the depression lifts, then allow him to enter group. However, if, and only if, a group of all depressed people is available, then group therapy can be the treatment of choice (Levine and Schild, 1969). If people get into crises, anxiety states, or depressive episodes while in a group, then the group can help them during this time. It is only upon entry and in early group meetings that people in a crisis, anxiety state, or depression create too much difficulty for themselves and the other group members.

Grouping for Therapy

No single activity on the part of the group therapist can influence the nature and destiny of a therapy group as much as the selection and matching of people for membership. The potentials, limitations, and balance of a therapy group are inherent in its composition. Once a group is together, there is some leeway in how much and how far the therapist can help the group develop, but the ultimate horizons for the group are formed by the membership (Hare, 1962: 206; Yalom and Rand, 1966:267-76). The central question in the determination of grouping is in what ways members should be similar or different. The kinds of similarities and differences among members that become significant for a particular group vary in relation to the purposes and structure of the group. Considerable literature deals with characteristics deemed significant for grouping and the range and balance of these characteristics. (See, for example, Wax, 1960; Northen, 1969:95; Redl, 1951:76-96; Samuels, 1964:411-420; Freedman and Sweet, 1954:355-64; Shepherd, 1954:3-4; Slavson, 1964:198-232; Yalom, 1975:246-75; Thelen, 1954:139; Glatzer, 1956:258-65; Cartwright and Harary, 1956:277-93.)

Group Composition. In general, *groups aimed at short term and/or supportive treatment should consist of people who share significant similarities; groups aimed at interpersonal or genetic insight should have a balance of people who are similar and different.* Differences among members of longer-term therapy groups are conducive toward intervention and change being built into the group process, but similarities are more immediately conducive toward group cohesion. Consequently, in long-term groups aimed at interpersonal and/or genetic insight development it is important to have different and diverse people, but each person should have at least one other person with whom he or she can readily identify.

Considerable research evidence supports the notion of similarity among group members being conducive to interpersonal attraction and mutual support and of differences being conducive to confrontation and change. Izard (1960: 484-85) found that personality similarity facilitates the mutual expression of positive affect and attraction. Harrison and Lubin (1965:286-301) had similar findings with respect to person orientation and task orientation similarities and differences. Smith (1974:261-77) found that when he formed groups where composition fostered confrontation, compliance to group was heightened. When he formed groups that combined confrontation and support, internalization was heightened. (Smith was employing Kelman's [1963:399-451] notions about the levels of group influence: compliance, identification, and internalization.)

Criteria for grouping begins with consideration of the intended purpose and structure for the group. *The shorter the term of the group, the more its purposes need to be clearly stated and common to all members. The longer the term of the group, the less its purposes need to be clearly stated and common to all the members.* Although a long-term group can have a clearly stated and common purpose, it isn't as crucial as it is for a short term group.

The clearest and commonest purposes arise from a common fate anticipated by all the members. If members are all facing the same or similar event in the *near* future, they will be able to readily identify with each other around that common fate and will feel free sooner to share their feelings openly about that fate. (Examples of common-fate groups include orientation groups, predischarge groups, pre-operative groups, and groups following serious illness with debilitating residuals.)

Next to common fate, common problems can serve as a viable basis for grouping, either into short-term or long-term groups, depending on what range or depth of helping is anticipated. Common problems often involve changes in life circumstances; they may center around social roles, life stage, or social and vocational task performance. (Examples are parent groups, posthospital groups, single mothers' groups, and postdivorce groups.)

Age of Group Members. After common fate and common problems the next most important factor in grouping is the age range of the potential members. In a study of twenty-four outpatient adult psychotherapy groups, the author found that age similarity was the one factor of many that was significantly related to interpersonal attraction and freedom of expression. Sex, marital status, parental status, religion, race, national origin, and educational and vocational levels were found to have little or no bearing except when they were combined with age differences (Levine, 1968).

Similarities in age function as a major force for cohesion in both short-term and long-term groups. Differences in age function as a major divisive force, particularly in short-term groups (Ziller and Exlin, 1958). The major problem with age difference is that a propensity exists for mutual rejection between people of differing ages. These people tend to keep their real disagreements and conflicts hidden from each other longer than people who are closer in age. People in the same age range tend to be more easily attracted to each other and feel freer to openly express their differences and conflicts sooner (Ziller and Exlin, 1958). As a consequence, almost all groups formed with a proximity of age will have an easier path to group formation and free expression. Unless there is some common fate which can strongly overcome the age differences, short-term groups (fewer than twenty-four weekly meetings) are most productive when members are in the same age range. The very differences that members might repress in short-term groups can and do become important facets of insight therapy in long-term groups (more than twenty-four weekly meetings). Thus, if the objective of a long-term group is insight therapy, a wide range in age is desirable.

The definition of wide or narrow age range varies within age categories and may also vary with the settings. Latency-aged children from six to twelve years old are best grouped within a one-year age span or school grade, but they can tolerate a two-year range without age differences having serious effects. For junior high children of thirteen to fifteen years, age disparity beyond a range of one year or one school grade can have an effect. If the members all come from different schools, a two-year age span might be tolerable. For high school freshmen, the one-year age span is best. Juniors and seniors in high school can tolerate the two-year span quite easily. Some sophomores can tolerate being with the juniors and seniors without the age span's having negative effects; others cannot (Sugar, 1975:43). Young adults can vary in age from eighteen to thirty without its having too much effect. However, when a group of eighteen- to twenty-two-year-olds includes those in college and those who work, then the differences in social role add to age difference phenomena. Young adults who are in college might be best served in groups whose members are all college aged and college-attending. Young adult groups that begin after college age can tolerate age spreads from the mid-twenties to mid-thirties without the age span differences taking effect. However, an age spread of more than twenty years will be likely to show the effects of age span differences.

Sex of Group Members. Sex as a factor in grouping doesn't generally create major difficulty except during the early adolescent years (thirteen to fifteen). Groups of latency-aged children can be coed; groups of older adolescents are often more effective when coed than when they are all one sex. In general and for most purposes, adult groups are better coed unless the members have a particular common problem related to sexual roles. In junior high and first-year high school groups, coed groups will take extremely long to develop. These groups are difficult enough to help become overtly productive without adding the burden of overcoming the stimulation of the opposite sex present in the meeting (Sugar, 1975). The problem is that more often than not, 12- to 15-year-olds cannot productively manage and express their feelings in therapy groups with the opposite sex. In any coed group, it would be important to have at least two of each sex; nearly half of each sex is still better.

Social-Emotional Capacity and Personality. Social-emotional level and capacity is the next most important factor in grouping. In general, it is best for group members to be in the same or similar social-emotional range for direct therapeutic purposes. Social-emotional level differences are of less consequence if the group is aimed at an immediate common fate or common problems. Group members in the chronic schizophrenic range generally do better in groups of other chronic schizophrenics or with a mixture of chronic and acute schizophrenics. Aside from the social-emotional level commonality, the probability is that there will be very different treatment objectives for people with chronic schizophrenia than for people who have more neurotic or characterological difficulties. People in the neurotic range of social-emotional function are often too uneasy and too frightened by chronic schizophrenics and find it too difficult or too frightening to identify with them as well as present their own thoughts and feelings. The decision about similarities and differences in social-emotional levels must be related to the anticipated mode of treatment as well as to the possible difficulties arising from diversity itself. If the objective is insight development, then only those people for whom insight development is useful as a major facet of treatment should be in the group. If the objective is supportive therapy or perhaps supportive therapy with some attempt at improving interpersonal relations, then there is less need to differentiate social-emotional levels. The process of insight development for those who are amenable to it might be too disturbing for group members unable to handle that degree or kind of insight (Kadis, 1974:59).

The above paragraph refers only to social-emotional level and not to personality types. By and large it is best to have diversity of personalities in any group (Glatzer, 1956:258-65). The very difference among varied personalities in coping mechanisms is a major source of benefit to all group members. If everyone in the group shares the same patterns of coping with emotions and life situations, it will sharply reduce or eliminate the vital differences in feelings and opinions that contribute to questioning and challenging existing patterns of behavior. In groups where members share too many personality or behavior patterns—as in groups of addicts of any kind (food, alcohol, or drugs)—the structure of the group must be altered to provide intervention into the modes of behavior. Ways to stimulate counter measures must be created or the full burden of intervention will fall on the therapist. It is helpful if each member of the group can find support in at least one other member for his mode of coping, but it is also important that differences and challenges to his coping mechanisms exist in the group, preferably through other members who differ, or else through structures that intervene.

Behavior Patterns of Group Members. A diversity in behavior patterns within the group can be useful to most groups. Differences among the members with regard to aggressiveness-withdrawness, domination-submission, expressive-constricted, and any other behavior pattern relevant to the particular group can provide an essential contrast and balance which enables members to grow through their interacting with opposites. Most important is that in any behavioral diversity at least two members share any extreme. However, for short-term groups, similarity in behavior patterns might lend essential support to members, especially when they are extremely withdrawn, submissive, or constricted. (Examples of such groups might be withdrawn groups and assertiveness-training groups.) In the short term, the behavioral differences can be shocking and not particularly productive, but in the long term the diverse members can gain a great deal from each other (see the discussion of children's groups later in this chapter). The group members need sufficient time to overcome the shock of the opposite behavior and then incorporate some of this behavior into their own modes of function (Slavson, 1950; Redl, 1951:76-96).

There are a host of other idiosyncratic criteria that can only be accounted for on a person-by-person and group-by-group basis. These criteria are sometimes found serendipitously and at other times may be anticipated. For example, in one of the author's private adult groups, a new member had a particularly difficult time entering the group, even though she seemed well matched with the group in many ways. It turned out that she was not as physically attractive as the other members. By chance all the other members of this open-ended group were unusually handsome and pretty people. This wasn't apparent to my cotherapist and me until the difficulty arose. While we didn't feel that this member was particularly unattractive, she didn't feel equal to the others in physical appearance. This turned out to be a major facet of her difficulties and she was unable to continue in the group.

Each open-ended group develops a character of its own based on who is in the group, what they experience together, and how they develop. As a therapist considers a new member for the group, it is important to consider how this particular person will or will not fit into the group. The therapist may also be interested in changing the character of the group by introducing new people that represent some differences. If a potential major change in character is planned, it would be well to fully process this anticipated change with the group beforehand and to add at least two people at the same time.

In sum, the process of selecting and matching group members is concerned with major similarities and differences. Similarities generally tend toward support, differences tend toward intervention. Any major differences create tensions in the group. Before introducing a possible factor of difference, the therapist should consider what the potential value of this difference is to all concerned, whether there is sufficient time in the projected life of the group for this difference to be of benefit to all concerned, and whenever possible, whether the group will have at least two people on each side of the difference. For major differences to be of significant therapeutic value, the group must be able to reach and resolve inclusion phase phenomena. In fact, major differences serve as the substance of inclusion phase conflicts (see Chapter 4, Part 2). In short-term groups, differences other than personality patterns will create severe tensions that can either directly or indirectly occupy all the groups' energies or lead to virtual or actual dissolution of the group. For example, if a therapist combined teen-agers and adults, the direct and indirect energies will all go into generation gap conflicts. If the purpose of this group is to deal with generation gap issues, then the combination would be good. If the group will deal with other issues, sufficient time must be allowed for the generation gap issues to be resolved before other work can be attended. How much time would depend on the particular teen-agers and adults and their relationships, if any, outside the group.

Because of agency purposes and functions, as in addiction programs, groups may inevitably have too many similarities among the members. The therapist must then introduce structures and purposes for providing the interventions that might already exist in a heterogeneous group.

Group Size. Homans (1950: 3) suggests that a group must be small enough for all the members to get around it. The number of people appropriate for therapy groups varies with the purpose, structure, and membership of the group. However, there are some overriding factors related to size. Considerable research and opinion by social psychologists and group therapists point to five or six as the optimum size for full and balanced interaction (see, for example, Bass and Norton, 1951:397-400; Slater, 1958:129-39; Hare, 1962:245-50; Shepherd, 1954:3-6; and Kadis et al, 1974:161).

Four is the minimum number of members for any therapy group. A membership of two would really mean three people in the situation, counting the therapist. As a result, each member would put an inordinate amount of energy into attempts at developing an exclusive relationship with the therapist. Most triadic relationships are extremely difficult: they are always a two and a one and are always in danger of becoming a different two and one. A membership of three raises the probability of triadic phenomenon among the three members (Golembiewski, 1962:146). The therapist cannot be the balancing fourth member, because if one member is felt to have a special relationship with the therapist, then the other two members will become both envious and competitive (Shepherd, 1964:3-4).

A minimum of four people, then, provides sufficient balance; if any two members form a pair, then the other two members can either form a pair or feel less excluded since they are both excluded from the pair. If a group has passed the inclusion struggles (see Chapter 4, Part 2), then the triadic effects will be minimized, if not totally absent. Consequently, a group can dwindle to three and even two members for a period of time—perhaps until new members are added or until the group ends. Indefinite continuing of a group of fewer than four members is not recommended.

The maximum for most intensive group experiences is eight members. With more than eight, it is almost impossible for each member to develop direct interpersonal relationships with every other member. Consequently, groups of more than eight always have subgroups and factions. Although at best these subgroups and factions might develop some internal intimacy, the larger group will have difficulty in developing any depth of intimacy. Thus, if any depth of intimacy is desired, a membership of between four and eight people is best. If the purpose of the group does not require any depth of intimacy among the members, more than eight people can be considered. (For example; some supportive groups, patient self-government groups, parent education or counseling groups can be larger than eight people.) On the other hand, people with lesser social-emotional capacities, such as groups of withdrawn adults or behaviorally disordered children, might need smaller groups both to provide more opportunity for individualized attention during meetings and to allow control (Geller, 1963:411-12).

When considering groups of couples the optimum number of couples is four. Two or three couples tend to develop some manifestations of the triadic difficulties found with two or three individuals. The couples interact with one another in the early phases of group development much as two or three individuals interact. More than four couples begins to overload the group with people and again reduces the possibilities for direct interpersonal relationships among all the members as individuals when the couples get past the pair interaction point in group development. After a couples' group has achieved some depth of intimacy, it can function with three and even two couples for a period of time. However, it is not recommended that a couples group continue with less than four couples for an indefinite period of time.

Group size will be considered more specifically under the various examples of group services that follow. Suffice to say that from four to eight members is the optimum size for most purposes and particularly for those purposes that aim at intensive interpersonal and/or insight development (Geller, 1963:411-12).

DIFFERENTIAL APPLICATION TO SPECIFIC SITUATIONS

The following discussion will demonstrate how purpose, grouping, and structure can be balanced to design group services appropriate to the needs and exigencies of many situations. The specific examples are of less consequence than the thinking about group design that is implied. While the designs presented below arise from the author's practice and consulting experience in the various settings, other similar settings may pose different needs and exigencies and consequently require different designs. This section illustrates the kind of thinking required to design group services and to evaluate and alter a design to suit the particular people in the particular setting with particular problems.

Children's Groups

Group therapy with children from eight to twelve years takes on a different character from group therapy for children of seven or younger. While groups of children seven or younger can gain some benefit, it cannot be expected, due to basic social-emotional developmental limitations, that most children under seven can realize any degree of group development as illustrated in Part 2 of this book. Rather, most children under seven, because they are in the parallel play phase of social development, will remain basically in a parallel phase and play next to each other with the basic relationship centered on the therapist. The objectives for most groups of children under seven cannot exceed coexistence with other children in relationship to a therapist or parent figure. However, many individual children may gain many benefits from the behavioral and occasional verbal interactions. The structure of such groups needs to focus on individual activity as children play next to each other, allowing spontaneous pair relationships to form. The structure of discussions centers around the therapist interacting with each child in turn with, perhaps, some bridging and interaction among the children. Generally, the major tools in younger children's groups are play and play materials. While some therapists recommend a planned progression of common activity for this age, other therapists suggest merely having a variety of play materials available and allowing each child to seek his or her own level of play and interaction (see, for example, Slavson, 1950:124-37).

Groups of children from eight to twelve years old present a different picture. Group psychotherapy with latency-aged children has been employed to serve a wide variety of problems and needs. (For examples see blind children, Raskin, 1954; severely deprived children, Scheidlinger, 1960; schizophrenic children, Lifton and Smolen, 1966; institutionalized children, Celia, 1970; Van Scoy 1972; Bardill 1973; autistic children, Coffey and Wiener, 1967.)

Generally, for intensive therapy experiences children's groups should have from four to six boys and/or girls. Children's groups with this age range are capable, in the long run, of resolving authority and inclusion phenomena as described in Part 2 of this book. The classic approach to such groups is to balance them with equal numbers of aggressive and withdrawn children and allow the behavioral conflicts to provide the therapeutic intervention (Redl, 1966:236-53; Slavson, 1964:211-14).

Structure for this classic approach to latency-aged groups is limited only by the confines of the room and the time available for meetings. Again, an array of play materials can be made available and each child allowed to pursue his own interests and his own level. The therapist does not demand interaction among the members. When interactions take place the therapist can become a supporter and mediator, being very careful not to take sides in favor of aggressive or con-strained behaviors (Slavson, 1950:137). Limits should be built into the room and the play materials to reduce the destructive potential and the necessity of having to set too many limits. For children to gain full benefit, such a group should run for the full school year with the same membership. Depending on the amount of time set aside for meetings, the structure can allow for "play time" and "talk time." Talk time is best kept under ten minutes in early sessions, then slowly increased as the group becomes able to handle it. While talking between therapists and members and among members goes on throughout play time, there is additional benefit to gathering all the members for the express purpose of talking, particularly about the group itself. Some groups seem to handle talk time better early in the meeting, some later. It is best to schedule talk time at either the start or the finish of the meeting. Two major benefits of talk time are, first, the progressive assumption of responsibility by the children for the control and direction of their individual and group behavior and, second, the progressive replacement of nonverbal with verbal expression (see, for ex-ample: Lieberman, 1964:455-64; Strunk and Witkin, 1974; and Sugar, 1974).

Ten- to twelve-year-olds are capable of developing and abiding by a consti-tutional type of government; however, the responsibility for self-control must develop in the group. If such a government is set up too early or artificially, assumption of responsibility by members could be self-defeating (Hallowitz, 1951; Karson, 1965; Rhodes, 1973). Only *after* the group begins to have some meaning to the members can setting limits on the whole group facilitate the development of group controls. This kind of group is the all-purpose children's group; it parallels the long-term adult psychotherapy group. Many children can gain great benefit from such a group within a one-year period, most within a two-year span. The problem is whether the therapist can tolerate the seeming chaos during the two- to four-month inclusion phase (Schreiber, 1969:138-146). If therapists are too uncomfortable with the chaotic conditions, the more structured approaches may work better for them (see, for example: Aranowitz 1968; Bruck 1966; Wordarski et. al. 1973; and Vinter 1967). Therapists who can tolerate the seeming chaos of the inclusion struggles can find the growth of the members very rewarding.

School settings are perhaps the most viable places for children's groups. Some of the recurrent purposes for children's groups in schools are to deal with behavior problems, isolation or withdrawal, and underachievement (see, for example, Frey and Kolodny, 1966). Homogeneous groups for withdrawn, iso-lated, and underachieving children can readily be formed. Although most children with behavior problems may be placed in homogeneous groups, they will require much more control than when they are mixed somewhat equally with withdrawn or underachieving children.

Structure for latency-aged groups must suit the needs and capacities of the children. One of the best structures, particularly for withdrawn children or those with behavior problems, is a ten- to fifteen-minute session before morning recess or lunch several times a week. With this structure many older latency-aged children can get together just to talk and, consequently, have less need for non-verbal activities. The reason for frequent short periods is that even the most impulse-ridden can quickly learn to handle ten or fifteen minutes and meanwhile have the opportunity to gain a positive social experience where they can control themselves and where they can release feelings verbally. Similarly, withdrawn children can often tolerate ten to fifteen minutes with other children without becoming unduly uncomfortable; thereby gaining a positive social experience that can help toward other positive social experiences. Much of the flagrant behavior reported in groups of latency-aged school children stems from the threat of too long a meeting. In an hour-long meeting, aggressive latency-aged children might spend a half hour to forty minutes in flagrant behavior in great part to fend off threatening discussions or experiences. Having less time to handle lessens their need for acting out. These groups are best as closed-end groups, either homogeneous or heterogenous among the two kinds of problems, single-sexed or coed, and running for nine or ten months of the school year.

Crisis groups in grammar schools generally focus on scapegoating and conflict situations among the children or between a teacher and a child or children. Anyone contemplating such a group might find the discussion of conflict in Chapter 1, Part 3 useful for planning and action. The membership of these groups requires that all parties to the conflict be included.

Groups of Early Adolescents

Groups of early adolescents ranging from twelve to fifteen years old, or seventh, eighth, and ninth graders, are perhaps among the most difficult for therapeutic purposes. Yet, such groups are also extremely potent as therapeutic agents. The reasons for the difficulty and the potency of early adolescent groups arises from the fact that peer group life is more important during early adolescence than in any other time of life (Osterrieth, 1969; Josselyn, 1971: 42-3; Erikson, 1968; Committee on Adolescence, 1968; Redl, 1966:247). The peer group becomes more important for early adolescents as they seek peer association and support in their strivings for independence from parents.

Many people's concepts of self in relation to peers is formed during early adolescence: popularity-unpopularity, leadership-followership, worthiness-unworthiness. The peer group serves as both the testing ground for oneself in relation to others and the source of peer opinions about oneself. Because the peer group is the context for normal growth during early adolescence, it follows that group therapy can serve as a viable corrective experience.

While there are a host of reasons for treating early adolescents in therapy groups, these reasons tend to center on the adolescents' handling of their impulses and their sexuality, on their relationships with peers, parents, and other adults, and on whether or how they will apply themselves to school. Sexuality, body image, impulses, and acceptability to the opposite sex are major concerns for seventh, eighth, or ninth graders. Because the areas of concern are so sensitive and the difficulties of sharing these concerns across sex lines so large, it is best to use single-sex groups for early adolescents. The presence of the opposite sex is so stimulating and threatening that any discussion of feelings becomes extremely difficult. It is difficult enough for early adolescents to accept and share their anxieties, even in single-sexed groups.

More than a one-year span of school grade also adds to the difficulty in discussing feelings. Eighth graders feel they must present a sophisticated image to seventh graders; and seventh graders are afraid that eighth graders will view them as infantile for what they say and feel. First year high school students also react this way with upper classmen and upper classmen with freshmen. Thus, for most purposes it is best to group early adolescents within a single sex and a one-year age or school grade span.

The structure of meetings is also very important. Meetings once or twice a week can be useful, but their length must vary with the readiness and capacity of the particular members. Twenty minutes is often sufficient for early meetings of junior high children. Some of the more anxious ones or those in greatest fear of risking too much will find any time longer than twenty minutes too much; they will miss meetings, come late, or act out disruptively to prevent the anxiety levels from getting too high. Once a group can discuss problems and issues and is increasingly comfortable with risking, the meetings can be extended to thirty, forty, or even sixty minutes, depending on the group.

While short-term groups serve many objectives with early adolescents, groups that last the full school year also have much to offer. Meeting over a full school year allows sufficient time for the group to reach full development and gives rise to social-emotional growth within the therapy group in a corrective peer group experience. Groups of early adolescents meeting over shorter periods of time can accomplish specific functions in reducing selected tensions, but will not provide the full growth experiences of the school year group.

Therapists have employed a wide range of meeting structures with early adolescents in short- and longer-term groups. The author favors the open discussion situation, which allows an unpressured discussion of whatever each and every member wants to discuss. Much of the early discussion is not directly related to the reason for including the members in the group; rather, it allows time for relationships to develop among the therapist and the members. As this relationship, particularly between the therapist and the members, develops, the therapist is able to progressively introduce more anxiety-laden issues, if the members themselves haven't already done so. It is important that the communication system allow a wide latitude, since most of the crucial issues for the members will arise from unlikely discussions and very often through jokes. Because unearthing anxieties and risking them in front of the other members is the most difficult, the joking and open discussion technique allows members to risk exposing their anxieties without too much danger of losing face if the other members deem the subject silly, stupid, or childish. However, once a subject has been raised, the therapist can easily suggest the universality of the issue for all teenagers. Most often, even under overt protest, the other members will accept the commonality of the concern and begin to relate to it in their own ways.

Unlike either older or younger groups, early adolescent groups do not generally dwell on even the most important subjects for any great length of time. More important, they do not seem to want or need lengthy or full discussion of each issue. They seem to benefit from a short unearthing, universalization, and dispensing with the subject, only to have it arise perhaps again at a future time. When the subject or issue recurs, the therapist is often surprised to see how meaningful the previous discussion had been, not only for the member for whom it meant the most, but also for the other members. Thus, while the elaborate discussion that can often be accomplished with a highly structured format might look more like adult processes, there is real question whether these adult-like discussions are as significant for the early adolescents as the short spontaneous dealings with their real concerns (Sheldon and Landsman, 1950: 210-15).

The other prominent feature of working with early adolescent groups is the recurrent feeling of futility therapists experience. A combination of the extreme use of denial and the seemingly chaotic process of early adolescent groups leads many adult therapists to despair that nothing meaningful is or can be accomplished. The author has left many an early adolescent therapy group meeting feeling that he could have been doing something more productive with his time. All this means is that the therapist has entered the world of the early adolescent and experienced the chaos of being inundated by emotions that the early adolescent hasn't fully learned to cope with yet and deals with through denial and flight in many forms. Just as they haven't learned to master their new and suddenly elongated and changing bodies, they haven't learned to master their new and often overwhelming feelings arising from the physiological and social changes that are taking place in and around them. It is extremely important for the therapist to note the changes that are taking place outside the group. A therapist quite often feels that little of significance is taking place in the group, yet after three to five months can see many signs of growth in school, at home, and with peers. The interaction and relationships among the children in the group and the therapist accomplish many changes *almost no matter what is or is not discussed in the group.* In early adolescent groups, the primary curative factors are the relationships and the behavioral interactions. Whatever direct discussions of significant problems, issues, and feelings take place are all to the good, but they are not essential for growth and change to result from the process. The therapist must enter the world of the early adolescent; he cannot require the early adolescent to function like an adult in groups.

Short-term groups with early adolescents can take either of two directions. One is a structured format for meetings. In this the subject is decided in advance and well universalized so that the members get the feeling that *every* adolescent might have the feelings involved; some means for entering the discussion also is provided. The second format is the rap session. Here members can opt for whatever they want to discuss without direct or indirect pressures to deal with anything in particular. The structured group should be very specific in its goals; the rap group can be very flexible, even for short-term groups.

Groups of early adolescents are capable of developing some degree of intimacy, but the capacity for intimacy, it must be remembered, is a product of adolescent growth rather than a characteristic of adolescents. The intimacy that a group of early adolescents achieves is like that seen in an adult group where intimacy is achieved prematurely through gimmicks or laboratory games. People share a good feeling about each other, but they need very stringent and narrow norms for their relationships and behavior with each other. The price of deviating from these norms, particularly when they first experience intimacy, is rejection. It takes considerable time, often three to six months, of meeting at least once a week for an early adolescent group to develop some degree of intimacy. Once they do it behooves the therapist to keep open continuously the latitude for differences in ideas, feelings, and behaviors. The therapist must constantly show his acceptance of what may appear to the group as deviancy from its norms. This process is no different from natural processes in early adolescent peer groups, except that the therapist is there to keep the possibilities for individual differences open.

Finally, most early adolescent groups require a minimum of five members and in long term groups can include as many as nine or ten. The reason for nine or ten is that there are frequent absences in adolescent groups and numbers are extremely important to the members. A membership of eight or nine gives more assurance that five or six members will appear at any given meeting. The reason for a minimum of five is that, again, the number of members is important and fewer than five seems like too few to most early adolescents. A group of five or more also provides greater probability that any deviancy from group norms in thoughts, feelings, or behavior will find some support from at least one other member. An indigenous leader in the group might be able to control one or two other members quite tightly, but he or she is less likely to be able to control four others over a long period.

There is a progression of focal issues in all adolescent groups. One initial focus tends frequently toward projection on and hostility toward parents and all adult authority. As the group develops, the adolescent concerns progressively change from external and adult focus to internal and peer focus (see, for example: Fried, 1956:358-73; Caplan, 1957:124-28; Gadpaille, 1959:275-86). Thus, the ultimate aim in adolescent group discussion is to help the members and group assume responsibility for themselves and rely less on projections. However, this change is very gradual and the therapist must go along with the projections until the group is *able* to shift. The group development from the parallel to the inclusion phase reflects and facilitates these changes (see Part 2, Chapters 2, 3, and 4).

Older Adolescent Groups

Groups of teen-agers ranging from ages sixteen to eighteen, or second through fourth year of high school, will vary considerably in their potential development with the kinds of problems to be addressed, their subculture, and the norms of the teen peer culture from which they come. Some teen groups function much like groups described under early adolescent, others will function almost on a par with adult groups. For example, a group of teen-aged girls, seventeen and eighteen, will often function much like an adult group in their relationships and processes, but a group of socially limited sixteen- and seventeen-year-old boys will often function like an early adolescent group.

Coed groups of teen-agers are often more productive than single-sexed groups. The boys in particular benefit since girls are often readier to discuss their feelings, which facilitates this process for the boys. In addition, single-sexed groups have a particular difficulty with feelings of intimacy that develop, since these feelings become confused with homosexual feelings at a time when sexual identity is a crucial question. The presence of the opposite sex allows members to reassure themselves in their sexual identities by at first emphasizing their feelings about the opposite sex in the group. Single-sexed groups often handle their homosexual fears by discussing their "exploits" with the opposite sex, particularly at times when they begin to have close feelings toward the other group members.

Because they need the feeling of numbers and they have a high tendency for absences from meetings, groups of five to eight members are best for most older teen-agers. Latenesses and absences from teen-aged groups can often be reduced by limiting the duration of each meeting to suit the particular members. The most common cause for lateness and absence is the degree of anxiety anticipated by the members. Thus, until the group can tolerate the anxiety of the meetings or learn to control the anxiety levels, a policy of shorter meetings helps attendance. The time can be increased as the group demonstrates capacity for longer meetings.

A major feature of teen-aged groups is the constant recurrence of authority-autonomy, and intimacy-isolation issues or, in the context of the framework of group development that follows, constant recurrence of authority and intimacy crises throughout the life of the group (Singer, 1974:429-38). It is no accident that these groups have these recurrent themes; the major goals for most teen-agers in groups are finding and actualizing their own initiative through relinquishing their dependency on adult authority and developing their capacity to act in their own behalf (Fried, 1956:358-73; Gadpaille, 1959:275-86). Constant rebellion toward authority is taken here to be little different from dependency on authority that is manifest in conformity with authority. Relationships with peers, particularly heterosexual relationships, are also of paramount importance for teen-agers; thus, the recurrent intimacy crises function to help teen-agers develop their capacities for relationships. The authority and intimacy themes are manifest in both content and process.

Groups of teen-agers are capable of considerable development along the lines of the model in Part 2. These groups can achieve some depth in development of a mutuality process. The major factor that determines the depth of mutuality is how capable the members are of moving beyond the early adolescent confusion of closeness and similarity. Teen groups may go through a more protracted period than adult groups during which they hold their membership to lockstep similarity in thoughts, feelings, and actions. As they develop more capacity for mutuality, they then relinquish this insistency on confomity. However, teen-aged groups need sufficient time to form as a group and go through a period of pseudo-intimacy before they become able to move beyond. Short-term groups of teen-agers will not pass the pseudo-intimacy phase. The range of structures for groups of teen-agers is almost infinite and runs from rap groups to intensive psychotherapy groups. Groups for underachievers and potential dropouts are quite common and generally effective. Some hard-core behavior problems in high schools are reachable in groups. A group formed of acting-out teen-agers per se will not provide sufficient balance for productive work unless they are also a natural group from the community, in which case there is a better chance that they will have means for mutual controls. Prior to group therapy these means for control may not have been operating to promote acceptable behavior, but because means of control exist, if a good relationship with a therapist is established, the group can exercise their controls toward maintaining the relationship and insuring the requisite kinds of behavior (Richmond and Schecter, 1964; Shellow, et al. 1958).

When starting group services in high schools it is well to not attempt to reach the most difficult teens first. Teens who drop out and have attendance problems may behave the same in the group as they do to their classes—that is, not come—until a relationship is established with the therapist. It is often best to start with underachievers and a few behavior problems in a heterogeneous group. Establishing a relationship with one group that is amenable builds bridges for establishing relationships with other teens in the teen community. "Good vibes" about the therapist and the group may interest other teens in seeking out the group or therapist's services. When a favorable image for the service has built up in the teen community, the drop-outs and attendance problems will be more likely to come to groups and stay in them. In general, teens have difficulty risking being first in anything until they know by peer consensual validation that it is acceptable to do something. Most drop-outs and delinquent-prone teen-agers have an even greater fear of risking than do other teens; therefore, it is best to make contact with other teens first to establish that the group service is an acceptable place for teens to be. Many a noble attempt to establish group services for teen-agers has faltered by trying to solve the hardest problems before the service is established. Worse yet is attempting to use group services to accomplish goals that haven't been tackled or even attempted prior to the service.

College-age and Young Adult Groups

College-age and young adult groups are perhaps the most exciting from a verbal process and developmental point of view. The needs of people at these ages to establish themselves with their peers is still strong enough to make peer group life extremely important and their psychosocial development is such that they can develop fully and deeply as a group over time. Groups for college-age and young adults provide, along with the growth in autonomy and intimacy, a most viable medium for discovering and firming up each member's identity. The product of group participation for each young adult in a fully developed group is a better sense of self and acceptance of self as well as others. Because these groups are capable of full and deep development as a group, each member's uniqueness becomes as valued if not more valued, to the group as the commonalities.

The full range of adult groups are possible with young adults; however, the question of their being combined with other adults is important. Those of college age who are either students or "temporarily" out of school view the world differently from those who are out of school permanently, have graduated, or are attending graduate school. The economic and emotional dependency of the college student brings forth very different issues in group therapy. While it isn't necessarily disasterous to combine college students with those who are out of school permanently in a long-term therapy group, the combination produces an intensity in the transferences among the members across the college versus beyond college subgroups that is extremely difficult to resolve. One of the important differences is that those beyond college can usually establish themselves economically and socially outside the family, while college students must sustain a continued, albeit hostile period of dependency. Long-term groups may allow sufficient time to employ the transferences for everyone's therapeutic benefit, but for short-term groups the differences can inhibit the more particular goals that may be accomplished.

Adult Groups

The possibilities for treating adults in groups are numerous. Classic to the adult therapy group is the long-term open-ended psychotherapy group meeting once weekly for from one to two hours, depending on the particular purpose, membership, and structures. The minimum number of people needed to start an adult group is usually four; six to eight people are the maximum allowable for an intensive group experience. Fewer than four people in the initial phases of group development will exacerbate the inclusion phenomenon and can even make the inclusion phenomenon insurmountable, resulting in either unnecessary drop-outs or the demise of the group. If an adult group has achieved some degree of mutuality, then by attrition dwindles to three or two people, it can continue for some time, depending on the nature of the relationships among the two or three people remaining. However, it is inadvisable to continue a group of two or three indefinitely. With more than eight people, an adult group is less likely to form as a total group. Permanent factions become more likely in groups larger than eight and intimate relationships among all the members become more difficult, if not impossible.

Long-term adult psychotherapy groups can tolerate a wide range of ages and differences, depending on the particular people involved and the reasons why they have come for therapy. The wide differences in the long run are productive, particularly of stimulating transference phenomena among the members, and help toward resolution of transference issues and identity issues. An adult group whose members are within a ten-year age span will form more quickly than one with a wider age span and can in the long run provide the same experiences for its members as a group with wide differences among the members. Transferences among people in the same age range at first tend to be from past sibling and peer relationships; however, over time, parental and authority transferences are also manifest among people in the same age ranges.

Since the theory of group development presented in Part 2 is based on the long-term therapy group with adults or young adults within the normal to neurotic ranges of personality, little more need be said about these groups at this juncture. Instead, Part 1 deals with organizational and procedural issues that may be useful for some of the many possible adult groups and their variations.

Most group psychotherapy literature is aimed at the intensive long-term adult psychotherapy group whose purpose is genetic and/or interpersonal insight development. Criteria for grouping in these works are consistent with the goals for long-term group psychotherapy. However, the criteria and suggestions for grouping in these works are not applicable for group purposes and structures aimed at people less capable of deep interpersonal or genetic insight (Yalom, 1975: 246-275; Slavson, 1964: 198-232).

Groups of Depressives

The author has come to view therapy in groups composed entirely of depressives as the treatment of choice for people with severe depression. These people cannot be placed in groups with nondepressed people since their intense needs for and imperviousness to the help of other people often draws non-depressed members in and then frustrates them to the point of destroying the group. However, when placed with others in the same range of severity of depression, the group allows a primitive empathy and a regaining of autonomy in ways not possible in the one-to-one relationship. Depression is different from other types of symptomatology in that people with very different kinds of personalities often become depressed. Consequently, as the depression begins to lift, a range of coping mechanisms inherent in the group members begins to appear (Levine and Schild, 1969; Miller and Ferone, 1966).

Groups of depressives are best kept at four or five people, since most, if not all, members need "time to talk." Particularly during the early phases members repeat their depressive stories over and over. Early structure can allow for the "round robin" format, where each member in turn tells how his or her situation is worse than anyone else's. Weekly meetings on an outpatient basis are most advisable; more frequent meeting will encourage dependency on the meetings. Groups of depressives, especially when they are of a single sex, tend to develop a mutal support network outside the group. This network most often consists of phone calls, but sometimes includes back and forth visiting among members and, best of all, going places with each other. In many groups outside contacts—particularly if they are across sex lines—create therapeutic difficulties; however, in groups of depressives outside contacts that develop a mutual support system can facilitate therapeutic objectives.

Life-Stage and Role Groups

Many therapy groups in family service agencies and outpatient clinics are formed around life stage and roles. These may be open or closed groups, depending on the number of meetings possible, the severity of the members' difficulties or, perhaps, other exigencies imposed by the supporting agency. Examples of such groups are: (1) Groups of thirty-five- to fifty-year-old women dealing with the identity crisis arising from their no longer feeling needed by their children. In carving out their new roles and identities, such women gain a great deal of support from each other. (2) Young mothers beset by the responsibilities and exhausted by the demands of young children. (3) Single parents, alone and coping with being both parents and providers. (4) Persons preparing for or adjusting to retirement. (5) Newly divorced people who are dealing with the loss of the relationship, questions of adequacy in their relationships, and re-entry into the "singles" whirl. A host of other possibilities arise when an agency detects a common need among several of its clients and brings them together around that common need. While most of these people could be well served by the long-term open-ended adult group, they do seem to gain a lot from relating to others in the same situation. When clients come with life-stage and role difficulties, if they are not treated in homogeneous groups, they should at least be matched with one person in a heterogeneous group. While treatment of those with stage and role problems in homogeneous groups could accomplish everything that a long-term open-end group might, homogenous groups tend to deal more fully with issues of common interest.

Medical settings offer a boundless array of grouping possibilities. Patients who face the same medical procedures, who have to follow the same medical regimen, or who suffer the same permanent incapacities have much to gain from each other. In addition, groups of various inpatients who are facing long-term hospitalization for protracted acute or chronic conditions for rehabilitation can be helped to maintain their social capacities and interest through participation in groups. Relatives of patients needing either specific instructions in understanding and helping the patient or help in dealing with the possible loss of function and changes resulting from illness and incapacity can be of profound help to each other in resolving both their own feelings about the medical problem and their relationships with the patient.

Groups for people in a crisis are more possible in medical settings than any other. People facing the same fate can readily and easily identify with each other. It must also be remembered that medical patients do not necessarily have emotional problems, but rather may be beset by their conditions. This means they have a ready base for identification and, with their good social-emotional capacity, these people can rapidly form as a group. The resulting group can be helpful in a very short period of time. Age, sex, and any of the other considerations for other groupings need not be major factors when grouping people who share the same or similar medical difficulties. Any number of meetings of any length are possible and can be experimented with in each setting. The number, frequency, and duration of meetings might be based more on the medical and institutional rationale rather than on group phenomena. Of course, similarities in age, sex, and life stage might add substantially to the mutual identification, but would be less cogent than the kind of medical problems and the consequences for the person's life. The author's own work with groups for pregnant adolescents and patients in physical rehabilitation services bears out how the commonalities of the physical problems and their emotional concomitants serve as ready bases for swift empathic bonding (Sharpe et al., 1969).

A major goal for any group in a medical setting is to deal with the feelings of loss resulting from the problem or illness. A mourning process is both the major objective and a necessity to clearing a path for members to cope with their predicaments. These processes undergo the classic pattern of denial, bargaining, depression, hostility, and finally, acceptance and coping. Because each member might be at a different point in the process and because each may follow a slightly different path through the stages, the phases of the mourning process may not unfold sequentially or evenly, but they will be present and amenable to help, particularly from the empathic process among the members.

30

Groups for Addicts (Drugs, Alcohol, Food.)

Because of the similarities in behavior patterns among the members, groups for addicted persons present particular difficulty. Behavioral similarities among people who are addicts do not provide the crucial differences in modes of behavior that are important to the group theraputic process. In heteregenous groups different people react to situations in their own ways, providing a necessary challenge to existing patterns of behavior and suggesting alternatives to those patterns. In groups of addicts, responsibility for challenging existing patterns of behavior lies mainly with the therapist. Consequently, other modes of intervention in behavior patterns are essential. The primary ways are either to provide a structure of rules, norms, and formats that intervene in behavior patterns or to bring in *reformed* addicts to challenge addict behaviors.

What all the structures for treating addiction essentially do is to offer relationships and acceptance. They use the addict's strong yearnings for relationships as the means for drawing them into the group, then they interfere with the tendencies for escaping anxieties of any kind through the structure of the group (Solms and Meuron, 1969). There are many variations with which the various self-help addiction groups and professionally led groups accomplish their goals, but in all, the basis is to employ the motivation for relationships as a means for helping addicts to sustain themselves and mobilize their coping efforts in anxiety-laden situations rather than to escape in the many ways addicts find to escape.

One common characteristic of groups of addicts is that the members often use the discussion of the addiction itself as the means for escaping anxiety in the meeting. Structure of meetings must support discussion of causal problems rather than allow addiction itself from becoming the major or only topic. A major danger is to fail to distinguish between "addicts" and "users." The extreme and sometimes severe confrontation and interventive techniques and structures essential for treatment of addicts are often employed for users of the various addictives and sometimes even extended to other kinds of social emotional problems. Users, however, as opposed to addicts, are generally better off in heterogeneous groups where they have the opportunities to deal with their problems in a setting where the variety of coping mechanisms found among the other members provides the needed intervention.

The use of authority in groups of addicts must be more protracted than in other groups. Two structures will enable the group of addicts to move beyond the authority crises and take more responsibility for itself. One is the use of rules; at first newer members are forced to adhere to the rules, then they become enforcers of them. The other is the use of those who have turned around in their addiction; such persons are used to control the addicts through counterdependence. Since interpersonal dependency is a common characteristic of most addicts, reformed addicts are helped to meet their dependency needs by counter-dependently looking after others who are still addicted. The former addicts gain support and mastery for their own controls over their addiction by controlling the behavior of other addicts. This phenomenon allows the exaddicts to meet their dependency needs through counterdependency while firming up their own controls. Thus, while the group process may remain in a comparatively primitive state (see parallel phase and authority crisis in Part 2), individual members of the group can be helped to achieve greater autonomy and to cope with authority through the structure of the group. The principle lies in the exploitation of dependency-counterdependency issues beginning in the parallel phase (Schual et al., 1971).

Chronic Schizophrenics in Groups

People who are classified as chronic schizophrenics can be offered effective therapy in homogenous groups if the therapist's accept the social-emotional limitations of the schizophrenic. Almost by definition, the schizophrenic is either fixated or regressed to the parallel phase of social-emotional development (see parallel phase in Part 2). Most difficulties in groups of schizophrenics arise from the therapist's expecting or demanding that they function at levels far beyond their capacity. The therapist must accept that any group composed of people who are all schizophrenic starts at a very primitive level and progresses very slowly from that point. After one to two years of treatment, groups of schizophrenics can achieve some resolve of authority issues and some degree of development in the inclusion phases. Subgroups of two, three or four people within the larger groups can achieve some degrees of intimacy and mutality but only after a long time. (Spear, 1960, describes the failure of an inpatient group-therapy program due to overexpectations of schizophrenics.)

In order to accept the lower social capacity in groups of schizophrenics, therapists must accept the centrality of their role for most of the group's life (Orange, 1955; Klapman, 1951). The resolution of authority issues and the inclusion processes become ends of therapy rather than means toward other therapeutic objectives. If a group of schizophrenics achieves some resolve of authority issues, it would mean that the members become able to assert increasing autonomy and initiative on their own behalf. It also means that members become able to express disagreement and hostility toward authority figures, and perhaps parents as well. Resolve of inclusion issues and movement into the inclusion phase means that members of a group of schizophrenics become able to express their negative feelings toward peers and accept negative feelings from peers without necessarily rejecting or feeling rejected. As they become increasingly comfortable with negative feelings and the air clears as a result of expressing these feelings in the group, schizophrenic members of groups can begin to have positive attachments toward each other. While positive feelings among the members in a group of schizophrenics are quite possible, real feelings of closeness are possible only within the limits of a very few relationships in the group and not all the members may be capable of more than that.

Thus, the structure of groups for schizophrenics must allow for their primitive levels of relationship and for slow progress (see, for example: Eisenman, 1965; Eicke, 1967; Payn, 1974). Format for meetings should allow for safe risking and building on areas of strength. In early meetings it is often important to accept whatever a schizophrenic offers in the way of discussion. More can be gained from the person's feeling adequate as a group member than from discussing another topic that might have a bearing on the person's plight. Any disallowal of what the schizophrenic offers in a meeting results in that member's feeling rejected and inadequate as a group member. Early meetings should focus on developing a communication system rather than employing that system for dealing with problems per se.

If there is to be a predetermined focus for groups of schizophrenics, it needs to be practical, clear, and limited in scope. Complex goals are as difficult for schizophrenics as complex thoughts. In the complexities of the mixed metaphoric background of the schizophrenic, it takes time for even simple thoughts to become untinged and untangled. A well conceived inpatient group for schizophrenics will provide structure, content, and interactive levels suitable for schizophrenics. (More elaborate ideas for meeting the therapeutic needs of schizophrenics in groups can be found in Fidler, 1965; Wolman, 1969.)

Groups of Couples

Groups of couples are among the most difficult to get started, but once they become functional they serve as a viable context for marital therapy. Some of the difficulties particular to the starting of couples groups, as opposed to other adult groups, stem from the increased difficulties in risking. In the early stages an individual finds it more difficult to risk in a group that includes another person who shares his or her reality outside the group. In groups of individuals, people can share their outside experiences without anyone else present who can suggest a different perspective on the situation. A couples group always includes both partners and, while they share the same outside situation, they also have some very different and perhaps conflicting views of each situation. In addition, the potential subject matter itself poses added risk in the early phases of couples groups. The prospect of sharing the intimacies of one's marital relationship with other people itself increases concerns about the risk. Very often, each couple comes to marital therapy feeling that its relationship is very different, that no other couples have the same kinds of difficulties. Couples entering groups have more intense fears of difference and deviance than individuals entering groups.

However, these very fears are most often the first feelings to be relieved during participation in a couple group. In the early phases, the universality of difficulties encountered by couples becomes apparent rather quickly and progressive risk-taking by each and all couples becomes much easier. In later phases, the different relational styles of the couples open alternatives for each couple to test in their own relationship.

Because of the intensity of the initial risk factors in couples groups it becomes extremely important for the therapist to pay close attention to group formation and the structure of early meetings. Therapists of couples groups must initially concern themselves more with inviting trust and risking in the early meetings than must therapists with many other kinds of adult groups (Flint, 1962).

Four couples is a good size for couple groups. Groups of three couples or fewer at the start will precipitate triadic and dyadic phenomenon that tend to increase the competitiveness and also increase both the fears and the real possibilities of rejection among the couples. In other words, during the early phases of the group three couples function much like three individuals. When a couples group has been together for a long time, it can dwindle to three or even two couples and still productively continue as a group. However, protracted meetings with two or three couples for an indefinite period of time is not desirable. Including more than four couples begins to make the group too large. Some therapists start with five couples, anticipating that one couple will drop out, leaving a viable group of four couples. However, if all five couples stay, the group may then be too large for full and deep relationships to develop.

Although age differences among couples is not a major factor, ideally each couple should have at least one other couple with whom they can identify particularly in age and status as parents. If three couples in a group are very much older than the fourth couple, there is a danger that the older couples, in the early phases, will tend to discount the problems of the younger couple and make them mascots. If three couples are younger and one very much older, the younger couples may tend to treat the older couple more like parents or inlaws. Although the latter phenomenon is potentially helpful to all concerned, the older couple may find it difficult to survive the bombardment from the younger couples without the support of at least one other older couple.

While roles as parents tend to take less discussion time and effort after the group becomes cohesive, the differences between couples who have or do not have children cause some factioning in the early phases. Having at least two couples with or without children in the early phases helps in the initial identification.

In open-ended couples groups, when one couple leaves a well developed group the therapist need not be as concerened about matching an incoming couple in age and parental status. Although ready identification with couples from the standpoint of age and parental status would still help a new couple, the level of the process in a well developed couples group would facilitate the induction of the couple as a couple regardless of possible differences in age and parental status.

In the early stages of couples groups, structures that call for safe risking and interaction, yet limit the amount of risking of very intimate information, help to build trust, comfort, and interaction. The therapist should be very active in the early phases and must control the process more than in the average adult group. Many structures can facilitate couple groups. One possibility is to ask each person during the first meeting, to think of a word or name to describe his or her marital relationship. In a second round, after hearing each person's name for the relationship, each person is asked to describe how he or she arrived at the name. In this way each person presents his or her view of the couple relationship and its nature without necessarily risking very many intimate details. The ensuing discussion leads to a greater identification among members as they explore the nature of their relationships and why they came for help. In a third round, if it is even necessary, the group might compare the names that each half of a couple had for its relationship and how the names might be conflictual or reconcilable. This last round could take place in the second or third meeting if necessary. Most couples groups don't need the third round.

A therapist for a couples group needs a background in marital therapy with one couple at a time as well as experience with groups of individuals. The complexities of the couples group can easily overwhelm the therapist who is new to either group therapy or counseling couples. The complexity of bringing together a group of people who have already established pair relationships can lead to many precipitous decisions unless the therapist well understands couple therapy per se as well as early group phenomena.

The drop-out rate in the early phases of couples groups can be rather high. A number of techniques may help reduce drop-outs. First and foremost is to have at least four couples at the first meeting. Second is to provide prior individual or couple therapy for one or both members of each couple. This helps the couples cope with the frustration and anxiety of the early phases. When one or both of a couple are new to counseling per se, a protracted intake might help the therapist form a relationship with the couple and prepare them for the early phases of the group. The therapist can help the couple anticipate the difficulties of the early phases, so that they realize that risking is difficult at first and that the process is frustrating because they may not be able to deal with what they really want to deal with for a while. Asking the new couple to try five group sessions before they decide whether it will be helpful takes some of the pressure off the therapist and group to prove the efficacy of the group; it also takes pressure off the couple to risk too much too soon.

During the first five meetings of the group many couples undergo a major crisis so that they not only consider leaving the group but they bring up the subject of separation or divorce. This pheomenon is most often caused by fears of the couple treatment process. It is well to advise the couple in advance to put off any major decisions about their relationship for at least two months, since the possibility of a precipitous decision is very likely during the early phases of couples group participation. It might also be well to see new couples as individual couples for a crisis session when these early phase crises occur. These crises can usually be allayed and the couple easily returned to the group. However, when these crises arise because one partner has already made up his or her mind about the future of the relationship, the crisis may be a fear either that the group will upset the plans or that he or she will inadvertantly reveal the plans in the group and precipitate the outcome.

The most crucial point in the development of couples groups occurs when members stop attempting to cast blame on the other half of the couple and instead accept their own part in the problems and processes of the relationship. This turn-around is facilitated by the universalization provided by other couples and their difficulties as well as the advent of deepening intimacy among all the members of the group. Very often, one partner comes to the group more interested in participating in the group than the other. This partner usually feels that he is "in the right" and casts blame for the problems on the other partner. The usual effect of the group on the partner being blamed is to alleviate his or her tendency to take all the blame and consequently, to increase his or her readiness to take more responsibility for improving the relationship. At that point, however, the former partner or blame-caster undergoes a crisis. He or she is at first afraid to continue in the group and must resolve feelings about being part of the problem. If and when the blame-caster can resolve resistances to being part of the problem, then the couples can make significant advances to the extent of their mutual capacities for relationship (Hastings and Runkle, 1963; Leichter, 1962 and 1973; Grunebaum and Christ, 1968). During the inclusion phase for the couple group, the power struggles within couples are mostly about who is to blame. If and as the group resolves its inclusion struggles, then the feeling of acceptance by other members facilitates each partner's acceptance of his/her part in the relational difficulties of the marriage. (For discussion of research and outcomes in couple groups see: Freeman et al., 1969; Hardcastle, 1972; Gottlieb and Pattison, 1966. For discussion of format, structure, and experiences in couples groups see: Freeman, 1965; Boas, 1962; Linden et al., 1968).

Groups of Parents

Groups of parents are formed for an infinite variety of purposes and with widely varying structures. By and large parent groups are among the easiest kinds of groups to form and start if the purpose and structure call for focus on their children. However, when the focus begins with or shifts to the parents and particularly to the relationship between parents, these groups in essence become couples groups and take on all the difficulties and complexities of such groups. Some people who come to parent groups are ready to focus on themselves, but others are extremely threatened by the shift in focus and many will not stay in the group or, if they do stay will strongly resist the focus. If the real intention for forming the group is to focus on the parents themselves, then the process of selection and intake should reflect this goal. In other words, only those parents who are interested in and amenable to coming into a group to work on either themselves or their marital relationship should be selected for the group. The group is not so much a parent group as a group of individuals or couples brought together for therapy who all happen to have a child in some similar plight.

When starting parent groups it is generally best to focus on the children and the relationship between parents and children. Most parents find it easy to come together to discuss their children, to try to understand them, and even to consider changing some of their ways of parenting. For short-term groups of parents a structured format is often useful. As therapists become familiar with the kinds of problems parents in the group need to deal with, they can set up a curriculum to provide a progression of focuses for the meetings (Winder et al.; 1965; Andrews, 1962, Criss, 1970). In developing such a curriculum the therapist must keep in mind some of the process issues that may influence discussions. For example, in any first meetings of parent groups the authority issues are a major preoccupation. Depending on the kinds of child problems which gave rise to the group, parents will be either anxious and guilty about their underlying angers toward the child's disability, or defensive over the feeling of having failed as a parent. Parents gathered because of some kind of accident, illness, or defects in the child are generally defending themselves from some degree of anger over the loss of a normal healthy child. These parents are inclined to fear that the therapist and other group members will detect their anger and feelings of rejection for the child and are very concerned with control and punishment. These feelings are manifest by a hostile but usually passive dependency on the therapist and initial concerns with disciplinary problems and methods for dealing with their children. In addition to the many practical issues that need to be worked out to help parents maximize the remaining potentials of the child for self-dependency, a major goal in these parent groups is helping parents unearth, express, and reduce the overcompensations for the anger over the loss of a normal healthy child. Where parents have not worked out these feelings, they are less likely to be able to reach that happy medium between overprotecting and underprotecting the child. In short-term groups for parents, the resolution of a parent's loss reactions to the child's problem is less likely to be worked out.,

For parent groups where the child has a social or emotional problem the parents approach the group and the thereapist with a great deal of suspicion, since most parents are aware that psychiatric literature and personnel hold them in major ways responsible for social-emotional problems in their children. These groups often start with the parents preoccupied with discipline and punishments for the child, a concern that often reflects their concern about being punished by the therapist for being "bad" parents. It is extremely important for the therapist to convey empathy for their plight as parents and engage these groups in a process aimed at working together for the benefit of the children.

Finally, a major issue is whether the marital situation should be treated within the group. One goal of working with parents is often to help them see difficulties in their own relationship that cause or contribute to the child's problem. As stated earlier, shifting the focus to the parents can turn a rather easy group developmental process into a very difficult and complex one. If and when it is discovered that the parental interaction is a primary factor in the child's problem, then perhaps the goal for working with those parents in the group might be to help them get help for the marriage outside the group. However, many aspects of the marriage can be dealt with in the group by virtue of the relationships between the here and now and the there and then. Particularly in groups where the child's problem is accident, illness, or defects, the parent's communication around the child and the problem can be employed as a partialization of the totality of parental interaction. Most often in such couples mothers tend to overprotect the child and fathers are inclined to encourage more self-dependency for the child. Because it is the mother who is involved with all the professionals, who gets their information, and who is primarily responsible for the care of the child, the fathers are often cut off. The support that fathers give each other in these meetings often begin to affect other aspects of the marriage. Other kinds of marital imbalances also become manifest in the communication around the child and can be dealt with in the same partialized way.

In groups of parents whose children have social and emotional problems it is not quite as easy to take the interaction around the child as a partialization of the marital difficulties, since the interaction around the child may be the way in which the parents avoid dealing with each other. However, in these groups either the contract needs to be directly aimed at treatment of the parents and their relationship or the groups need to be of long enough term for the focus to shift from child to parents.

In groups of single parents or parents who are severely socially and emotionally deprived, the shift to discussing themselves often presents little problem. These parents are frequently so in need of something for themselves that they readily welcome the opportunity. In fact, some such parent groups seldom get to discuss their children and, consequently, the members require help with their guilt for coming to group on their own behalves. (Further examples of the varieties of parent groups can be found in Heffrin, 1973; Finger, 1966; Mowatt, 1972; Winder, 1963.)

Inpatient and Residential Groups

Inpatient and residential populations lend themselves to many different kinds of groups. Problems with residential groups are that they are often too multipurposed and inappropriately structured to accomplish their purposes. A major factor to consider informing groups in residential situations is the anticipated length of time each person will remain in the institution. The trend toward shorter stays in most children's and adult institutions reduces the possibilities for long-term psychotherapy groups. However, many other kinds of purposes might be served by inpatient groups.

The milieu meeting (a meeting between staff and patients) is perhaps the base for any inpatient or residential program. Purposes for milieu meetings must be clear if the base of participation is to include more than the staff and a few of the more vocal residents. Generally, the purpose of the milieu meeting is to develop and enhance relationships among the patients and between the staff and the patients. When milieu meetings are concerned primarily with issues and interactions on the milieu there is a larger base of participation among both staff and patients. If the milieu meeting is approached as a town meeting it encourages everyone to come to the meeting as citizens of a community and to have their say. Staff can come in full force and not overwhelm the patients, since the staff are not at the meeting as therapists, but as members of the community who occupy staff positions. Staff can be free to raise their ideas about the community just as patients or residents should feel free to voice their concerns and seek solutions to conflicts. Attempts to turn large milieu meetings into insight therapy sessions are perhaps the largest problem, often inhibiting the processes of the meetings. The town meeting structure can accommodate large numbers of patients and staff. The frequency and duration of meetings must be experimented with, adapted to the particular institution, and balanced in relation to other programs and therapies.

The essence of milieu therapy is to combat the regressive and dependency-causing effects of hospitalization, to help patients and residents develop their capacities for self-control and mutual control of behavior, to facilitate growth in the patients' capacities for interpersonal relationships through the use of the milieu as a microcosm of the interpersonal world outside the hospital, and to help develop and support individual autonomy and initiative in coping with the milieu and outside society. Problems in milieu therapy stem from attempts to accomplish all or some of these goals in a single group structure rather than providing differentiated structures to accomplish specific ends. A more rational approach might comprise different group structures to accomplish the several goals at different times for different members of the milieu. If the large milieu meeting becomes the base for patient-to-patient and patient-to-staff communication and decision-making, then other kinds of group services can be built around the milieu meetings. Orientation meetings can help new people adjust to the milieu, while predischarge and postdischarge services can help prepare people to leave the milieu. During the middle phase of institutionalization and hospitalization, verbal and nonverbal therapy groups can include groups with a range of goals from establishing interpersonal communication and relationships (withdrawn groups) to the development of interpersonal and/or intrapsychic insight. Only those in need of and appropriate to the several groups should be included in such services. The average hospital unit may have only enough patients capable of intrapsychic insight to form one such group at a time. To weaken such a group with people who do not belong in such a group is a disservice to all concerned. (Tanaka, 1962, discusses the structure, range, and rationales for group services in a psychiatric milieu, while Heitler, 1973, and Hadley et al., 1963, report on unusual variations to meet specialized milieu needs.)

Transitional states serve as a viable base for short-term open-ended or closed groups. The transitional states in an institution generally consist of entering the community, leaving the community, and any major steps or transfers within the program. Thus, orientation groups help people move into the social interaction of the community; predischarge groups can then prepare members to leave the community. Especially in treatment communities where an idyllic social climate is developed, predischarge and postdischarge groups are often essential to help individuals readjust to the world outside and also to insure that they more directly transfer some of the growth that they experienced while an inpatient. The membership of these groups is usually of little consequence, since everyone is facing the same immediate fate. The frequency, duration, and number of meetings must be a matter of experimentation and related to the practical realities of the community.

Some residents of therapeutic communities have difficulty adjusting even to the idyllic social climate that often becomes a part of such communities. For people who have difficulty adjusting to the community, special groups can often help them become more a part of the community and maintain a good level and broad base of social interaction within the community. (Hadley, 1963; Heitler et al., 1973. Homogeneous groups consisting of four to six withdrawn patients meeting three to five times a week for fifteen minutes to a half hour can go a long way in socializing the withdrawn to the community.

Any particular objective that the community has for some of its members can be facilitated by forming a homogenous grouping to give the residents a chance to support each other in the endeavor. Some areas such groups could deal with include passes, home visits, vocational preparation, and grooming, for example. Many medical and psychiatric settings have groups dealing with peer review of weekly progress. These groups help to induce and support motivation for growth as well as provide social reward for effort. (See, for example, McNeil and Verwoerot, 1972; Towey, 1966; Pinsky and Levy, 1964; and Rees and Glatt, 1955).

Patient government is a much used and often abused form of helping inpatient communities. For patient government to be both effective and therapeutic, residents must have a clear definition of what authority for decision-making is granted them. Careful consideration must also be given to what authority the residents want and are able to handle (see the authority crisis in Chapter 3, Part 2). For example, patient decisions about passes and discharges are unrealistic in most settings. Generally, when patients become involved in these decisions they become more involved in politics than in issues of the growth and readiness of the person under consideration. In any event the legal responsibility for these decisions is usually vested in the medical profession and the patients know this.

However, when patients are asked to help evaluate a person's readiness for passes and discharges and when good criteria are drawn up and shared with the patients, the discussion and opinions about the prospective pass and discharge can be a realistic evaluation of the patient, helpful not only to the patient but to all those discussing the issue.

If, instead of being told unrealistically that they make the decisions, patients are aware that the staff, or more specifically the doctor is interested in their opinions and will use them as a guide in making decisions, they usually respond to and use the pass or discharge meeting more favorably.

Realistic patient government in a residential situation can support and enhance patient autonomy and initiative more effectively than any other technique. The principles in developing a sound patient government are to give realistic authority to the patients and reserve for staff that authority which it cannot legally or socially relinquish, then make standards for guiding deliberations as clear as possible. Of course, patients can be extremely helpful in drawing up clear and realistic standards but, staff often must temper the too strict or too rigid standards and rules that patients develop.

2

Preparing
Individuals

Most prospective members of most types of therapy groups can benefit greatly from individual interviews preparatory to group therapy. Some evidence supports the notion that pregroup interviews help prevent early drop-outs (Ormont, 1957); further evidence supports the notion that pregroup interviews contribute to group development (Yalom, 1966; Yalom et al., 1967). Pregroup individual interviews can accomplish at least four major purposes. They can

1. initiate a relationship between the therapist and the prospective member;
2. find out why the person has come for therapy as well as what motives, expectations, and resistances to therapy the person has;
3. prepare the person for entry into the group by exploring and reducing fears and resistances to the group and by anticipating the difficulties arising in early phases of group participation;
4. gain an initial impression of the person's strivings, difficulties, background, capacities, and suitability both for group therapy and for the particular group under consideration.

Pregroup interviewing can range from a single session to a full course of individual or family therapy prior to entry into the group; however, a single interview will often suffice. Intake interviews protect both the new individual and the group. For the new individual, they can either help prepare the person for entry into the group or result in the person's not coming into an inappropriate group or not coming into group therapy inappropriately. The intake interview also helps protect the group from members who either don't fit or would be apt to drop out, taking time and energy away from the group to little avail.

INITIATING RELATIONSHIPS WITH THE THERAPIST

One primary function of the intake interview is to intiate a therapist-member relationship that can support the new individual entering the group. The initial relationship with the therapist helps the member feel that the therapist, at least, is available even if the other members aren't. The a priori acceptance in the therapist-member relationship reduces the emotional energies that might otherwise go into making contact with the therapist in early group sessions. However, there is danger that the pregroup individual contact will increase the member's wishes for an exclusive relationship with the therapist. Unconflicted support by the therapist for the member to enter the group and establish relationships with other members, along with an empathic understanding of the individual's ambivalences about sharing the therapist and entering into relationships, can serve to reduce the conflict.

Particularly during the often bombastic processes of the inclusion phase it is important that members feel they can turn to the therapist as a port in the storm. Thus, establishing a relationship between patient and therapist in the intake interview, while it has its dangers, serves as a support for entry into the group and as a bridge to relationships with other members (Levine, 1965). It is important to view the movement from relationship with the therapist to relationships with other group members as a dynamic process essential for individual growth rather than as something to be avoided for the sake of better group processes.

Without a prior relationship with the therapist a person may enter the group so anxious that the anxiety may push him to participate and risk rather quickly. The new member would become immediately active, but to what avail? If initiating relationships with other people and entering social situations is difficult, as it is for many people coming for group therapy, then protracting the entry process by permitting the haven of an individual contact with the therapist might result in an unfolding of the very difficulties that the individual has in making contact with other people. If the relationship with the therapist is viewed in its psychosocial framework, the individual first establishes a relationship with the therapist as a parent figure, then matures into venturing out toward other people just as the infant first relates to the nurturing parent and then develops sufficient trust in the world outside himself to reach out beyond the parent. Thus, the entry process becomes a recapitulation and reworking of early psychosocial development. To the degree that people have had difficulty trusting in the world outside themselves and outside the relationship with a nurturing figure, to that same degree they may need to cling to the therapist while they grow to where they can reach out to others. The re-enactment of this process is important to the individual since it provides opportunities in the early group meeting for working through some of the conflicts remaining from those periods in the person's life when he or she was attempting to establish their autonomy separate from their parents. In the long run, the group process that evolves from growth of the members rather than an approach of "sink or swim" holds firmer and provides corrective re-experience of unresolved growth issues. The development of the group provides both a bulwark against untoward dependency as well as an environment that makes reaching out beyond the member-therapist relationship both easier and more desirable.

EXPLORATION OF GOALS AND EXPECTATIONS

This aspect of the intake process differs little from initial interview for individual therapy. The therapist must learn some of the individual's background so that he or she can assess the person's difficulty, gather some initial information which may prove useful in facilitating the development of identification and empathic bridges to other members in early sessions, and give the individual an opportunity to begin talking about himself with the therapist as a preparation for self-initiative and revelation in the group. The therapist's nonjudgmental and empathic acceptance of the person and his plight in the intake process can serve as a building block for participation in the group. As a result of a positive intake interview the individual can feel that at least one person in the group accepts, understands, and may be able to help.

This process of finding out about the individual will not be elaborated here, for the principles of individual diagnostic interviews are to be found elsewhere (see, for example: Hollis, 1972: 247-348; Garrett, 1970: 7-59). For this discussion it may be well to concentrate on the differences of this process for groups. Most important is that the therapist conducting intake interviews must keep in mind that a little information can be useful to both therapist and client, but a lot of information might lead to some of the dangers cited under initiating the relationship. Just as in an intake or initial interview for individual therapy, the therapist doesn't expect to get all the information in one sitting. However, group therapists doing intake interviews might become anxious to get all the information right away, since the balance may be slow in coming once the person is in the group. This kind of anxiety might lead the therapist toward drawing the individual into telling too much at intake. Just as in individual treatment, the major unfolding of pertinent information can and must take place in the group.

It is important for the therapist to get basic data on the problem and precipitating events that bring the person for treatment, and how the person thinks therapy might help. Some people coming for group therapy, particularly when they have had prior individual or group therapy, have definite ideas of what they would like from the group experience. A contract to work toward their goal is all that is necessary in such instances. Others have ideas of what's the matter but are not sure where and how therapy can help. Part of the contract with these people might be to have them figure out while in the group what they might get from therapy, especially after they, the therapist, and other group members get a better idea of what the problem is. A third group of clients have little or no idea of what's the matter, never mind what to expect from the group. These people often come for therapy either because someone sent them or because they just don't feel right and wonder why. Their contract might be to figure out both what is the matter and what can be done. These people can often gain some knowledge of their own situation by first experiencing in the group what is causing difficulty for others. Children and adolescents, particularly, often need exposure to the group before they can allow themselves to realize or experience their difficulties.

Reconciling the goals of the member with those of the therapist begins with the intake interview and continues during either the formative part of the group for those in closed groups or during the entry process for those in open-ended groups. A mechanistic statement of goals on either the member's or the therapist's part is of little consequence, since both can only be tentative in what they perceive as the goal until they more fully understand and appreciate what is the matter. However, *the shorter the term of the group, the more specific the goals should be.* If a member is being interviewed for a short-term and, consequently, very circumscribed purpose, then a clear delineation of the goals for the group and its possible limitations in meeting all of the client's other possible needs must be made. It is important at intake to align the contract and goal for the individual with the purpose, structure, and membership of the group. Aligning goals requires dealing not only with the substance of these goals, but also with the limitations for the process if the group is less than a long-term open-ended one where people can continue until they complete their quest.

PREPARING FOR GROUP PARTICIPATION

In group therapy, there is the additional aspect of preparing people to participate in a group to gain the help that they are seeking. The therapist can help the individual to get ready to participate in a therapy group in two major ways. The first is to gain knowledge of the person's past group experiences with the aim of understanding positive experiences that may be useful in the group and, with this information, to help reduce some of the possible fears and resistances to the group stemming from past experiences (Gerard, 1956). The other is to anticipate the early processes that the person will be exposed to and help the person prepare for understanding and coping with these processes. Nash et al. (1957) make obvious the need for preparation for group phenomenon in their finding that people with lesser social resources tend to drop out of groups unless in marked distress.

Considering that most people who come for therapy have had some negative experiences with other people in their family, romantic, peer, or work relationships, the problem of helping them prepare for using group relationships for their therapy is compounded. However, it also follows that difficulties in relationships might be ameliorated in a situation that provides relationships for corrective social-emotional experiences. In preparing people for participation in therapy groups the problem is to help them see how groups can provide what they are looking for and to help them to sufficiently overcome fears of groups stemming from past experiences so that they can venture into a group.

While most people have had some interpersonal experiences which help to compensate for problematic or conflictual relationships, few have experienced the kinds of relationships that develop in a therapy group. When considering group therapy usually people consciously harken back to their adolescent peer experiences or classrooms. Memories of early adolescent peer groups with their strict pressures for conformity with peer culture and high risk of rejection for deviation can add to the fears that an individual might have about entering group therapy. The major fear is that the group will insist on conformity and not allow individuality. A prospective member may listen but not fully believe that a well developed group of adults not only grows to allow individuality but also highly values and supports it.

In addition to their interpersonal experiences, of course, most people coming to therapy groups have parts of their intellectual and emotional life that they reject and which cause them great discomfort. While, on one hand, they may be coming for therapy to alleviate the burden of these thoughts and feelings, on the other hand, they feel unacceptable to others because of these thoughts and feelings. The threat of having to reveal these thoughts and feelings to others in order to gain relief poses many fears. In spite of some awareness of the possible universality of these thoughts and feelings, which must be stressed during intake, each person finds it difficult to believe, in advance of group participation, that other people really have the same or similar thoughts or feelings. Consequently, each member harbors the fear that if and when others find out what is really happening inside him or her, others will reject them. Perhaps just as difficult, each member fears that he will see himself as worse than other people.

A third range of threats comes when people know that something is not going right for them, yet they have no awareness of what their underlying feelings might be. Such a person may trust a therapist to let him or her know in a gradual and sensitive way while allowing the person sufficient time to become aware of his or her underlying feelings. However, a person cannot feel as trusting that a group will allow him or her to deal with underlying feelings at their own rate of readiness (Wolf, 1963; Ormont, 1957). Thus, the possible embarassment and shame both over the overt symptoms and manifestations and over the possible unknown and covert symptoms contribute to the potential group member's fears and despair of gaining help from a group.

Some of the other major fears of entering group therapy stem from people's expectations of themselves for growth and change. When considering group as opposed to individual therapy, people become concerned that others may place too high an expectation for growth upon them, while an individual therapist might be more patient and understanding with the person's rate of progress.

Many people are preoccupied with the confidentiality of the group. These people might trust a therapist to maintain confidentiality, but can't be sure that other group members would. Such people need reassurance that they do not have to risk information until they trust the group to maintain their confidences

(Wolf, 1963). While the problem of confidentiality might seem irresolvable to nongroup therapists and new members, the fact of the matter is that there is seldom any difficulty with violation of confidentiality. Progressive unfolding of confidences leads the group member to risk only what he or she is ready to have known. Then the universality that one experiences in the feedback from other members leads a member to become less concerned about who knows their inner thoughts and feelings. The phenomenon of quasi-public disclosure of disdained or feared inner processes in the therapy group helps to make a member less fearing and disdainful of these thoughts and feelings and, consequently, less concerned about who knows them. Lowered concern about confidentiality in the group must not be viewed as justification for not giving the question full attention. Members must contract to maintain the confidentiality of others and need the assurance that others will do the same. Contracting for maintaining confidentaility can begin in the intake interview and can be discussed further when the group meets.

Finally, many people come to therapy with mixed feelings about relinquishing some of their neurotic patterns of behavior (Spotnitz, 1952; Wolf, 1963; Ormont, 1957). While these people seek relief from their pain, a big part of them doesn't want to give up their ways of doing things. These people fear group therapy; they think an individual therapist might allow them to continue their behavior pattern while helping to relieve their pain, but that other members of a group may not be as understanding and lenient with them.

The task of the therapist in the pregroup interview is to help the person unearth and come to grips with their particular fears and resistances to group therapy. Again, the therapist should bear in mind that the task in pregroup interviews is to help reduce fears and resistances sufficiently to enable the person to enter the group situation. There is plenty of time for working through the causes of these fears and resistances while the individual is in the group. The therapist might point out the universality of the fears for all people when they enter groups and also point out how these fears are not fully founded for therapy groups. The therapist should also consider that the fears under discussion are the more manifest and conscious ones, whereas the deeper fears, stemming perhaps from primary family or current life experiences, are the major objective of the corrective emotional experience. In most cases, the underlying fears cannot be resolved until the person has been in therapy long enough to gain conscious awareness of them.

Some overt fears that prospective members have about groups and participation are well founded. Their experiences in the early group sessions very often confirm some of the fears. Consequently, during the intake interview it is important that the therapist prepare the member for the early group processes (Yalom, 1966; Ormont, 1957). Prior to entering the group, inclusion processes are often what people consider the most ominous. The major fears center on the member's comfort or discomfort with expression or fear of being the object of aggression and hostility. Immediately underlying the fears of aggression and hostility are the fears of rejection (Snoek, 1962). Reassurance that everyone entering group therapy has some fear of aggression, hostility, and rejection can be helpful. What is different about group therapy as opposed to other group membership is that if members stay with it through the inclusion processes they come to the other end, which is a comfortable acceptance by the group in an atmosphere where they feel accepted and free to express themselves and live in decreasing fear of affective expression.

Though most people are not usually aware of it, fears of intimacy often prove more overpowering than fears of hostility. Most people feel that they desire intimacy with others, but as intimacy descends upon a group many fears emerge, which give rise to a multitude of still other fears and often results in drop-outs (Yalom, 1966). Since most premature drop-outs from therapy groups are brought about by inclusion and intimacy issues, it is well to prepare the person for these phenomena as fully as possible, but always remembering that the group experience itself will provide the opportunities and support for overcoming these fears more fully. While preparing people for the difficult work of becoming group members it is also well to point toward the hopeful aspect of group, the idyllic middle phase of mutuality with its comfort, support, and empathy balancing the confrontation and conflict. Without some notion and hope of a silver lining to the often stormy entry struggles, the intake preparation may paint so dark a picture of group therapy that it becomes not worth pursuing. The instillation of hope during intake interviews as a factor in continuance in treatment is supported by the findings of Ripple (1964) and Goldstein and Shipman (1961). People's past experiences with family, school, and peer (particularly adolescent) experiences, as well as their romantic and work group relationships, may cause them to despair over the possibilities of a group becoming a comfortable nurturing and growth producing experience. It is important to explore the person's experiences with any of these relationships to understand both what helpful capacities they have for relationship and what fears may remain from earlier experiences. It is best to concentrate on the particular experiences and fears of the individual while helping the individual anticipate how a therapy group may differ from and possibly corrective for these past experiences.

INITIAL ASSESSMENT OF NEEDS AND
CAPACITY FOR GROUP THERAPY

Therapists must come to some initial conclusions about the client and his needs as part of the intake process. Depending on what these conclusions are, the therapist either prepares the client for entry into the group, decides on a protracted preparation process, or helps the person consider alternatives to group therapy. The manner in which the therapist assesses the person's difficulties depends on his/her psychosocial school of thought and mode of treatment he/

she employs with a group. Regardless of how a therapist reaches conclusions about the person and his plight there are some considerations that follow from these conclusions. In addition to assessing the individual and the presenting difficulties, the therapist must decide:

1. the individual's need for therapy;
2. appropriateness of group therapy for the person and problem;
3. appropriateness of the available groups for the person and the problem.

Therefore, the group therapist must determine the nature of the person and problems being presented and make professional determinations about what needs to be done to help, regardless of treatment modality. If the therapist determines that psychotherapy is needed, then the next question becomes whether group therapy is appropriate.

Beyond generalization about who is amenable to group therapy and who needs protracted individual preparation for it lies a host of specific judgments that the therapist must make during the intake process; he must determine whether or not the particular person will fit into a particular group in ways that will be productive for both the individual and the group.

First is the basic consideration of whether the person shares the same goals as the other members. If the group is a long-term one, then the question is whether the individual's goals are compatible with those of the other members. Compatible goals need not necessarily be similar and, indeed, might well be different but complementary. For example, in the balanced children's group one child's need to develop controls complements another's need to be freer to express himself.

Next consideration is whether the individual can identify with at least one other person in some major ways (Smith, 1974; Levine, 1968). In the example of the children's group, other children also need to develop controls. A comparison must be made of age, sex, subcultural, vocational, educational, intellectual, and any other vital characteristics that may be or become significant for the particular person in the particular group.

Also to be considered are behavioral patterns and characteristics: do they blend or contrast (Redl, 1951)? Is this person the only one with his or her kind of behavioral pattern? What does this similarity or difference mean for this person and this group at this time?

Finally, does the state of the particular group lend itself to incorporating the new member? A group in an early intimacy crisis is inclined to resent and reject a new member. A group in the depths of inclusion struggles will accept a new member, but a new member who is extremely afraid of his own or other people's hostility will soon be frightened off by such a group. A group in a solid state of mutuality will be most likely to classically work through the inclusion of a new member. However, if the group in mutuality is in the middle of a separation crisis, it might displace some of the hostility on the new member.

In conclusion, the decision about placing a person in a group must be based on the general principles of purpose, grouping, and structure, as well as careful consideration of who the individual is and how this individual will fit into a particular group at a particular time.

3

Preparing
Therapists

To be effective, group therapists must know about themselves in the helping role, about dynamics of individual dysfunction and amelioration, and about
dynamics of therapy groups. When therapists approach groups without either
knowledge of or readiness to learn about all three areas, consequences for the
group, individual members, and perhaps the therapist as well are unfortunate.
The therapeutic role calls for two very different kinds of responses from the
group therapist: nurturing parent and empathic facilitator. Complicating the
group therapist's role is that at times the therapist is required to be nurturing to
some members and facilitative to others, depending on the respective levels of
function of those in the group.

Most groups begin with individuals needing nurture. As they develop the
individuals in them need less nurture and more personal and interpersonal facilitation within an empathic atmosphere. Some groups advance so rapidly that a
period of nurture is almost unnecessary; others never grow beyond needing
nurture from the therapist.

For group therapists the problem is to appropriately assess the level and
needs of the group in order to provide what is actually required. Among the
major problems group therapists confront are their tendencies to nurture groups
when empathic facilitation would be more appropriate and to provide empathic
facilitation when nurture is called for. This chapter elaborates the more critical
learning issues for group therapists in differential leadership of therapy groups
(Yalom, 1966; Lakin et al., 1969).

Therapists' personal and professional backgrounds strongly influence their
preoccupation with roles that are primarily facilitative or primarily nurturing
(Williams, 1966; Goodman, 1968; Berger, 1974). Some define their roles in ways
that allow mostly nurture for individuals, with perhaps some empathic facilitation. Others define their roles as empathic facilitators to the entire group and
view nurture to individuals as fostering dependency. While these stances are
often well rationalized through adherence to or creation of a theory that underlies their role behavior, the basic difficulty is that their personal background has
led most therapists to fear, distrust, or discount the possible therapeutic value of

group processes or to use group processes to hide from any depth in their relationships with the individual members (Williams, 1966).

Since a therapist new to groups is unlikely to have all the attributes essential for the role at the outset, it is difficult to anticipate what he or she needs to learn before starting a group. However, before listing the qualities essential for a group therapist who would perform at a high level of professionality, it might be well to say that neophytes should at least be open to recognizing which qualities they possess and open to supervisory help as they learn and grow in their abilities. Ebersole et al. (1969) reports on a study of two groups of psychiatric technicians who were involved in a group therapy program. Half were trained and supervised; the other half left to their own devices. The trained group improved as group therapists over a six month period; the others showed some evidence of declining in their abilities. Authoritarianism, emotional isolation, and fears of loss of control were among the major increasing problems found in the untrained group of leaders.

KNOWLEDGE OF INDIVIDUALS

It matters little what school of psychology or psychiatry the group therapist espouses; it is important that the therapist have some means for evaluating individual behavior and dynamics to assess strengths and limitations. Without it, the therapist lacks the means to realistically assess and accept the individual member's level of function and to determine how much can be expected in the ways the individual functions, currently and in the future, within and outside of the group. Without knowledge of individual dynamics, there is danger that the therapist will not be able to assess the impact of group processes on the individual and the reactions of the individual to these processes.

Powerful forces are operative in therapy groups. These forces can work toward growth and can help the members, but occasionally they can devastate certain individuals. A group therapist without knowledge of individual dynamics is like a midwife delivering a baby. As long as there are no serious complications the midwife can tend the delivery. If serious complications develop, then an obstetrician is needed to assess and tend the situation and perhaps, to save the lives of mother and child. Similarly, a group therapist without knowledge of individual dynamics is unable to recognize and act upon complications that develop for individuals (Lieberman et al., 1973: 430-4).

An often repeated rationalization from some sensitivity group leaders is that if a person comes to a group, then whatever happens is the person's own responsibility (Lieberman et al., 1973: 437). This rationale is presumed to clear the trainer in advance of any responsibility for his or her acts of omission or commission that may result in harm to individuals. It is most interesting that this philosophy emerges in an era of consumerism with its ever increasing concern and protection for consumers of goods and services. The rationale of client responsibility may help in absolving the trainer from guilt over difficulties arising from sensitivity groups—but does it really speak to the responsibility of professional helpers to provide services that are potentially curative rather than harmful? Of course, a therapist may do all that can be expected within sound professional knowledge and the individual still might not benefit and could even be hurt by the process. The crux of the matter is whether the therapist took all due precaution based on sound clinical judgment and practices and, more fundamentally, whether the therapist used sound clinical judgment and practice.

Finally, if the purpose of group therapy is ultimately to help individuals, then it behooves therapists to have some understanding of what help is needed and when and if that help has been rendered. Since the group is an open learning and growth situation, a therapist may not be aware of all the learning and growth that has taken place for the individual. Still, however, the therapist should have awareness and understanding of those aspects of difficulty and function that the person brought for work and/or were deemed to be objectives by the therapist. Only in this way can the therapist monitor and assess progress or regression to consider what further or different help might be necessary for the individual. If a therapy group exists to help individuals, not to build better groups per se, then knowledge of individuals is essential.

Experience in helping individuals, particularly with the kinds of problems that beset members of the group, is important for the group therapist. If the group therapist is to be helpful to individuals in resolving their individual problems, then the experience of helping through individual therapy provides the opportunity to see all the ramifications for the individual—how the problem came to be and what it took for the individual to resolve the problem. Because the group process often makes it less necessary to explore more fully the nooks and crannies of a problem to achieve the same degree of amelioration, a therapist without individual experience may not fully and deeply appreciate the impact of causitive factors—as well as the difficulties in individual growth and change.

A therapist without individual treatment experience may not fully appreciate the weight of the helping relationship on the therapist. In most therapy groups, the direct impact of people and their plight on the therapist is diluted because the helping burden is shared by the other members and perhaps even co-therapist. Without well-supervised experience in one-to-one helping, therapists might not fully appreciate their own feelings and reactions as helpers. While it is possible to gain the full appreciation of the weight of helping relationships in group therapy, wary or unknowing therapists can shunt away in many ways the full impact of the helping responsibility in the group situation. Therapists who need to protect themselves from the weight of helping responsibility might tend to keep the group at a relational distance with many possible negative consequences for the group and the individual members. Therefore, it is important for new group therapists to experience themselves in some depth as helpers in one-to-one relationships. This will insure their readiness and capacity to carry fully the weight of helping relationships in the group.

Some knowledge of group dynamics can be important for the therapist starting a group. Such knowledge can be obtained in courses on group therapy and by participating in a training group or a therapy group. Courses in group dynamics, however, are often not very meaningful to most therapists until they themselves have been either therapists or a member of a group. Most therapists are grounded in individual psychologies; therefore, they often underestimate or discount group dynamics, although group dynamics are often more readily visible than individual emotional dynamics. It seems that if dynamics are easily visible many therapists feel that they couldn't be important or powerful. For this reason it is important that the person studying therapy group dynamics do it concurrently either with a group experience or while leading a group. If the student therapists have places to apply the didactic learning, they seem to gain a fuller and deeper appreciation of the group dynamics.

A caution about gaining all of one's knowledge about groups from either classroom group exercises or training groups: potential group therapists may come to expect that all groups will function the way a group of therapists functions or that therapy groups can and should function like training groups. There might be many similarities when compared to a group of outpatient neurotics, but few similarities when compared to groups of children or people with lower levels of psychosocial function. A group composed of all mental health professionals or would-be mental health professionals has some peculiarities seldom found in other groups. The level of self awareness of the members and the interpersonal sophistication allow the members to more readily identify and deal with group issues. On the other hand, groups of mental health professionals often have more difficulty in overtly expressing early conflicts. They often feel that they are "beyond" having such conflicts or they feel some responsibility for being "maturely" patient with each other and counterdependently allowing others to go first, "patiently waiting for their turn." Moreover, risking of significant material is often more difficult among other professionals. Both the member risking and the other members are more likely aware of the full implications of what is said or done; therefore, the danger of being clinically judged is higher. Mental health professionals do not fear being judged right or wrong, good or bad, so much as being judged normal or abnormal.

In the author's opinion the best opportunity for learning about group processes lies in a group supervisory process in which each member of the supervisory group leads or coleads a therapy group. In the group supervisory process, guided by a competent group therapy supervisor, the members can experience group processes both as members of a group and as therapists. The dangers of expecting therapy groups to be like training groups are reduced because the differences can be discussed as they are experienced, both within the group one is leading and with those leading other groups. Similarities and differences among groups can be brought out more fully and deeply in a group supervisory process than anywhere else. In addition, supervisory group members come to better appreciate the assets and liabilities in different people with different personalities and to understand their particular impact on group processes. Most important, through the group supervisory process, group therapists can become more comfortable with how their own personalities effect and affect their helping and the processes of the group.

SELF-AWARENESS

Self-awareness is one of the major facets of the therapist's role in the group. Therapists are entitled to the same range of human emotions and reactions as any one else. But the two major questions are: are those reactions based on perception of the group or clouded by phenomena the therapist brings to the meeting? Is the therapist prepared to recognize the difference in order to facilitate accurate assessment and appropriate therapeutic action for the members and group? A therapist's "gut" reaction is often extremely useful in perceiving the group situation; however, at other times the reaction may be caused by the therapist's own personal needs for security. Only experience and careful scrutiny with supervisory help can help the therapist learn the difference.

Regardless of the therapist's school of psychology or group therapy, there is little doubt the therapist's own personality has profound impact on the group. (See, for example: Haythorn et al., 1956; Williams, 1966; Bandura, 1956; Astrachan et al., 1967; Klaf, 1961; Lewin et al., 1939; Berger, 1974; Shatan, 1962.) The ways in which the therapist's feelings and reactions can facilitate or inhibit the group processes are endless. In the author's experiences with supervision and training of group therapists, a number of crucial characteristics often occur. In general, these characteristics are closely linked to developmental phenomena in groups. While these phenomena will be more fully elaborated upon in Part 2 where and as they arise as issues in group development and therapist reactions, it may be well to merely list them at this juncture:

1. Self-reliance. Is the therapist reasonably self-reliant but able to give and get help appropriately? Or does the therapist have unmet dependency needs that he might seek to have met by group members either through a frank dependency on them or through counterdependent helping in which the therapist vicariously gratifies his dependency needs by meeting those of others?
2. Authority. Is the therapist reasonably comfortable in asserting and accepting appropriate levels of authority? Or will the therapist inappropriately capitulate his authority to the group or autocratically dominate the group?
3. Acceptance. Is the therapist reasonably satisfied with his acceptance by other people? Or will the therapist seek to make up for a feeling of lack of acceptance by attempting to gain acceptance from the group

members, by being overly fearful of rejection by group members, or perhaps even by seeking rejection by group members?

4. Expression of emotions. Is the therapist reasonably comfortable with his own and other people's expression of emotions? Or will the therapist seek to prevent the members from expressing feelings (particularly angry ones) or seek to have group members express emotions for him?

5. Intimacy. Does the therapist have sufficient capacity for and opportunities for intimacy in his own relationships? Or will the therapist become too uncomfortable with intimacy in the group or seek to meet his needs for intimacy in the therapy group?

6. Separation. Is the therapist comfortable with separation? Or will the therapist, because of his own unresolved feelings, seek to either suppress separation and termination phenomena or seek its expression beyond the group's needs or capacities?

The therapist's leanings with regard to the above characteristics can be gleaned from past and present relationships as well as prior individual and family treatment experiences. However, individual and family treatment relationships sometimes don't bring out the same issues as group treatment. For example, many therapists who see themselves as not controlling because of their experience with individual therapy often either run headlong into controlling the group or display intense anxiety over their felt lack of control of the group. The problem seems to arise from the therapist's feeling that he could allow individuals more latitude than he can allow a group because he had confidence in his ability to regain control of the process at any time with individuals but he doesn't have that confidence with a group.

COUNTERTRANSFERENCE, OVERIDENTIFICATION, AND NEGATIVE IDENTIFICATION

Countertransference and identification are two of the major ways in which the therapist may react emotionally to individual members and the group. Any of the phenomenon in the preceding discussion could cause or interact with transference and identification of the therapist.

Countertransference in this discussion is used to mean the attribution of unfounded feelings and reactions to a group member or the group. Countertransference can be positive or negative. The essential problem is that feelings and reactions that arise from countertransference may cause the therapist to misperceive the member or group and act toward the person or group in ways that are unrelated or inappropriate to the person's real feelings and needs. The possibilities for countertransference in group therapy are limitless: a therapist can see in group members his own parents, siblings, children, spouses, friends, bosses, and peers, and, consequently, view the group or individual members from the vantage point of his past experience.

Overidentificiation occurs when the therapist attributes unfounded similarities in feelings and reactions to group members. A major problem with over-identification is that the therapist again may act toward the person in ways which are unrelated to the person's actual feelings and needs.

Negative identification is a little different from overidentification in that the therapist's perception of the group member may be accurate, but the member's similarities in feelings or behavior may remind the therapist of feelings and reactions in himself which he would like to disown. To the degree that the therapist is unaware of these feelings and reactions in himself, the therapist may react negatively and perhaps even punitively toward the person or persons who remind him of the part of himself he would like to disown. These phenomena are well explicated in many sources on individual and group therapy. Many authors on group psychotherapy underscore the existence, function, and need of professional awareness of these pheomena. However, various authors use differing and overlapping concepts when referring to these phenomena. See, for example: Slavson, 1964: 446-449; Schwartz and Wolf, 1964; Rosenthal, 1953; Goodman et al., 1964; Berger, 1974; Winnicott, 1960).

The only additional aspect of these phenomena in group therapy are the possibilities of the therapist's reacting to current situations in the therapy group on the basis of past experiences with another group rather than on what is actually happening in the group at the time. The classic example occurs when a therapist encounters an early conflict in the group during the inclusion phase and harkens back to past experiences where a conflict among people resulted in some bad outcomes. Thus, the fears aroused in the therapist by the conflict in the group may be due more to past familial, peer, romantic, or even therapy-group experiences than to what is happening in the group.

Countertransference, overidentification, and negative identification mostly arise after the group is in progress. Although they are sometimes instantaneous more often they develop as the relationships deepen. These reactions cannot easily be anticipated prior to the therapist's working with groups but may be the subject of supervisory help during work with groups. These same phenomena occur even with very experienced therapists and such therapists should be aware of the possibilities and ready to seek another person to help evaluate the situation. Cotherapists can check out perceptions with each other and can often help each other recognize and cope with these reactions.

GROUP-ORIENTED THERAPISTS

In my experience supervising and training many group-oriented therapists, many characteristics seem to recur. An examination of their adolescent peer experiences usually shows that they were either in the center of their peer groups or somewhere on the periphery, not in between.

Peripheral status in the adolescent peer group was manifested either by frank isolation from the peer group or a sense of being above or beyond their peer group's interaction. In leading therapy groups, these people are often trying to gain the acceptance and inclusion that they either couldn't get or held themselves back from during adolescence, and perhaps long before that in peer and family experiences. Although they can be extremely empathic with the interpersonal difficulties that group members encounter, they also tend to overidentify with their clients. Most of these seek acceptance by and inclusion in the group and have difficulty allowing members to express hostile and rejecting feelings toward each other and the therapist. Some of these therapists harbor anger at groups for past rejection or exclusion and focus incessantly on issues of anger. Or these therapists may incline toward "hot-seat" approaches, in which everyone in the group flails away at each member in turn. This is not to infer that there is never indication for use of hot-seat approaches, but rather implies that inappropriate use of the hot seat may result from the therapist's need to "get even" with groups for past injuries. While overt limit-setting may be difficult, if not impossible, for this therapist, limits are set covertly, especially on aggression and hostility, through his exuding displeasure or discomfort. Groups led by these therapists can at best develop to the pseudo-intimacy level of the normal adolescent group. As a result everyone comes to the meetings with good feelings about each other and grows to feel even worse about any feelings of rejection or hostility that they may harbor. Many of these therapists gravitate to the philosophies that render the therapist as being without a special role—essentially one of the group members. They often prefer nondirective approaches, yet end up in firmer control of affective expression than most other therapists.

Group-oriented therapists who were very much the center of peer group life during their adolescent years are often motivated by a search for the intimacy they missed by being at the center of things (Chapin, 1950). However, just as they did in their peer experiences, these therapists tend to opt for control of the group as a substitute for acceptance. Again the basic issue is the search for acceptance and intimacy, but the fear of being rejected leads many of these therapists to adopt more autocratic methods to structure the situation and reduce the possibilities for rejection. However, these therapists are benevolent despots in that they are often extremely sensitive to the overt and covert wishes of the members and give the members what they want, so long as the therapist feels secure with what's desired. When the therapist conflicts with what a member desires, the therapist will either attempt to convince the members that there is no conflict or manipulate the group to control or overwhelm the individual member. Thus, the individual either must accede to the "group" wishes or drop out. A good deal of what goes on in the group is aimed at pleasing the therapist. Individual and group growth often takes place to the extent that the therapist is comfortable with and only to that extent (Mann, 1967: 120-145). If this therapist has some notions of group development, the group will most often grow in the way and at the pace the therapist wants. Thus, this kind of group can often seem to achieve a full development by virture of having gone through various stages but the development is very superficial.

The major problem in this kind of group development is that instead of members achieving a firmer sense of their own identity vis-a-vis other people, they often end up with still another experience in which they had to sacrifice their autonomy in order to gain acceptance by the therapist. As in any auto-cratic process, the members hardly ever develop a sense of completion or self-sufficiency and need to keep coming back to the therapist for further advice, permission, and particularly, approval. Often these therapists spend an inordi-nate amount of time on goal-setting and structure in order to maintain control of the process and prevent anything they can't deal with from happening. How-ever, most of these therapists either gravitate toward philosophies that support an autocratic stance for the therapist and that don't allow for group develop-ment or, while giving lip service to freedom and democracy, skillfully maintain autocratic control (Bandura, 1956; Hollister, 1957).

One characteristic that many group-oriented therapists have in common is their fear of the dependency, intimacy, and depth of one-to-one relationships. This very often leads them to reject or ignore theories of individual dynamics in favor of interpersonal and group theories. It can also lead them to favor relation-ships with the group as a whole rather than individual relationships with all members. These therapists often have difficulty differentiating between one-to-one interaction between therapist and group members aimed at deepening the affective level of the group and treatment of one person in front of the others.

INDIVIDUALLY-ORIENTED GROUP THERAPISTS

Since most group therapists switch to group therapy after first learning and doing individual therapy, the possible influences of current and past life experi-ences on their approach to group therapy are often further confounded by their first having learned a way of helping in which they have knowledge, skill, and conviction. However, some recurrent issues became obvious as the author helped many therapists make the transition from individual to group therapy. The com-monly held notion that most people become therapists in order to rectify some-thing from their past life might very well hold true.

The primary problem for most individual therapists turning to group therapy is that they have had little theoretical background in group develop-ment; they rely more on the often vast amount of information they have accu-mulated on individual growth, dysfunction, and amelioration. Since much of what they have retained has been confirmed by their practice, they are less inclined to see their understandings as theories and perspectives than as unre-futable fact. Since the task of linking individual and group dynamics is far from complete, there is no fully satisfactory way to help those who formerly special-ized in individual therapy to transfer their theoretical understandings of individ-uals to groups. Some of the early group psychotherapy theories were based primarily on individual dynamics spread around the group. Although many formerly individually oriented therapists have used these theories as a bridge to group therapy, these knowledge bridges are often restricting because they do not explain group phenomena per se. Consequently, individual therapists are often resistant to accepting even the theoretical possibilities that group dynamics can be primary forces acting upon individuals. A recurrent example arises in classes where the author uses a very safe and circumscribed exercise to bring out how those in groups where members perceive significant commonalities are freer to risk. The class is divided into homogeneous and heterogenous groups for a ten-minute sharing of certain feelings. The heterogenous groups always have more difficulty risking than the homogenous. In spite of explanation of the group dynamic involved, the members are inclined to feel that their individual personalities caused the lower levels of sharing rather than the group phenomenon.

Control is a major factor in the transition from individual to group therapy (Williams, 1966). While most individual therapists view themselves as people who do not exert a great deal of control on their clients, it appears that they seldom feel far from being able to control an individual interview. In other words, even if a therapist doesn't particularly control the process during individual therapy the therapist often feels able to gain or regain control at will. When confronted with a multiple person situation and the fact that it is a new situation, the therapist fears that the group will get out of control. Often the fears of loss of control are reduced in actual experiences in the group. With some therapists, the need for control and fears of loss of control persist and require some exploration and understanding before the therapist can relinquish control to the group.

The prime resistance of many individual therapists who start to work with groups is often related to their counterdependency needs. Therapists who over-exploit their counterdependency needs in individual therapy often persist in this trait in treating individuals in the group situation, preventing the member's dependency from shifting to the whole group. The choice between meeting individual need or allowing that need to excite responses and spread to other members is a constantly recurrent situation in group therapy. The reflex reactions of the individual therapist are to respond to an individual's need or anxiety, either relieving the pain or helping the individual to employ that energy for coping. Many former individual therapists who are operating from intense counterdependent needs have difficulty in allowing the individual's anxiety to spread to the group and feel impelled to respond to the individual themselves rather than allowing the group to help first.

In the author's experience it has usually been easier to help formerly individual therapists to make the transition by proceeding gradually. Allowing the individual therapist first to treat individuals in front of the others in the group makes the therapist more comfortable in the group situation. Then as specific instances of treating one person in front of the others arise, it is often easier to help the therapist gradually learn how to engage the whole group or simply allow the process to engage the whole group. Most therapists who are acting from habit and intellectual orientation can soon recognize and understand the difference in group therapy. Therapists who are acting from intense counterdependence or control needs often have more difficulty in making the transition; in these cases, their own feelings as they relate to group situations should then be explored.

PART TWO

Bion (1961) posits three major group dynamics, which he calls assumptions, and gives credence to their recurrent development in groups, but he also
suggests that these dynamics or assumptions need to be interpreted away for the
"work group" or fully formed group to develop. In order for the real work of
personal and interpersonal insight to take place these assumptions must be
defeated. It is interesting to note that many group development theorists see
Bion's basic assumptions as sequential and leading to group development (Hare,
1973; Tuckman, 1965). The assumptions of dependency, fight-flight, and pairing
are viewed as sequential in group development and correlate well with the more
sequential theories of group development.

Whitaker and Lieberman (1964) go furthest in balancing the intrapsychic
phenomenon with the interpersonal by developing a focal conflict theory based
upon the theories of French (1952). Their theory of group development is cap-
sulized in their Proposition 18:

> The development of a therapy group from its inception to its termination
> is characterized by the recurrence of basic themes under progressively ex-
> panding cultural conditions (p. 117).

The only deference that Whitaker and Lieberman pay to sequential group development is that basic themes in the early development might differ from later
recurrence of the *same* themes. The essential ingredients of the recurrent focal
conflicts are the progressive expansion of group norms to allow for increasing
depth of revelation, relationship, and insight.

Yalom (1975) takes a middle ground between the recurrent and sequential
group development theorists by positing three developmental stages: orientation,
conflict, and cohesiveness. These stages appear to correlate with Tuckman's
(1965) early developmental stages. Yalom suggests that once cohesiveness has
been achieved, there are no parameters by which to assess and compare fully
developed groups since each proceeds in very unique ways.

Another school of thought predicates their theories of group development
on the finite structure and brief tenure of the training group. Most training
groups are organized so that the members can study themselves in the development of the group or learn about group development and themselves as group
members. Schutz (1966), Tuckman (1965), Bennis and Shepard (1974), Slater
(1966) and Mann (1967) are representative of this school of thought. Schutz
(1966) is the only one who posits recurrent cycles of group phenomena, which
are inclusion, control, and affection. The control and affection phenomena are
reminiscent of Bion's (1961) fight-flight and pairing phenomena as is their recurrence through the entire life of the group. The only change that takes place in
the recurrence of these phenomena is that toward termination there is a reversal
so that intimacy gives way to fight-flight, which in turn gives way to exclusion.

All the other training group theorists subscribe to the sequential stages of
group development. They are all very much in agreement on an initial stage of

1

An Overview
of Dynamics
# of Group Development

This chapter sets forth the basic theory of group devel
assumptions, tenets, and objectives. The aim is to provide an
theory that can be readily applied to therapy groups. For thos
groups and group therapy, the overview may suffice for get
chapter introductions for each segment of the theory of group c
help to further specify the major dimensions of each phase
experienced group therapists and those who learn to identify
crises as they occur may want to explore more deeply and
manner in which dynamics operate in each phase and crisis. T
and crisis dynamics are also intended as a reference for thera
volved with a group and at a loss in explaining a particular situa

TOWARD A THEORY OF GROUP DEVELOPMENT

The search for a theory of group development that will be co
plete for all groups is the subject of much theorizing, investig
and controversy. There appear to be several schools of thou
group dynamics in therapy groups. One school consists of th
psychotherapists who predicate most of their ideas on the l
therapy groups aimed at emotional growth and/or depth of int
and insight. Authors like Slavson (1957) and Durkin (1964)
dynamics are at the best inconsequential and at the worst serv
group therapeutic processes. Slavson (1964:64-66) suggest
problem with group dynamics is that the conformity and
manded by the cohesive forces of group dynamics serve to r
development of insight and individuality. What Slavson is desi
tive effects of cohesion is what many authors call initial intim
condition lasts, the author calls it "pseudo-intimacy" (Slavso
groups as well as other kinds of groups can and do develop
intimacy with concomitant increasing freedom for deeper a
tiated exploration of the individual members (Schroder and H

dependency, followed by intragroup conflict, then cohesion, and finally group maturity. The major difference lies in Tuckman, and Bennis and Shepard seeing the struggles among the members following the rebellion against the leader while Slater and Mann see the struggling among the members as preceding the rebellions against the leader. Mann refers to this phenomenon as premature enactment and suggests that the real struggle for control takes place after the rebellion against the leader.

A third school of thought arises from the social group work theorists who predicate their theories of group development on the supportive treatment and socialization groups they primarily work with. In general, these theorists subscribe to the sequential form of group development. Coyle's (1930) contributions to the group work field facilitated the integration of group dynamic concepts into the supportive treatment and socialization groups. Most prominent among these theories is the "Boston model," which was developed by a faculty committee of the Boston University School of Social Work (Garland et al., 1965). The model has five stages of group development: pre-affiliation, power and control, intimacy, differentiation, and termination. Hartford (1971) and Northen (1969) posit similar developmental stages, but they emphasize the struggle with the leader during the control phase, where the authority struggle is not as clear in the Boston model. Hartford also posits a stage that is the pregroup phase: the leader does the work conceiving the group and bringing it together. Sarri and Galinsky (1967) posit a seven-phase theory that matches the other group work theories except for what they call Intermediate Phase I. This phase appears to be a minor intimacy phase before the control struggles emerge. Otherwise the remaining phases correlate somewhat with the model of Garland et al. There is a strong resemblance between the group work stages and the sequential models of Tuckman and Bennis and Shepard.

It appears from the above discussion that the longer-term intensive therapy group tends to defy sequence in development, while the shorter term training, supportive, or socialization group can lend itself to sequential classification. A major reason for the discrepancy between the two kinds of groups lies in the fact that the same phenomena that are achievable in the short-term group for more definitive purposes have many levels and ramifications that can only fully emerge in the longer-term intensive process. For example, wresting or transfer of authority from the therapist to the members can take place in a short-term group in sufficient quantity for the members to assume major responsibility for a circumscribed task. However, in the long-term intensive therapy group the initial transfer of authority is only the beginning. The unsettled issues and conflicts from each member's past can and do recur each time the group reaches new depths of revelation and work. As both Whitaker and Lieberman and Slater attest, the coping with authority by the members is a progressive process throughout the life of the group. The relinquishment of dependency and the increase of member autonomy is inherent in Bion's (1961) recurrent dependency assumption, in Whitaker and Lieberman's recurrent focal issue of the wish for sole possession of the therapist, and in Slater's postulate of progressive decreasing libidinal involvement with the leader and increasing libidinal involvement with the other members. (Slater, 1966:85) Rather, the initial shift of power from the therapist to the members may be sufficient for group members to take some control of their group and vie for that control, but it requires many more shifts of power for the members, many of whom were perhaps rendered powerless by their life experiences, to gain sufficient feelings of power to cope with their outside environment. To this end, the concept of the recurrent authority crisis throughout the life of the group is posited.

Similarly, the development of intimacy in a short-term circumscribed group can facilitate a certain level of openess and sharing of affect. However, the intimacy essential to the work of an intensive therapy group requires depth far beyond that of a short-term or circumscribed goal. In addition, there are continued and new authority issues inherent in each group venture into deeper intimacy. Particularly, the work of Whitaker and Lieberman (1964) addresses itself to the constant struggle for opening normative constrictions on intimacy. Perhaps, Bion (1961) and Slavson (1957) were relating to the resistence levels of deepening intimacy and exploration when they warned against group processes. To the end of the constant deepening of intimacy, the concept of the recurrent intimacy crises is posited. Initial resolution of intimacy crises give rise to early cohesion, but subsequent resolutions of intimacy crises progressively deepen the affective bonds through the life of the fully formed group.

Similarly, the omnipresence of separation phenomenon arises from the initial fears of rejection and expulsion by the therapist, through the fears of rejection and expulsion by the other group members, to the recurrent events of absences and terminations (Slater, 1966:70). The concept of separation crisis is employed to describe the recurrence and progression in dealing with separation phenomena.

While the authority, intimacy, and separation issues are recurrent throughout the life of the therapy group, there are some sequential phenomenon that describe the formation of any group, whether short-term and circumscribed in purpose or long-term and multifaceted. What appears basic to the above discussion is: (1) In every process of group formation there is an initial knitting together of the group members into a cohesive group entity, (2) Fundamental to the process of members knitting together is the transferring of sufficient power from the therapist to the members. (3) Control struggles among the members during the formative stages are a direct consequence of and *require* a power shift from the therapist. (4) Group cohesiveness and its concomitants in group formation are a direct result of successful resolution of control struggles among the members. (5) Power ceases to be a major issue among group members once cohesion develops. (6) The directionality of communication, interaction, and relationships moves from therapist-members at the outset toward member-member as cohesion develops.

A four-stage sequence of phases that parallel the major sequential theories discussed above are employed to describe the development of therapy groups. The phases in brief are: (1) the parallel phase which describes the leader-centered dependency phase; (2) the inclusion phase which describes the process of members knitting together through intragroup struggles after the first resolution of an authority crisis; (3) the mutuality phase which describes the mature group after the initial resolution of group intimacy crises; and (4) the termination phase. These phases and their interaction with the crises will be further elaborated throughout the ensuing discussion.

In sum, this theory of therapy group development attempts to accomplish three major tasks. First is to identify and reconcile the sequential and the recurrent developmental phenomena in short- and long-term groups. The concepts of phases and crises, their inherent phenomena, and their interaction are offered as a step toward the development of a consistent and complete theory of therapy group development.

The second major task is to more fully explain how the dynamics of each phase work to complete the developmental tasks of the phase and give rise to the next phase. The concept of inclusion phase with its subgrouping and factioning or flocking and fighting might shed more light on how intragroup struggles give rise to group cohesion. Hare (1973:300) points to the dirth of theory explaining how one phase gives rise to the next.

A third major task not directly related to the above discussion is to more fully integrate developmental dynamics of individuals with group phenomenon. The guiding principle for this integration is that there is a recapitulation of individual development in the development of a therapy group. However, this recapitulation is not a direct linear one since several developmental levels may be inherent in it for each member in each group phenomenon. For example, Gibbard and Hartman (1973) suggest after their study of the oedipal paradigm as an organizing principle for group development that both oedipal and pre-oedipal processes may be present and operative at one and the same time.

BASIC TENETS FOR THERAPY GROUP DEVELOPMENT

Fundamental to any theory of group development are Homans' principles of small group development. *The more often people get together, the more they interact. The more that people interact, the more they like each other. The more that people like each other the more they interact.* (Homans, 1950:112-13) While Homans draws on some of the major social psychological research available at that time, several subsequent small group studies have confirmed the positive relationship between interaction frequency and the development of relationships (for examples see Hearn, 1957; McIntyre, 1952). Thus, what any therapy group has working for it is the probability of its coming together over time through natural processes. Support and facilitation of these processes may ensure the group's development. However, acceleration of or interference with these processes can prevent or distort group development. Schroder and Harvey (1963:152-62) point to how acceleration or interference can prevent or distort group development.

Social development is recapitulated in the course of therapy groups in two major ways. First, *each and every member recapitulates his social development in the process of becoming an integral member of the group.* Second, *therapy group development itself parallels the ontogenetic development of individuals.* Fundamental to individual and group development is the principle derived from biological and evolutionary theory, which is that growth progresses from undifferentiation to differentiation. The genetic development of individuals from the undifferentiated single cell to the highly differentiated adult complex of interdependent cells is paralleled in the social-emotional development of individuals and the development of groups. Werner (1948) brings together considerable research and theory to demonstrate how cognitive and emotional development of individuals follows the principle of differentiation. Schroder and Harvey (1963) develop the principle of differentiation from the cognitive and behavioral standpoints in the development of personality, with particular emphasis on the functions of authority and dependence on authority to the development of autonomy and openness to alternatives in thought and action. Schroder and Harvey also make some cogent connections between the social manifestations of progressive differentiation in individual development and their counterparts in progressive differentiation in groups. They propose that differentiation for individual and group development is a function of increasing and consistent freedom for autonomous thought and behavior. For individuals, freedom for autonomous thought and behavior is brought about by the child's progressive gaining of freedom from parents. Constrictions on freedom of thought bring about rigidities and preclude autonomous development; allowing freedom of thought inconsistently or too liberally or too soon brings about other distortions that center on either uncertainty or the constant search for unanimity.

The group parallels posited by Schroder and Harvey are the processes of members differentiating from the leader, followed by the processes of the members differentiating from each other. They connect the differentiation process to several group developmental theories and ascribe the major differentiation work to power struggles of the formative stages of groups. They also point to the initial differentiation being one of tolerance, gradually building toward the mature group situation, which places value on both similarities and uniqueness.

Tucker (1973) studied Schroder and Harvey's theory and found that people whose freedom of thought and action was either constricted early in life or was inconsistent or premature did not undergo differentiation of selves from leader and other members; however, people who had in their development progressively attained autonomy did indeed recapitulate their differentiation from the leader and other members. The interesting result was that all the groups evidenced differentiation phenomena, but individuals only recapitulated their life experiences to the point of their own development, then apparently were carried along by the group.

The implications of the principle of differentiation of thought and actions for therapy group development are endless. Most important among the implications is that a therapy group is predisposed to dependency on authority and, through the process of individual and interindividual differentiation, can grow in autonomy and mutual interdependence. Directive forms of group therapy accept the autocratic role easily accorded the therapist at the inception of the group; nondirective forms of group therapy deny the essential state of dependency on authority at the beginning of the group and assume that the group has the capacity to govern itself and will do so if the therapist doesn't allow the group to be dependent.

A therapist who maintains autocratic control of the group throughout its life will usually inhibit the process of differentiation and recapitulation by not allowing the crucial differentiation from the therapist, thus endangering the process of differentiation among the members. Most nondirective therapists leave the group to its own devices. If the members have achieved a high level of differentiation in their past lives, then the group can well take hold and handle the process of differentiation by themselves. If some or all the members of the group have not achieved a high degree of differentiation, then, at best, the members who fill the breach in leadership can carry the group through the process of differentiation; however, there is doubt that those members who have not achieved similar degrees of differentiation in their lives will gain anything from the process except another experience where they fuse with other people undifferentiatedly (Tucker, 1973).

Well-timed and progressive transfer of political power from the therapist to the members is an extremely important phenomenon for the social-emotional growth of the members for group development.

Interacting with and surrounding the process of differentiation throughout the life cycle are the emotional developmental issues for individuals and groups. The individual developmental theories of Erikson (1968) very closely parallel the developmental phenomena experienced in therapy group development. Three of Erikson's major concepts are particularly relevant to group development: trust versus mistrust, autonomy versus shame and doubt, and intimacy versus isolation. The basic capacity for trust is developed during the first year of life (Erikson, 1968:96). Subsequent life experiences enhance or detract from the initial capacity developed during the first year of life. Similarly, the trust-mistrust issue is the first important emotional dilemma to be resolved in groups. However, just as in psychosocial development, trust-mistrust is a constant dilemma throughout the life of a group.

With sufficient trust the individual can move toward the establishment of autonomy. Perhaps more directly relevant to group development is the Eriksonian idea of autonomy versus shame and doubt (1968:107-14). This dilemma becomes manifest in the early phases of the group, first in relation to dependency on the therapist, then in relation to dependency on other group members. Thus, the fundamental dilemma in the group becomes dependence on authority versus autonomy. Erikson's concepts of initiative, industry, and identity follow from the individual's establishing sufficient levels of trust and autonomy in the group.

Finally, the dilemma of intimacy versus isolation has its counterpart in group phenomena. Erikson points to the development of identity as a precondition to the development of capacity for intimacy (1968:135). Perhaps in psychosocial growth the development of identity precedes the capacity for intimacy, but in group development the two interact. While the tendency in groups is for a recapitulation of individual development, individuals bring their current developmental level to the group with their achieved levels and compensations for unresolved developmental issues (Slater, 1966; Gibbard and Hartman, 1973; Tucker, 1973). Consequently, the recapitulation takes on a simultaneous multilevel reenactment. A major difference in group development is that intimacy can often preceed further differentiation and identity formation or reaffirmation.

The two major fears of intimacy in groups stem from the difficulties of incomplete identity: fear of engulfment by others and fear of rejection or abandonment (Slater, 1966; Gibbard and Hartman, 1973; Schroeder and Harvey, 1963). The fears of both rejection and abandonment stem from experiences in which love was given on the condition that the individual remain an undifferentiated mass or be punished or abandoned for asserting autonomy or difference. Through the experience of progressive development of autonomy and differentiation within the climate of acceptance, first by the therapist, then by other group members, each group member can grow in both identity and capacity for intimacy. Thus, by fostering intimacy and individuality the group climate is conducive to completion of two growth phenomena that are fundamental to mature psychosocial development: identity and the capacity for intimacy (Beck, 1958).

The interaction of differentiation and intimacy in therapy groups is crucial to the group's development and the treatment outcomes of the members. When intimacy is imposed or accelerated beyond the readiness or capacities of the members, members tend to seek refuge in the undifferentiated mass. Because the affective contact is not really present in premature intimacy, members will create and cling to notions of similarity, lack of difference, and absense of conflict in the group. Autonomy and individuality are threats to premature intimacy; therefore, they are controlled. Those who threaten the illusion of similarity are subject to punishment, rejection, or abandonment. Thus, premature intimacy can cause members to reexperience and deepen their fears of intimacy—that is, their fears of engulfment or abandonment. While engulfment and abandonment are the two major extremes in fears of intimacy, group members may manifest some lesser forms of either or both in a modified way.

Differentiation without intimacy can foster the development of narcissistic preoccupation with an individual's own needs and not help the individual to achieve the experience of mutuality in which differentiated individuals can reciprocally meet their own and each other's needs within a close relationship. Differentiation without intimacy is a danger in therapy groups where full affective contact among the members is not allowed.

An example of premature intimacy arises in groups that, through intimacy exercises, are accelerated toward premature affective contact. Such groups quickly renounce difference, hostility, and conflict, developing norms which perpetuate expression of only positive feelings and agreement among the members.

An example of differentiation without intimacy is the directively led group in which the exercises facilitate individual freedom and self-actualization but do not provide experiences of reciprocity and mutuality. At best, these groups foster freedom for narcissistic pursuit of an individual's own needs along with counterdependent meeting of the needs of others. However, a differentiated "we-ness" is not achieved (Hacker, 1956).

THE THEORY OF GROUP DEVELOPMENT: AN OVERVIEW

The theory of group development presented in the ensuing chapters divides the life of a therapy group into four distinct phases. A major feature of each phase is the directionality of relationships among the members and the therapist. In each phase the direction of relationship has distinctive characteristics not found in other phases. It is important to understand that this discussion is about relationships and not necessarily about overt behavioral and verbal interactional patterns. Verbal and behavioral interactional patterns may or may not manifest the actual direction of relationships.

There are three phenonmena called crises. Although they interact with the phases, they can and do occur throughout the life of a group. The resolution of the crises as they arise represent points of change in the directionality and emotional quality of relationships. Thus, the four phases represent the achieved directional and qualitative change in relationships. The change in direction of relationships represents movement from one phase to another; the recurrent crises represent changes in quality of relationships at the start of and during each phase.

Phases of Group Development

The four phases of group development are (1) parallel phase, (2) inclusion phase, (3) mutuality phase, and (4) termination phase. In the parallel phase the direction of relationships all funnel to the therapist. The name *parallel phase* is derived from the parallel play concept of social development in preschool children.

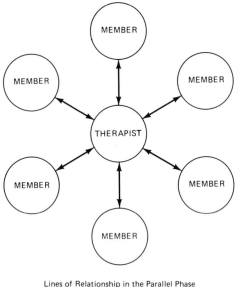

Lines of Relationship in the Parallel Phase
(Extreme Situation)

Figure 1.1. Lines of relationship in parallel phase.

Parallel Phase. Although there may be verbal and/or behavioral interaction among the members during the parallel phase, this interaction, overtly directed toward the other members, is really intended for the therapist. An adult group of outpatient neurotics meeting on a weekly basis may spend from a few minutes to a few weeks in the parallel phase before moving on; how long will depend on the therapist, style of leadership, and structure of the group. Many groups of children below the age of eight or groups of chronic schizophrenics spend their entire group existence in the parallel phase. Most groups of latency-aged children spend from a few meetings to several months in the parallel phase. The basic work in the parallel phase is for the members to increase their levels of trust in the therapist, the other members, and the group situation in order to free their autonomous strivings and actions.

Inclusion Phase. The inclusion phase is the period of group formation. During the inclusion phase there is a decrease in the centrality of the therapist in the group relationships and an increase in the member-to-member relationships. Affiliations among the members begin with pairing and subgrouping, generally along lines of perceived similarities. The inclusion phase begins with pairing and subgroupings; it ends with most or all members of the group having relationships with most or all other members of the group. The centrality of the therapist in relationships decreases as the group members establish relationships with each other. However, the therapist maintains relationships with each member and with the pairings and subgroupings as they develop.

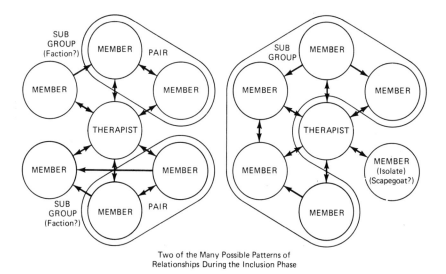

Two of the Many Possible Patterns of
Relationships During the Inclusion Phase

Figure 1.2. Typical lines of relationship in the inclusion phase.

The name *inclusion* is derived from the central tasks of the phase, which are for members to become accepted by the other members, accept other members, and share in the power of the group. Although some theorists are inclined to emphasize the conflicts and power struggles, which are an important and integral part of the processes during the formative period in group life; however, underlying all the conflict and power struggles is a quest by all members for inclusion in the group as fully accepted members who have some degree of influence on the group. Another major dimension of the inclusion phase is the distribution of power among the group members.

Achievement of full membership for all members and management of group power is about as far as most latency-aged groups and groups of chronic schizophrenics can develop. If a group of chronic schizophrenics achieves a full measure of inclusion phenomenon over a period of one to two years, it would mean that the members, or at least those who achieve this level, would be capable of trusting interpersonal situations sufficiently to make contact with some of the other members and be able to assert some of their autonomy in the group. Groups of older latency-aged children are capable of constitutional government; they develop formal rules or informal norms that govern their behavior and to which they all adhere at the risk of actual or virtual expulsion from the group.

Mutuality Phase. The mutuality phase represents the middle phase of adult groups with capacity for intimate relationships. Most of the life of long-term closed-end or open-ended adult groups is spent in the mutuality phase. The directionality of relationships in the mutuality phase extends from most or all

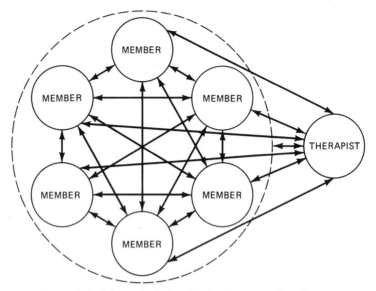

Figure 1.3 Lines of relationship in the mutuality phase.

members to most or all of the other members and the therapist. Therapists have a relationship with each member and to the group as a whole.

The name mutuality is derived from the nature of relationships during the middle phase. At the start of the mutuality phase everyone who is a part of the mutual processes feels accepted and included in the group, shares in the power and affect of the group, participates in the process of give and take, and develops initial empathy. Depending upon who is in the group, what personality and style the therapist has, and how long the group meets, the empathy deepens progressively as do other facets of relationships among the members during the course of the mutuality phase. While all members progressively become more emotionally linked to each other during mutuality, members also become emotionally freer to be unique or differential in their thoughts and affects. In contrast to the inclusion phase in which all members have to identify with either one set of people, thoughts, and feelings or another, during mutuality each member is increasingly freer to share thoughts and feelings of any and all members of the group. From the standpoint of the differentiation process, the undifferentiation of the parallel phase grows to the gross acceptance or rejection in the inclusion phase, then to the partialized and particularized acceptance and rejection of the mutuality phase.

Since group development is fundamentally accomplished by the mutuality phase, the group puts in less work on the system itself and can put most of its effort into work on therapeutic tasks and relationships within and beyond the bounds of the group itself. The major tasks are the deepening of the relationships.

Older adolescent and adult groups composed of members capable of mutuality in relationships will accomplish most of their therapeutic work and spend most of their group existence in the mutuality phase. Older latency-aged groups and early adolescent groups can achieve some degree of mutuality if they are together long enough (from two to six months of weekly meetings, depending on the nature of the members), but they will remain very dependent on the therapist for keeping open the freedom for diversity and deviance from the group in thoughts, feelings, and behavior. The difference between the early adolescent groups and adult groups in the depth of intimacy achievable is due to the difference in capacity of the respective groups for depth of intimacy.

Termination Phase. The termination phase is mostly a phenomenon of closed groups although it can occur toward the end of open-ended group sessions. Some termination phenomena is associated with a members leaving an open-ended group, mostly for the member leaving. Members of open-ended groups experience more of what can be called separation crises. Again, the directionality of relationships is the key factor in the termination phase. Members begin to disengage in their relationships from the other group members and the therapist and move toward their relationships outside the group.

Ideally, the termination phase represents a point where the member and/or group have completed their major goals for therapy and begin to move out of the group. However, in limited- time or short-term groups the termination phase is precipitated by the prospect of the group coming to an end. This means that the termination phase ideally begins during the mutuality phase and progresses until the group ends or the individual leaves. However, due to the realities of ending dates, the termination phase can occur in the middle of any of the other phases, from parallel and inclusion to mutuality. The nature of the termination phase will depend on the achieved level of relationships among the members of the group when it begins. Perhaps more important, the nature of the termination phase will reflect the quality and degree to which the authority, intimacy, and separation crises have been resolved.

The Crises

There are three recurrent crises in the life of therapy groups: authority, intimacy, and separation crises. While all three can and do occur at any point in the life of a group, the crises serve specific transitional functions from phase to phase, and then serve to deepen the nature of relationships after the first crisis is resolved.

Authority Crises. Authority crises generally arise first. The essential ingredient of the authority crisis is the challenge to the centrality and political power of the therapist. Authority crises will begin to emerge in the parallel phase and the initial authority crises may not be resolved. The resolving of the first authority crisis generally marks the end of the parallel phase and the start of the inclusion phase. Resolution of the authority crises means that some political power has passed from the therapist to the members, that the therapist ceded this power and the group accepted the power. If the therapist does not cede the power or the group doesn't accept the power, then the authority crisis is not resolved.

Groups can and do move on to the inclusion phase without resolution of an authority crisis but the nature of the inclusion phase phenomena will be rendered extremely narrow and shallow compared with a group in which there was reasonable resolution of initial authority crises. Most important, the ceding of political power to the group and its acceptance by the group also represents the giving of permission and allowing room for individual and group to develop autonomy. If political power must be wrested from the therapist without permission, then it creates doubt in the minds of the members as to the legitimacy of their autonomy and their fears of punishment and rejection mount. If political power is ceded to the group without their being ready for or seeking it, then the group has power and autonomy that they cannot use well and it runs the risk of its members failing to exert that power and autonomy, with a consequent return to the therapist as the repository of power and to the concomitant dependency.

Authority issues are not settled the first time an authority is crisis is resolved but recur during the inclusion, mutuality, and termination phases. While the overt process manifestation of early authority crises is the transfer of power, the process of ultimate equalization of power between therapist and individual group members brings about fundamental growth in individual members' capacity for self and interdependence and frees them for basic autonomy and initiative strivings. Finally, authority crises which are concommitant with intimacy crises during the mutuality phase serve to progressively resolve the dilemma between attachments to authority (parents) and attachments among group members (friends, lovers, etc.). Intimacy crises, like authority crises, can and do occur throughout the life of a group. Early intimacy crises are set off by the potentiality of affective contact among the members. Later intimacy crises are set off by the potentiality of new depths of affective contact, mutual revelation, and empathy. Resolution of an intimacy crisis allows the members to make or deepen affective contact.

Intimacy Crises. A major difference between this and the sequential theories of therapy group development is that intimacy is not viewed as a discrete phase, but rather as a recurrent process more like that posited by recurrent developmental theorists. The main reason for this is the notion that pair and subgroup intimacy begins to develop in the inclusion phase and reaches a peak with the first resolution of an intimacy crisis for the entire group. Thus, the first resolution of an intimacy crisis for the entire group is similar to what the sequential theorists view as the intimacy phase. Since the work of deepening intimacy continues through the mutuality phase, all that can be said about the resolution of the first intimacy crisis is that it establishes initial intimacy and creates the base for further deepening of intimacy and differentiation.

Intimacy crises can and do occur as early as the parallel phase. However, these early intimacy crises generally are not resolved, rather, the members are inclined to back off from early intimacy. If early intimacy crises are resolved or accelerated too early, the resolution, of necessity, has to be superficial. Either stringent norms and boundaries are set to control the intimacy or members flee into an intellectualized process that gives an appearance of intimacy but in reality they maintain their distance. If intimacy is resolved before the inclusion process has run its course, members will be constrained in the latitude of their affective contact and welded into the roles they occupied at the time of the resolution. In such a group change becomes difficult and very unlikely.

The first resolution of an intimacy crisis serves as a transition from the inclusion phase to the mutuality phase. Since affective contact is the basis of the mutuality phase, the function of intimacy crises is to initiate and deepen affective contact during the mutuality phase. A group can enter the mutuality phase with a low degree of intimacy but will require subsequent intimacy crises to gradually deepen the level of affective contact. The level of intimacy for a group during mutuality is infinite and depends on the nature of the people in the group and the length of time they have been together.

Late latency and adolescent groups achieve a state of pseudo-intimacy that is appropriate for their level of development. The capacity of children of these ages for intimacy is limited by their social development. Late latency and early adolescent groups substitute similarity for intimacy. These age groups require that all the members think, act, and behave alike, demonstrating to themselves and others that they are together. The need and interest in showing outsiders that they are intimate suggests the shallowness of the process. When adult groups develop psuedo-intimacy it is often because the therapist or some of the members forced intimacy on the group before they were ready. While the pseudo-intimacy of the younger groups can serve as an age appropriate level for developing capacity for intimacy, in an adult group pseudo-intimacy can sharply reduce the degree of mutuality phenomenon that will be achieved. In the pseudo-intimacy of adult groups the most notable omission is the absence of negative feelings and overt conflicts. The greatest danger in pseudo-intimacy in adult groups is that each of the members leaves the group feeling that the others experienced something they played at experiencing; consequently, they feel bad about their lack of capacity for intimacy.

Separation Crises. Separation crises arise at any phase of group development and are set off by fears of the therapist, fears of other members, absences of therapists or members, termination of members or therapists, and termination of the group. Separation fears are also inherent in authority and intimacy crises. The function of separation crises is to deal with loss or potential loss of other people in the group situation and, ultimately, to deal with separations and losses that members might have or will experience in their lives and in their termination from the group.

Separation crises are resolved if the members are able to deal with their

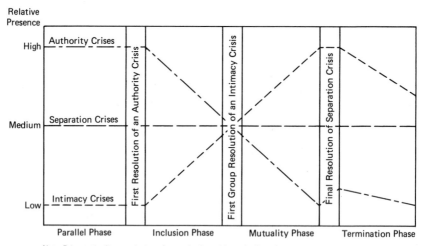

Figure 1.4 Interaction of phases and crises.

Note: Prior to the first resolution of an authority crisis, authority crises are present
but do not get resolved. Prior to the first resolution of an intimacy crisis by
the group, intimacy crises abound but do not get resolved except between
individual members. Separation crises become increasingly resolved during
the life of the group and build toward final resolution preceding the
termination phase.

feelings and reactions to the separation that precipitated the crisis. Separation crises are not resolved if the members do not deal with their feelings about separations and continue to deny and repress these feelings. The later in the phases of group development the separation crisis, the more chance that the group will have the capacity for resolving separation crises and will have developed ways of doing so.

There is usually a progression in the way groups deal with separation crises and they develop their capacity to deal with them as they recur in the group.

Figure 1.4 is a conceptual rendering of the relative presence of the three crisis phenomena during the four group phases. The smoothness of the lines may be taken as averages; fluctuations and variations will occur from group to group and within each group. However, such major variations as premature intimacy during the parallel or inclusion phase and premature authority crises will cause major distortions in group development. Many of the possible distortions, their nature, and amelioration are discussed in the text of the respective phases and crises. Suffice to say that Figure 1.4 represents a conceptual model for the interaction of phases and crises.

Dimensions of Group Process

The discussion in the ensuing chapters describes and analyses each phrase and crisis from the standpoint of thirteen dynamics operative in therapy group.

Definitions and summaries of each of these dimensions is provided below, but their full operation in each phase and crisis is left for the respective chapters.

Affective Polarities. Affective polarities refers to the valences in emotions that underly each phase and crisis. Although many emotions are inherent in each phase and crisis in group development, there are critical emotional dilemmas concerned with the significance of the particular phase or crisis of each individual. These valences of emotion are not only important at the time of the meetings in which they are afoot but for each member's prior, concurrent, and future social-emotional life. It is the reworking or further development or growth of these affective polarities that are the primary contributors to the therapeutic benefits of the group. Each of these polarities must be viewed as an almost infinite continuum along which every individual might be placed. Progress simply means that a member or group moves a reasonable distance along the continuum.

For example, every person comes to a group with his own level of trust. No person is totally lacking in trust, nor is anyone completely trusting. The objective of the parallel phase is for each member to increase their levels of trust so that they can feel freer to approach others and ultimately take initiative in the group. The level required for each person to take initiative will differ for each person. Examination of the chart on pages 86-87 shows the major affective polarities for each phase and crisis. These polarities reflect recapitulation of social-emotional growth that takes place for each individual in the course of group development.

Major Behavioral Features. While a wide range of behaviors might be manifest at any point in group development, there are recurrent behaviors or behavioral themes characteristic of each phase and crisis. The behavioral level is closely tied to the affective dimension in that the behaviors both reflect and alter the affective polarities. In discussing behavioral features it is assumed that both verbal and nonverbal interactions are part of the behavioral process. In adult groups the preponderance of interaction is usually verbal; in children's groups the preponderance of interaction is usually nonverbal.

Examination of the chart on pages 86-87 shows the behaviors most characteristic of each phase and crisis. These and other behavioral features are discussed in the ensuing chapters. Of note in an overview is that the progression in behavior from the parallel through the inclusion phase demonstrates how the members progress into interaction with each other and, while the feelings are manifest in the behaviors, they are not an integral part of the process itself. After the first resolution of an intimacy crisis, behavior and affect begin to merge, in that both verbal and nonverbal behavior more consciously and overtly express the feelings of the members as a consequence, feelings surface for the remainder of the group's life into the overt processes of the meetings.

Sources of Gratification. At different points in the life of the group, members seek to have their needs met from different people. While some members might come to the group readier to seek gratification from other members, most members come to group therapy to gain gratification from the therapist. The meaning and function of the sources of gratification at each phase and crisis is discussed in their respective chapters but it is enough to note here that members progress from seeking gratification from the therapist, to seeking gratification from each other and the therapist, to seeking gratification from self and others outside the group.

Relational Issues. Relational issues are concerned with the quality and directionality of the interactions themselves. While the specific issues for each phase and crisis are found in the chart on pages 86-87 and in the respective chapters, two major dimensions pervade the process through the life of the group. The first is the progression from contact to affiliation in pairs and subgroups and finally to intimacy. Second is the progression of dependence-counterdependence through dominance-submission to free give-and-take. Dependence-counterdependence are ways in which members in a parallel process interact with each other without actually relating to each other. Dominance-submission are the ways in which various members choose to handle the power and acceptance struggles of the inclusion phase. With the affective contact and growing bonds of empathy, members become able to freely give and take in ways that preclude both dependency-counterdependency and dominance-submission.

Self-other Concept. Individuals come to know themselves through their interactions with other people: first the family, then peer group and outside world. As people grow they form conceptions of themselves in relation to other people. In addition to the obvious contrasts like male-female, younger-older, people begin to rank themselves in comparison to other people and at the same time assign ranks to the other people. This ranking occurs on many levels: better-worse, smarter-dumber, superior-inferior, similar-different, and so forth. The self-other concept as employed in this work is concerned with the individual's feelings and ideas about himself as compared with other people. These feelings and ideas also include the individual's concept of how others think and feel about him. Most people who come to group therapy arrive feeling different from others and feel inferior. Some recognize the universality of their needs, problems, and feelings but seek and need validation for their ideas. Some feel superior to others but these feelings often cover feelings of inadequacy. Thus, the unearthing, experiencing, and changing of a person's concept of himself in relation to others is a major therapeutic task of each individual member. On most issues over the course of full group participation members develop a more realistic appraisal of their capacities in relation to those of others in the group and elsewhere with perhaps some increased comfort resulting from the comparison. However, the crucial development in self-other concept arises as they experience the universality of feelings among people. A group member deeply joined in the empathic bond comes to appreciate that all human beings have similar feelings and reactions to things, although perhaps they differ in degree or intensity. Consequently the member feels more at peace with his own feelings and on a more equal, if not fully equal, basis with the others in the group and with humanity.

Power Relations. Interpersonal power is defined essentially as the capacity of one person to perform an act that will change another person. For the purposes of therapy groups, the concern with power centers mostly on the capacity to influence others in the group. The meaning of power to individuals and group development is discussed under the respective chapters for each phase and crisis but is important to note that interpersonal power among the members is central in importance during the inclusion or formative phase of the group and fades into insignificance during the mutuality phase. During mutuality any and all members can assert power at will. Some may opt for more use of power than others but the group in mutuality is open to all members having access to power in the group.

Another major trend in the group over time is the gradual transfer of power from the therapist to the group members, beginning with the first resolution of an authority crisis and continuing through the life of the group with subsequent authority crises. The experience of gaining power from an authority figure and sharing in the wielding of that power with peers has profound significance for the recapitulation of social-emotional growth in the group. Group members who have not themselves experienced progressive reduction of parental power as well as group members who have not had good experiences either with being accorded power or with holding power with peers can benefit from corrective experience. Still other group members who have substituted wielding power for gaining acceptance in their lives can find corrective experiences in gaining direct acceptance and relinquishing power in interpersonal situations.

Conflict. Two kinds of conflict are of concern in therapy group processes. First are the interpersonal conflicts between or among members of the group or group members and the therapist. Second are the conflicts within each person—the conflicting emotions, needs, and drives. The two types of conflict are integrally related. This relationship is discussed under conflict in each of the respective phases and crises as well as Chapter 1 of Part 3. Suffice for this discussion to consider that interpersonal conflicts emerge through the life of the group. During the parallel phase they are covert. The emergence of conflict is an essential condition of the early authority crises and the inclusion phase. When the first intimacy crisis is resolved, the nature of the interpersonal conflicts begins to change. Members become freer to conflict because they are less fearful of rejection from the group. During the mutuality phase and as intimacy deepens, conflicts may be intense but they tend to involve fewer people as adversaries and more people who can relate to both sides of the conflict. Most important, during mutuality members grow to recognize the dualities in their own emotions and have less need to polarize.

During inclusion members tend to form factions around the issues or sides to the conflict. In the mutuality phase the tendency to factionalize slowly disappears as the members become secure in their acceptance, grow in their abilities to conflict, and more quickly recognize the polarities in their own emotions.

Cohesion. *Cohesion* refers fundamentally to the degree to which members are attracted to the group. There are many bases for cohesion in therapy groups and as the group progresses, the bases tend to deepen. Cohesion starts in the parallel phase with bases like commonality, perceived similarity, and common goals and expectations. During the inclusion phase affective bonds and aversions begin to form between and among individual members. As the inclusion phase conflicts and intimacy crises are successively resolved, the affective cohesiveness spreads among all the members, although to what degree will depend on the size and composition of the group. In the depth of mutuality the basis of cohesion becomes empathic contact among the members. In fact, the depth of empathic contact in large measure determines the strength of group cohesion and its ultimate impact on the members.

Group Controls. The term *group controls* refers to the way the group as a whole exerts power or influence over members. In a therapy group, group controls are concerned with interpersonal as well as intrapersonal controls. A major therapeutic benefit of groups for many people is the participation in controlling other people's behavior and, from that experience, gaining in their own capacity to control. Through participation in the development of group controls, each member begins to develop his own ego controls. For some people with too high a degree of control, the experience of relinquishing some personal controls and relying on the group controls as a bridge between their constricted range of controls and chaos, gives them greater freedom in their range of behavior.

The major vehicles of control in group therapy are inclusion and acceptance in the group. Exclusion and rejection during the parallel and inclusion phases are the major threats. As the group develops depth of mutuality, exclusion and rejection are no longer necessary and the exertion of controls by the group is gradually replaced by the individual members taking more responsibility for their own control. As acceptance by the other group members is felt, the capacity of the group to influence each member's behavior without resorting to threat increases. The therapist has primary responsibility for control during the parallel phase; the group develops increasing responsibility for controls during the inclusion phase; finally, all individuals share control of themselves and others in the mutuality phase.

Norms. Norms have the same implications for therapy groups as they do for any group. Norms are the typical patterns or traits of individual and group behavior that develop in therapy groups. Group norms begin with tentative individual behaviors based on each individual's expectations of himself in the therapy group situation. Initial setting of norms during the parallel phase is vested in the therapist. Members look to the therapist to set the kinds of norms that the members themselves would like to set for the group. During the inclusion phase the members struggle among themselves to set the norms for group behavior. Finally, during the mutuality phase the norms for group behavior are well established. The nature of norms during the mutuality phase are primary determinants of how therapeutic the group can and will be for the members. Group norms during mutuality can either allow for depth of interpersonal contact or restrain that contact to very superficial levels. The norms may allow some forms of expression but exclude others. The essential struggle in the group is to establish norms that will not be constricting but rather that will free the members in their behaviors, expression, and interpersonal contacts. Norms are the biggest factor in change resulting from therapy group experience. The kinds of norms that develop in a group can enhance those behaviors that facilitate emotional well being and change those that interfere with social-emotional well being and growth or they can inhibit change and reinforce the prohibition on those behaviors that facilitate health and growth of individuals.

Norms for therapy group behavior are primarily products of the authority and intimacy crises and the inclusion phase. Each resolution of an authority or intimacy crisis represents progress in the development of norms that foster initiative and intimacy among the members. Each resolution of an inclusion conflict results in norms that incorporate the desired behaviors of most, if not all, members.

The experience of participating in a group with progressively freeing norms counterbalances unfavorable influences from an individual member's past and gives him the social support to behave differently with other people. The acceptance of this new behavior in the social context of the group supports the individual member's capacity to behave in similar ways outside the group in other social situations. The opportunities for growth and change come about through the development of norms in the group. More often than not it will happen before insight is developed. That an individual changes in the group and receives support and validation from the other members provides him with the opportunity to behave differently. Moreover, it paves the way for him to understand why he behaved as he did before and to resolve the feelings that the new behaviors arouse.

Goals. Individual and group goals are the core of group function. Goals refer to what the members want from the group for themselves and what they want the group to direct its efforts toward.

In short-term groups (those lasting for less than three months or with fewer than twelve sessions) it is imperative that the several goals of individuals be synthesized before the group can pull together and achieve its common goals. In long-term groups, the longer the term, the less important is the synthesis of goals, more important is the allowance of goals. Thus, in long-term groups there is a process of ferreting out individual goals during the inclusion phase to deter-

GROUP DIMENSION	PARALLEL PHASE	AUTHORITY CRISES	INCLUSION PHASE
Differentiation	Undifferentiated	Members from therapist	Members from each other
Affective polarities	Trust vs. mistrust	Autonomy vs. fear of therapist	Acceptance vs. rejection; aggression vs. flight
Major behavioral features	Approach vs. avoidance	Challenge to authority	Fighting, vs. flocking, vs. fleeing
Source of gratification	Therapist		Therapist and other members
Relational issues	Contact vs. isolation	Therapist vs. member dominance vs. submission	Member-member affiliation vs. isolation and dominance vs. submission
Self-Other concept	Commonality vs. difference; superiority vs. inferiority	Reduction in therapists omnipotence	Uniqueness vs. uniformity
Power relations	Vested in therapist	Therapist vs. group	Members vs. members
Conflict	No overt; covert developing.	Member(s) therapist	Surfacing of member-member conflicts
Cohesion	Primary ties to therapist		Pairs and subgroup bonding & exclusiveness
Controls	Vested in therapist	Shifting therapist to group	Member and subgroup struggles for control
Norms	Covert, tentative, therapist determined	Challenge existing norms	Norm setting and redetermining
Goals	Covert, diffuse, individual, and tentative	Challenge to therapists	Overt and/or covert goal deliberation
Roles	Tentative role taking	Emerging indigenous leadership; modification of therapist role	Assumption and assignment of roles

DEVELOPMENT

INTIMACY CRISES	MUTALITY PHASE	SEPARATION CRISES	TERMINATION PHASE
	Within and among members		Members from group
Autonomy vs. intimacy	Intimacy vs. isolation	Autonomy vs. abandonment	Hostility vs. guilt
Affective contact and flight	Emergence of affect	Depression or super self-dependence	Regression, recapitulation, decathexis, and separation
	Therapist, other members, and self		Self, group, and extra group
Affective contact	Intimacy vs. isolation and free give and take	Freedom vs. object losses	Loosening and breaking of bonds
Equality	Acceptance of individuality mastery vs. futility	Identity crisis	Separation of self and others
Resolve of major power struggles	Balance among therapist and members	Individual vs. group	Relinquishment of power
Hiatus	Partialized conflicts	Staying vs. leaving	Disengagement
Whole-group exclusion of others	Deepening whole group bonds; lessening exclusion		In group and out group ties in balance
Emerging group controls	Shared by members and therapist	Tightening vs. breaking out	Incorporation of group controls
Normative crisis	Restrictive or freeing norms	Developing separation norms	Selective incorporation or rejection of norms
Emerging goal syntheses	Therapist, group, and individual confluence	Achievement of major goals	Individual goals external to group
	Increasing fluidity and interchangeability	Return to early roles	Relinquishment of roles

mine whether they are compatible with the individual goals of others. The product of the inclusion phase, then, is the development of group goals that allow the achievement of individual goals. The degree to which individual members can hope that the group will meet their goals is the same degree to which the member will feel included in the group.

In short-term groups, the achievement of the group goals triggers the final separation crisis and termination phase. However, goals are not always achieved in short-term groups since the termination phase may be triggered by the fact of the approaching end of the group. Consequently, some dealing with the loss of not fully achieving the goals of the group becomes a major part of the separation and termination processes. In long-term groups, the achievement of major individual goals generally precipitates the final separation crisis and termination of an individual member.

Group goals set during the parallel phase may or may not be the real goals an individual member has for the group. Even some early agreements on goals during the parallel phase may or may not result in a real contract among the members and the therapist. The early authority crises and the inclusion phase provide a major opportunity for individual members to indentify real goals for themselves in the group and for the group.

Finally, it must be emphasized that most goal struggles and determinations in therapy groups are covert and indirect. Very few therapy groups openly and directly negotiate their goals. More often goals are inherent in the behavior and focuses selected by the members. Opposing or divergent goals are inherent in the support of alternate or opposing focuses or in disruptive behavior that inhibits or prevents the work toward achievement of goals inherent in the prevailing focuses.

Roles. A role is an individual's performance of a set of expectations for behavior in the therapy group. Roles assumed by members are based on their expectations of themselves in the group situation and their perceptions of the expectations of others in the group. For a person to occupy a permanent role in the group, the individual has to not only assume the role but also be assigned that role by the other members.

In the parallel phase, members assume roles that, based on their past experiences, help them define the group situation and help them meet the expectations they perceive or assume the therapist has for their role performance. Other members may assign early roles to an individual either through default or because they temporarily want someone to perform some function. The actual process of assumption and assignment of roles takes place during the recurrent authority crises and in the inclusion phase. Roles reach their peak in importance as the group begins to develop some level of intimacy. As intimacy deepens during the mutuality phase, roles become less fixed; they are increasingly shared by some, if not all, of the other group members. In fact, one of the hallmarks of a well-developed group is the fluidity and interchangeability of roles. In a well-developed group members can move in and out of roles rather easily and, perhaps most important, perform those roles in their own unique ways.

The freedom in role performance during the mutuality phase is extremely important to the growth and change that results from therapy group experience. The new roles and new ways of performing those roles, coupled with the acceptance of being in these roles by the other group members, is a major way in which members can experiment with new behavior and prepare for behaving in new ways outside the group. The fluidity and interchangeability of roles characteristic of the inclusion phase is sometimes confused with the overt freedom for individuals to occupy roles in the parallel phase. The major difference is that in the parallel phase members are inclined to allow others to assume certain roles temporarily before the group becomes more meaningful and before the members trust the therapy group situation enough to take the initiatives they would really like to take. Allowing another member to take a role is very different from assigning that person a role. To the degree that a role is not really assigned to a member by the group, to that same degree will the member have to assume the role more rigidly, not allowing others to share in the performance of the functions associated with that role.

2

Parallel
Relations Phase

... we are obedient to whomsoever
is set in authority, and to the
laws, more especially to those
which offer protection. . .
      —Hippocrates

Every group formed by a therapist begins in the parallel relations phase. A therapy group may remain in the parallel phase anywhere from a few minutes to its entire existence. Whether a group moves from the parallel phase to a higher level of development depends on several factors: ages and ego states of the members; composition, structure, and purposes of the group; and leadership style of the therapist.

Almost all theorists of group development agree on the existence of a first phase of group development, although they disagree on which features are most characteristic of this phase. Hartford (1971) and Northen (1969) emphasize the trust issues. Bion (1961), Tuckman (1965), Bennis and Shepard (1974), and Mann (1967) emphasize dependency on authority. Garland et al. (1965) and Tuckman (1965) emphasize the testing issues.

Parallel relations is a term drawn from the concept of parallel play of young children. (Isaacs, 1933). Three- to eight-year-old children generally play next to each other, perhaps even interact with each other, but they do not in essence relate to each other. Instead, in the prepeer relationship the child will use other children to his own ends or allow himself to be used as an object in the other child's play. Naturally, children show increasing cognizance of the other children as they get older, but qualities of relationship like sharing affect or collaboration are rare. Interaction is based largely on one child's vesting the other child with qualities useful to his immediate ends and he becomes upset if these ends are frustrated.

Primary relationships during this phase are with any adults who are present in the play sphere or immediately available to the children. Most direct relationship with other children takes on the nature of the direct gratification a child usually seeks from a parent or parent substitute or, counterdependently, a child becomes a parent substitute for the other child. In counterdependent behavior the child meets his own needs for parenting by parenting the other child. Thus, the relationship with other children during this phase is a substitute for parental relations, not a direct peer relationship. With an adult present, the peer is easily sacrificed in favor of seeking gratification from the adult.

One of the most overt manifestations of parallelism in children under the age of seven is their identifying their groups by the name of the leader: for example, "We are Mary's group," or "We are John's group." From age eight upward, many children continue to identify their groups by the group leader's name until the group reaches a degree of cohesion, then they call themselves by the group name. Very often the leader designates a name for the group, but as cohesion grows the children are interested in changing the name. Another sign of parallelism: before the age of eight, a child can be placed with almost any other child. From eight onward, who is and who is not in their group becomes very important for most children.

The essential point of this discussion is that a recapitulation of the parallel stage of social development takes place at the start of any formed group. This phenomenon has implications for the necessary centrality of the group therapist and the low level of relationship among the members.

LEADER DEPENDENCY

Centrality of the therapist and dependency of the members on the therapist most typify the relational system during the parallel phase (see Bion, 1961; Tuckman, 1965; Bennis and Shepard, 1974; Mann, 1967). There may or may not be interaction among the members in the parallel state. More important is whether members experience a connection to one another or whether they are merely using each other or endowing each other with qualities necessary for their own ends. Crucial to therapy groups is whether the members have affective ties to one another in either sharing common affect or opposing valences of affect. In other words, therapy group members can be considered in a parallel state with one another if they interact but do not have affective communication and bonds. Affective communication consists of sympathy, empathy, positive identification, and negative identification. These phenomenon will be discussed more fully in the chapters dealing with later phases.

Basic to the centrality-dependency of the therapist during the parallel phase are the initial affective bonds of the members to the therapist. While sympathy or empathy may be offered by other group members, it is most often disregarded or depreciated compared with affective contact from the therapist. Members perceive the therapist as the sole source of gratification and will disregard or even reject affective contact from other members. (If they were to express their feelings they might say, "I'm only interested in what the therapist has to say. How can you or I help each other since we both have problems?")

Other factors inherent in the group dependency on the therapist arise from the member's vesting all of the power in the therapist. The therapist is accorded power for determining the kind of help necessary for the group and the way in which that help is proffered. He or she is also given the responsibility for controlling the process and protecting the members from themselves and from each other. In other words, responsibility and power for complete control of the situation are vested in the therapist. When each member concedes power to the therapist it is usually with the hope or expectation that the therapist will use that power to do what each individual member wants done: "Why don't you tell us to. . .?" "Make everyone stop. . ." "Should we be. . .?" "I wish that everyone would. . . ." The hope is that the therapist will carry out the individual's desires; then the individual doesn't have to deal directly with other members to realize his wishes.

A number of fears are associated with receiving help from anyone but the therapist. Most prominent is the fear of loss of the therapist (Weigert, 1960: 121-31). If an individual's needs are met by other members, the individual might fear that the therapist is less likely to be a source of need gratification: "If the other members tell me what's the matter or what I should do, then I might not find out what the therapist thinks." Perhaps a major reason why therapy had become necessary for many group members is that a fear arose early in life from parental prohibitions forbidding the child from receiving help or even forming relationships with anyone outside the family. The members may attribute these same prohibitions to the therapist and be fearful of punishment for reaching out to peers.

The nature and duration of leader dependency will vary with different kinds of groups. Groups of people very low on the psychosocial development scale, such as adult chronic schizophrenics or adult retardates, will remain dependent on the therapist throughout the life of the group. While the members of an adult group with a low psychosocial level of development will take on some self-dependency over time, the therapist remains fairly central in the relational system and remains the main source of gratification, initiative, and control.

Groups of latency-aged children can become somewhat self-dependent over time but usually require the leader to mediate conflicts, remain a major source of gratification, share in the initiative, and at least be a back-up for group controls. Often, the therapist must be the one to soften the too stringent controls that latency-aged children will exert upon each other.

In both groups of low functioning adults and latency-aged children the therapist must accept the dependency of the group for as long as necessary and remain central in the process and relationships. Expecting the group to function on a less dependent level than it is capable of can create an atmosphere of futility and failure for the members. At best this is unhelpful; at worst, it can lower the self-esteem of the members. The direct help and support that individuals and subgroups receive in becoming progressively self-dependent in minute steps can be one of the major benefits of the group experience. Even in the parallel phase, as other members experience one member's becoming more self-dependent with the permission, help, and support of the therapist, they too can vicariously gain some increased readiness for their own self-dependence.

A fundamental way in which the therapist can accept the centrality and dependency required both by the parallel phase phenomena and particularly by lower functioning groups is to create an atmosphere in which the therapist provides initial direction and control but opens the process to member's saying *no* to the therapist's suggestions, directions, and initiatives. Posing questions and initiatives in the form of "Would you like to tell us about. . .?" "Would you like to respond to what he just said. . .?" rather than "Tell us!" or "Respond to. . . !" provides the option for members to easily refuse. During the parallel phase, members of lower level groups may only be able to say *no* to what is suggested; they may not have alternative wishes or may not be able to express them directly. If and as the *nos* are accepted by the therapist, members may begin to experience the freedom to assert their autonomy in the situation and prepare for transfer of power and responsibility from the therapist. In groups of schizophrenics and adult retardates, however, the experience of saying *no* and trusting the therapist to accept *no* without rejecting or punishing the negative response may require a great many repetitions.

In general groups of adolescents and moderately well functioning adults can more readily assert their own wishes for the group and it is more a matter of increasing readiness to either depose the leader as an authority or accept the transfer of power from the leader to the members or both. The parallel phase in groups of such adolescents and adults might last from less than a few minutes to a few meetings. Unless the therapist or the members balk at the transfer of power, these groups can be helped through the parallel phenomena with relative ease.

AFFECTIVE POLARITIES

The same sense of trust that begins in the crucial first year of life becomes a critical dilemma during the parallel phase of group development (Erikson, 1968; p. 96). From the outset, each member struggles with the affective dilemma of whether to trust or mistrust the group. While the trust-mistrust polarity continues through the entire life of the group, its initial resolution in the parallel phase serves as the basis for further group development. Failure of the members to resolve the dilemma in favor of trust will seriously hamper the group development and perhaps result in dissolution of the group.

Each member's entry into the group is based on first establishing a relationship with the therapist. Therapist-member relationships become a bridge for each member to reach others in the group. Thus, the quality of the therapist-member relationship can either help or hinder the individual member's contact with the other members of the group. Basic to the initial therapist-member relationship is the degree of trust the member brings to the group experience. Initial trust of the therapist leaves emotional room for the member to begin to determine the trustability of the other members of the therapy group.

Increased trust of the therapist comes out in two major ways. First is the member's own interaction with the therapist, which suggests to the member that trust is deserved by the person the therapist appears to be and by the way the therapist treats the individual. Second, by perceiving the interaction of the other group members and the therapist, the individual member forms conclusions about the safety or the danger of the therapist. As the therapist is confirmed as being trustworthy, then the individual member can begin to consider whether the other members are trustworthy. He might express his thoughts as, "When I saw how nice the therapist was to the member who was crying I knew that she was a good person and then I wondered what the other group members were like."

Trust development in groups is a much used and abused phenomenon. Common notions of group development suggest a watershed moment that separates trust from mistrust. Many sensitivity trainers would even suggest that this watershed moment can be experienced by some simple exercises that allow the individual to experience trust sensations. The implication is that, once these trusting sensations are experienced, the person will from that time forward trust the group. For example, if a person assuming a rigid posture falls backward and allows himself to be caught by other group members, then the sensation of trust in the other group members is considered to carry over the life of the group. Certainly, the experience would help a person trust the group members to catch him again. Perhaps it would elevate his trust level in the members to some degree, much like any other experience would suggest to the group member that the other group members can be trusted. However, this small increase in trust can in no way mean that the person trusts the other members in all ways and at all times.

It is safe to say that, even after being in a group for years, no member would completely trust any of the other members. Each member might have a high degree of trust in the other members, and perhaps more than they experience in other situations, but it is never complete. Trust development must be considered a long continuum, with each person having his own starting point based on his past experiences, then moving to sufficient trust levels to enable him to approach the group situation.

Each phase of group development has its requiste level of trust, necessary for the increasing depth of relationships and revelations in the group therapeutic process. In the parallel phase trust is a prerequisite for resolution of the approach-avoidance behavioral dilemma. To the degree that a member trusts the group a member will chance approaching the situation. To the degree the person mistrusts the situation the person will tend to avoid it or flee from it.

Sufficient trust for approaching the group would include confidence that the therapist will not harm or punish the members and confidence that the therapist will protect the member from undue punishment by other members in the group.

Trust in other group members develops as the individual gains confidence that they accept his presence, his initiative, and the substance of what he says. The major fears of rejection, harm, and punishment are slowly reduced as the other members demonstrate by their behavior that these are not forthcoming. Conversely, to the degree that rejection, harm, or punishment are present in the group, the individual will tend to mistrust the group situation. In sum, the individual obtains enough data on the behavior of the other members to begin to know what to expect. A new member will trust the other members but how much or how little he trusts will depend on the real expectations he develops.

Trust development is the first emotional building block of the infant. The first object of trust is the parent or mother figure. A sufficient degree of trust in that mothering figure is necessary for the child to become interested in and aware of the outside world. If this initial trust is not forthcoming or is thwarted, autism or retreating inward results. The assumption must be made that no one develops complete trust or complete mistrust during this first year of life. Consequently, in the initial phases of group development, we are dealing with the level of trust developed by the individual during the first year of life and perhaps modified toward more or less trust since then. The group experience itself can be a vehicle for ultimately increasing the basic capacity for trust of parent and peer figures. From the level of trust that people bring to the group, we could anticipate whether they will require more or fewer or trustworthy experiences to increase their trust of the leader and other members. Thus, people with tendencies toward autism or paranoia require many more experiences and much longer periods to establish sufficient trust in the group to approach the situation.

BEHAVIORAL FEATURES

Pseudo-interaction

Central to the behavior in the parallel phase is the phenomenon of group members existing next to each other but relating primarily to the therapist. Most or all communication is aimed at the therapist. Members may address each other in their overt communication, but the messages being sent are intended for the therapist. Return messages from other group members may be received, but it is really the therapist's answers that are sought. In other words, group members may talk to each other, but they are looking over their shoulders to see what the therapist thinks about what they have said or done.

This pseudo-interaction can range from a frank silence, with everyone watching and waiting, to a bubbly hyperactivity with a lot of words passing among the members. Characteristically, each member pursues his own subject in tandem to subjects mentioned by others, but each is directing the conversation toward his own interests.

More aggressive or more anxious members can tend to dominate the discussion during this phase. This domination is often allowed and encouraged by the other members, since it allows them to watch what happens to the dominator without having to risk themselves. However, the domination may or may not produce significant material for the group. Very often the dominator merely filibusters the interaction space to prevent anything threatening from being discussed. The other members allow and encourage the filibuster in hopes of maintaining a low degree of threat and demand in the situation.

A very anxious dominator in the parallel phase may be pushed by anxiety into expressing many of the very matters that the others most feared talking about. This phenomenon is dangerous for both the dominator and the rest of the group. If the therapist stops the dominator from telling too much too soon, then the dominator will feel somewhat rejected and the other members will fear that the same might happen to them if they talk too much. If the dominator is allowed to continue, then he may tell more than he wants to and become embarrassed after the meeting. Members who tell too much in initial meetings often do not return for subsequent meetings, if ever again. It is very important to limit too effusive members somewhat in how much they say, to universalize their revelations as much as possible, and to seek the reactions of the other members to what they say.

Approach-Avoidance Conflict

The approach-avoidance conflict is the major behavioral dilemma for each of the members (Garland et al., 1965; Tuckman, 1965). We have already discussed how trust is the foundation for approaching the group, but it is through the group interaction that data for increased or decreased trust are developed. Members each come with their own individual wants, needs, and fears seeking gratification from the therapist. Each member fears that, at best, the therapist will disappoint them and, at worst, punish them for seeking satisfaction. Many even fear that the therapist may help them, and this arouses past fears of disloyalty to parents. Parents have often given children prohibitions against seeking help elsewhere or even seeking help from the other parent in the family.

In addition to fearing the therapist, individuals fear reaching out for gratification because of possible envy and hostility from other members (Whitaker and Lieberman, 1964: 19). Many, from their past experiences, feel unworthy of receiving gratification from a parent figure or have grown to put their sibling's needs ahead of their own to the extent that they cannot accept help until their siblings' needs have been satisfied. Thus, individuals fear being singled out for help because of possible wrath and punishment from the other members. Many of these fears become founded for each member because they experience feelings of envy and hostility toward other members as these others reach out for the group. When members check these fears in themselves, the result is a tendency to be overly nice to one another. "Company manners" prevail in most groups during the parallel phase.

Thus, each venture out toward the group and the therapist is frought with fears. Each step toward the group involves a risk. Each risk taken becomes a feeler for the member to see what happens when he says or does something. As he observes the reactions and feedback from the group, he gets either a feeling of safety, which encourages more risks, or a feeling of uncertainty or fright, which makes him more wary and less venturesome.

Other members watch the individual who is venturing and may vicariously gain a feeling of safety or wariness, depending on what they see happen to the other person. Still other individuals are watching both the person venturing as well as the reactions of others. They are concerned not only with how the therapist and group react to the members but also with how the member handles the venture. For example, when a member is pushed by anxiety and tells too much, the other members worry whether the same might happen to them if they start talking. The concern is whether they will be able to tell enough to get something, yet not so much that they might lose control and regret having talked.

Approaching the group is not to be confused with overt activity. Much of the activity, talking, and behavior during the parallel phase is risking and responding to risks; however, much of the activity is aimed at keeping the situation safe and unthreatening. Subject matter that is remote to real concerns, idle chatter, or perseveration on relevant but less consequential issues tends to keep the situation safe and away from more anxiety-provoking issues. When many group members join in these discussions they are casting votes for maintaining a safe and distant atmosphere. It is often necessary for a group to go through long periods of safe nonthreatening interaction to gain experience in existing next to each other. Extended periods of peaceful coexistence can help more distrustful or fearful people to become more relaxed in the group situation.

Communication Skills and Networks

Another function of the parallel interaction is building communication skills and networks. If group members are not adept in communication, it is often helpful to let them spend extended periods in safe discussions in order to develop their skills and establish a base of talking to each other. As the group develops, these skills and communication networks might serve very well. The only danger is that the group might develop norms that preclude meaningful discussion. The question of whether extended light discussion is useful or not must depend on the nature of the members and the goals for the group. In general, the lower the psychosocial level of the group members, the more time might well be spent on the group developing its communication system—just learning to talk to each other—rather than on material that might be more directly related to their problems.

Meetings during the parallel phase are very disjointed and pluralistic. Many overt themes can run through the topics of discussion. Group themes are covert in that the members will act them out by testing and reaching for the therapist. Immediate confrontation of the group with underlying themes is generally not useful during the parallel phase. Pointing them out might cause the members to attempt interaction that they are not ready for. The result would be heightened fears or feelings of having failed as a group and as group members. The therapist should keep early underlying themes in mind when helping the group and individual members, but confrontation may work better in later phases.

The subjects, while usually in the then-and-there time sphere, have significance here and now for the group. The classic example of an initial subject appears almost universally in parent groups; in early meetings they want to discuss discipline. What they say about discipline usually has implications for the therapist as their parent in the group situation and what the therapist should or should not do about punishing them for being "bad" parents or "bad" group members. Many possible connections can be made between controlling children's behavior and controlling their own behavior and that of other members in the group. Often, the discussion of parallel responsibilities also contains messages for the therapist, and through it group members suggest how they think the therapist is supposed to relate to the group members.

SOURCES OF GRATIFICATION

The therapist is the primary source of gratification during the parallel phase for many reasons. Fundamental is the parent-like role ascribed to the therapist at the outset of a group. Just as in early childhood the group member sought gratification from parents or parent substitutes, the group member will be likely to attribute the major capacity for need gratification to the therapist (Mann, 1967; Gibbard & Hartman, 1973).

Individual Expectations

When people come to any form of therapy they usually have the doctor-patient image. They expect to tell their story to the therapist and they expect the therapist to decide the nature of the problem and suggest curative solutions. Members will bring the doctor-patient image to group therapy, especially during the parallel phase.

There is an additional image that members bring to the group. The classroom is the closest situation to a therapy group that most people have experienced in the past. Again, the classroom image has implications for the primacy of the therapist in relationships with the members. In most classrooms, the teacher is the primary source of gratification. Most classrooms even have prohibitions against members' seeking help from each other since, even though many teachers subscribe to the idea of mutual help, they often view such efforts as misbehavior or cheating. Thus, group members are predisposed to seek gratification from the therapist in the group and, because of prohibitions from the past, they may fear seeking help from other group members.

Direct seeking of help from the therapist presents a very mixed picture. Sibling relationships and classmate images are stirred up for the members when they want to reach out for help from the therapist. Depending on his past experience, the member might feel entitled to help from the therapist or might feel that the other members are more entitled. Getting the help may bring up feelings of preferred sibling or teacher's pet, with the concomitant fears of envy and retaliation by the other members. Some members will instead try to offer help to other members to counter their own wishes and avoid the possible wrath of the other members for getting special attention.

The degree to which the therapist offers gratification to individual members is a matter of controversy in the group therapy field, with range of opinion varying from no help whatever to the major source of help throughout the life of a group. This author's position is a middle one. *The therapist should provide some initial gratification, especially during the parallel phase, then facilitate the process of mutual gratification among the members.*

Rationale for the middle position arises from the concept that the group experience is a recapitulation of the individual's social development. As an infant the individual first received gratification from the parent, later he learned to seek it from other adults, and finally, from peers. Experiencing or re-experiencing the therapist gratifications like those of the first year of life helps awaken the member's desires for gratification that he hopes will be forthcoming in the group situation. Just as the gratification from primary sources during the first year of life leads to trust and interest in the outside world, so does initial gratification from the therapist in the group. In other words, initial gratification from the therapist to the individual group members will lead to trust in the therapist and becomes a bridge to trust in the group for gratification.

Opponents of this view suggest that the group will become and remain dependent on the therapist for gratification and will not seek it from others. The question becomes whether nurture provides sustenance for the person to grow or whether readily available nurture creates and sustains dependency. The author's contention is that, for most groups, initial nurture of the group members, combined with increasing bridging among members for mutual nurture, will not create an untoward dependency and will, in fact, better facilitate the development of a group atmosphere in which giving and getting among members reaches a high level.

Groups of young children or severely emotionally deprived adults will by their very nature tend to fixate at the stage of seeking all gratification from the leader. However, helping them to seek beyond a parent figure may indeed be an end for the group therapeutic process rather than a means for therapy.

Dependency-Counterdependency

When the therapist does not provide initial gratifications for members, groups tend to set up a dependency-counterdependency network. Some members become the older siblings, substituting for the gap left from ungiving parents. Counterdependent members may then get into their pattern of re-enacting their usual ways of helping others as they would like to be helped. As they gain status from this role they may be reluctant to receive help from the group. The dependent members might then become the group mascots or objects of pity and get locked into a possibly familiar position of having to be dependent to have others gratify their counterdependency needs.

> Ellen was a young woman locked in a debilitating hostile dependency on her mother. In the group, Ellen quickly learned to push other people along in dealing with their issues by asking them very pointed questions and providing hasty solutions. The objective of this counterdependent helping was to speed up everyone else's help so Ellen could claim the remaining time in the session. Even though at times Ellen's help to others was well conceived, the underlying hostility was indirectly transmitted to the other members. Other members found they resented Ellen's help, yet felt very bad since she seemed to be attempting to help them. Ellen was, of course, assuming her mother's mode of helping. Other counterdependent people often get gratification from helping others; however, Ellen and her mother would give gratification solely to create emotional indebtedness. Other counterdependent people in the group most often won't seek any time and attention for themselves but rather will attempt to meet all of their own needs through meeting needs of others.

The phenomena of dependence/counterdependence is well developed by Bordin (1965). Bordin suggests that the nurturing of dependent patients facilitates the therapeutic progress; nurturing counterdependent patients interfers with their therapeutic progress.

RELATIONAL ISSUES

Co-existence of individual members is the dominant feature of the parallel phase. Depending on the nature of the group, there may or may not be interaction among the members. Member-member interaction is often confused with member-member relationships. Certainly, member-member interaction is an essential step toward the development of member-member relationships, but the nature of the interaction determines whether it is parallel interaction or interaction reflecting a relationship between members. During the parallel phase, member-member interaction provides opportunity for contact that might lead toward the mutual interest and affinity characteristic of a relationship. Contact among members may come about through ways other than overt interaction. Members may begin to identify with feelings and attitudes manifest in both the general behavior and the verbal behavior of other members. Contact results when one member develops an initial affective awareness of another member. When the affective awareness becomes mutual, a relationship is begun.

Initial relationships are developed between the members and the therapist. The member is either attempting to communicate with the leader by telling something to another member or wanting the leader to communicate something to him. During the parallel phase, the members are generally looking for approval or disapproval from the leader for the actions and content of the communication. They are asking for the therapist's interest, but are very much afraid of getting it. As the therapist demonstrates his interest and concern both behaviorally and verbally, the members become more secure in the relationship with the therapist and develop more interest in gaining the interest of other members. Once members gain feelings of initial acceptance by the therapist, there is more energy available for contact with other members.

The length of time required for members to feel initial acceptance by the therapist will vary accordingly with (1) the age of the member, (2) the psychosocial capacity of the members, (3) the homogeneity of the group, and (4) the purpose for the group. Latency-aged children will require more time for developing and sustaining a relationship with the therapist before moving out to other members, merely because they have not matured much beyond the parallel phase of their back psychosocial development. Early adolescent groups eleven to fifteen years of age will require a long time to develop a relationship with the therapist, largely because of their need for separation from adult control and for room to flex their own autonomy. In particular, they need reassurance that the therapist will not inhibit their autonomy beyond reasonable expectations. Adult groups will, depending on their nature and psychosocial capacities, move into a relationship with the therapist rather quickly. The variables for adult groups depend on the degree of deprivation the respective members experienced during the very early years of life or the degree of their negative experiences with parents and past authority figures or both.

A homogeneous group provides an easier base for contact among the members, since such a group requires less reaching out for overt and covert contact among the members. Heterogeneous groups provide more threats, since the likelihood of acceptance by other members is less sure and more security in the relationship with the therapist is a necessary precondition to reaching out to other members.

The purpose and structure of a group will influence the length of time it stays in a parallel state. A group of very short duration (fewer than eight sessions) will cause members to ponder the relative values of investing in relationships when the harvest might be meager. (Is the risk worth the possible gain?) The longer the duration of the group, the more people will be willing to invest in member-member relationships. Depending on the purpose of the group, members will be inclined to assess the relative danger or safety of relating to the other members. A long-term therapy group aimed at insight development will hold more fear than a short-term educational process in which the expectations are lower and clearer.

To summarize, if we accept that contacts are the beginning and building blocks of relationships and that contacts are moments of mutual awareness, then initial contact generally occurs between members and the therapist and, with the support of the member-therapist relationship, members begin to contact each other. Relationships in the parallel phase are primarily developed with the therapist. The final test of this relationship arises in authority crises. After the first resolution of an authority crisis, members can contact each other more directly. As members contact each other, the group is moving into the relational pattern of the inclusion phase. Initial contacts among members are often characterized by statements like: "I didn't realize that others felt like I do," or "You took the words right out of my mouth." Initial aversion to contact among members is epitomized in groups of depressed people by such comments as, "If you think that's bad listen to my situation. . ."

SELF-OTHER CONCEPT

The individual members' concept of self in relation to other people is perhaps the most difficult aspect of entering a group, although it becomes a major source of therapeutic gain in group therapy. Before entering groups and during the parallel phase, most members are concerned with how they compare to other members of the group. Since most people come to groups because of some felt failures or deficiencies in their lives, they believe that everyone else in the group is somehow better than they are as competent people and competent group members. Initially the most relieving quality of group therapy is the sense of commonality that each member gets from hearing or perceiving that others have similar or equivalent kinds of difficulties. The universality of human difficulties plays a key role in the gain of initial comfort that each member derives from the group.

The experience of commonality with at least one other member begins a feeling of universality and affinity for that other member. Thus, the importance of having at least one other member in the group with whom he can identify begins to help the individual feel less bad about his plight and more on a par with others.

Some people need to feel that they are different from others in the group. They will deny any similarities between them and other people. There are a number of people who must see themselves as different. The differences are usually deemed to make the individual either inferior or superior to the others. A person who tends toward the extreme paranoid side of the paranoid-depressive continuum will see himself as superior to the other members and as not having the same problems. The extreme is indeed that their problem is other people and not inherent within themselves. People who tend toward the depressive end of the continuum will see themselves as inferior to everyone else and will reject all possible signs that the other members are as bad or as bad off as they are. Both the very paranoid and the very depressed will reject commonality with others and resist any attempts on the part of others toward mutual affinity. In groups composed entirely of depressed members there is often an initial process in which they fight over who is the worst in the group (Levine and Schild, 1969).

Thus, the social comparison process of the parallel phase is a relieving phenomenon for most people and a threatening phenomenon for some people who tend toward extreme paranoia or extreme depression. Most often the therapist will prove helpful to the members if he points to commonalities and allows the members to develop an affinity by means of these comparisons. In the case of people who need to see themselves as different, allowing their perception and the concomitant distance and aversion to others will permit these people to find their niche until such time as they may feel comfortable enough to find their affinities to the other members.

POWER RELATIONS

During the parallel phase, group members individually and collectively vest all the power in the leader. The leader gains some of his power by virtue of his position as expert helper and by being endowed with power by the members.

Members are quick to endow the leader with power for many reasons. First, most members come to the group because of some feelings of helplessness over at least some if not all, aspects of their lives. Thus, endowing the therapist with all the power stems from a wish for the therapist to have sufficient power to make things right for them. Another reason to endow the therapist with power is to handle the members' fears of their own incapacity to control and the feared incapacities of the other members to control. Thus, if the therapist has all the power, each member will feel protected from his own and other peoples' impulses.

As group members develop ideas about the nature and direction of the group, they often attempt to influence the therapist to carry out these ideas. Each member holds the therapist responsible for making the group do what that member wants the group to do. They say, for example, "Shouldn't we be. . .?" "Don't you think that the group should. . .?" "Why don't you tell us to. . .?" Attempts to control each other or help each other, even if directed from one member to another, are very tentative, since the members are not sure they have or want the authority to act toward or upon each other. They might say, "Is it okay for them to. . .?" "Shouldn't they. . .?" "I'm not sure I'm supposed to say this. . ." Members also fear that the leader does not want them to usurp any power for control or helping, as evidenced by such remarks as "Is it okay for me to tell them that. . .?" "I'm not the therapist but I think that. . . ."

The therapist must accept the power position until the members feel more comfortable in the group and more able to exert their own power. The therapist has to provide help and permission for the group members to gain, use, and distribute the power in the group. Realization of power in the group is one of the major ingredients for helping members to overcome their feelings of helplessness and to gain more confidence in their own abilities to handle their life situations.

If the therapist abandons the power position too quickly, members will become fearful of themselves and each other, with resultant distortions in the group process. The need for centralized power in the group will become manifest as everyone keeps a very safe distance (often in excruciating silence) or as more power-prone members take over. Usually when a power-prone member takes over, the mode of leadership is autocratic. Just as when a child is forced to be an adult prematurely, such a member may handle the responsibilities, but the resiliency and latitude of their handling those responsibilities will be extremely constricted. The group will have to function in a very narrow range with little or no opposition to the member authority figure and, ultimately, with little or no difference of opinion or allowance for individuality. The group may even develop an overt bond knit tightly around the dictates of the indigenous leader, excluding to the point of complete rejection any who differ. The therapist or any member becomes an object for scapegoating. Conformity to the indigenous leader's dictates becomes paramount, since members fear to differ because of the real possibility of being the next scapegoat. Those people who are inclined toward being scapegoats, of course, may help to develop and perpetuate this situation, since they are more comfortable in this role.

Thus, gradual assumption of political power by the group increases the possibility that this power will be exerted in more resilient and supportive ways by the group. Gradual relinquishment of power to the group by the therapist will facilitate a healthy development of group power. The therapist can use his power position to prepare the group by granting wishes of the members while insuring that a balance of wishes of all members is incorporated in initial dictates. The demonstration and assurance of equal opportunity for all the members builds the basis of an open and balanced system after the group begins to wield its own power.

Initial ceding of power to the group or a member arises as the therapist accepts a negative response to a suggestion. A second level of the therapist's ceding power to the group arises when the therapist says, "Joe is suggesting that we. . . . Can we try Joe's suggestion?" or "What do the others think about Joe's suggestion?" A third level of ceding power to the group arises when the therapist suggests, "Joe, why don't you ask the other members if they would like to procede your way?" At a fourth level, the therapist remains silent and lets the others react or not react to Joe's suggestion.

The level of ceding power must be related to the capacity of the group members to exert and accept power. A fourth-level ceding of power in a group only capable of a first-level response might well reinforce fears of assuming power.

CONFLICT

Overt conflict during the parallel phase is usually nonexistent. Potential conflict is always present in any multiple-person situation. In the early phases of groups most people are in a temporary hiatus from overt conflict. "Company manners prevail," (Slater, 1966: 7-23). Members patiently wait their turns and back off from disagreements, since they are generally uncertain of themselves and uncertain of the reactions of other members and the therapist. Members adopt a wait-and-see attitude for early disagreements or attempt to gain the therapist's support for their own contention or wish, rather than directly challenging the opinions of the other members (Ormont, 1968).

The search for commonality and the fear of difference that prevail in the parallel phase cause people to shove under the rug a great deal of potential conflict. However, the potentials for conflict grow with each passing minute that the group is in existence. The disjointed nature of early meetings caused by the covert differences in seeking gratification from the therapist and the competition for gratification from the therapist itself are the bases for rivalry. Minor conflicts will initially emerge over the focus of discussion. These conflicts will be manifest in an individual's not listening to others unless what the others are saying directly relates to the individual. When another has finished talking the member will then begin to talk about his interest or concern almost in disregard of the other members.

In groups of severly withdrawn patients, in the author's experience, the members would simply all talk at the same time. In adolescent groups the conflict is manifest in disruptive acting-out or in diffusion of the group into many little conversations. In adult groups, the phenomenon is manifest in turn-taking and subject-changing.

At first, the therapist must be a communication center for picking up the divergent pulls and opinion while offering compromises and accommodations. As the communication center, the therapist offers the group models for resolving conflict, insures that all sides are heard and respected, and provides the members with the satisfaction of having their desires respected in the solutions. This activity helps to build means for conflict resolution and points the way for the members to do the same more independently when the group takes more responsibility for expressing and resolving conflict. To the degree that each member feels that his own interests are respected by the leader, each member will feel more like offering further opinions and, eventually, fighting for their own opinion. Thus, although conflicts are covert, in the parallel phase the therapist helps conflict ultimately emerge by providing support for all opinions, providing creatively satisfying solutions, and demonstrating ways in which members may eventually achieve their own satisfying solutions to conflicts.

The first step for the therapist in handling conflict is to recognize both sides: "It seems like Joe would like the group to. . . and Jim would like the group to. . . ." Then the first level of handling the conflict might be a suggestion: "Let's take up Joe's point, then Jim's point." A second level of handling conflict might be, "How can we do what both Joe and Jim would like us to do?" A third level of handling the conflict might be, "What are we going to do about the two ideas?"

COHESION

Cohesion among the members is almost nonexistent during the parallel phase. All that members have binding them together as a group is that they meet in the same place at the same time for possibly similar reasons and they have someone in common from whom they are seeking help. Initial cohesion is mostly a feeling between the members and the therapist. This initial cohesion is facilitated by pregroup contract between the member and the therapist and at this time the member may develop some good feelings about the therapist as a possible support in moving into the group.

Children's groups often manifest this early form of cohesion by calling their group by the name of the therapist. It is no accident that the members use the possessive for the leader—until the members experience more power over the destiny of the group and an affective bond with each other, they are coming to *his* group.

The earliest form of cohesion arises from feelings of affinity for other members in the group. This early affinity is based on perceived commonality with one, some, or all of the other members. It may stem from an affinity in age and sex, from similarities in behavior patterns, from a fate shared with other members, or from the knowledge that other members have experienced similar difficulties (Stotland et al., 1960).

Members will also experience from the outset some aversions to other members of the group. Most members will have an aversion to members who represent the opposite of the member to whom they feel an affinity. Particularly wide differences in age will tend to produce an initial aversion between members. However, depending on how the individual is feeling about a particular characteristic in someone else, the affinity or aversion to that person will reflect his own comfort with or rejection of that characteristic in himself. For example, a person who is withdrawn will tend to feel an affinity to someone else who is withdrawn. However, if the withdrawn individual is highly desirous of emerging from his withdrawness, he may develop an affinity for someone who is aggressive. In the parallel phase, affinities are mostly with people whom the individual sees as being like himself. In later phases, affinities and aversions take many different forms, depending on how the person is feeling about particular characteristics in himself.

In summary, during the parallel phase members begin to feel drawn toward some members and to feel aversions to others. These feelings are the forerunners of subgrouping in the inclusion phase.

CONTROLS

During the parallel phase controls are all vested in the therapist (See Hartford, 1971: 74-80; Northen, 1969: 128-29). Control of self, control of others, and control of the group process are all matters of concern for all new members. Some members either feel incompetent to control or would rather be controlled by others so as to be accepted. Because these members have low control needs, they will cede all responsibility for control to the leader. Other members come to a group with high needs for control of themselves, of others, and of the situation. These members hope that the therapist will control them and the others, but their estimates of what constitutes sufficient control and the right kinds of control will be rather high. To the degree that the leader exerts the nature and degree of control that these members want, they will feel comfortable. If they do not perceive the leader as sufficiently controlling, then the member with high control needs will first attempt to make the leader exert the kind and degree of controls that the member would like. If the member feels no hope that the leader will maintain this nature and degree of control, then the member will attempt to take over control of the group. Tucker (1973) and Schroder and Harvey (1963) delineate clearly the varying needs and wishes of members for control by the therapist.

For most members with high control needs, a feeling of having some degree of influence over the process and direction of the session will lessen their fears and reduce their consequent need to control. However, if their control is threatened, they will attempt to take over the group or will have to withdraw from the group through silence, inactivity, or abortive termination.

Very often the person with high control needs will attempt to dominate the group sessions through what essentially becomes a filibuster. That is, the member comes to each meeting and talks incessantly witout allowing others their chance for participation. Intervention by the therapist in this situation is precarious. On the one hand, if the therapist directly stops this member, the other members will feel protected but at the same time will become fearful that the therapist may come down on them if they get carried away or say the "wrong" things. This would inhibit the entire group. In dealing with the domina- tor it is important for the therapist to support one facet of what the dominator brings for discussion and limit the rest. It may require interrupting the person on an *and,* since such people often do not pause between sentences. By accepting one part of what the individual brings up and limiting the rest, the therapist demonstrates acceptance of the person and what the person may be asking for, but sets limits on the quantity of discussion. This approach not only has less chance of frightening the other members but also helps the dominator feel some sense of control over what is discussed. Asking the group to react to one facet of the dominator's input gives the other members openings for talking on ground already broken by the dominator. The therapist might say, "It appears that John is asking the group if. . . . What do others think about. . . ?" A dominator who cannot respond to repeated efforts like the above may be so fearful of the group that he is impervious to other people's wishes and it may become necessary to drop him from the group—if he does not voluntarily withdraw after being limited in a supportive way.

The therapist thus must accept the responsibility for controls by attempt- ing to be the initial vehicle by which individual members can realize their control interests. To the degree that the several members' control objectives can be incorporated the group will be able to feel more in charge of the situation. Most group members do not need to feel in complete control of the situation but need only to feel assured that threatening situations will not arise until they are ready for them.

Here again if the therapist accepts the role of being the initial controller and the vehicle through which members can realize their desired controls, he most probably can incorporate controls desired by a variety of members. If the therapist only battles attempts by members to control the process, then the therapist is open to a scapegoating situation as described under power relations in the parallel phase. The problem would stem from the group's having responsi- bility for its own control before there is a balance in the group and a readiness to both assert and accept group controls.

Ultimately, in later phases of group development, members submit to control by the group if they (1) have a part in developing those controls, (2) feel accepted by the group, and (3) feel some degree of power in the determination of group means and ends. Early efforts at self-control must be supported, but they must also be balanced for input by a broad base of membership.

NORMS

The functions of norms and goals during the parallel phase are perhaps the least understood phenomena yet the most crucial building blocks for long-range group development. Norms are what group members expect of themselves and of other people in an interpersonal situation. With clear-cut norms, a group member knows what behaviors will be accepted by other members and what behavior and response to expect from other members. Norms can be violated but, when group members understand the norms, they know when they are violating them and what possible risk is involved. The risk may be worth the anticipated difficulty in violating the norms. However, more than anything else, norms can facilitate group development and therapeutic productivity or hinder and constrict the behavior of the group so that growth and development are brought to a halt. (Almost the entire theory of Whitaker and Lieberman (1964) is devoted to normative development and expansion of freedom.)

Central to the normative problems in the parallel phase is that members generally do not know what is expected of them in a therapy group or what to expect of the leader and the other members. Members who have had prior group therapy experience will bring anticipations from that experience to the new group. If their past experiences with therapy groups were positive, then they will anticipate enabling and freeing experiences. If their past therapy group experiences were negative, then anxiety and fear will be heightened and as a result, they will anticipate norms that reduce risking and promote maintenance of very safe behavior. Such expectations can restrict group growth and therapeutic productivity.

Members who have no prior experience will rely on the most relevant past experiences to understand the current group situation. Preset attitudes that many people bring to group therapy come from their teen peer-group experiences, doctor-patient and student-teacher relationships, and primary family experiences.

Family relationships are the basis of the way in which individuals have learned to behave in the doctor-patient, pupil-teacher, and teen peer-group experiences. Thus, during the parallel phase individual behavior will be influenced mostly by the ways in which people have learned to deal with peers and authorities outside the family; they will not be a direct reflection of family relational patterns per se. At the outset, members are all looking to the therapist to confirm or disapprove acceptability of behavior (Garland et al., 1965; Tuckman, 1965). With each behavior and interaction in the first meetings, tentative norms that are being developed hinge mostly on whether the therapist seems to approve or disapprove of the behavior. A lack of response from the therapist will raise the uncertainties of the member who took the risk and the other members, who are all watching.

Initial Risk-taking

Initial risks are usually aimed directly at the therapist. If the therapist responds to the initial risk in an accepting way—that is, if he or she answers the question or acknowledges the communication—then the member will more than likely feel safe and will begin to form some direct ideas about the acceptability of behavior in the current situation. If the therapist rejects outright the first risks in a group—that is, if he or she disparages the communication in any way as inadequate or inappropriate—this will heighten the fears of all the members and block the impetus for further risking. Some members will tend to take counterphobic measures; that is, they will act out their worst fears to see what might be the worst that happens to them. Generally when members take a counterphobic tack, they go to an extreme, revealing much more than they really want to or raising the standards for participation in the group to such heights that they far exceed the trust level of an initial group. This behavior is usually manifest by members who take the therapist's role in either supporting or depreciating what others have to say. If another member shares a problem the counterphobic member will suggest that it is not the real problem; if another member shares a feeling the counterphobic member will suggest that the feeling is superficial and will ask for the true feeling. As a result the norms for participation become so stringent that few, if any, group members can meet the expectations and they become extremely anxious and fearful. When this happens it is important for the therapist to directly temper the stringent test for communication with realistic expectations for the group's stage of development. Pointing to the future desirability of fuller and deeper revelation to the group while bringing in the reality of trust levels of members at the early meetings will help to establish more realistic norms.

Role of the Therapist

The degree to which the therapist actively sets norms for the group must be related to the group's capacity to develop norms of its own. In groups whose members have a lower level of psychosocial development, the therapist may need to suggest norms very actively; in groups with higher levels of psychosocial development the group can more easily evolve its own norms. For example, a first level of norm setting in lower capacity groups might be for the therapist to suggest. "Can we each take a turn and tell about. . .?" "Would you like to introduce yourselves to each other?" Posing the normative suggestion as a question opens the possibility of members rejecting the suggestion of the therapist and thus beginning to participate to some extent in norm setting. Members could also reject the therapist's norm by simply not doing what is suggested or by interfering with the suggestion in operation, (for example not waiting for their turns). A second level of norm setting by the therapist might be for the therapist to pose the alternatives: "It looks like you would rather not conduct our meeting by taking turns but would rather talk more spontaneously," or "It seems that some of you want to take turns and others want to talk more spontaneously. Which should we do?" This second level begins to pose normative conflicts for resolution between the group and the therapist or among the members.

Beginnings of Authority Crisis

As the group gains in comfort and security in the situation, the members inevitably begin to question and/or challenge the initial norms set by the therapist; this is part and parcel of the authority crisis. Ideally, the modeling and norm-setting by the therapist has given the members the opportunity to develop sound ideas about how the group might be helpful to them. In addition, if the therapist has taken each member's initial behavior as a vote for the manner in which the group conducts itself and has helped to insure that these votes are tempered by realistic expectations, then the group will already be functioning, in large part, according to the members' own desires about how it should operate. This increased security will facilitate the group's beginning to take more direct responsibility for norm-setting, which is an integral part of the first authority crisis.

The more crucial norms in the parallel phase are concerned with (1) how long to talk, (2) how often to talk, (3) how much to risk and reveal, (4) how much to reach out for each other and how much distance to maintain, and (5) how much help to ask for. The behavioral manifestations of these norms have been discussed under behavioral features of the parallel phase.

At first all members feel protected by the blanket of active nonthreatening discussion brought about by the anxious, needy, and depressed members. Then other group members begin to covertly resent the fact that the very active ones are taking up the time and, at the same time, the counterdependent ones become additionally angry because the active members cannot or will not accept their help and be satisfied (Frank et al., 1952). This underlying dissatisfaction and anger is the impetus for a change of norms in the first authority crisis and during the inclusion phase. If not expressed, this underlying hostility and conflict can cause members to drop out feeling that the group will never do what they would like. The underlying hostility will at first be manifest in the members' wanting the therapist to do something about controlling the balance of participation. A policy of crediting the member with the idea and supporting the idea with the rest of the group will help the member feel that he has had impact on the process. The latter effort is a building block toward the member's bypassing the therapist and dealing more directly with the other group members.

GOALS

Fundamental to a member's commitment to a group and its efforts is the degree to which the member feels that this goals are incorporated into the group goals. On the other hand, if a member feels that there is little room for his goals in the group, he is faced with the dilemma of either fighting for his goals or fleeing, either by being inactive in the group or by leaving it. The fight-flight dilemma is part of the inclusion phase; however, a member may begin to experience concern about the potential or lack of potential for the group to help him achieve his goal during the parallel phase.

The process of goal development for individuals is facilitated by the intake process. During intake it is helpful for the therapist to unearth the member's goals and perhaps resolve any disparities between the goals perceived by the therapist and those perceived by the member. The therapist's acceptance and support of the member's goals from intake might help insure the member's hope that his goals will be served in the group.

In Short-term Groups

There is a wide disparity in how goals will function in short-term homogeneous groups and how they will function in long-term heterogenous groups. Because short-term groups should have limited goals, capable of accomplishment within the allotted time span, and common to all the members, the commonalities in goals can serve as a unifying force in the group process. For example, in a predischarge group at a psychiatric inpatient facility, all the members can readily support each other in their aims, plans, and feelings about leaving the hospital. However, when one hospital combined a predischarge group of patients who were motivated with others who were unmotivated, there was a great deal of difficulty. When the patients with questionable motivation were separated into a homogeneous group with the goal of dealing with the question of whether or not to leave the hospital, the group was considerably more effective in helping many of the patients with questionable motivation decide to leave the hospital. Thus, in a short-term group (from four to eight meetings) the goal disparity between those who wanted to leave the hospital and those who did not was too great to reconcile in the available time.

In Long-Term Groups

In a long-term group, the goals run deeper and are generally more multifaceted. Members come to long-term therapy groups with wide variations in their goals. They may for example, seek relief from high levels of anxiety, from general malaise, or from particular symptomatologies like overeating, sleeplessness, or depression, or they may want help with specific problems, perhaps concern over lack of relationships or concern with specific relationships with family, lovers, friends, or work associates. The very divergence of goals can be productive for all concerned, but only if there is sufficient time for members to realize how the concerns of others might have implications for their own coping efforts. Another example: a member coming into a group may want to work out problems in relationships with the opposite sex a second member is concerned with parental relationships. The second member could help the first to experience how relationships with parents can interfere with relationships to the opposite sex and vice versa. However, during the parallel phase, both members might feel that discussion of the other person's problem is a waste of time, that it is something they have to bear to get "their turn." As members of a long-term therapy group gain increased comfort for experiencing, expressing and pursuing their goals, they see the relevance of other members' goals and the potentials for gaining from the group relationships themselves. As a result they undergo both a clarification and an expansion of their goals. Thus, in a long-term process, individual goals expand and become incorporated into the goals for other members and perhaps the entire group.

In long-term groups goals are seldom negotiated through direct discussion. In early group meetings the goals are usually manifest in what people choose to talk about. The diversity in goals is also apparent in the disjointed nature of early meetings as each person waits for others to finish so that he can take his turn. There is little sustained development of an issue raised by one member, unless perhaps there is an attempt to quickly solve that member's problem. If this disjointed process is viewed only as resistance to any particular topic, then it discounts the so-called resistor's vote for a change in direction. If the therapist takes the view that interference or subject-changing is only resistance, then the therapist will suggest that one member's topic is more important than another and will strongly influence the group's perception of what its goals should be. Other members will either begin to aline their goals with those of the therapist or will become discouraged and feel rejected by the therapist because their interests seem illegitimate. In the predischarge groups discussed above, for example, members who did not share the goal of leaving the hospital became either silent or disruptive because they felt they could not discuss their goal of remaining in the hospital. If the interruptions and lack of participation by these members were recognized as votes for alternative goals, then these members might have been able to deal with their feelings about staying and leaving. For that matter, those who were more motivated to leave might also have dealt more effectively with their mixed feelings about leaving if the therapist had allowed expansion of the group goals.

As Preparation for the Authority Crisis

Basic to the members' preparing for the authority crisis is their coming to feel that what they want from the group is legitimate enough so that they can inisist upon it. Whether or not the therapist has shared his own hopes for the group and its members, the group members will attribute certain goals to the therapist. If the therapist supports each member's expression, direct or indirect, of his hopes and aspirations, then the members will be better able to challenge their concept of the therapist's goals during the authority crisis. Persistent nullification of individual goals during the parallel phase will lead either to perpetuation of the parallel phase, dissolution of the group, or full-scale rebellion against the authority of the therapist. While a full-scale rebellion may eventually free the group to move ahead, not many therapy groups are immediately capable of such a step. Therefore, unless each individual gets help and support for his or her goal, the group is likely to dissolve or remain in the parallel phase.

ROLES: THE INITIAL APPROACH

Initial role-taking in the group is a tentative process that may or may not reflect the major roles members will occupy during the life of the group. Determinants of roles during the parallel phase are the open or constricted atmosphere provided by the leader and the capacities and predispositions of the members to occupy the various roles. While the possible roles of each member during the life of a group are numerous, many roles are recurrent and significant for forwarding or inhibiting group development. The true determination of roles will be negotiated and determined by the inclusion phase. Initial roles may last until the inclusion phase, then either be affirmed by the group or be assumed by and assigned to another member or members. For any role to be permanent, it must be both assumed by the individual and assigned to the individual by the rest of the group.

During the parallel phase some members assume and hold roles with only the toleration of the other members. This situation does not really represent assignment of those roles by the group or full acceptance of the person in the role. Some roles may be tentatively assigned during the parallel phase and either affirmed or disaffirmed during the inclusion phase.

Covert Indigenous Leader

The most important and too often overlooked role during the parallel phase is that of covert indigenous leader. The forces that combine to create this kind of leadership are not as yet well understood, but this does not belie the existence of this phenomenon. The best partial explanation of this role comes from the flocking or herding instincts in birds and animals. Studies of initial encounters among animals have shown that when two animals first encounter each other, both can immediately determine which will dominate the situation. Two geese will decide instantaneously which is the leader, which the follower. If the decision is not instantaneous, either the geese will fight to determine which is the leader or one or both flee the situation (Crook, 1961). In the parallel phase of group development the followers are often more aware of the covert leader than the covert leader himself is. Some covert leaders, especially those not used to prominence or dominance in social situations, may be unaware that others are looking to them for signs of authoritative permision or rebuke. Other covert leaders are well aware of the power of their presence and use this presence to control some of the early process in the group.

In the absence of overt communication or behavior from the covert leader, other members will attempt to pick up signals of approval or disapproval from this person. Overt communication by the covert leader will have more influence on the group than communication by other members. Some of the more obvious qualities or characteristics that contribute to the covert leader's initial influence have to do with what the group perceives as their superiority in whatever is deemed important for the group situation. Sometimes they are particularly attractive or menacing in their appearance; sometimes they are aggressively quiet. In initial group meetings some people are frankly quiet and withdrawn. Others are painfully reticent; they demonstrate a great deal of anxiety or anguish, but do not communicate anything verbally. The covert leader, if verbally inactive, exudes power that the others cannot overlook.

As they begin to feel at ease with the therapist and are prepared to approach the group situation, members then look to other members for signs of threat to determine whether the situation merits trust or distrust. The covert leader or leaders are then the members to whom the others look for approval. A frown or feeling of displeasure from the covert leader can cause any member to drop a subject or hold back from risking something that brought displeasure for someone else. In other words, the covert leader controls the norm development for the group. When a covert leader is detected in early sessions, it is important for the therapist to facilitate that person's overt expression of attitudes and reactions. If these attitudes and reactions are expressed, the other members are more apt to be freed to challenge them and approach the situation in ways they desire.

Overt Indigenous Leader

Leadership by group members in the parallel phase is accomplished as people with more propensity for leadership seize the power from the void left by the therapist. During the parallel phase other members can be seen as allowing or defaulting to initial leadership but not necessarily assigning those functions. It is important for the therapist to leave some room for indigenous leadership to arise, but it also behooves the therapist to support leadership that leads in the direction of facilitating group growth and to intervene with leadership that inhibits group growth. Sometimes it is hard to tell the difference.

Indigenous leadership that moves toward approaching the situation and that encourages others to do the same will facilitate group development. Indigenous leadership that seems to lead toward openness and communication but begins to set *too high standards* for premature expression and revelation will have a big impact toward making the situation threatening for the other members and can cause them to pull back from participation. The too highly demanding indigenous leader must be questioned by the therapist because, if his standards for performance remain unchallenged, the group will be cut off from progressively opening up, particularly about their feelings and other sensitive matters.

Indigenous leaders who frankly oppose revelation and expression can do the group a great service if the therapist respects their frankness and explores what such a position and such resistances imply for the indigenous leader and the other members as well.

Dominators

The initial dominator is often confused with initial overt or covert leader. The dominator is often a person who, because of intense need or anxiety, is driven to take up most, if not all, of the group's interaction space. Early dominators are a major problem for the therapist. The other group members allow and support the dominator at first because it gets them off the hook, on one hand, and because they do not feel that it would be proper to limit him, on the other. During the parallel phase, the therapist most often is left to deal with the dominator.

Initial domination presents a two-pronged threat to the therapist. If the person is abruptly limited, then the other members begin to fear the same possible response to them when they talk. If the dominator is allowed to continue indefinitely, the chances are that the other members will not overtly oppose this domination and will become extremely angry. If after a period of time this anger is not expressed, the other members will consider dropping out of the group. The best protection from this situation is to consider having at least two people in the group who dominate. Two dominators will undoubtedly vie for time, allowing room for others to get into the interaction. If the therapist is faced with a single dominator in a group, one approach is to focus on an initial question or issue in the dominator's ramblings and attempt to engage the rest of the group in discussing the issue. Asking the dominator to be available for feedback continues to give support to the other member's concerns while limiting the dominator and opening the interaction field for others to respond. For example, the therapist might say, "It seems that Mary is saying that. . . . Have others had any experience with. . .?"

Superior and Inferior Beings

In the initial quest for commonalities most group members will seek to find the common plights and experiences as people being to talk about their reasons for coming to group therapy. Two extreme kinds of people tend to hold themselves off from the commonality search. These are people who tend to occupy extreme positions on the paranoid-depressive continuum. Where people fall on the paranoid-depressive continuum is determined by how they tend to attribute blame for their plight. Most people accept some responsibility for their plight, while seeing others as contributing to the problems. People who tend more toward blaming others will see themselves as superior to the others in the commonality search. As the commonalities unfold, they will feel and present themselves as above and different from the others in the group. To the degree that this difference is unreal, this perception constitutes a problem for the person and the group. During the parallel phase, the therapist should allow this person to experience the difference and give him time to feel more comfortable. In time, unless the person is too highly structured in his paranoia to be in the group, the "superior beings" begin to accept in themselves what they see in other group members.

Persons who tend toward the depressive end of the continuum will persist in presenting themselves as the worst off in the group. They will occupy the role of "inferior being" in the group. They cannot be easily dissuaded from this position and, if very persistent, should be allowed to occupy the worst-off role until they feel more comfortable in the group. Again, if this person is severely depressed, perhaps he should not be in a group unless the other members are all equally depressed. Other people who occupy the inferior-being role in the group are those who have experienced a great deal of threat in being adequate. They have experienced love for having problems and loss of love when manifesting adequacy or achievement in their primary families. However, these people will be able to join in commonality testing, while reserving the right to be viewed as the least adequate. They must, under all circumstances, not be seen by the others as threatening in any way.

Nonverbal Members

Two major kinds of nonverbal members are those who cannot talk and those who will not talk. If the nonverbal member simply has difficulty talking or lacks social experience, direct support and assistance will usually help him get into the process—unless, of course, the inability is due to autism. With those who are nonverbal out of fear and reluctance to talk, patient waiting and creation of a climate in which they feel comfortable in talking will be most useful. It is always important to approach such a member in ways that allow him to easily refuse an invitation, saying, for example: "Would you like to comment on that?"

The pregroup relationship through the intake process is crucial for helping the nonverbal member in the group. Ideally, pregroup contact will have helped to establish a relationship and will have provided the therapist with understanding of the reason for the nonverbal position, as well as with knowledge of which subjects the nonverbal member might be most comfortable with. Prior knowledge of comfortable subject areas will give the therapist opportunitites for inviting the nonverbal member to participate.

Scapegoats

Scapegoats serve many purposes for groups at various stages of development. Scapegoating at any time occurs so that some or all of the other members can avoid dealing with each other on some crucial issues. But during the parallel phase the scapegoat will undobutedly be a person who seeks the scapegoat role in most social situations. They feel that if they get everyone mad at them for what they have done, then they will not be rejected for other reasons. It is easier for the scapegoat to handle rejection for their deeds than rejection for other reasons. Because the scapegoat does not feel worthy of love and acceptance by the others, his scapegoating interactions are a way of having contact and not being ignored. During the parallel phase it is important for the therapist to firmly accept that the scapegoat contributes to the development of the situation. At this point in group development, it may be best for the therapist to limit both the scapegoat and the other members equally, leaving the full resolution of the situation to a time when the group can better deal with it.

A host of other roles can be described, especially during the early phases of group development. Many are important for facilitating the work of the group but do not necessarily create development problems. These are what can be called "task roles" and are important for specific consideration in a task-oriented group. Although they help in the interaction of a therapy group, they need not occupy space in this discussion.

3

Authority
Crises

Your presence, strength and love
stopped, simply,
and the sky lost its patterns
and reflected light of earth-colors.
—Jerilyn Elise Miripol

Authority crises occur throughout the life of a group. The first resolution of an authority crisis serves as an essential condition for the transition from the parallel phase to the inclusion phase. For individual members, the first resolution of an authority crisis begins the process of separation and differentiation of selves from the therapist and opens the possibilities for further differentiation of self from the other group members during the inclusion phase (Schroder and Harvey, 1963). Authority crises begin to appear in the parallel phase. If early authority crises are not resolved, the group remains in the parallel mode. When an authority crisis is resolved, then the group enters the inclusion phase. Subsequent resolutions of authority crises serve to deepen the members' feelings of autonomy and differentiation through the inclusion and mutuality phases.

All theorists of group development take cognizance of the authority struggles as a major and crucial aspect of group development. The sequential theorists tend to view the authority struggles as more fixed in time and either as a prerequisite to group development or as an integral part of the power struggles among the members (see, for example: Tuckman, 1965; Bennis and Shepard, 1974; Mann, 1967; Garland et al., 1965; Hartford, 1971 and Northen, 1969). The recurrent therorists see the authority struggles as recurrent and progressive throughout the life of the group (see, for example: Whitaker and Lieberman, 1964; Bion, 1961; Schutz, 1966). Slater (1966) elaborated on the Freudian concept of decreasing libidinal involvement with the leader by pointing to the initial gaining of power and autonomy from the rebellion against authority (pp. 55-60) and later to the needs of members to rebel against authority to gain sexual freedom (pp. 109-129).

Some groups take on inclusion phase characteristics without resolving their authority crises. Mann (1967) calls this phenomenon premature enactment. Unless or until the group has subsequent resolutions of authority crises, premature enactment will not lead to growth in autonomy or differentiaton of members from each other, but rather undifferentiated banding together of the members in scapegoating the leader, other members or people outside the group.

The essence of a successful resolution of an authority crisis lies in the transfer of some political power from the therapist to the group. Political power refers to the power to decide on the means (norms) and the ends (goals) of the group. In the parallel phase the therapist held and was granted all the power by the members. In the inclusion phase the members begin to accept, distribute, and wield increasing power of their own. If authority crises are not resolved there is no power for the group members to share. Successful resolution results when the therapist cedes power to the group and the group accepts or takes the power from the therapist.

Two major reasons for unsuccessful resolution of authority crises are that the therapist does not give up any power and the group does not accept or wrest power from the therapist. If the therapist cedes power to the group and the members accept or wrest power from the therapist, the authority crisis can be resolved in a relatively smooth fashion.

If the therapist overtly or covertly retains power and fights attempts by group members to wrest power, there are several major results. First, the group may simply return to and remain in the parallel phase.

Second, the group may become very angry and displace their hostility on people in the group or outside the group. Constant hostility toward one or more members of the group without resolution is often a vehicle for displacement of anger that the members are fearful of expressing toward the therapist for his retention of power and control of the group. Another variation of the displacement of hostility is constant hostile references to people outside the group. The difference between displacement and pure ventilation about these "other" people is that ventilation often leads to a reduction in hostility and resolution of the issues, but displacement must be continued, so possible resolutions are rejected. A third possibility when the therapist refuses to give up power is the direct expression of hostility toward the therapist. This takes the form of rebellion in which the group wrests power from the therapist for distribution among the members. The latter could lead to a successful resolution of the authority crisis or a constant unending battle for power throughout the life of the group, depending on the response of the therapist.

If the group members overtly or covertly refuse to accept power and responsibility for the group, because they feel unable to handle the power or fear loss of power to other group members, then the group may profoundly regress and return to the earliest form of the parallel relations phase. If the members' refusal is based on unwillingness to accept power and responsibility for themselves, the result may be constant scapegoating of people in or outside the group or scapegoating of the therapist. The difference between a group rebellion and scapegoating the therapist lies in the fact that in the scapegoating of the therapist the group attempts not to gain power but rather to leave the power vested in the therapist, while rejecting the therapist and his efforts to help. Overt scapegoating under these circumstances will take place outside the group meetings and the only manifestations in the group meeting will range from passive resistance to hostile dependency. A group scapegoating the leader can unite as an entity against the leader and develop in a very precarious and shallow way. Inclusion struggles may be submerged, and shallow, constricting intimacy may develop in which the group feels united but undifferentiated; the range of individuality in expression and behavior is extremely narrow.

One of the major reasons for allowing and helping a group to develop lies in the myriad of emotional and interpersonal forces that are unleashed, not the least of which are the processes of developing autonomy and differentiation. Autonomy and differentiation cannot be directed by the therapist, but only allowed, supported, and facilitated.

Individual reasons for the group to refuse power are many. Foremost among the causes are: (1) incapacity to handle autonomy due to developmental limitations, (2) fear of autonomy, (3) fear of loss of dependency, (4) therapist's need to retain omnipotence, (5) fear of rejection or punishment from the therapist, (6) fear of loss of control of self and others if therapist's power is reduced, and (7) fear of engaging with other members.

Successful resolution of authority crises thus calls for the therapist first, to be aware of and deal professionally with his needs for and feelings about control; second, to support and nurture communications and actions that tend toward increasing autonomy during the parallel phase; third, increasingly cede more autonomy to the group; fourth, give explicit acceptance and permission for autonomous behavior in the group. Therapists must accept the fact that timing in granting and supporting autonomy is crucial to successful resolution of the authority crises. Too much too soon or too little too late are both problems. A therapist can expect to err on the side of either too little or too much as the group increases its capacity to handle autonomy. It is more important that the therapist be attuned to early feedback that suggests where he is in error than to hold himself responsible for always being accurate.

Finally, resolution of an authority crisis may or may not include all of the members of the group. Members who may be at a lower psychosocial level (for examples of pre-oedipal, see Gibbard and Hartman, 1973; or less differentiated, Tucker, 1973) may not experience or re-experience the gaining of autonomy with the rest of the group. For the members with lower levels of psychosocial development, it is important to facilitate their experience of resolving the authority phenomena in ways more suited to their level and capacities. For example, in groups of young children or groups of adult chronic schizophrenics, the members may first have to assert their autonomy by rejecting or disagreeing with the therapist even though they have no ready alternatives or support for their positions. It is the act of not accepting authority that becomes important (just as it is with two-year-olds) rather than the substance of the disagreement.

When individuals of lower developmental levels are left behind by others in a therapy group, it is important for the therapist to provide opportunities for them as individuals to assert their autonomy vis-a-vis the therapist perhaps even long after the others are further along in their relationships.

AFFECTIVE POLARITIES: AUTONOMY vs. FEAR

Central to the authority crisis is the desire for individual and group autonomy counterposed against the fears of deposing the leader. Freud suggests that in order for a group to develop, the members must first come to terms with authority. He points out that the members must tokenly annihilate the leader before they can become a brotherhood (Freud, 1960: 67-77). This Freudian insight is borne out in therapy groups and its manifestations reach a peak during the first resolution of an authority crisis. Before group members can experience a peership, they must feel more on a par with the authority figures.

Both the quest for autonomy and the feelings about the therapist or authority figure are saturated with conflicts from past experiences. The quest for autonomy begins with the negativism of the two-year-old whose only way of gaining autonomy is to say *no* and resist what he is asked to do (Erikson, 1968: 107-109). During the oedipal period the rivalry with the parent of the same sex and its outcome directly affect the relative freedom the person feels toward self-assertion and dealing with authority figures. While the anal and oedipal stages of development basically affect the emotional readiness of the individual to vie with authority for power, psychosocial experience most akin to the authority crisis in the group is the "fallen idol" stage of the seven- to nine-year-old.

Eight-year-old children begin to see that their parents are not the pillars of strength they seemed to be in earlier times. As the parents tumble from apparent omnipotence, the child then begins to firm up his own autonomy and become a miniature adult in his behavior. To the degree that parents fight to maintain their omniscience and to the degree that they are successful in keeping him in awe and fear as a child will that person as an adult fear and be reticent to accept power from the therapist, much less to wrest power from the therapist. While the child's predisposition for coming to terms with parental omnipotence is basically determined by the anal and oedipal experiences, the fallen idol age is another opportunity to correct past distortions.

Experiences subsequent to the fallen idol age, particularly during adolescence and young adulthood, may also influence the readiness or unreadiness of the individual to cope with authority crises. Indeed, compensatory experiences with the family or other authority figures and perhaps even a profound adolescent rebellion, might correct the distortions of earlier experiences. However, the well-timed development of autonomy and differentiation from the therapist in the group can serve to help toward the resolve of autonomy and differentiation conflicts stemming from past experiences of members.

The emotional components of the authority crisis thus run wide and deep. For those groups and members in whom these issues are reasonably resolved the authority crisis in the group will be a quickly passing phenomenon. For those in whom there remain many unresolved autonomy issues with parents and authorities, the authority crisis will loom large and will be a source of deep therapeutic benefit if and when resolved in the group. These basic psychosocial issues determine the capacity of the group to meet and resolve authority crises or flee from them. Consequently, the resolution of an authority crisis is extremely important for the group to continue on its developmental way. However, for most group members issues of deep significance will linger and subsequent authority crises will be necessary for a full and deeper resolution of autonomy issues for each individual.

Essentially, when children are thwarted in their two-year-old negativism by too constricted parental control, they tend to remain very dependent upon parental direction (Erikson, 1968: 107-114) and have difficulty differentiating self from parents. These people can gain from well timed development of autonomous strivings in group to gain the feeling that autonomy doesn't lead to disapproval or rejection. In other words, actualization of autonomy with acceptance from the therapist is what can facilitate growth.

When children are allowed too much freedom in their two-year-old negativism, they tend to seek their ultimate limits through constant testing and rebellion, particularly in relation to authority. Autonomy for these people is uncertain, as is their sense of self and others, since the boundaries have not been sufficiently delineated (Erikson, 1968: 107-114).

Meeting some limitations from the therapist in a progressively fought and won struggle for autonomy can help such individuals to affirm both their autonomy and their differentiation of self vis-a-vis authority, as it is confronted in parents, therapist, teachers, bosses.

Self-awareness Issues for the Therapist

The therapist's own developmental experiences with authority and autonomy can influence the therapist's reactions to authority issues in the group. Strong needs for control can cause the therapist to gain and hold the authority position directly or indirectly. The direct way of holding on to authority is to lead with an autocratic style and/or philosophy. The indirect way of maintaining control over the group is to overtly allow the group a great deal of freedom, perhaps too quickly; and create a situation where the group flounders, thus justifying the need for a high degree of control from the therapist.

BEHAVIORAL FEATURES: CHALLENGE TO AUTHORITY

The singular outstanding behavioral feature of authority crises is the challenge to the therapist's authority by some or all the members. Usually the challenge arises when a member disagrees with the therapist on what or how the group should be. More primitive forms of challenge arise when the members refuse or question a suggestion by the therapist: "Do we have to. . .?" "Are you sure this is the best way?" "Why must we. . . ?" The most primitive form of challenge is for members to either not do what the therapist suggests without overt challenge, remain silent, or begin disruptive behavior. More developed forms might arise in which members suggest or insist on alternatives to what is already happening or proposed by the therapist: "Let's talk about . . . instead?" Very often instead of asking or telling, members simply shift the discussion from that proposed by the therapist.

Authority crises can occur in many indirect ways. A there-and-then focus on authorities or parents outside the group might bring to light many of the concerns that have bearing on the group situation itself. Exploration of those reactions to authority might facilitate direct dealing with similar problems in the group. Here-and-now manifestations of the authority crisis occur when people refuse to form the group in quite the way the authority has asked them to, come late for meetings, miss meetings, refuse to participate, or dwell on and belabor inconsequential matters.

A classic way in which members often bring an authority crisis to the surface is by talking about how another group or other situation was better than the current one. Again, by exploring this other situation the therapist might help disclose what the member wants from the present group.

As the first blow for freedom is struck by the first members, a host of reactions will be set off in the group. Other members experience feelings in sympathy with the first person, but some may experience more of the fear than the desire for more autonomy. Those who experience more fear tend to protect the therapist and the group in the ensuing discussion; the others are more likely to join the rebellion against the therapist.

Role of the Therapist

Whatever form the challenge to authority takes, the therapist must be attuned to the critique or suggestion and do whatever is possible to see that some constructive suggestion arises from the encounter. If the therapist ignores, discounts, or fights the challenge, the message to the group will be clear: the therapist does not want to allow this kind of autonomy to the group. The various possibilities discussed in the introduction to the authority crisis might then occur. Basically, the members will either accept the counterchanllenge and fight for their autonomy or be frightened into reverting back to a parallel mode of behavior, leaving the therapist clearly in command of the group.

Finally, therapists must be careful to determine the difference between resistance and challenge to authority. What may indeed be a resistance may often also represent a challenge to authority. Working through or not allowing a resistance can at the same time, by ignoring the challenge, defeat the autonomy of group members. In groups where autonomy of members is less of an issue, the resistances might well be explored. In groups where members need much by way of growth in autonomy, then it may be well to allow the resistance to stand as a successful vote to challenge the therapist's wishes.

SOURCE OF GRATIFICATION:
A BREAKING AWAY FROM THE THERAPIST

The first resolution of an authority crisis represents a major change or transition in sources of gratification for the members. Until resolution of an authority crisis, most or all members will have looked to the therapist for all gratification. As a result of an authority crisis resolution, the members are, at first, at a loss. They are not sure that the other members can or will help and feel less certain of help emanating from the therapist. Members who have experienced parental rejections for autonomous striving will particularly fear punishment or rejection by the therapist. One of the major reasons for members to back down from a challenge to the therapist is that they fear the therapist will no longer help them if they are hostile. By supporting the members in their challenge, the therapist demonstrates a continuity in helping which may allay the fears. However, the members are best left with some anxiety about the therapist's helping role, since this anxiety may help them to explore the possibilities for help in other members.

The therapist treads a very fine line when he insists upon mutual gratification among the members and supports their challenge to his authority. This dual posture could be felt by the members as withdrawal of gratification in retaliation for the challenge to the therapist's authority. As already mentioned, support and acceptance of the rebellion offers some signs of continued helping; at the same time, support for the early mutual helping efforts will also give the members some feeling that some gratification will still emanate from the therapist. Because the mutual helping system is still rather formative, the members will be very uncertain about the group's capacity to provide the help.

Fundamental in the authority crisis is the dependency/independency issue. The wish for autonomy is balanced against the loss of the leader as a major source of dependency-need gratification. Therapists' own counterdependent needs (that is, to meet their own dependency needs by having others dependent on them) become crucial during authority crises. Awareness of their own counter-dependency needs is essential if the therapists are to relinquish the role of primary gratifiers of member needs.

RELATIONAL ISSUES: CHANGING DIRECTION

The first resolution of an authority crisis is the watershed for the direction of relationships in the group. Before this all the relationships are primarily with the therapist or through the therapist to the other members. The first resolution of an authroity crisis results in the development of relationships among the members. Failure to resolve the authority crisis will seriously impede, if not preclude, the development of relationships among the members.

Centrality of the therapist in the parallel phase is also accomplished by the dominance accorded the therapist by the members. If the therapist's political dominance is maintained either by the therapist's own efforts or by the persistence of the members in keeping the therapist dominant, there is little chance that the members will be free to develop their own status and role structure in the inclusion phase. If the therapist loses a significant part of the political dominance, the members are free to negotiate and vie for roles and positions in the group.

The relationship between the dominance and centrality of the therapist vis-a-vis the freedom of the members to form relationships with each other can be traced back to family structure. Domineering parents most often succeed in limiting their children's contacts with other people. Children who conform to this dominance often do not have many peer relationships or have very shallow relationships with peers. Children who rebel against this dominance have relationships with peers, but these relationships are so frought with overcoming parental strictures that parents become a constant negative consideration in these relationships. Since most people coming to therapy groups have had some degree of difficulty in the development of their autonomy with respect to parental authority, the authority crisis awakens many basic and unresolved issues.

If authority and autonomy issues have not been resolved before adolescence, the adolescent peer group experiences often help toward resolution. However, even if a person has these issues reasonably resolved, there is considerable enactment of the authority issues in school and work situtions, so that the overcoming of these issues in the authority crisis is replete with meaning. By the same token, the resolution of the authority crises as they are in the group facilitates the understanding and resolution of the authority and autonomy issues in peer and authority situations in life outside the group.

One of the major phenomena of authority crises is its effect on the member's feeling that the therapist is omnipotent. As in the first eight or so years in the family the child attributes omnipotence to parental figures, during the parallel phase the members are inclined to both attribute and wish for omnipotence in the therapist. With successful resolution of authority crises the therapist progressively falls from the pedestal, with consequent increase in autonomy of the members (Erikson, 1968). Initial resolution of authority crises also starts the process of member-therapist differentiation (Schroder and Harvey, 1963).

It would be difficult to say which comes first—the rise in members' self-esteem or the fall of the leader's seeming omnipotence. Most likely, some members own self-esteem must begin to rise before they can engage in overturning authority; for other members, the overturning of authority allows the necessary room for a rise in self-esteem. In either event, reduction of leader omnipotence will support feelings of self-esteem on the part of the members.

Self-awareness Issues for the Therapist

Relinquishment of the omnipotent aura presents many difficulties for therapists. It is flattering to the therapist's own self-esteem to be held in such high regard. The therapist's task in self-awareness is to understand what motives might make him perpetuate a situation in which he is held to be omnipotent. Some groups need to feel that the therapist is omnipotent for longer periods of time than other groups. The time for stepping down should be closely related to the readiness and needs of the group. That is why it is extremely important for the therapist to separate his own needs for the onmipotent role from the timing of the omnipotence reduction for the differential needs of the group members. Premature diminishment of therapist omnipotence could lead to panic on the part of the members. If the members are not ready to handle the resulting anxiety, they could feel worse about themselves rather than better.

It is most important to consider that the only loss is the therapist's omnipotence. This does not necessarily mean that the therapist goes from everything to nothing instantaneously. Usually, the group still perceives the therapist as an expert professional who has much to contribute to the helping process; he is simply no longer viewed as all things to all people. For many members, chinks in the omnipotence of the therapist are tantamount to the therapist's being rendered totally inept and incompetent. If the therapist is clear about and comfortable with the reality of his human assets and limitations, he is in a good position to help the members deal with a less than omnipotent therapist and perhaps then the member will be in better position to view himself in a realistic range of human potential.

POWER RELATIONS:
A SHARING BETWEEN THERAPIST AND MEMBERS

Almost by definition the crucial group dynamic of the authority crisis is the shift from the therapist's having all the power to some degree of sharing that power with the members. Power ceded by the therapist and or won by the members serves as the very basis of the inclusion phase. A major dimension of the inclusion phase is the struggle among the members for a share in the power of the group. For many group members, sharing in the power of the group and being included are almost the same phenomenon. Without a sharing of power, the members have to rely on the therapist for all the group's function. Increasing the amounts of power held by the members is basic to their taking responsibility for the nature and direction of the group. Participation in wielding the power in the group is closely allied to individuals beginning to feel more powerful in themselves and serves to lessen members' feelings of helplessness.

The close tie between power and responsibility for the group brings mixed reactions from different members. Some members, because of the difficulties that brought them to therapy, would rather not have power. They realize, on one level or another, that assuming the power would be a responsibility and, if they participate in handling that power, they would have to relinquish their feelings of helplessness. Others more motivated to take initiative on their own behalf grow as a result accepting and wielding the power.

The First Overt Conflict

Prior to the authority crisis, all group conflict is submerged. The first overt conflict appears as part of the authority crisis. The dilemma for each member is to express his thoughts and feelings without opening himself to possible punishment from the therapist and other members for disagreeing with them. Since members possess no real power before the first resolution of authority crises, there is very little reason for conflict among the members. Consequently, until there has been a successful resolution of the authority crisis, any conflicts may be viewed as having authority crisis implications (Slater, 1966; Mann, 1967).

During early authority crises, members feel that any disagreement with the therapist will bring on the therapist's total rejection of them. If early authority crises are successfully resolved, then the members feel that they will not be totally rejected by the therapist for having their own feelings, behaviors, and opinions.

Role of the Therapist

Dealing with conflicts before and during early authority crises thus requires a great deal of support and acceptance by the therapist for the very persons opposing him and a wealth of self-awareness on the part of the therapist so that he does not feel vanquished or feel he must prevail over the members in the conflicts. It is particularly difficult for the therapist to remain neutral during the early authority crises, since potential factions supporting and opposing the therapist often develop among the members. Siding with the faction favoring the therapist could impair resolution of the authority crisis. Siding with the opposing faction could confuse and frighten pro-therapist factions. Only by supporting both sides of this conflict can the therapist facilitate the sound resolution of the authority crisis that will result in group members gaining an amount of power requisite to their collective capacities.

COHESION: A TRANSITION

The authority crisis is the transition from the cohesion of the parallel phase centering on the therapist to the building of cohesion among members in the inclusion phase. Since the therapist is the center of acceptance and cohesion prior to the authority crisis, the threat of losing the tie to the therapist looms large in each member's feelings about rebelling against the therapist. Because many group members have experienced rejection by significant authority figures for exerting their own autonomy, their difficulty of asserting themselves in relation to the authority in the group is increased. Sufficient feelings of acceptance, permission, and support from the therapist for the reaching out of group members bolster the member's security in reaching out to other members.

Thus, the ties to the therapist are under severe stress during the authority crisis. In addition to the therapist's possible needs for power, omnipotence, and control, the therapist must be able to use his acceptance of the members as a base and a bridge for member-to-member contact and development of affective ties. This support by the therapist of an individual member's autonomy also comes at a time when the therapist is necessarily losing his exalted position in the group.

Many members cannot trust the permission they are given to reach out to other members. Their prior experiences with acceptance have been tantamount to control and suffocation, so that being accepted and free to relate to other people is an unknown experience.

CONTROLS: SHIFTING RESPONSIBILITIES

Prior to early resolutions of authority crises, group controls are primarily vested in the therapist. Part of the problem in the authority crises arises because group members have the difficult task of rebelling against the authority figure while they look to the authority figure for control. Thus, support for the rebellion against the therapist is essential. Very often both support for the rebellion and some setting of limits are the crucial combination required, since the members may need the help of the therapist to keep their rebellion within constructive bounds. Members often find it difficult to differentiate between essential rebellion and threatened loss of control.

Self-awareness Issues for the Therapist

One of the most important areas in which the therapist needs self-awareness is in the area of controls. The therapist's feelings about control are most important during early authority crises, the first point in the group development where the therapist begins to lose control over the processes. One of the major reasons for groups to get fixated in the parallel phase is the reluctance of the therapist to relinquish some control of the group (Williams, 1966). Most often the therapist is not aware of his fear of giving up control and this compounds the problem. One of the classic control phenomena is the overt insistence by the therapist that the group is free to do whatever it wishes, while at the same time his behavioral and covert messages demonstrate to the members that he means for them to stay right where they are. A carte-blanche invitation to group members during the authority crisis to do whatever they wish must of itself be suspect. People who have had difficulty with too many or too few controls in their lives are inclined to become overwhelmed with sudden and boundless freedom (Fromm, 1969). Thus, granting too much freedom before the group is ready to handle it can either firm up the therapist's control or destroy the group.

In this situation the therapist would most appropriately concentrate with the group on very specific areas of disagreement and rebellions. He would grant support for the members' opinions and feelings and give the members permission to challenge his authority on the specifics, setting reasonable limits when necessary. After repeated experiences with a few specific issues, the members realize that they can gain more control of the group and that the therapist really wants to share the controls with them.

Development of Group Controls

As early authority crises are successfully resolved, members begin to exert their own controls on the group. The development of group controls is a major part of the work in the inclusion phase. If the members see from the authority crisis that they have the room to exert their own controls, they then have to deal with each other on the what, how, and why of control in the group.

In groups of latency-aged children, the therapist may need to maintain control over menacing or destructive behavior while he helps the group to decide the focus of discussion or activities for themselves. Behavioral issues and control are often the sum and substance of children's groups in the inclusion phase. Groups of adolescents often need some behavioral controls from the therapist but can be engaged in developing their own control more quickly than younger children.

Groups of schizophrenics often need the therapist's controls to help them handle their own feelings of loss of control. As schizophrenics increase their feelings of autonomy in the group they often feel better able to control, unless some critical feelings like anger become too threatening to their controls.

NORMS IN THE AUTHORITY CRISIS

A major feature of early authority crises is the challenge to the group norms developed during the parallel phase—norms associated with the therapist whether or not the therapist indeed developed them. The challenge brings into question whether members must behave according to their perceptions of the therapist's and the group's expectations for behavior or whether members can have more direct influence on determining the norms.

While many norms in the parallel may well have been initiated by group members, the perpetuation of these norms is actually—or is felt by group members to be—at the discretion of the therapist. During the parallel phase the members do not feel powerful enough in the group to be responsible for norm-setting. Even members who have in large part been responsible for norm-setting in the parallel phase are often unaware that they have done so. Norms and goals are the major areas for overt or covert decisions in a therapy group. Norms are a major part of the determination of how a group will function; they guide the way in which members work and relate in the group. Therefore, the therapist must carefully consider each norm as it is subjected to challenge in authority crises and must develop awareness of the kinds of norms that will enhance the process of the group and those that will inhibit the group's development.

Self-awareness Issues for the Therapist

The therapist must be professionally aware of his own propensities for power, control, and omnipotence so that he or she can allow the group members to begin to develop a working climate most suited to their own particular personalities and manner of behavior. If as the primary guideline the therapist insists that the group function in ways most comfortable for himself, then there is danger that the group may not be suited to that mode of functioning and danger that the group will be held back from taking responsibility for its own functioning. The failure of the therapist to allow the group to set its own norms, or the failure of the members to challenge existing norms and initiate their own norm-setting during the authority crisis, places the very processes of the group squarely in the jurisdiction of the therapist. The therapist takes on the responsibility for initiative and control and the group remains dependent.

Initial success of the members in challenging existing norms and developing their own peculiar norms will set the stage for members to develop the nature of their relationships, interactions, and manner of working together.

Challenge to the norms may be a matter of direct discussion or, more often, it may be inherent in the behavior or discussion of the members about seemingly unrelated topics. When norm-setting is a matter of direct discussion, the therapist can best facilitate maximum contribution to norm development by involving all the members in those discussions. When norm-setting is more covert or simply inherent in discussion and behavior, the therapist's responses to the behavior or discussion will help to either support the new implicit norm or alter its development. The first order of action is for the therapist to give clear messages to the group about the legitimacy of the norm from his standpoint. Once the other members perceive that the therapist accepts the new mode of behavior, discussion topic, or manner of expression, they will be more willing to follow the lead of the member or members initiating the new norm. If the new norm is objectionable to any members, their capacity to challenge the norm is basic to the inclusion phase of the group. The therapist needs to support these dissenting views and help the group negotiate which norms will prevail and perhaps allow individual members to go about their participation in the group in their own unique ways.

Norms to Increase Individual Freedom

At stake in the authority crisis is the first test of whether, in the ultimate development of the group, each member will be allowed to think, act, and talk in his own unique ways.

Whitaker and Lieberman base most of their theory on group normative development and the gradual increase of freedom and acceptance in the group climate (Whitaker and Lieberman, 1964). Most of their normative development themes center on authority and intimacy issues. Thus, a major product of the recurrent authority and intimacy crises is the development of that increase freedom.

A typical challenge to the therapist's norms arises in children's groups when a child might say, "Do we have to talk about problems? I'd rather have some fun." Although this may indeed be the expression of a resistance, it is also a suggestion that may run counter to the norms and expectations of the therapist. In a group needing help with the development of initiative and autonomy, a response from the therapist might well be to accept the suggestion: "O.K. let's have some fun." In a group that has developed some initiative and autonomy, the response from the therapist might well be to help the group deliberate the issue: "How do others feel about this? Do you want to talk about problems or have some fun right now?" In a group that is both dealing well with problems and showing initiative, the therapist's response might be explore the resistance: "Why don't you feel like talking about problems? Is there something about this problem we're talking about that you don't like" Or the therapist might confront the challenge: "I think you don't want to talk about this problem because you. . .

SURFACING OF GOALS

Early authority crises are the times when the goals of the members surface. Surfacing of goals may begin with members challenging or questioning the therapist's expressed goals for themselves and the group or challenging the goals that the group members attribute to the therapist. Most often the expression of goals is inherent in what members actually do and whether they cooperate with what is happening in the group. Most goal challenges are not carried out through direct discussion but rather by some members moving in one direction and other members either joining them or attempting to move in other directions.

During early authority crises the question is whether the goals of the group members are in consonance with the goals of the therapist. Assuming that there will always be some disparity in goals between the therapist and the members, the authority crisis is the first critical point at which the members can find out whether the direction of the group can be what they desire. If the therapist does not allow members' goals to influence, modify, or change the direction of the group, the group may be stultified in its development and members will lack room to negotiate their goals with each other during the inclusion phase. On the other hand, if the therapist allows rooom for members' goals to shape the group goals, then members can assert their goals and negotiate the direction of the group. To the degree that members feel they have influence on the direction of the group will they be committed to and feel part of the process.

Self-awareness Issues for the Therapist

Perhaps with goals, more than with any other issue, the therapist's professional self-esteem is on the line. Despite the many protestations of therapists about not predetermining their client's fate, despite disavowals by some schools of thought about goals for clients, many therapists get caught in overt and covert goal disputes during the authority crisis and few give way to members' goals easily. Self-awareness on the part of the therapist calls for his being aware, as much as possible, of the overt and convert goals he has for individuals and the group and not allowing these goals to interfere with the development by members of their own goals for themselves and the group.

The task of allowing room for members' goals does not mean that the therapist must forsake his own goals for the group, but rather that he must enter into negotiations with the members and attempt to have his goals integrated with the members' goals in carving out the direction for the group. However, the real test of whether the therapist is negotiating goals or imposing them is whether the therapist is ready to lose out on influencing the direction of the group. That is, can the therapist allow his own goals to be rejected by the group even temporarily, if not permanently?

One major way in which therapists impose their own goals on a group is through the abuse of pointing out resistances. While the author subscribes to the notion that resistances, especially in the early phases of a therapy group, do exist and are a deterrent to individual and group progress, differentiating between a resistance and a vote either against the therapist's goal or a vote for an alternate goal is often hard to do. Many embryonic challenges to the authority and, particularly, to goals of the therapist, are squashed by being labeled resistance. The therapist can be more certain of the difference if he thoroughly explores noncompliance with his own wishes or fully discusses the alternatives posed by the members. However, the attitude of the therapist during the exploration is crucial. If he is truly ready to change direction on the basis of what he hears from the members, then he is likely to be able to differentiate between resistence and votes for other goals and directions.

When a child group member asks, "Do we have to talk about problems? I'd rather have some fun," essentially, the child is questioning the perceived goal of the therapist to solve problems and suggesting that the group be for fun. Pursuing fun might have some inherent goals, such as getting more comfortable with the therapist and the other group members, gaining control of the situation, or stopping a threatening discussion. Initially, the therapist might well go along with the suggestion. Negotiation of goals takes place indirectly when group members, either through direct discussion or through behavior deliberate between working on problems and having fun. However, at some point it may be essential for the therapist to initiate a discussion of what the group is for and how much the members want to pursue the goals of problem-solving and how much they want to pursue the goal of having fun.

ROLES: RISE OF THE INDIGENOUS LEADER

Early authority crises mark the beginning of serious role-taking and role assignment in the group. The most important roles are those of the indigenous leaders. Those who offer the initial challenges to the authority of the therapist assume the indigenous leadership role. However, the first challenge may or may not come from the real indigenous leader. Rather, some indigenous leaders will allow or set up other members to make the first challenges. After perceiving the response of the therapist to the initial challenge, the real indigenous leaders will determine whether to come out directly and assert their leadership or continue to work through others to their own ends (Redl, 1966).

There may be at least two indigenous leaders during the authority crisis, one representing the forces for challenge of authority and the other representing the forces for protecting the therapist. Other members will be inclined to line up behind these leaders; on which side will depend on how strong their ambivalence about the therapist remaining in power is. The emergence of indigenous leadership and the sharing of power with the members begins to reduce the dominating and central role of the therapist. Although this process begins in the first resolution of an authority crisis, through successive authority crises other powers of the therapist's role decreases as these powers are shared with the members.

The successful rise of indigenous leadership starts the process of role and status struggling most characteristic of the inclusion phase. The battle for indigenous leadership is not ended with the successful resolution of early authority crises; indigenous leadership becomes more attractive with real powers and, therefore, more of a coveted entity. Accordingly, the struggle for indigenous leadership begins with the first successful resolution of an authority crisis and starts a whole process of scrambling for roles and statuses within the group.

4

Inclusion
Phase

For souls in growth,
great quarrels are great
emancipation.
　　　－Logan P. Smith

The inclusion phase comprises the major formative work of the members toward becoming a group. A major *product* of the inclusion phase is the knitting together of the members into a cohesive unit called "the group." While all theories of group development attest to the existence of this phase and process, little is actually understood of how the interpersonal struggles of this phase result in a cohesive unit (Hare, 1973).

The theories of Werner (1948) as further developed by Schroder and Harvey (1963) in combination with the interpersonal balance theory of Heider (1958) lend major support to the ideas that follow. In other words, the processes of group and individual differentiation (Werner, 1948) and the balance between people's feelings about each other and their tendencies to agree and disagree with each other (Heider, 1958) help to explain the dynamics of the inclusion phase.

The word *inclusion* is employed to emphasize the flocking aspect that underlies this phase. Acceptance by the group and accepting other members of the group is the underlying quest of all group members during this phase. However, because group members enter this phase in a relatively undifferentiated state they are inclined to see themselves as either totally accepted or totally rejected by others and are also inclined to totally accept or totally reject others. The basis of this total acceptance begins with perceived similarities between themselves and others in thought, affect, and behavior and particularly in the ways that these relate to norms and goals for the group. Members begin to join in pairs and subgroups with those they perceive as similar; they begin to reject those individuals, pairs, and subgroups they perceive as different. Thus, the first point of differentiation among the members begins with the polarizing and factioning around perceived similarities.

Those issues group members polarize around in the inclusion phase tend to be issues over which the members have much ambivalence. For example, in the protherapist factions that develop during the authority crisis the members often harbor much hostility for the leader but, because of their developmental background, have many prohibitions against expressing disagreement or hostility toward authority figures. These members identify with others who are inclined to "protect" the therapist and reject those who oppose the therapist. Those in the faction opposing the therapist fear being rejected by the therapist for their rebellion and reject the members who seek favor of the therapist by supporting him. As the two factions struggle with each other, they can each begin to perceive parts of the polarity that exists within themselves. If the conflict is resolved, they can come to accept not only the other faction but also that part of the polarization that was rejected within themselves and represented by the other faction. With increasing acceptance of both poles of the ambivalence within each group member, there is increasing acceptance of other members and increasing feeling of being accepted by each member.

Thus, through conflict and the bipolar identification resulting from conflict resolution does the pairing, subgrouping, and factioning facilitate the processes of both acceptance and differentiation. The acceptance of other diverse people and diversities within other people parallels acceptance of diversities within oneself. According to Heider (1958), people who differ are under tension to either agree or to dislike each other if the issue has importance to both. Also, people who like each other are under tension to agree or to dislike each other if they disagree. Without means for unearthing and resolving conflict, a group has to maintain a posture of at least overt agreement or reject and exclude those who disagree from the group. Thus, a group without means for unearthing and resolving conflict cannot grow and its members cannot gain the experience of differentiation in their thoughts, feelings, behavior, and relationships.

Other products of the inclusion phase are the merging of overt and covert goals into group goals and the development of norms and controls that lead toward the achievement of those goals. Most of the group functions are centralized in the therapist during the parallel phase. During the early authority crises there is a shift from complete power vested in the therapist to more power available to group members. Much of the struggling in the inclusion phase centers on the distribution of the therapists' power among the members.

Almost all groups of children younger than eight will spend their entire existence, no matter how long they meet, hovering among parallel and inclusion phenomena with recurrent authority crises. These children may develop some cohesion around the therapist and within pairs or small subgroups but will seldom reach a depth of intimacy.

Most groups of latency-aged children (age eight through eleven) will spend a great deal of time (three to six months of weekly meetings) in the inclusion phase with some development of a shallow level of intimacy within pairs, sub-groups, and in the group as a whole, particularly when the group is small (four to six members). Resolution of inclusion phenomena for latency-aged groups can arise in an uneasy adherence to rules and norms developed by the group and to some extent enforced by the new group itself but often falling back on the leader. One need only watch a sand-lot baseball game of latency-aged children and note how much of their time is spent arguing about infractions of the rules to see this phenomenon in action.

Groups of early adolescents (twelve to fifteen years old) spend consider-able time resolving inclusion phenomena. However, belonging to the group is of such paramount importance to many early adolescents that they will readily forsake their own wishes for norms and goals that will enable them to be in-cluded. The difficulty of risking with peers and the intense needs for inclusion combine to interfere with full resolution of inclusion phenomena; hence, when and as the group develops its form of pseudo-intimacy, it is rather unstable. The major factor in the instability of early adolescent pseudo-intimacy is the omni-present fear of rejection, particularly because of differences from their peers. In groups of adults in the normal to neurotic ranges of psychosocial develop-ment, the resolution of inclusion issues basically lays to rest the major fears and dangers of rejection by the group. In groups of early adolescents rejection serves as a major vehicle for group controls.

Over a two-year span of weekly meetings groups of adults in the schizo-phrenic range of psychosocial development will achieve some resolve of inclusion phenomena. These people have difficulty developing the autonomy and initiative essential for confronting and resolving inclusion issues; they also have difficulty with affective contact. Some levels of intimacy might develop among pairs and subgroups and, if the group is small enough (eight members or fewer), might develop some degree of intimacy in the group as a whole. However, the resolu-tion of authority and inclusion phenomena is a major accomplishment for long-term members of groups of people who are schizophrenic. Groups of adult retardates function very similarly to groups of adult schizophrenics.

Groups of older adolescents and adults most often enter and cope with inclusion phenomena in three to six meetings. Some groups might enter into inclusion in the first meeting while others, depending on the purpose and structure of the group, may never resolve inclusion issues. Each successive resolu-tion of intimacy crises reduces the amount of inclusion phenomena and increases the mutuality phenomena in a group of adults.

It is important to note that premature drop-outs are most likely to occur during the inclusion phase. Reasons are all related to the fundamental processes of acceptance, power, and status. Feared or sensed rejection is one major reason for premature drop-outs; another is unasserted power or frustrated desire for power, particularly power to influence group norms and goals. Frustrated desire for power can lead an individual to feel rejected by the group. If the group disagrees with his wishes, particularly for what the group should accomplish and how it should work, then the member feels rejected.

Unasserted power is also closely related to feeling rejected. The individual member fears that the others will not accept his suggestions or that what he wants is so far removed from or inconsequential to what the others want that there is no point in even asking the group to consider his suggestions. Sometimes, however, the member's perception may be very accurate and dropping out of the group may be appropriate if the group is not dealing with what he wants.

When power is not asserted strictly because of fear of taking initiative for one's self, a great deal of repressed anger builds up. While this anger builds up for all the members and serves as a motivator for initiative in the group, some members become immobilized by the anger. They fear that if they continue in the group their controls would break down and they would have to express the anger. This fear is one of the major causes of flight from the group during the inclusion phase.

Thus, a crucial job for the therapist during the inclusion phase is to insure that wishes of all group members are expressed and to demonstrate some acceptance and respect for the wishes of every member. As the alliances and factions build around the different goals and norms expressed or implied by the members, the therapist's role is to keep alive all opinions, whether one member or several hold that opinion. The therapist's preservation of all opinions about goals and norms for the group serves many immediate and crucial developmental purposes. In the early inclusion phase, it serves to give all members support to express their opinions and provides at least the minimum of recognition for the individual's opinion, which gives the individual a base of acceptance in the situation. In the long-range development of the group, the therapist's preservation of opinions helps to establish norms that encourage the toleration of differences among the members. The toleration of differences is crucial to full development of the group in the mutuality phase. If the group does not grow to tolerate differences among members, then the mutuality phase will become very superficial and the norms for behavior and expression will be extremely narrow. Ultimately at stake in toleration of difference is whether or not the group will help and allow members to be their unique selves and to grow, each in his own way.

Self-awareness Issues for the Therapist

The major issues for therapist self-awareness in the inclusion phase are basically an extension of the possible control needs of the therapist. High control needs may cause the therapist to disregard opinions of some of the members about norms and goals, particularly if those opinions differ from those of the therapist. Another danger is that the therapist might side with one faction of the group over another faction. The therapist must be aware of his own biases toward certain kinds of group norms and goals in order to allow the members to create their own unique group climate. Even the norm suggested above, the toleration of different opinions among the members, must be demonstrated and carefully negotiated with the members in order that it not be imposed but rather soundly developed. The therapist must demonstrate other norms and goals through his own behavior and carefully negotiate them with the group rather than impose them. To negotiate the acceptance of a norm, the therapist must be prepared for the alternative, rejection of the particular norm or goal by the group either temporarily or permanently. Repeated rejection of particular norms by the group may be indicative of the group's low capacity for social development. Such a group requires a differentially lower level of group therapy aimed at developing relationships, rather than therapy per se.

Usually, the therapist's full acceptance of all opinions, especially those that differ from his own, will set a model that the group members will emulate sooner or later. On the other hand, the therapist's rejection of differing opinions and his control of the process of norm and goal deliberation will stymie the group's development of a capacity to free individuals to be themselves.

AFFECTIVE POLARITIES:
ACCEPTANCE AND REJECTION IN THE GROUP

The wish for acceptance and the fear of rejection by the other group members is the central affective issue in the inclusion phase. Closely tied to the quest for acceptance is the primitive dilemma of initiative versus fear (Erikson, 1968). Having gained some certainty of acceptance by the therapist during the parallel phase and then some winning and granting of autonomy from the authority crisis, the group members now must deal with the other group members. The central question becomes whether the degree of acceptance and autonomy achieved in relation to the therapist during the parallel and authority crisis can be achieved in relation to the other group members.

The inclusion phase calls forth many past and current emotional experiences: the social expansiveness of the three- to five-year-old, the pairing and peer orientation of the eight-year-old, the immersion in the peer group of the early adolescent, and the separation from family of the young adult. Each member brings to this phase of group development his successes and failures with each of these socially expansive life experiences. It is each member's degree of past success that will determine his capacity to handle the very difficult tasks confronting him in the inclusion phase. His past failures with these experiences can be remedied through re-enactment, with potentially more successful and gratifying results.

Self-awareness Issues for the Therapist

The self-awareness issues for the therapist arise from his own experiences with trust, autonomy, and initiative issues during his own life. A therapist who fears his own aggression will tend to exert too much or too little control of the group process during the inclusion phase. Since his role calls for high degrees of acceptance of the members, the therapist must be comfortable with the unfolding aggression of the members and be able to set supportive limits without rejecting the members for their demonstrated traits. The therapist's judgment of unfolding aggression may be hampered by his own degree of discomfort with aggression. This discomfort with aggression may cause the therapist to either freeze in the face of aggression or cut off the expression of aggressive impulses at a level too low for the members to gain satisfaction from the group. The therapist must be free to perceive whether the aggressive behavior is requisite or signals potential loss of control. The complicating factor is that, for many members, the inclusion phase may be the time they first express some of their aggression and, consequently, they may go to an extreme. Setting premature limits will tend to signify rejection to the member as well as to establish norms that restrict full expression and group development. Setting limits on extreme or excessive behavior, although it will also cause some feelings of rejection on the part of member, will set some norms that will be reassuring both to the members who need control and to the rest of the group.

MAJOR BEHAVIORAL FEATURES:
FLOCKING, FIGHTING, AND FEELING

Flocking, fighting, and fleeing serve to sum up the major behavioral features of the inclusion phase. *Flocking* refers to the pairing and subgrouping that takes place in the inclusion process. Individuals cannot relate to a new group of people all at the same time. Instead, the knitting together process begins with the formation of pairs and subgroups along lines of perceived similarities. The similarities might be based on age in groups that have a wide age span, on sex in groups that have both sexes, on social roles and status in groups in which social status is a variable, and finally, in both homogenous and heterogenous groups on comparable desired norms and goals.

Just as important in the affiliation process are the early aversions that people develop to other members in the group. These early aversions are mostly based on differences in age, sex, social status, and desired norms and goals for the group. Very often, certain pairs and subgroups will be formed because they share the same aversions to another member or subgroup. At other times, subgroups may be formed of people excluded from another alliance. In either event, the opposing groups that form tend to support the views of each of its constituents and each subgroup has the essential support to both express its feelings and opinions and defend itself from the opposing factions.

In each controversy, or *fight*, the emergence of both sides is crucial since the more intense the conflict, the greater the strength of both sides of each individual's ambivalence. It is through this mutual support of the alliance that the individual can express his feelings and opinions. He is assured that at least some members in the group accept him and his opinions (which he considers one and the same during inclusion) while tolerating the other side of the mixed feelings and opinions represented by the opposing view. Through the subgroup, each member can gain a feeling of influence upon the group's means and ends and thus feel more a part of the group. Resolve of interpersonal and subgroup conflicts are the building blocks toward intimacy in the group. Initially, members feel more akin to those on their side but, as the conflicts are resolved, they develop affective contact with the opposing factions around the common underlying feelings.

Thus, in group therapy, flocking and fighting are part of the same phenomenon: members form alliances and oppositions around their feelings of ambivalence and, through the conflicts, knit themselves into a cohesive group-as-a-whole. The conflicts tend to deepen the affect which surfaces in the overt process and resolving the conflict results in affective contact among all the members of the group.

The *flight* reaction can occur in relation to either the flocking or the fighting aspect of the inclusion phase. People can feel unworthy of an alliance with other group members. These members will not seek alliances with other members and will reject those who attempt to either ally with them or draw them into an alliance to support their position. The increasing emergence of hostility in the group will further threaten people who already feel unworthy because of repressed anger.

Members who have not resolved their trust, acceptance, or autonomy issues with the therapist will also resist forming alliances in the group. These members try to maintain their own direct relationship with the therapist to the exclusion of the other members. Particularly when intermember conflicts surface in the group, the members who are not ready to interact may attempt to maintain the "good child" image with the therapist or may see themselves as being above the goings on in the group. Chances are, these members adopted the same pattern of behavior during the critical points in their lives when other children were venturing away from parents into relationships with others.

The therapist can only hope that members with repressed hostility can stay with the group long enough to get drawn into member-member relationships. Unfortunately, unless such members are able to either join a subgroup that will express their anger for them or express their own anger, the situation may become too overwhelming and cause them to drop out of the group. During the inclusion phase, every group member goes through at least one crisis in which he is in an expression-inhibition quandary with respect to his underlying feelings. Once a member has had the experience of expressing his feelings and has experienced acceptance by and influence on the group, he begins to feel included in the group.

Some members can express their feelings very quickly; others wait a long time. Those members who wait are probably expressing their feelings vicariously through others in their subgroup or even through people they see as opposition. If a member's feelings are not expressed directly or indirectly, he is more likely to drop out of the group.

Expression of Aggression and Hostility

As in the parallel phase and authority crisis, members may be expressing aggression and hostility with the aim of alienating themselves rather than of resolving issues. The extreme of this expression is again found in group scapegoats. They feel that a negative contact allows them to be in the group without being ignored, yet frees them from taking the risk of rejection by seeking acceptance. Since the fear of rejection is universal during the inclusion phase, other members will be inclined to use the scapegoat as a means of focusing the rejection, therefore standing less chance of being rejected themselves. The resolution comes as the conflict is worked through and the scapegoat shares his fear of rejection with those who are doing the rejecting.

When inclusion battles appear to be endless and members back away from resolving them, group members in all likelihood have intense fears of intimacy. In a sense, they are all taking the pattern of the scapegoat and perpetuating conflicts to avoid intimacy.

Although conflicts are important phenomena throughout the life of a therapy group, they are more highly charged during the inclusion phase than before or after. This is because members feel that if they lose a conflict during the inclusion phase they will be rejected. The feeling or opinion at stake is a representation of the individual person's whole being and if it is rejected, then the whole person feels rejected. In later phases, members feel a basic acceptance by the group and when they lose a conflict they can partialize the issues and not feel totally rejected.

Self-awareness Issues for the Therapist

During the inclusion phase the therapist must be comfortable with both hostility and conflict. Also the therapist should not have an unrealistic bravado about his capacity to endure hostility or conflict. This bravado could lead to misjudgment in allowing too intense conflict to go unabated. On the other hand, the therapist who is too uncomfortable with hostility and conflict will be inclined to stop or smooth over too many conflicts. Not allowing sufficient conflict in the group gives members the message that the group is not allowed to have group autonomy or differences. Not allowing conflict will also lead to member's feeling increasingly guilty because of their hostility.

At stake in the inclusion phase are group norms that can set the ultimate parameters of the therapeutic process. If aggression and differences are not allowed to emerge, then the group is limited to a narrow range of feelings and behavior. Many therapists and groups attempt to avoid the inclusion battles by employing techniques that accelerate affective contact among the members. If these techniques are employed before the group has had a chance to work out its inclusion process, the resulting norms for behavior will tolerate only those behaviors that seem to enhance togetherness and positiveness. Premature togetherness and positiveness in a group will be gained at the expense of individuality, negating the use of the group as a medium for members to tolerate a wide range of feelings in themselves and other people. Because the negative feelings of each person are not allowed into the group, a depth of intimacy and mutuality would be precluded.

Role of the Therapist

During the inclusion phase the therapist supports the group's developing autonomy by facilitating the development of alliances, unfolding and resolving conflicts among the members, and helping each member resolve ambivalences toward expression rather than inhibition. Particularly important is the therapist's acceptance of the member's expression of hostility and conflict. The biggest danger for the therapist is to opt for peace in the group or to side with one faction of a conflict over another. If the therapist takes sides during an inclusion phase conflict, the conflict might never be resolved, and the losing faction will feel totally rejected by both therapist and group.

In a five-member group of nine- and ten-year-old boys for example, a basic inclusion conflict developed between the two boys who were rather hostilely aggressive and the other three who were rather constricted and withdrawn. As the three withdrawn boys developed their friendship they became increasingly resentful of the acting out by the other two boys. Finally, in one meeting the three withdrawn boys asked if they could have their own group apart from the other two. In the ensuing discussion there was a great deal of name-calling and accusations on both sides. Finally the therapists suggested that they all had to be in the same room at the same time but they could each have separate parts of the room for themselves. The separate but equal division of the room lasted a few weeks with occasisional verbal and attempted physical flareups. More important, however, was continued discussion among the boys and the therapists of each side's wishes to be somewhat like the others. The withdrawn boys wished they could be more aggressive and expressive and the acting-out boys wished to have more control of themselves. In time the group did get together, the withdrawn boys became better able to deal with the aggressive boys and with each other, and the aggressive boys developed more controls of their behavior in the group.

The inclusion issue over norms for behavior in the group was built into the group in its very matching of members. The mutual rejection between the two factions represented a positive identification of the boys with others who resembled them in behavior and a negative identification with the opposing faction, those whose behaviors they overtly rejected but covertly envied. At first the mutual rejection was so complete that they wanted separate groups. However, the withdrawn boys, by joining forces and acting out aggressively against the aggresive boys and by verbally dealing with their own mixed feelings about aggression, came to a better acceptance of their own aggression and the aggressive boys. The aggressive boys, in their longings for acceptance by other boys in the group and elsewhere, were at first able to accept control by the group in order to be members and then, having experienced acceptance, were able to maintain more controls in hopes of gaining friends in other situations as well.

Most important during this whole process was the stance of the therapists; they continued to accept both factions and did not favor either behavior pattern. Support of "good behavior" would have meant rejection of the "bad boys" and the aggressive parts of the "good boys." The resulting norms for behavior in this group ultimately incorporated some of each side's ways of behaving.

SOURCE OF GRATIFICATION: EXPANSION TO OTHERS

Although the therapist continues as a major source of gratification in the inclusion phase, other members become alternate sources. From the perspective of the individual member, as other members become acceptable, they then become objects for need gratification. That is, the other members become sources of acceptance, support, advice, control, and empathy.

Members may differ widely in their capacities and willingness to accept other members as sources of gratification. Many accept the additional support, welcome it, and use it immediately. Others tend to negate the potential usefulness of fellow members as sources of gratification and cling to the therapist as the sole source of gratification. Still other members will seek the support of fellow members exclusively and negate the potentials for the therapist as a source of gratification. Finally, many members will negate their needs for gratification from other people and counterdependently serve as sources of gratification for others. Counterdependent members attempt to meet their own dependency needs by meeting other peoples' needs.

Each member's particular pattern of seeking gratification from other group members is directly related to his life patterns and experiences. Members who negate the potentials of other members as sources of gratification are generally most primitive in their attachments to parents. Very often, these members have grown to fear any reaching out to other people because of the danger of loss of parental acceptance or rejection by their parents. Their past experiences with parents have primed them to seek only their parents as sources of gratification and to feel illicit in any significant contact outside the immediate family. Other members simply have not been able to experience nurture from anyone other than parents because the conflictual nature of the nurturing process with their own parents stymied their growth and left them with the mandate to perpetually seek parents for primary gratification.

During the inclusion phase, members who negate the potential gratification from other members tend to perceive the therapist as the parent figure and will direct all of their seeking for need gratification to the therapist. Some will talk only to the therapist at meetings. Others will talk to the other members, but only superficially; their primary intent is to convey to the therapist their need for gratification.

Experiences in gaining gratification from other members can be a source of growth for these members. Despite early efforts on the part of other members to respond and help, members who feel that the therapist is the sole source of gratification negate the help of others, no matter how abundant it is. The therapist must be prepared to provide some of the gratification sought while supporting the member's reaching out to others and receiving help from others. An important ingredient in helping a therapist-dependent member to reach out is the granting of clear permission from the therapist to seek gratification from others. In the absence of clear permission, the member will be inclined to interpret the therapist's actions as a desire for him to seek gratificaton only from the therapist and he may even see the therapist's pushing of him toward the other members as rejection.

Members who exclusively seek the help of other group members have often had very negative or conflictual experiences with parents and, as a consequence, have developed fears of seeking gratification from parents or parent figures. Many are also rebelling against authority figures and need to gain their gratification from peers rather than parents. The group, particularly during the inclusion phase, is the primary support for these members to carry out their necessary rebellion and come to terms with seeking help from the therapist when they have established themselves in the peer group. Teen-agers and adults who have not had a successful teen-age rebellion can gain mastery of the life task of moving out of the family into peer association for primary relationships through resolving the issues of the inclusion phase and the resultant intimacy crisis.

Members who take the counterdependent approach to need gratification have the most difficult time during the inclusion phase. These people usually have had unsatisfying relationships with parents and peers; they have been disappointed severely, often enough to fear reaching out. They have learned over the years to meet their own dependency needs by meeting needs of other people. The classic problem with counterdependency as a total way of relationship is that it usually does not meet enough of the individual's needs. If an individual is allowed to set up and sustain a counterdependent role in the group, he is not likely to gain much from the process and the longer the pattern persists, the less likely its interruption. Disallowing any counterdependent behavior will make the person too uncomfortable and possibly precipitate his leaving the group. Allowing the counterdependent member to complete his helping before inviting him to discuss the relationship of the problem at hand to his own life and functioning can best bring about a balance between allowing the individual to maintain the counterdependent defense and helping him to gain experience in seeking gratification from the group.

Self-awareness Issues for the Therapist

There are many issues in the sources of gratification during the inclusion phase that require a high degree of self-awareness on the part of the therapist. Foremost is the therapist's need to be a source of gratification, a need that is perhaps one of the major reasons people choose to become therapists. In relinquishing responsibility for need gratification to the group the therapist is sharing an extremely important area of his gratification. Thus, therapists must be aware of their desire to remain the primary source of gratification. Gratification in facilitating a growing mutual helping system can substitute for direct need gratification.

Directly related to the need for giving gratification is the fact that therapists very often have developed counterdependent patterns of relating to other people. This counterdependency serves well to help the therapist function in the interests of other people and keep his own needs, other than for counterdependent gratification, out of the helping process. However, it is important for the therapist to deal with relinquishment of the counterdependent gratification. His reluctance to give up this gratification will feed in to those members who need to negate help from peers or will prematurely force those members who are reluctant to depend on the therapist to rely on him as a source of gratification. It can contribute to competition with counterdependent members or cause the therapist to overlook the counterdependent member's inability to ask for anything from others.

During the incluson phase the therapist must not only continue to be a source of gratification but also must facilitate the mutual helping process that is developing among the members. The developing capacity of the group to provide mutual help is a major step toward individuals' learning how to meet their own and other people's needs as well as to successfully seek and accept gratification from others. This process underlies the giving and getting essential to the middle phase of group therapy, the mutuality phase.

RELATIONAL ISSUES: TOWARD GROUP-AS-A-WHOLE

Development of relationships among the members is the central process in the inclusion phase. Individual members seek acceptance from others and determine their own acceptance or rejection of others. Since no person can develop relationships with all others at the same time, a process of selection develops in which individuals begin to pair up with others. Pairing gives way to subgrouping, in which several members form an affiliation. Finally, the subgrouping grows into a group-as-a-whole. While the basic trend in small groups is toward growing together, the process of this growing together does not follow a direct path. A member's experiences with oedipal and sibling relationships strongly influence predispositions for power and acceptance (Slater, 1966; Gibbard and Hartman, 1973).

Power Relationships

Of paramount importance to the indirect path toward development of a group as a whole are the power relationships among individuals. As described earlier, people's needs for inclusion combine needs for acceptance and power. For many, the relation between power and acceptance becomes confused. Some feel that acceptance by others is achieved by giving all the power to others. Still others fear probable rejection and seek power as a substitute. Finally there are those who seek rejection and powerlessness for their acts rather than risk being rejected for themselves. These latter people (scapegoats) have usually been frustrated in their efforts to gain acceptance and would rather be overtly rejected by the group than attempt to gain acceptance and be rejected. They have developed some feelings of safety in the scapegoat role.

Fundamental to how he pursues inclusion is the person's self-concept. People with very low self-esteem feel unworthy of acceptance by others and, indeed, wonder about anyone who finds them acceptable. Most others feel acceptable to some degree and their fear of rejection is based on past experiences with acceptance and rejection by others. People who seek acceptance through power often overtly feel acceptable (or even superacceptable), but covertly fear unacceptability and avoid possible rejection by controlling the situation so that they are in charge and so that they determine who and what is acceptable.

Attraction-Aversion

Initial attractions among members are generally brought about through their perceptions of similarities in opinions, feelings, behavior, life roles, situations, and problems. Positive identifications ("I'm just like you") and

148

positive transferences ("You're just like my mother") serve as the next level of affiliation. Finally, relationships are sealed by the emergence of empathy ("That's exactly how I feel") between members. The end of the inclusion phase comes as empathy grows to include all the members in an empathic bond. The first time all the members make empathic contact, the first intimacy crisis is set off. Partial resolution of intimacy crises will lead the group to maintain many inclusion characteristics (particularly the threat and fear of rejection) along with some characteristics of mutuality.

Equally important to the inclusion process is the early exclusion process. Initial affiliations are formed as much from aversions to certain members as from attractions to others. Initial rejection of people with differing opinions, feelings, behaviors, life roles, situations, and problems serves to narrow the number of people to whom each member is initially attracted. Factions form around the opinions and perceived differences. As differences of opinions give way to negative identifications and transferences, the composition of factions will change or deepen, depending on how similar these negative identifications and transferences are to the differences. On a deeper level, the negative identifications and transferences serve as an underlying basis for conflict. While resolution of negative identifications and transferences serves as major therapeutic media in the mutuality phase, initial empathic contact resulting from conflicts in the inclusion phase set the stage for resolution.

Self-awareness Issues for the Therapist

In order to be helpful to members during the inclusion phase, the therapist must be well aware of his own relational pattern so as not to impose that pattern on the group or reject members for manifesting too similar or too objectionably different a pattern of developing relationships. A therapist with a great need for power may be inclined to conflict with members who attempt to gain inclusion through dominance. A therapist with little need for power may be inclined to either allow the dominant members too much room or to reject them for trying to establish their niche in the group. Therapists with high need for acceptance and inclusion might be inclined to submit to the domination of an indigenous leader at the expense of equal support for a rival faction. The therapist's need for acceptance might also cause him to reject members when they reach out to each other rather than to the therapist for acceptance. In other words, the therapist must be well aware of his needs for acceptance and domination to avoid being drawn into the factioning that takes place in the group.

SELF-OTHER CONCEPT: OVERT UNIFORMITY

A member's self-concept determines his or her feelings of acceptability to other members. However, since most people coming to therapy groups suffer some degree of low self-esteem, the question of self in relation to others in the group becomes important in the determination of one's feelings of acceptability to others. For most members, the perception of similarity between themselves and other members tends to reduce their fears of being unacceptable. The discovery of other people's low opinions of themselves particularly helps each member feel more on a par with everyone else. The experience of empathy with other members is the ultimate leveler. As members work through to affective contact, with empathy at the very peak in this contact, the question of superiority or inferiority is finally laid to rest. The universality of the feelings among the members serves as the base of uniformity which allows all to feel equal and be more comfortable with their areas of uniqueness (Yalom, 1975). However, until the base of empathy is reached at the end of the inclusion phase, members stress overt uniformity as the equalizer. For most members during parallel and inclusion, being unique is tantamount to being unacceptable to the others. This phenomenon is one of the major reasons why people will affiliate with those who seem similar and reject those who seem different.

Members who tend toward the severe depressive or highly structured paranoid ends of the paranoid-depressive continuum tend to retain their feelings of uniqueness and reject notions of uniformity. The depressive needs to remain unique from the others in order to maintain the depressive feelings of helplessness, hopelessness and, in this instance particularly, worthlessness. Recognizing uniformity with others in the group suggests to the depressive that others are not so content and consequently he is not so depressed.

The highly paranoid person needs to reject uniformity with others since this uniformity might puncture the very shaky overt feelings of self-esteem and impute causation for difficulties to himself. Other members may have some resistances to recognizing uniformity, but as long as they are not impervious to the others, as in the two examples above, the uniformities will become obvious.

Thus, except for extreme cases, most members seek overt uniformity between themselves and others as a means to raise their own self-esteem. As information about other members unfold, members tend either to get reinforcement for their uniformity with others or to develop feelings of being very different, which usually carries a negative connotation and tends to lower their concept of self in relation to others. As members fear or become more fearful of their possible uniqueness, they will tend either to resist from exposing their possible uniqueness or to aggressively make the group more uniform. Which path members take will vary according to their capacity for aggression and assertion of power. Until or unless empathic universality of feelings emerges in a group, the members will content themselves with a lockstep narrow range of expression and behavior that is intended in part to preserve each member's self-esteem. The idea is that if the group looks, thinks, and acts alike, then no one needs to feel less worthy than anyone else.

Self-awareness Issues for the Therapist

The therapist's comfort with his own uniqueness can be a major factor in how accepting he will be of each member's uniqueness. Overconformity or over-rebellion by the therapist in his own social behavior can lead to disallowing each person to be unique and can certainly preclude helping the person to become comfortable with areas in which he feels unique. Overconformity or rebellion may also preclude the therapist's allowing depressive or paranoid people to sustain their uniqueness until such time as they no longer need it.

The role of the therapist during the inclusion phase is to help people find areas of uniformity, but he must also be accepting and supportive of uniqueness as he helps other members to allow and accept uniqueness. Often it is the therapist's own acceptance of the person's overt uniqueness that serves as a bridge to the rest of the group until the basic coming together through the empathic bond. The therapist's acceptance can sustain people through this phase in relation to their self-other concept.

In the boy's group described earlier in this chapter, the therapists' rejecting neither the constricted children nor the acting-out children provided a base that, while disconcerting to the two sides, also freed both sides to accept the alternate parts of themselves as well as the other boys.

POWER RELATIONS:
EXERCISING AND DISTRIBUTING POWER

Power relations among members is a major facet of the inclusion phase. In the parallel phase, all the power is vested in the therapist. Central to the authority crisis is the passage of power from the therapist to the group. A central issue in the inclusion phase is how the power will be exercised and what will be the power distribution among the members.

Initially, the power goes to the more aggressive members, simply because in the early inclusion phase they push their views on the others. As the group develops, other people begin either to support the members who demonstrate power or to oppose them and vie for power. Those who cannot or will not assert their demands on the group must either find some more dominant members with whom they agree and whom they can support or find their views completely disregarded by the group. If these members are overlooked for too long a period they will soon drop out of the group.

There are four areas for which power in the group is important: accept-ance process, focus of discussion, norms for expression and behavior, and goals of the group. These four areas are all interrelated. If there is balance among factions in the group, any faction gaining control of one area may be defeated by other factions on other areas. If one faction gains control of group goals, other factions can defeat those goals by developing norms that impede work or by controlling the focus and aiming it in other directions.

Some subgroup formation during the early part of the inclusion phase is based on similar ideas among members for focus, norms, and goals. Indigenous leaders of these subgroups may represent positions in relation to focus, norms, and goals. Acceptance or rejection of other members is then based on whether they share or oppose these positions. However, many members respond to overt acceptance from the indigenous leaders and take positions based on their desire to sustain that acceptance rather than on how they really feel about the issues. As inclusion moves forward, and if there are at least two indigenous leaders, then other members begin to experience their own real ideas for focus, norms, and goals. As these members begin to assert their opinions and get support for them, some realignments in subgroup structures take place in accordance with the new decisions about norms and goals.

Most inclusion struggles are not explicit in the content of the group discussion. Instead, when some members start to discuss one topic, other members subvert that discussion in overt or covert ways. Or other members simply attempt to talk about something completely unrelated to the first topic. Here the group disagrees about focus. The norm suggested is that any member can stop or change the subject at any time. The implication for the goal of the group is inherent in the subject in focus.

In order to balance the power in the group and insure every member direct or indirect access to power the therapist must maintain a neutral position in relation to the various factions. Giving equal weight to all ideas or initiative, no matter how many or how few in the faction, demonstrates a norm of having to deal with and reconcile the differences. Individual members' feelings of power or hope for being able to influence the group in their own desired direction will make the difference in whether they feel accepted or rejected in the group and will certainly affect whether they feel that the group can be helpful to them.

Self-awareness Issues for the Therapist

Again, the therapist's own feelings about power and about sharing it with group members is put to the test. A ready substitute for the therapist's power is to identify with one power faction over another. If one subgroup stands for the focus, norms, or goals that the therapist is really interested in, the temptation is to help or allow that faction to dominate, while the other faction gets defeated. One of the major causes of group resistances is a therapist directly or through a faction forcing his will on the group without full negotiation with the members. In the author's experience, much (not all) of the group resistances represent a power struggle between the therapist and some or all of the members. Consequently, if the area of focus that the group is resisting were open to a discussion in which the therapist is prepared to modify his view from the negotiations, there would be fewer resistances. Once resistances are present, it is not too late to negotiate the implications for different focuses or goals, provided the therapist is prepared to modify his position in the negotiations. If the therapist merely defeats the opposition, different and perhaps deeper resistances are more than likely to develop.

What many therapists, particularly those new to group therapy, often overlook is that the interaction between the members and the therapist may be more important then the subject matter deemed so critical by the therapist at the time of the struggle. Even resistances in their pure form are an expression of autonomy akin to the negativism of the two-year-old. Accepting initiatives contrary to the immediate goals of the therapist may have more therapeutic value in the emotional growth of the group members than the very goals of the therapist. Power struggles among the members are a more advanced state of emotional initiative and aggressivity. Again, attention to members' succeeding in gaining influence through the power struggle may provide greater long-term benefit in self-understanding or direction than the content of the issue might have.

CONFLICT: INTENSE AND FACTIONALIZING

Surfacing of conflict is a major characteristic of the inclusion phase. Before the inclusion phase, hostilities and disagreements build within individuals, but they remain submerged. Successful resolution of early authority crises demonstrates to the group that aggression can be expressed with positive results and perhaps few if any of the negative results they feared. The autonomy aroused and expressed in the authority crisis leads the group members to feel a little more comfortable and hopeful of having influence over the group. The divergent feelings, opinions, and reactions to each other that were being repressed can now be experienced. Initially, however, only the aggressive members who are more comfortable with their hostile and aggressive impulses can express their disagreement with others.

Conflicts during the inclusion phase are the most dramatic and fearsome conflicts in a group because losing a conflict is tantamount to rejection. Members do not partialize their opinions or their feelings but rather feel that if their side of the conflict is rejected by the group, then they are rejected by the group. After the group has come together affectively in the mutuality phase, the conflicts become partialized and particularized (differentiated). While mutuality conflicts may be bombastic, the members do not feel total rejection when they lose and do not fear rejection or a potential loss.

Adding to the intensity of conflicts during the inclusion phase is the tendency for the group to factionalize around issues. During the inclusion phase members either express their positions directly or tend to support one side of the issue against the other. In conflicts of more developed groups, members are more inclined to see both sides, leaving the major adversaries as the only major contenders. Thus, if fear of rejection is still inherent in the potential loss of a conflict, it is only rejection by the opposing party and not by the whole group.

Thus, the intensity of conflict during the inclusion phase is based on the fear of rejection and the need and tendency for all the members to line up on one side or the other of the conflict. Conflict is one of the most formidable and essential processes in the inclusion phase and the resolutions of major conflicts are the building blocks by which the inclusion process encompasses the entire group. Initially, through conflict, individuals who appear opposed to each other let each other know where they are at odds; then, through conflict resolve, they come to empathize around the feelings they share. Later, whole factions begin to settle their differences and to develop affective bonds through discovering the common underlying feelings at the base of their conflicts. The resolution of conflicts between factions opens the door for the unearthing and resolving of differences among the subgroups that were formed by simple flocking. These groups often submerge differences among themselves in order to keep a united front. Once they successfully resolve differences with the opposition, the dangers of rejection are reduced and the members of each side are freer to confront each other.

Avoidance of Conflict to Escape Intimacy

Because they help reconcile differences and unearth common underlying feelings, thereby establishing a base for empathy, the surfacing and resolution of conflicts among group members in the inclusion phase are major vehicles for group movement toward intimacy. However, the very vehicles for helping a group knit together can also become vehicles for preventing intimacy. Perpetuation of inclusion conflicts can prevent the development of intimacy in a group. Many group members fear intimacy more than they fear conflict. A major way of avoiding intimacy is to avoid the common feelings that underlie the conflict and thus prevent any full resolution. Consequently, issue after issue will arise within the same general conflict.

Another way of avoiding conflict and intimacy in groups is to make a scapegoat of one member or of someone outside the group. As long as the group perpetuates the enemy, they can even become a faction of the whole. However, the faction of the whole tends to exist within a very narrow band of norms, with interpersonal conflicts within the faction being repressed and intimacy being very shallow. Intimacy under circumstances of scapegoating must remain shallow, since all the members, including the indigenous leader, fear that the rejection process will turn against them.

In order to break up these knots of conflict, the therapist has the hazardous job of opening up the interpersonal conflicts among the members of a faction. The major hazard is that the therapist might be made the scapegoat in order to protect the position of the faction. However, there is less danger that the faction will be able to perpetuate scapegoating of the therapist at this stage of development, as opposed to scapegoating the therapist during the parallel phase. The fact that the group has successfully resolved its first authority crisis suggests sufficient autonomy among the members to untangle the conflictual bind. Like two individuals in a conflict, two factions in conflict share the same ambivalences and common underlying fears. Pursuing the ambivalence and underlying fears in the faction can help untangle the system that is using conflict to hold the faction together. In sum, while it is best to allow factions to dissolve after they resolve their differences through conflict resolution, interfactional conflicts can also be resolved by unearthing and resolving the intrafactional conflict.

Self-awareness Issues for the Therapist

In the inclusion phase the therapist must be aware of his feelings about conflict within individuals, within subgroups, and among individuals and subgroups. Only experience with unearthing and resolving interpersonal conflicts can really help the therapist gain comfort with conflict and confidence in both the efficacy of conflict and his ability to help groups resolve conflicts. However, the therapist's personal style with conflict may also influence his readiness to risk even allowing groups to conflict. Group conflict is closely related to the establishment of autonomy for individuals in the group and, if the group is not allowed to have and resolve its conflicts, it must remain dependent on the therapist for its functioning.

A therapist with unresolved feelings about conflicts can also allow a group to have too much conflict too soon without intervening. If a group is allowed to deal with conflicts they are not ready to resolve, they will frighten themselves into dependency on the therapist and avoid further conflicts. It is difficult enough for a therapist who is comfortable with conflict to judge whether it is too soon or too late to resolve a conflict. In groups with a reasonable degree of social capacity, two major symptoms of covert conflict are the total absence of conflict and either a narrow range of tolerable behavior or norms that emphasize only positive feelings. These two characteristics would be found in groups where conflict was not allowed as well as in groups that experienced too much conflict without the therapist's support or setting of limits to keep the conflict within tolerable bounds.

In helping a group handle conflict in the inclusion phase, the therapist must support all sides. This support must be real; lip service will not help resolve the conflict. The therapist must facilitate the full expression of both sides of the conflict and assist in reception by the opposing sides. The therapist must set some limits on the full expression of the factions during the inclusion phase: the norms and controls of the members are not yet sufficiently developed to do so and few, if any, neutral members will take the middle position and enforce controls. Finally, the therapist must help unearth the common underlying feelings on both sides of the conflict to facilitate the full resolve of the conflict. During inclusion the common underlying feelings are usually related to fears of rejection.

A few major conflicts and many minor conflicts will usually bring the group to some initial empathy. Then, when there is empathic touching by all the members, an intimacy crisis ensues.

> In a summer workshop for professional therapists the participants were divided into four autonomous groups to have limited experiences in group development. In the second session, three of the groups began to experience some inclusion conflicts. The fourth group very efficiently accomplished the assigned task and spent the rest of their group time joking about the apparent conflicts going on in the other three groups. In the feedback session for all groups, the efficient group gloated over their accomplishment, suggesting that they were all mature people, above the silly bickering of the other groups. Members of the other groups felt requisitely bad about their groups and their lesser productivity. However, between the second and third sessions, members of the more argumentative groups told me that they were enjoying the workshops very much and were getting to like the other people in their small group. Two of the five members of the efficient group asked if we couldn't spend more of our workshop time in lecture-discussion rather than the small groups, since those didn't seem to be sufficiently productive. In talking further, it became apparent that they were very angry with one very dominant member who dictated their process. I pointed out how they may have overlooked some points of disagreement with this dominant member and perhaps that is why they felt unsatisfied with their small group experience. In the third session, while the other groups were beginning to experience some cohesion and intimacy the efficient group began to address their submerged power struggle. From that point forward the initial indigenous leader took an uneasy back seat during small group meetings while the other members went on to develop as a group.

COHESION: A DRAMATIC CHANGE

The nature of interpersonal cohesion changes dramatically through the inclusion phase. At first, there is little cohesion beyond the ties between therapist and individual members. By the end of the inclusion phase the group verges on becoming a single entity. The process between is the progressive development of cohesive networks, starting with pairing, then subgrouping, and finally the group-as-a-whole or "we" feeling that comes with growing intimacy.

Early bonds among some members must exclude others. As each pair and subgroup develops, the member must identify the group by who is and who is not in it. The reasons for which members are included and which are excluded can be many and varied. Just as some of the usual reasons for early bond formation arise from similarities in opinions, feelings, behaviors, life stage, situations, and problems, some of the usual reasons for excluding people arise from differences in these same areas.

Later bond formation is based on shared affect, with particular emphasis on empathy. Although initial empathy may arise from pairs and subgroups that started with perceived similarities, then deepen into empathy, empathic bonds may and often do form across subgroups and directly result from initial perception of differences, which gives rise to conflict, and results in empathy from resolve of the conflicts.

The strength and depth of cohesion among the members is inversely related to the degree to which the pair or subgroup must exclude or reject other members. Early cohesion requires some degree of exclusion. As the cohesion increases, the need to exclude others decreases. If both cohesion and exclusion seem to increase, then the cohesion is at the expense of at least some, if not all, members of the subgroup. The degree of exclusion is indicative of the underlying fears among the members in the subgroup. Emphasis on exclusion is often used by subgroups to take attention away from possible differences and conflicts within the group. If a subgroup needs to perpetuate the exclusion, quite probably they are hiding some interpersonal strife from themselves.

Self-awareness Issues for the Therapist

The self-awareness issues for the therapist in relation to cohesion in the inclusion phase arise from the therapist's own needs for inclusion. As the members begin to develop their mutual bonds, the primary bond to the therapist from the parallel phase is diluted. The therapist may experience some loss as the primary bond is loosened and some envy of the bonding among the members. If the therapist is unaware of his own feelings about this process, he may give overt or covert signals to the members not to get together or he may attempt to force people together prematurely, which would frighten them and cause them to back off from each other and fear getting closer.

Many group members have retained parental prohibitions about making affective ties to people outside the family and any reaction from the therapist that confirms this prohibition will certainly slow down, if not stymie, the development of ties among the members.

The therapist's role in relation to cohesion during the inclusion phase is to allow and help bonding to take place among the members but not to force bonding to the point where members become too frightened. All group members to some degree fear getting close and some of these fears may need attention even during the inclusion phase. A major clue that these fears are present is unremitting conflict in which the parties to the conflict do not seem to want to settle the issues and certainly do not want to share their common underlying feelings or even allow others to know what these feelings are. The primary adversaries in such unremitting conflict during the inclusion phase may very well be fending off a mutual attraction that is difficult for them to accept. Fears of closeness may not be the only reasons for unremitting conflict during the inclusion phase, but they are a major reason.

One other major fear that can result in unremitting conflict is negative identification between two or more people. One or both parties remind the other of something in themselves that they find particularly objectionable. In this instance, resolving the conflict would mean accepting the similarities between them.

CONTROLS: GROUP DEVELOPMENT

A major product of the inclusion phase is the development of group controls. After the resolution of early authority crises, some responsibility for control shifts from the therapist to the group. At the outset of the inclusion phase the group is not ready to exert its own controls. Members show varying interest in and capacity for control. A struggle ensues and members attempt to gain control of the group and do battle with others who are also attempting to take control. Part of the basis of subgroup formation arises as members join forces for the purpose of controlling the group. As the several factions struggle for overall control of the group, many control issues are worked out, allowing the group to emerge with controls for itself.

Control of Self and Others

There are two kinds of controls at issue in the group. One concerns one's own and other people's behavior. After the authority crisis the therapist is no longer the major source of controls for behavior. Members become concerned with their own potentials for loss of control and fear that others may lose control. Fears of loss of control are exacerbated by the emergence of the hostilities and conflict of the inclusion struggles. In addition, people often come to therapy groups because of real or felt inability to control their own behavior. Consequently, members look to the therapist or the group for control of their own and other people's behavior. Major growth can arise from participating in developing group controls as well as experiencing group control. Both are steps toward increasing each member's capacity for self-control. For many group members, particularly children with difficulty in impulse control, a major area of growth results from the group control process. (Redl, 1966)

Control of Group

Another kind of control concerns the destiny of the group. Control of the group's means and ends is at stake during the inclusion phase. Members seek to have the group meet their needs by attempting to control the group's development of norms, seeking norms that provide comfort for themselves in the group, and of goals, again seeking ones that promise to meet their own needs.

Acceptance and rejection serve as the major implements of control in the inclusion phase. Acceptance or rejection of each other's behavior and each other's wishes for the group's destiny becomes a basis for pair and subgroup formation. Similar desires for the nature and destiny of the group can be expressed and enforced by joining with others to have a greater impact on the group.

In the early part of the inclusion phase, the more aggressive members will tend to control the group mostly because others fear them. Aggressive members may encourage others to join them to avoid being the objects of aggression. Other members may join in opposition to the aggressive members to gain protection from aggression through numbers. However, as the inclusion phase develops, the basis of control shifts from the aggressive members to those who are successful in norm-setting. Norm-setters gain their power to control through becoming the initial judges of behavior, feelings, and opinions, with concomitant acceptance or rejection of others for their behavior, feelings, or opinions.

In some groups, the skillful norm-setters begin to take control of the acceptance and rejection process during the parallel phase. If the early norm-setters succeed in preventing aggressive members from exerting leadership, there is a danger that the group will be hampered by too narrow a range of behavior and expression.

The development of healthy controls in a therapy group depends on the balance of aggressive and norm-setting members. Two or more opposing norm-setters and two or more opposing aggressive leaders, or at least a norm-setter opposing an aggressive leader, is important for balance in the struggle for group controls. If any one of these members gains and holds power unopposed, the danger is that the resulting group controls will be too narrowly shaped to the indigenous leader's wishes and will preclude a range of behavior that will allow room for every member's mode of behavior. If no one opposes the aggressive leader or norm-setter, it behooves the therapist to open up the question of controls, letting other group members participate in development of norms and controls.

Self-awareness Issues for the Therapist

The task of the therapist is to balance the various factions, whether they be aggressive leaders or norm-setters. The group needs the divergent opinions of the members to develop controls that permit a climate of progressive expression.

Central to most control controversies in therapy groups during the inclusion phase is the question of expression versus inhibition. Forces in both directions are essential for the group to fully work out facilitating norms while maintaining limits so that the degree of expression will not exceed the readiness of most members.

The therapist's awareness of his own needs for control of self and others is crucial during the inclusion phase. The difficult task of recognizing realistic levels of control can be complicated if the therapist cannot comfortably allow the group to assume responsibility for its own control. The therapist is in danger of assuming too much or too little control for the group's level of development. Many therapists are inclined to dislike factions that control through aggression and to overlook norm-setters. It may help to realize that usually, sooner or later, aggressive control is countered by aggression from opposing subgroups, but norm-setters are often more difficult for members to oppose. Aggressive controllers threaten only punishment for opposition, but norm-setters threaten full rejection for opposition.

A classic example of the norm-setter is seen in many groups when one member expresses a feeling, only to have the norm-setter respond with, "Tell us how you *really* feel." The norm-setter is suggesting that there is a more profound way for the other member to express that feeling and perhaps more profound feelings to be expressed. Even if there are more profound feelings to be expressed, they are not likely to be forthcoming early in the group process. The net result is that the member is made to feel inadequate as an expressor and both the member and other members become more fearful of expressing any feelings. If successful, the norm setter can, at best, cause everyone in the group to look to him for approval of actions and, at worst, cause all members hold back from participation. Whenever members begin to make qualitative assessments of another member's behavior, it is important to ask them to clarify what the suggested expectation is. What, for example, is a *real* feeling?

THE SHIFT IN NORMS

A major shift in norms takes place during the inclusion phase. Tentative norms of the parallel phase come up for questioning and change and the direction of change can either enhance the therapeutic work of the group or close off the possibilities for productivity. Norm-setting and norm-breaking during the inclusion phase are both products of the inclusion struggles and major tools in those struggles. Members and subgroups who gain control of the norms generally control the acceptance process and thus become more influential in determining norms for the group.

Expression vs. Inhibition

Of the many norms that develop during inclusion, those concerned with the dilemma of expression versus inhibition are most important. Two sides usually develop, one representing the thrust for full and deep expression and the other representing the withholding of meaningful expression. This dilemma exists within each member, although each does lean toward one side or the other. That both sides exist is extremely important, since the balance between expression and inhibition will allow the group to progressively reveal themselves within tolerable limits for most, if not all, members.

Domination of the forces for expression will lead to premature revelation with its concomitant danger that people will become frightened from telling too much too soon. Even those who strongly push for full and deep expression become frightened by premature revelation and are often the first to flee. Domination by the forces for inhibition, however, can close up the process and prohibit the revelation of problems and difficult feelings. Thus, a balance of these opposing forces represents a polarization of each person's dilemma and provides the opportunities for expression along with limits appropriate to most group members.

Those members who directly balk at expression can be inhibitory forces, but often more so are those members who counterphobically push for premature full expression. These members are often the ones who fear expression most but, by being the leaders for expression, they get in the vanguard and are able to set norms for expression that preclude areas they find threatening. With the presence of strong directly inhibitory forces, the counterphobic members are held back, and the result can be a full dealing with and reduction of the fears of all members for self-expression and revelation.

Conflict and Acceptance

Other crucial normative development concerns the surfacing of conflict and the acceptance-rejection process. The degree to which conflict can emerge and how conflict can be resolved are closely tied to the normative development of expression. Norm-setters can lead toward norms that suggest only positive expression is allowable and exclude hostility between members and differences of opinion. If the "positive" norm-setters prevail, then those who express only positive feelings and agreement are accepted and others are rejected. Such circumstances will preclude the expression of hostilities and conflict, keeping the group at a quasi-parallel level. If this situation is perpetuated, then the uniqueness of individuals and any real closeness among the members cannot emerge.

161

Forces for and against conflict will facilitate the gradual emergence of conflict and provide the group with opportunities for developing norms dealing with conflict.

Members who have already achieved a high degree of status and acceptance by the group are more likely candidates for setting norms that the others accept. However, a member with high status can overstep his popularity and lose status and acceptance by actions that are extremely threatening to others. As the inclusion phase goes on, norm-setters generally enhance their status with the other members and serve as the indigenous leaders.

Role of the Therapist

The task of the therapist in relation to normative development is to help in the unfolding and development of norms. Some norms will be directly discussed in the group with members giving opinions on what should or should not happen. Other norms develop as members simply act in certain ways and the others follow. Initiating new behavior is perhaps the most common method of challenging norms and introducing new ones. The therapist's reactions to these behavior initiations are crucial, since an inappropriate reaction can cause members to desist from this behavior. Ultimately the possible acceptance or rejection of the individual for the initiated behavior is the major determinant of whether new behaviors will be perpetuated. Acceptance by the therapist can go far in supporting unpopular behavior as long as the therapist also recognizes and accepts the reasons for the unpopularity.

Self-awareness Issues for the Therapist

Self-awareness for the therapist with regard to normative development is directly related to the therapist's own ideas of how a group should proceed. Ideas from past experiences or training can be useful if they fit the particular group. However, it is important for a therapist to realize that no two groups are alike and that each group, because of its unique combination of individuals, must have its own ways of functioning. The therapist can suggest and model enabling norms for the group but must always be prepared for the group to develop its own ways, which may be very different from those the therapist would prefer.

Constricting norms are a very difficult aspect of norm development for therapists. Rejecting a restrictive norm is tantamount to overlooking the need of some members for that norm; ultimately it is seen as rejection of those members. If there is no ready opposition to the constricting norms in the group, the therapist might explore the reasons for the norm's existence and make it less necessary by helping with the underlying fear rather than by defeating the norm politically. Defeat of the norm (that is, getting other group members to support the therapist's norm rather than the group member's norm) will result in persistent resistance by the members subscribing to the defeated norm, and perhaps by the rest of the group as well. Although the other members may overtly support the therapist, they may participate in covertly defeating the therapist's norm through resistance.

In the earlier example of the group of constricted and aggressive boys (pp. 144-45), if the therapists had favored the conforming behavior of the constricted boys, then the aggressive boys could at best have conformed to the therapists' wishes; however, they would have continued to rely on the therapist for control and would not have gained in their ability to control their own behavior.

DEVELOPMENT OF GROUP GOALS

A major product of the inclusion phase is the development of group goals. A long-term therapy group might develop very broad goals, whereas shorter-term groups must, of necessity, clearly define what the group will do within a short period of time. The most effective use of a short time period makes clarity of goals a pressing issue for the members. Goals in long-term therapy groups are more related to notions about what the group is for and which areas of life it will pursue. For example, a long-term group might decide that (a) the group is to help everyone work out his problems, (b) the group is to help everyone work out his relationships with other people, (c) the group is to help everyone be able to do better in his work, (d) the group is to help everyone feel better about himself, (e) the group is to help everyone get a better sense of his own identity.

Most group goals in long-term therapy groups are related to feelings of self-worth, anxiety, functioning, and relationships. Long-term goals are usually defined in terms of life roles, stages, developmental tasks, and significant relationships. Individual members' goals are often more specific aspects of the roles, stages, and so on.

Arriving at Group Goals

During the inclusion phase, members engage in a process of negotiating their individual goals in an attempt to influence the group toward developing goals that promise to meet their own needs. However, during the inclusion phase, individuals often become clearer about what they want and need from the group therapy experience. Often members come to the group with one idea of what they want and need but during the inclusion struggles find that their wants and needs have become very different.

Early pairings and subgroupings are often formed on the basis of shared concerns, but individuals may shift their overt concerns because of the influence of the subgroup upon them. These individuals often subordinate their goals to gain acceptance by other members. Stronger leaders may superimpose their goals on the group in attempts to validate their often shaky conviction about what they need. Thus, through the processes of people defining and redefining their goals and by superordinating and subordinating goals, the group develops a synthesis of the varied goals. In long-term groups, since there is time and space for a wide variety of goals, there is less conflict and less urgency for resolution. In short-term groups, because of time limitations, the goal deliberation is highly charged.

Sometimes, groups will engage in direct discussions of what the group is or should be for. During the parallel and early inclusion phases, these discussions are superficial, and are as much influenced by what other people will accept as by what a person really understands of his own quest. Overt goal discussions in the later part of the inclusion phase are more realistic, since members feel freer to express their real wishes and are more in touch with what those real wishes are. Aside from interaction around their goals vis-a-vis other people's goals members have had more experience with the therapy group process and have a better idea of what they might get from this process.

More often, goal deliberation takes indirect routes. Members opting for discussion of particular issues as opposed to other issues, or simply refusing to engage in certain discussions while proffering other questions and issues for discussion, is the more usual pattern for goal negotiation. Resistance to certain discussion areas may also be votes against making that area a group function. If resistances are at first treated as votes against an area rather than as prevention, there is a better chance that alternatives and compromises may result from the discussion. As their feelings of control and influence on the group increase, members are often more inclined to lower their resistances.

The therapist's role is to support all direct and indirect votes for group goals and to support individual goals related to those group goals. To the degree that each member feels the group is responding to his wishes will the member become invested in the work of the group both for himself and for others. It is the therapist's responsibility to insure that everyone's wishes for the group are heard, recognized, and incorporated into the resulting group goals. However, if a member's goals are too far apart from the actual intent of the group, the therapist must consider terminating that member and providing some other help if the member has not already considered leaving the group himself.

Self-awareness Issues for the Therapist

The major area of self-awareness for the therapist concerns the therapist's own goals for the group and individual members. From prior and early group contacts with members, the therapist may well have set out some therapeutic tasks for himself in relation to the members and the group. The best time and place for the therapist to exert influence on the goals of the group is in the mixing and matching of members as the group is formed. After the group is together, the therapist can rely on the mixing and matching of individuals to carry the group to determination of goals best suited to its concerns. However, if the group was not developed through sound initial grouping or careful selection of new members, the therapist must be prepared to negotiate his goals for the group with the group. Imposition of the therapist's goals will seriously hamper the self-determination of the group and create severe problems with dependency and resistance.

Goals are the very backbone of the group process and the provision of therapy to groups. If members have a part in determining the goals of the group they will have more feeling of being included in the group and, even more important, a feeling that the group belongs to them. These feelings are fundamental to the intimacy crisis and the mutuality phase of group development.

ROLES: ASSUMPTION AND ASSIGNMENT

Roles are more important during the inclusion phase than before or after. The tentative role-taking during the parallel phase gives way to the struggle for roles during the inclusion phase. Members may keep roles they assumed during the parallel phase, but they usually have to vie with others for those roles. Usually roles change as fuller expression and conflict emerge. During the parallel phase members need only to assume the various roles in the group and generally the group allows them to keep those roles until the resolution of authority crises. After resolution of authority crises, along with increased flexing of autonomy by the members, roles are occupied less by assumption and more by assignment. The process of assumption and assignment of roles is an integral characteristic of the inclusion phase.

Group members can take on infinite numbers of roles during the life of a group. Some of those more important for therapy group development and life are discussed below, but an exhaustive list is impossible and unessential.

The Indigenous Leaders

Indigenous leadership or members of the group who perform leadership functions are perhaps the most important roles to be considered. There are many kinds of indigenous leaders, and in most groups the leadership tasks are divided among them. The most obvious indigenous leader is the aggressive leader who pushes for his own way early in the group process. Members allow such a leader to take over for two major reasons. One is that the aggressive leader picks up the slack after the authority crises and allows the other members to wait before exerting their own initiative. The second reason is that other members often fear the early indigenous leaders because they usually rule through the expressed or implied threat of punishment for those who do not follow.

Another indigenous leader is the norm-setter. The norm-setter may or may not be aggressive, but more often is a skillful manipulator. With a few direct remarks or innuendos the norm-setters can make the group turn completely around and not even realize why. They might disparage certain modes of behavior or set certain standards for behavior and expression that the group inadvertently follows. When the group follows the norm-setter, this person becomes extremely powerful, being in position to determine whether people are acceptable or rejectable on the basis of whether or not they have adhered to the norms. The basis of the norm-setter's control is expressed or implied rejection of people who differ.

Still another indigenous leader is the emotional leader. The emotional leader is the first to risk his feelings. Emotional leadership often shifts during the inclusion phase, depending on the emotions at issue at the time. Some emotional leaders are first to risk warmth, anxiety, or fear; others may be better at risking initial hostility. Very often the first emotional leader will fight to maintain that leadership because the expression of anger is difficult and the positive emotional leader's domination is for the purpose of keeping angry expression at a minimum.

Dominator

The dominator of the parallel phase might very well attempt to continue into the inclusion phase. During the parallel phase, the dominator serves many functions for the other members by taking up the time so that the others do not have to risk. As the other members become more interested in risking and receiving from the group, they withdraw their support of the dominator. However, if the dominator is also the aggressive leader and/or the norm-setter, the task of controlling the dominator becomes much more difficult. Although it is best if the group handles the dominator, many times the therapist must step in and control the dominator to give the others a chance to participate. The therapist must be aware of the mixed feelings that the other members have about dominators. Part of each member wants room to interact, but another part is afraid and is happy to have the dominator fill the time. By the time others are ready to drop out because of the dominator it is certainly time for the therapist to step in strongly. Some dominators do not respond to other members, no matter how hard they try to control. Some of these dominators might have been mistakenly put into groups.

Group Thermostat

The group thermostat may combine other roles discussed above or may function solely as the thermostat. A primary function of the group thermostat is to detect emotionally laden situations and prevent their development. Detouring emotionally laden situations can be accomplished in many ways. Acting out behaviorally, joking, or simply interjecting relatively unimportant focuses are three major ways in which group thermostats operate. Thermostats may or may not be in conscious touch with their own feelings, but usually they are not. They sense impending danger in the anxiousness, seriousness, or heaviness of the situation and avoid it for themselves and the group by diverting the energies. Like the dominators, thermostats have a mandate from the group until the other members are ready to deal with more emotionally laden material. When the other members no longer need the thermostat, conflict may ensue. In the early phases of the group, thermostats play an important role in keeping the situation tolerable for everyone. Later in the group development a thermostat may at times come in handy, but usually they become resented by the other members if they are overly persistent.

Isolated and Withdrawn Members

Isolated and withdrawn members take on importance during the inclusion phase. When the group members are new to the exertion of their initiative they often become concerned with the isolated and withdrawn members. The isolated and withdrawn members represent the part of the active members that would like to withdraw and play it safe. After some early risks the other members are also bothered at having shared some of themselves without learning much about some of the other members. The question really boils down to what the isolated and withdrawn members think about the others and to their concern about possible rejection. Isolated and withdrawn members become important again as the group enters the intimacy crisis. Again, the isolated and withdrawn members represent the side of each member that fears intimacy and would like to hold back.

The Scapegoat

Scapegoats are common during the parallel and early inclusion phase of the group. If the scapegoating phenomenon does not hold back the group's development, the time comes in the later inclusion phase when the other group members will no longer need or want the scapegoat. If the scapegoat persists after that position is no longer needed in the group, the group will attempt to limit or ignore the behavior rather than feed into it.

Mascots

Mascots and objects of pity occupy the opposite roles from those of scapegoats. Where scapegoats get the hostility of the group displaced on them, mascots and group objects of pity get the flow of positive feelings toward them. In order to perpetuate the flow of positive feelings toward them, the mascots and objects of pity must sacrifice their own initiative and influence on the group. Mascots, on the one hand, are not to be taken seriously or else they lose their role. When they try to be taken seriously the group will inadvertently discount their opinions or feelings. Objects of pity, however, can, if they choose, manipulate the group to do their bidding by merely letting wishes be known. Since hostilities and disagreement with an object of pity is not allowed, the group is inclined to be manipulated quite far by objects of pity until the unexpressed anger builds to such levels that it bursts. A skillful object of pity can then make the group feel very guilty and start the cycle over again. Sooner or later the group breaks the cycle or the object of pity finds other ways to relate to the group. This cycle is most often broken by the direct expression of anger by other members toward the object of pity.

Minor Roles

Many minor roles played during the inclusion phase are based on the members' personal behavior patterns and how they might help the work of the group. Some of these roles are the logical thinker, who reasons everything out for the group; the catalyst, who is closely in touch with his own feelings and facilitates the expression of affect; the anticipators, who must clearly understand each step they and the group are about to take; and the plungers, who impel themselves and the group into situations and then work them out.

Finally, there is the junior therapist, who is a counterdependent person who tries to help everyone else in the group but does not risk much about himself or ask for anything for himself. The junior therapist provides a great deal of help to others and sets some norms for everyone participating in the helping process. However, the junior therapist needs to be helped to get something for himself. The best way to facilitate this help is to allow the junior therapist to fully complete his helping of others and then ask what the meaning of the problem or situation is for himself. The idea is that if someone becomes involved with someone else around a problem or situation, that person probably has some stake in the problem for himself.

Self-awareness Issues for the Therapist

It is crucial for the therapist to remember that each role is both assumed by the member occupying that role and assigned to the member by the other members. If there is no need for the role in the group, it will not last long. If the therapist takes it upon himself to reduce or eliminate a particular role, especially one that seems to be holding the group back, the therapist will most often be surprised to see someone else take the role or to find that the anticipated freeing of the group does not happen. However, at times a role is perpetuated by a member long after the group needs the job performed. When a member has not sensed that his role is no longer needed or when he persists anyhow, the group most often will become angry with the person and the ensuing conflict might help to reduce the objectionable behavior. It is important during these struggles that the therapist support the person occupying the role as well as the other members who want to eliminate it. The therapist must be aware of the needs that the role once served for all the group members and must help everyone understand both what the former role meant and what the change means.

Summary

Any particular person's occupation of a role is a function of that person's predisposition for the role and of who else is available to fill it. Leadership, for example, is a function of the person's predisposition for leadership and the availability of others in the group who might also be predisposed for leadership. The relative capacities of the several candidates for the job and their degree of acceptance by the other members will determine who wins the leadership struggles.

Roles continue to develop and redevelop until the first resolution of an intimacy crisis. During the intimacy crisis, roles become rigidified and slowly lose importance during the mutuality phase. Roles become less clear as the group fully develops. Everyone shares more of all the tasks that might have been relegated to particular roles during inclusion.

5

Intimacy
Crises

Sharing your sense of regard, of color
and of pain,
I grew.
     — Jerilyn Elise Miripol

The first intimacy crisis to be resolved is the watershed between the struggles of the inclusion phase and the often idyllic existence of the mutuality phase. While other intimacy crises follow throughout the life of the group, the first successful resolution of an intimacy crisis serves to establish the affective bonds among the members and lays to rest some of the more basic fears of rejection that powered the turmoil of the inclusion phase. Prior to the first resolution of an intimacy crisis, members live in fear of total rejection for what they say, feel, or do. They might phrase it, "If you don't like my ideas, feelings, or actions, you don't like me." After the first resolution of an intimacy crisis, members feel more basically accepted and less afraid of rejection. Rejection becomes more partialized or differentiated toward particular statements, feelings or actions. A member now might say, "If you don't like my thought, feeling, or action, you don't accept that part of me, but you might still like the rest of me."

Development of intimacy is generally accepted as a major and essential component of group development. However, theorists differ on the place of intimacy in group development. The sequential theorists are in substantial agreement that intimacy follows and is a product of the formation phase of group development (see, for example: Tuckman, 1965; Bennis and Shepard, 1974; Northen, 1969; Hartford, 1971; Garland et al., 1965). While the sequential authors are in substantial agreement with the intimacy phenomena described below, they are inclined to view the advent of intimacy as more of a singular phenomenon, fixed in its sequence between group development and the full maturation of the group, which in this discussion is called mutuality phase. The fact of the initial development of intimacy being a phase in itself holds true in the kinds of groups that the sequential authors base their theories on— that is, relatively short-term groups with limited goals and focus. (Examples are

170

found in the goal of developing as a group for the training group purposes, and the myriad of short-term and supportive goals of the group work authors.) Groups of latency-age children, if they do reach a modicum of intimacy, may achieve a more primitive intimacy appropriate to their age, which is like pseudo-intimacy described below for groups of normal or neurotic adults. Early adolescents can achieve some degree of intimacy in their process and will indeed spend considerable time in a state resembling pseudo-intimacy. However, pseudo-intimacy is age-appropriate for adolescent groups and its development in adolescent groups can serve as a growth experience for the members.

The recurrent phenomenon theorists like Bion (1961) and Schutz (1966) more aptly describe the recurrence in their respective pairing and affection dynamics. Whitaker and Lieberman (1964) take a further step in basing their entire theory of group development on the constantly recurring progression in the group developing a climate of intimacy through the resolution of many focal conflicts. Slater (1966:86-89) also supports the omnipresence of intimacy issues in the life of a group in his notion of members' progressively decreasing libidinal involvement with the therapist to increasing libidinal involvement with peers.

BEGINNINGS OF INTIMACY

If the core of intimacy between and among the group members can be defined as shared affective contact or empathy, intimacy begins with the pairing and sub-grouping of the inclusion phase. Intimacy crises are the watershed phenomena that follow occurences of shared affect among most or all the members of the group. Intimacy crises can and do arise at any moment of the group's life. They become more critical toward the end of the inclusion phase. A group may have several intimacy crises during the inclusion phase without resolving these crises. By not resolving an intimacy crisis, the group members regain and sustain their emotional distance. When group members do resolve intimacy crises, they move toward acceptance of intimate contact and develop norms for sustaining and gaining more affective contact. Not resolving an intimacy crisis is akin to Whitaker and Lieberman's notion of a restrictive resolution to a focal conflict; resolving an intimacy crisis is akin to their concept of an enabling resolution.

While affective contact between members may have begun during the parallel and inclusion phases, some major differences are seen in affective contact during and after intimacy crises begin to be resolved. Before resolution of intimacy crises, members may have the same feeling: "I feel the same way you do," "I have often felt the same way," "You mean you feel the same way?" These affective contacts are the bases of the important universalizations or legitimizations of feelings through consensual validation during the parallel phase. During and after resolution of intimacy crises members are more inclined to share feelings rather than simply acknowledge that both have similar feelings: "I felt your pain, while you were expressing your anger at Joe. I found myself getting angry at him too. It reminded me of how angry I am at. . . ." Empathy becomes the basis of affective contact after intimacy crises begin to be resolved. Empathy may begin between pairs of members or subgroups during the inclusion phase and members may experience some crisis phenomena after empathetic contacts. However, as the empathy grows to encompass most, if not all, the group members, then crises of intimacy become more pronounced. Resolution of intimacy crises become increasingly essential if a climate of empathy is to be achieved and maintained.

Early Barriers to Intimacy

Before entering groups, most people fear the possible hostility, punishment, or rejection they might experience in the group. However, once in the group, many people find that they have more difficulty accepting and tolerating intimacy. The many fears of intimacy stem from past experiences in which intimacy harbored many concomitant dangers. Resolution of intimacy crises entail the identification and reduction of the fears each person experiences on approaching intimate relationships (Slater, 1966; Gibbard and Hartman, 1973). For intimacy to progress in the group, the group must reduce or resolve some of the initial fears sufficiently for members to maintain contact with each other. In subsequent intimacy crises, which take place frequently during the mutuality phase, more fears of intimacy are reduced and the capacity of members for intimacy in relationships is enhanced through intimate experiences.

In the first intimacy crisis, members must resolve to at least maintain contact and move toward each other to find out if their worst fears are indeed confirmed in the group. Perhaps one of the most therapeutic and growth-producing experiences of intimacy crises arise from the corrective emotional experiences that group members have with intimacy. Many of the conflicts arising from past intimacies either do not arise in the group or, if they do arise, are much more easily dispelled than the member had hoped. The resolution of intimacy crises is one of the most frightening and growth-producing experiences in group therapy. No matter what each member came to therapy for, the development of intimate relationships in the group is bound to prove helpful.

Self-awareness Issues for the Therapist

The therapist's own capacity for and fears of intimacy are extremely important aspects of how well he will be able to cope with intimacy crises. Two major functions of the therapist in an intimacy crises center on *allowing* and *helping* the group members to develop intimate relationships. Therapists who are well capable of intimacy and comfortable with it can allow members to make contact with each other and develop empathic bonds. Therapists who have their own conflicts about intimacy are inclined not to allow members to solidify intimate relationships despite overt efforts to support intimacy or they are inclined to force intimacy prematurely or too deeply too soon, exacerbating fears to the point of panic within and among the members. In either event, the resolution of the intimacy crisis will be hampered, if not prevented. An additional factor besets therapists during an intimacy crisis in that they may experience some feelings of exclusion or at least envy of the members for their growing closeness. If the therapist's relationships outside the group are not sufficiently gratifying or are in a state of turmoil, there is danger that he will seek closeness with the group to meet his own needs or will disallow intimacy among the members in order to retain the primary relational ties of the members to the therapist. Group members are highly vulnerable to the feelings of the therapist with respect to developing intimacy (Slater, 1966) and very small signs of prohibition from the therapist can cause major impediments to the development of initial intimacy among the group members.

AFFECTIVE POLARITIES: A CONVERGING OF ISSUES

Many affective issues converge on an intimacy crisis. Central to the affective convergence in intimacy crises is the search and longing for intimacy counterposing the fears of loss of autonomy. Every member of every group has at least some fear, if not a great deal of fear of intimacy. When considering a group for therapy, most people express fears of the possible hostilities, punishment, and rejection and they express concern over loss of autonomy. They might ask, "Can I be myself in this group?" However, after going into group therapy, most appear to handle the hostility, punishment, and rejection possibilities with more ease than they thought possible, and the fears of intimacy loom much larger than they would have anticipated.

The list of intimacy fears is endless, since nothing else in group therapy life conjures up more affect from past and concurrent life experiences. The particular fears for a given individual will depend on the kinds of experiences that individual has had or is having with others outside the group.

Fears of Loss of Autonomy

Loss of autonomy serves as the major focal point of most intimacy fears (Slater, 1966; Gibbard and Hartman, 1973). The association between intimacy and loss of autonomy is based on past experiences with intimacy, beginning very early in childhood. Early child-parent relationships are often characterized by threatened rejection for expressions of autonomy and initiative. Thus, when children assert their individuality, they run the risk of rejection. If group members have had early experiences in which rejection was the price for autonomy, they fear intimacy as a plunderer of autonomy.

Another major life experience that builds toward the autonomy versus intimacy dilemma is the early adolescent peer-group experience. Intimacy in early adolescent peer experiences is often synonymous with sameness. Moreover, even people whose parents allowed autonomy within a close relationship may have had subsequent peer experiences in which autonomy and intimacy were juxtaposed. Among adolescents, this might be phrased, "If we look, think, and act, alike, we are close. Anyone who is different is out." People who had early experiences with parents in which autonomy and intimacy were at odds may have had these experiences further supported during early adolescence.

Early childhood and early adolescence are not the only times when individuals experience a conflict between their inner strivings toward autonomy and their quest for intimacy. During latency and after adolescence they may have had experiences in which loss of autonomy in intimacy was confirmed or disproved. However, even if the individual's later experiences were supportive of maintainance or development of autonomy within intimate relationships, each person still brings those remnants of experiences to the contrary to a therapy group.

Fear of Loss of Identity

Another major fear of intimacy is tied to a more advanced form of autonomy versus intimacy. Fear of loss of identity in an intimate relationship takes many forms during the intimacy crisis. Most important of the fears of loss of identity concern the loss of sexual identity (Slater, 1966). As group members experience warm feelings toward the other group members, these feelings are highly sexualized. While sexual feelings may indeed be a part of the warmth and closeness that members experience, there is a major presexual element of the affective attachments developing in the group (Gibbard and Hartman, 1973). Those members with sexual conflict may experience some threat in their feelings of attraction and attractiveness to the opposite sex. Some members will attempt to act on these feelings so as to prevent any deeper or more basic attachment from developing. However, of greater concern are the feelings of warmth to members of the same sex. In heterosexual groups, group members will often focus on feelings toward the opposite sex to preclude feelings toward members of the same sex. Earlier alliances that may have developed along sex lines during the inclusion phase will often give way to heterosexual pairing in order to compensate for warm feelings that may have developed toward members of the same sex. These heterosexual feelings may be manifest in attempts at seduction in the group or by intense interest in discussion of heterosexual problems or exploits outside the group. In either event, the heterosexual intensity is aimed at reassurance of one's self and others of one's own heterosexuality. Resolution of the intimacy crisis often requires much work on the reducing of sexual fears inherent in mutual attraction.

Fear of Loss of Control

Loss of control is another widespread fear. Many group members fear that they may lose control and also that other group members may lose control. Loss of control directly relates to the basic feelings of loss of autonomy in relationships. The specific fears of the individual are that loss of control will arise when he becomes overwhelmed with the relationship and that he will either be rendered powerless or plunge headlong into relationships without restraint. The concomitant fear is either that other members may take over, taking advantage of his loss of control, or that the other members may pursue relationships with a vigor that he would find difficult to stop.

The fear of being swallowed up by other members or the group is directly related to the loss of autonomy and the loss of control. Ultimately in the fear of being swallowed up is the fear of being forced back into relationships which members have found smothering and in which they must relinquish their identities. The fear of helplessness in close relationships is also tied to the fear of being smothered.

Other Fears

In group therapy fears of ultimate punishment, rejection, or abandonment also arise in the intimacy crisis. Fears of punishment and rejection stem from many sources. Parents of some members may have prohibited a person from establishing meaningful relations with people outside the family. Such members often feel disloyal to the family and the therapist when they move into relationships with peers and they fear that the family and the therapist will punish and reject them for establishing such relationships. Other fears of punishment and rejection stem from member's own feelings about themselves. Since most people come to group therapy with some inner feelings they feel very bad about, they fear that in close relationships the other members will discover their inner feelings and punish or reject them. The members may or may not be aware of these inner feelings that make them feel they are basically bad people, but many group members have some sense of inner rot they feel must not be discovered by others (Ormont, 1968).

The fear of abandonment arises from the pragmatic perception that the group will not last forever and that ultimate separation from the other group members is inevitable. The nearer the approaching end of the group, the more people hold back from investing in relationships. Other fears of abandonment may stem from real-life experiences with death and separation from significant relationships and the fear of entering new relationships with the same possible consequences.

Finally, among the more recurrent problems of intimacy is a basic distrust of other people. Although trust issues permeate all of group development up to the first resolution of an intimacy crisis, for most members intimacy comes about because of increasing trust levels among the members. Persons with a high degree of distrust (verging toward the paranoid) will have extreme difficulty tolerating a close situation. Many such people must either leave the group or do things that cause them to be dropped from the group, if indeed they have survived in the group to this stage. Once affective contact is made with a highly paranoid person, that person will either begin to let down the barriers or be forced to leave the group.

Role of the Therapist

The therapist's role during the intimacy crisis is highly complex. Therapists must give support and *permission* for members to sustain affective contact while sensitively reducing fears of intimacy through unearthing and examining these fears. Problematic for therapists is the relinquishment of the primary affective attachment between them and the individual members. The therapist's own longings for and fears of intimacy loom large and can stand in the way of his granting permission and support for the members to join together affectively. Both his longing for and fears of intimacy could cause the therapist to hold the group back from making contact. He could accomplish this through punishment and rejection of members for getting intimate or through forcing too much intimacy too soon, which would cause the members to either flee or develop norms that would allow them to seem to be making contact while in reality they emotionally withhold themselves from the experience. The process might then become an intellectualized one in which members behave as if they were intimate but they remain essentially not emotionally involved in the process.

After the first resolution of an intimacy crisis, feelings become a part of the overt process of the group. If an intimacy crisis is not resolved, feelings basically move back into repression and the group either frankly regresses to the inclusion of parallel phase or proceeds on a very superficial level. The group pairs or subgroups may experience a few intimacy crises before resolving one. After resolving the first intimacy crisis the group will experience more intimacy crises during the mutuality phase. Each subsequent crisis gets progressively easier for the group to resolve and results in deeper levels of sharing affect. Thus, the first resolution of an intimacy crisis is the crossroads for affect. Successful resolution starts the progressive integration of affect with overt behavior in the group.

MAJOR BEHAVIORAL FEATURES

Initial affective contact, followed by flight, and ending in reapproachment are the most pronounced behavioral features of intimacy crises. Before the first resolution of an intimacy crisis individual members may have had some affective contact with one or several other members, but not with everyone in the group. A moment of empathy among most or all the group members will trigger an intimacy crisis.

Initial Affective Contact

Some common examples of initial affective contact arise in groups of parents when one parent first expresses angry or hateful feelings toward a child and the other parents readily emphathize; in groups of presurgery patients when one begins to express fears of the surgery and others join in with the same or similar fears; and in groups of young adults when one expresses how very lonely he feels and the others respond with their loneliness.

Initially, the members may pursue the empathic experience for the duration of the meeting. However, initial intimate contact often takes place toward the end of a meeting. Members usually leave the meeting in which the affective contact took place in a good mood with a good feeling about the meeting. Comments like "This has been the best meeting so far," might be plentiful.

In the meeting following the initial affective contact there may be an initial attempt to regain the moment of the proceding meeting, but usually there is not. Members most often seek distance from each other and regress in both the content and process. If they were to express their feelings, it might sound like this: "What happened last week? I wasn't sure I was coming today. Where are we going in this group?" The group members are frightened and need to gain distance from each other so they can carefully consider whether or not to attempt further contact, and how to go about it. If the group members are allowed to maintain their distance in the meeting and are not forced to pursue the intimacy too quickly, then a gradual process of moving toward each other will begin again. Depending on members' capacities for verbalizing, they might begin to discuss their desires for continued closeness and their fears of closeness. Groups less able to deal with issues verbally will progressively attempt to renew intimacy. At any rate, the movement toward intimate contacts may or may not take place in the meeting following the initial contact.

Before any further intimacy can develop, the group members must understand the meaning for themselves and others of the prior intimate contact and must establish understandings (norms) about further intimate contacts. Renegotiation of norms, or what is called a normative crisis (Garland et al., 1965), is part of the members' efforts to develop what is expected and not expected of themselves and others if further affective contact is to take place. The substance and boundaries of affective contact are thus determined. The nature and boundaries negotiations, in which each member expresses his own wishes for intimacy and finds out what others' wishes are, may take place directly or indirectly.

Direct and Indirect Approaches to Intimacy

When the normative crisis occurs through direct discussion, the desires for intimacy, as well as expectations and limits for other people will be expressed: for example, "If I were to . . . what would you do? How would you feel? What would you think?" When the normative crisis is dealt with indirectly, through then-and-there content or through behavior, it will be characterized by talking about situations that reflect the wishes and boundaries or by testing intimate contacts and reacting to them. A member might say, I know this guy who . . . and when he does that other people. . . ." The testing and reactions essentially are the expressions of wishes for intimacy and the boundaries that the members place on intimacy: "We should . . . or we shouldn't . . . when someone. . . ." When the intimacy crisis is handled indirectly, fears are reduced either through what the therapist and what members have to say about those situations outside the group or through their reactions to the tests in the group: "It's okay if we. . . ."

Essentially what the members must find out from the intimacy crisis is, first, that their wishes for intimacy are legitimate and that they are shared by the other members and, second, that they will be able to maintain sufficient control of the situation to have some control over their involvement. In other words, if and as members find that they can have intimate contacts without sacrificing their autonomy or identity, they will continue to move toward each other.

Readiness for Intimacy

Within any group members will differ in their readiness and capacity for intimacy. When some members are extremely far behind the others in either readiness or capacity for intimacy, the group may be slowed in the development of intimacy. At first, initial intimacy will usually take on an inclusion-like aura; this, because a major subgroup will form around intimacy within the group and will tend to reject the individual or subgroup that is holding back the intimacy. However, as the major subgroups resolve intimacy crises, they will have increasing tolerance for those individuals not included. If intimacy in the large subgroups is solid, it can allow others who are not ready to be intimate to remain where they are while extending a constant invitation for those members to join in. However, if that invitation becomes an insistence that the member either join or experience punishment or rejection or both for not joining, then the solidity of the intimacy is in question. To the degree that the intimate subgroup is pre-occupied with those who are not intimate with them, there are unresolved intimacy fears belaboring the intimate subgroup.

Often, as is seen in early adolescent groups, members sustain early intimate contacts by becoming a subgroup of the whole and rejecting everyone outside the group. The enemy are usually adults, but often other groups or other adolescents outside the groups are prime targets for group displacement of their intimacy fears. If and as the members become more comfortable with their own intimacy, the rejection of outsiders within and without the group decreases. In a sense, as the group accepts itself as a social entity, it is better able to accept others.

Role of the Therapist

The role of the therapist in relation to the group process during intimacy is mainly concerned with faciliating affective contact, reducing fears of intimate contact, and giving permission for the group to have intimate relationships. It is important that the therapist accept the initial regression and flight in the face of the initial affective contact and to help the members sensitively reapproach each other. If the therapist does not accept the regression patiently or, particularly, if he forces intimacy, accelerating the development of intimacy will either cause further flight and regression or will drive the group into a pseudo-intimate process in an attempt to please the therapist. Pseudo-intimate processes result in very narrow ranges of expression and behavior in the group, and could develop into a pleasant but perennially superficial atmosphere. The group will find comfort and acceptance, but at the expense of individual autonomy and identity. Members might express their feelings thus: "We all agree and like each other. We have no hostilities among us." Deeper emotional conflict will not be allowed to emerge and be resolved in the group.

Full resolution of intimacy crises serve as the bases for the group to accept itself as an entity, accept others outside the group, and finally provide an atmosphere in which each individual member can better accept himself.

SOURCE OF GRATIFICATION: SELF AND PEERS

Successful resolution of intimacy crises bring a sense of inclusion and autonomy for the individual member. To be included, while retaining freedom for autonomy raises the spectre for individuals that they themselves are another source of gratification. During the authority crisis, the individual experienced a partial loss of the therapist as the prime source of gratification and began to see the group as the possible source of gratifications. With the resolution of the intimacy-autonomy dilemma, the member feels support as well as responsibility for the initiative on his or her own behalf. The feeling of more responsibility is accompanied by some feeling of loss of the other members as prime sources of gratification.

Although fears of loss of autonomy pervade the intimacy crisis, the individual also fears autonomy. When people have been subjected to many experiences in which autonomy is achieved at the price of rejection in relationships, they also come to fear the actualization of autonomy, as they feel unable to be autonomous. These people are actually more than ready to sacrifice their autonomy for inclusion so that they do not have to take responsibility for themselves (Tucker 1973: 270). Thus, when the group includes these members and allows them their autonomy, with that acceptance they experience some loss of dependency on the group.

If all goes well in resolution of intimacy crises, the members will then see the therapist, the other members, and to some extent, themselves as sources of gratification. A member who continues to deny needing the therapist and/or the other members as sources of gratification may be just as uncertain of himself as a source of gratification as the members who are more frankly traumatized by the prospect of being free to take initiative.

> Victor, a young man who had spent many years in hospitals with a serious childhood disease, came into an adult group to gain some ability to relate to other young adults. At first, Vic was very clear about wanting the therapist and other members to reach out to him. When they did, Vic would reluctantly respond almost as if he were a little boy and his parents were asking him to say something in front of strangers. After considerable confrontation by the other members, Vic began to take more initiative for himself and slowly began to reveal some of his inner torments about his illnesses and other people. The first time that Vic shared some of his deeper feelings with the group, he received considerable affective support. But when he came to the next meeting, he announced he was quitting. The group helped him through the first intimacy crisis but a few weeks later Vic again shared a great deal with the group and admitted that this was the first time he had shared these feelings with any one other than his mother. When Vic returned at the following meeting he was again determined to quit the group, this time citing the group's failure to take initiative in reaching out to him anymore.

Vic's crisis was, indeed, that he experienced his ability to gain emotional support from other people on his own behalf and if he went further he would have difficulty justifying his hostile dependency on his parents in which he gets them to provide most of the initiative for taking care of him.

RELATIONAL ISSUES: INITIAL INTIMACY

Almost by definition the main relational feature of the first resolution of an intimacy crisis is initial intimacy among the members. Although intimacy between individual members and within subgroups builds up during the inclusion phase, the first experience with empathy for the whole group touches off the intimacy crisis. The first successful resolution of an intimacy crisis through sustained affective contact among the members begins to lay to rest the dominance-submission struggles of the inclusion phase.

Relinquishment of the dominance-submission strivings follows from the reduction of the fears of loss of control and from feelings of freedom and autonomy in the group. The need to dominate or be dominated during the inclusion phase directly relates to the need to maintain control as a manifestation of acceptance or the need to relinquish control to be accepted by others. Affective contact that promises to be sustained or regainable at will provides members with feelings of security in their basic acceptance by other members. With acceptance secured, members feel less need to gain dominance over others and less need to trade submission for acceptance.

The more members begin to share affectively, the closer and the more accepted they feel. Through successive resolutions of intimacy crises, the members broaden and deepen their ties to one another by sharing more of their affect and strengthening the empathic bond. Shared fears of intimacy themselves become bases for further empathic bonding.

Insurance of acceptance and inclusion in the group is the most significant contribution of the intimacy crisis for group development. Assured acceptance brings to climax the processes of the parallel and inclusion phases and sets the foundation for the remainder of the group. Once a group has assured acceptance for all its members energies are freed for other work and not consumed by the need to survive with others in the group. Less effort is needed for developing and maintaining the system and more effort can go to forwarding the goals of the group and its individual members. Thus, the scene is set for the major work of the mutuality phase. With acceptance within the group assured and energy freed for other work, the members are free to pursue their goals in depth in an atmosphere in which they feel relatively trustful and secure.

The significance of resolution of intimacy crises for each member's own life situations is monumental. Assuming that every person who enters a group has some reservations about intimacy in relationships and that developing the capacity for intimacy is a life task for everyone, the experience of developing and sustaining intimate relationships in a group can serve as a basis for members to develop intimate relationships outside the group.

SELF-OTHER CONCEPT: EQUALITY

The empathic sharing of feelings beginning with the intimacy crisis is a major factor in bringing about feelings of equality among all the members of the group. The more overt signs of commonality, superiority and inferiority, and uniformity on which self-other concepts were based during the parallel and inclusion phases give way to the basic humanity inherent in the commonness of shared feelings. Sharing and acceptance of feelings in self and others gives rise to feelings of equality among the group members.

The only holdouts from feelings of equality resulting from shared feelings in the group are those people who tend toward either in paranoid or depressive ends of the paranoid-depressive continuum.

A major factor in the leveling effect of the empathic sharing of intimacy crises is the reduction of the core of rotten feelings in each individual. As each member fully realizes that everyone else shares the feelings that made him feel he was rotten, other measures of inferiority-superiority, difference, uniqueness, and such become inconsequential in comparison to the commonality of feelings. The basic perception and acceptance of the common core of feelings within all members of the group during the first and subsequent resolution of intimacy crises pave the way during the mutuality phase for individuals to accept their uniqueness and the uniqueness of the other members.

POWER RELATIONS:REDUCTION IN POWER STRUGGLES

Intimacy crises themselves are often touched off by the resolution of major power struggles among the members. Basic to the power issues that beset any group during the inclusion phase is the issue of acceptance with autonomy. The individual can say, "I can be myself and assert myself and still be accepted. With resolution of a power struggle and the affective contact that results, the affective bond that develops between the adversaries, along with assurances of power for both sides, brings with it implicit permission for autonomy with acceptance. The very assurance of acceptance with autonomy reduces the impetus for further power struggles, so that remaining struggles have less intensity after the initial affective contact resulting from major power resolution. Thus, the power struggles of the inclusion phase serve as vehicles for developing intimacy with autonomy; the struggles become extinct because of the resolution they bring about.

Intimacy brought about without resolve of power issues leaves both acceptance and autonomy in doubt. Consequently, until and unless those power struggles are resolved, no depth of intimacy is possible. People who fear intimacy and cannot assuage their fears in intimacy crises will need to perpetuate power struggles in the group. Having and retaining power is felt to be insurance of acceptance and autonomy. The individual tells himself "If they do as I say, maybe they accept me." Those in power feel in charge of the acceptance process; they feel they can therefore determine who is accepted or rejected and the power over the others is in itself assurance of autonomy.

Role of the Therapist

A difficult task for the therapist during intimacy crises arises from the need to perceive the fear in people who hold onto and brandish power while the other members draw together. It is often difficult to distinguish between those

members with true needs to hang onto power and those who are simply perpetuating conflict in order to preclude intimacy. Both fear the approach of intimacy,
but those who are simply perpetuating conflict are more easily helped with their
fears than those who must cling to power. The therapist's own feelings about
power and the degree to which his feelings about power and autonomy conflict
will influence whether he can sensitively help the power-fast members with their
underlying fears or allow the power struggles to gain renewed vigor. To be helpful it is crucial that the therapist accept both those who more easily relinquish
power and those who do not.

Resolution of the power struggles in the intimacy crisis means that power
will be shared by all members and the therapist. The sharing of power among the
therapist and members supports each member's acceptance with autonomy. In
addition to laying the groundwork for full group development, the achievement of a balance of power in the group gives all members the experiences of
relationships in which they are accepted with autonomy intact and in which
they can relate to others, accepting them with their autonomy.

CONFLICT: HIATUS

Since early intimacy crises are often set off by resolution of major inclusion conflicts there is a a hiatus in conflict during the crisis itself (Bennis and Shepard,
1974). Prior to the intimacy crisis, each conflict held the ultimate threat of
punishment, rejection, or exclusion from the group for difference. After the intimacy crisis the fears of punishment, rejection, and exclusion become much less
of a concern for adversaries in a conflict.

The relative absence of overt conflict during the intimacy crisis does not
mean that conflicts do not exist. Inclusion struggles have reasonably settled the
questions of inclusion, norms, goals and members have begun the task of differentiating themselves from each other. There still may be smaller issues to settle
with regard to norms, goals and differentiation, but the basic feeling of inclusion
for all members makes it easy for further work on norms, goals and differentiation to flow easily. Beginning with the first resolution of an intimacy crisis,
members feel freer to assert their desires for the group and to express disagreement with the desires of others. Due to the bonds established during the
resolution of intimacy crises, disagreements are easily settled since members are
more receptive to compromises that grant each member his wishes. Power issues
no longer prevent members from being receptive to alternate opinions and
opposing ideas.

Thus, the hiatus in conflict during the intimacy crisis is brought about by
the feeling of acceptance, feelings of freedom to assert one's own opinions, and
receptivity to other members that, due to resolution of power struggles, all
members experience. The successful resolution of the intimacy crisis sets the
stage for the easier flow of conflict during the mutuality phase.

Prohibitions of Conflict

Groups tend to prohibit conflict somewhat during the first resolution of an intimacy crisis and some distance beyond. Often members fear losing the intimacy if they become disagreeable with and to others in the group. If intimacy is forced on the group prematurely, either by the therapist or by some of the members, then the group is more likely to disallow conflict. The reasons for the disallowal of conflict during the intimacy crisis stem directly from the fact that the intimacy is premature, that it has not been established on the basis of resolution of inclusion conflicts. Therefore, exclusion fears, power struggles and, particularly, the question of acceptance with autonomy have not been settled. Although members experience closeness, they continue to fear both rejection and taking initiative. Reworking the inclusion issues may be difficult for such a group because they have all experienced acceptance, even though it may have cost them their autonomy. Dominant members fear the loss of their dominance that could come in any further struggles since they fear that full resolution of inclusion issues will result in loss of their power. Reopening of inclusion issues by the therapist could result in scapegoating the therapist as a means of preserving the status quo and precluding the rejection of the members themselves. Members are often inclined to choose the less satisfying but safer superficial intimacy rather than risk the hazards of reopening inclusion strife.

In the same way that drop-out potential is highest during the inclusion phase, a re-opened inclusion struggle harbors many possibilities for drop-out due to fear of rejection. For those members wielding power, intimacy while in the power position supports their prior feelings that power insures acceptance. Threatened or actual loss of that power may seem to them tantamount to rejection and may be too great a blow for them to continue in the group.

Pseudo-intimacy

If a group persists with the facade of intimacy, this will have impact on the nature and range of expression that the group is capable of. Constricting norms will develop which prohibit conflict and promote overt agreement (Whitaker & Liberman, 1964). Members may even feel bad about their private disagreements, thinking they are the only members holding such thoughts and, therefore, they are unacceptable and even pathological. To perpetuate the myth of intimacy, members screen out their negative feelings and express only their positive feelings toward the group. Some groups go as far as to screen out negative feelings toward anything and anybody outside the group, afraid that allowing the entry of any negative feelings might threaten to call up negative feelings within the group. Most groups, however, allow some negative feelings toward objects outside the group and some groups even engage in a scapegoating process to control the negative feelings by focusing them outside the group or on the therapist if the therapist threatens the myth.

Early adolescent groups in particular handle their intimacy by disallowing conflict and difference. This is an age-related phenomenon; early adolescents are generally not capable of a higher level of intimacy than perpetuating a facade of intimacy through lockstop commonality. But even in early adolescent groups the therapist can work on broadening and deepening the intimacy to allow for difference and its concomitant improved self-acceptance as major goals for work with the group.

In adult groups where pseudo-intimacy is perpetuated, the therapist is faced with the decision either to re-open inclusion struggles or to hope that, over time, members will become sufficiently certain of their inclusion and differentiation to slowly develop capacity for tolerating conflict, differences, negative feelings and opinions and, ultimately, individuality. In either event it remains the task of the therapist during and after resolution of intimacy crises to support differences as they emerge and to reduce fears of negative expression in the group.

Self-assessment Issues for the Therapist

The therapist's own feelings about intimacy, conflict, and negative expression influence greatly whether the therapist also seeks comfort in the pseudo-intimacy or helps the group toward deepening the intimacy. Danger to the therapist is real, since re-opening the inclusion struggles could cause the dominant members to fear the therapist and could lead to full-scale scapegoating of the therapist.

The development of pseudo-intimacy is the other side of the group avoiding deep intimacy. During the inclusion phase, some groups will avoid intimacy by perpetuating inclusion conflicts beyond the point at which they could reasonably be resolved. In both instances, unending conflict or absence of conflict, the therapist must consider the capacity of the group for intimacy and the many fears that can prevent real intimacy. Latency-aged groups generally have a low capacity for intimacy and will have long, drawn out inclusion struggles; reaching some degree of pseudo-intimacy would be a reasonable expectation for this age. Early adolescent groups might get caught in prolonged inclusion struggles, but then can shift into pseudo-intimacy with a minimum of conflict; again this would be within reasonable expectations. Adult groups within the normal and neurotic ego levels can be expected to resolve the inclusion struggles and achieve a full measure of intimacy if they are not prematurely forced into or prevented from intimacy by the therapist or fearful group members. Groups of adult schizophrenics can develop a good feeling about other group members and may need to submerge conflict to preserve that good feeling. Adult schizophrenics need a great deal of direct help on the issue of separating disagreement and conflict from rejection.

COHESION: BEGINNINGS OF TOTAL GROUP

Resolution of early intimacy crises mark the beginning of total group cohesion. Prior to the resolution of early intimacy crises, feelings of "me and them" (parallel phase) and "us and them" (inclusion phase) give way to a total "we" feeling in the group. From the intimacy crisis through the remainder of the life of the group, members in the group become "we"; "theys" are people outside the group.

This initial cohesion is intense among the members. Members feel a tie not only to all the other members but to the group itself. Subordination of one's own interests in favor of the group comes easily to most members, since they also feel part ownership of that entity.

The "we" feelings in the group are a direct extension of the former "we" feelings within the subgroup in earlier phases. While the feeling of unity is still new for the entire group, the boundaries of the group become extremely important. Who is included in the group is as important as who is not. Significant outside relationships, affiliation with other social entities, and anyone outside the group are highly suspect. That is why the introduction of a new member during the first resolution of an intimacy crisis is undesirable. The new member is likely to be rejected and excluded by the group if introduced during initial intimacy. In addition to the natural and usual hostility that the new member encounters upon entering a group, the new member will find a wall enveloping the group. If the new member is introduced to the group after the group has sustained their intimacy and cohesion for a period of time, then the entry will go much easier.

Self-awareness Issues for the Therapist

During initial intimacy, the therapist is as likely as the other group members to reject the new member. Having nursed the group through the process of formation and perhaps liking the fruit of his labors, the therapist may also feel some threat to the existence of the group as it is. The therapist usually shares the satisfaction of achieving organizational development and fears its change or destruction by introduction of the new member. Potential pain and frustration from the possibility of re-opening the inclusion struggles and regression from the newly found intimacy and cohesion easily cause the therapist to join the group against the new member. While the therapist may well be aware of the threats of the new member, taking a new member in the group during initial intimacy and cohesion would still be unwise from the standpoint of the group itself.

Depending on the degree to which the group resolves the inclusion struggles, the group cohesion after resolution of early intimacy will either grow and deepen or will be subjected to further tests of its solidity. Assuming that no phase in group life is ever completely resolved, there may be some major or minor tests of the group's solidarity during the mutuality phase. Generally, if the group has achieved intimacy as a result of reasonable resolution of the inclusion struggles, then further crises of cohesion and intimacy will be resolved more easily. Each time the group members touch on new and deeper levels of feelings, major crises of intimacy may be set off.

CONTROLS: POWER OF THE GROUP

Group controls begin with the resolution of the early intimacy crises. Before this, controls are more a matter of individual and subgroup struggles; after, controls become a matter of the group's preservation of its nature and boundaries. Before the resolution of early intmacy crises, individuals and subgroups battle for influence upon each other, with threats of punishment and rejection for noncompliance; after, group members submit to group controls because they feel they are an integral part of the group and a part of the establishment of the norms over which controls are exerted. Thus, resolution of early intimacy crises brings a shift in the nature of controls from attempts by part of the group to enforce their will on the whole group to voluntary submission by the members to the group power. While punishment may still be a part of group controls after intimacy, threat of total rejection and exclusion cease to be an active means of control.

After the resolution of early intimacy crises, group controls are exerted on behaviors that threaten the continuity of the group as an entity. Since each member is assured a place in the group, controls are aimed mostly at those behaviors of individuals that disrupt or threaten to disrupt the group. Punishment through verbal chastisement serves as the major force for control, but most often attempts to influence and dissuade a member from violating group norms serve as the major pressure for conformity. In other words, conflict of a particularized nature focuses on the questioned behavior and the attempt to gain the individual's accordance with the prevailing feeling of the group is the major vehicle for group control.

A major difference between control in the inclusion phase as opposed to control during the postintimacy crisis, is that during the inclusion phase, the issue is not just control of behavior but also involves a question of domination by those attempting to control. After the intimacy crisis, control is aimed at preserving organizational systems of which the deviant member is an integral part. Thus, both the member and the group have a stake in controlling the deviant behavior. By the same token, the deviant behavior by the member may be an important initiative for the group (Redl, 1966: 155-196). Since the major vehicle of control in a therapy group is the conflict over the behavior, at issue is the importance of the deviant behavior to the system. A full conflict, in which the members attempting to exert controls get in touch with the same underlying feelings in themselves that the deviant behavior expresses, will help to resolve the issue. A consequence of each attempt at control can be either inhibition of the deviant behavior or incorporation of the deviant behavior into acceptable behavior in the group system. In this way, the boundaries of the group can be tested and either held or extended.

Role of the Therapist

At issue for the therapist in the emergence of group control is the permanent loss of the capacity to exert full control of the group. After the emergence of group controls, the therapist can at most mediate between the controllers and the deviants or negotiate with the group on issues of control deemed important to the therapist. It would be difficult, if not impossible, for the therapist to continue control of the group.

When the therapist takes responsibility for control of deviant behavior, he or she is discounting not only the possible implications that deviant behavior may represent a new direction for the system's growth but also the meaning of the deviant behavior to all the members of the group. The therapist is, in a sense, ruling out one side of the issue of deviancy in the group and attempting to assume responsibility for control. If the therapist does take sides on the issue and wins, then further control of that behavior will reside with the therapist or with members acting for the therapist. Those acting for the therapist will lose as much by not dealing with the same issue in themselves as those who are limited in their behavior.

Sometimes it behooves a therapist, even at the risk of group regression, to exert controls on the group or on its members no matter what phase the group is in. However, the therapist must realize the kind of intrusion this behavior is into the growth both of the group and of individual members and must work to help the group regain its capacity for exerting its own controls. If the therapist cannot, because of personal, therapeutic, or institutional reasons, accept certain behaviors, then the therapist might well set a direct limit and not try to bring the group around to accepting his point of view. The group needs to understand the therapist's point of view and also needs understanding from the therapist for the group point of view. An agreement to disagree with the group yet demand conformance will better preserve group capacity for control than a process of negotiation in which the therapist cannot accept any and all outcomes.

Some groups, despite the emergence of controls on many issues, will continue to rely on the therapist for certain controls. Although the therapist may have to accept responsibility for some of these controls it is important that he or she be aware of the significance of these control issues for the members and for the group and to watch for the proper time to transfer the responsibilities for these controls to the group.

The significance of controls for a therapy group is profound. Many persons who come to therapy groups tend toward emotional constriction with too much control; others tend toward impulsive behavior with too little control. Through full participation in a therapy group, people with too much control tend to soften their harshness with themselves and those who are impulse-ridden tend to gain more control. Beginning with the resolution of early intimacy crises, members who tend toward either extreme will begin to moderate toward the range of controls that the group develops. The middle range of controls will vary from group to group, since every member participates to a greater or lesser extent in development of the ultimate range of controls. Consequently, by participating in the group controlling efforts and acceding to the controls of the group, members enhance their capacities to control their own emotional expression and behavior (Redl, 1966).

NORMS TO ACHIEVE INTIMACY

A major part of the process during intimacy crises focuses on the development of norms that will allow members to achieve the degree of closeness they desire. Norms during the parallel phase mostly concerned "company manners"; norms during the inclusion phase mostly centered on the rules for fighting and fleeing: no norms have yet developed for the expression of and response to initiate feelings. With the advent of intimate feelings, the need to establish the expectations for expression and response to such feelings becomes a crisis in itself. The very establishment of norms for the flow of intimate feelings is the crux of the intimacy crisis (Garland et al., 1965). If the norms allow the flow of intimate feelings, the intimacy crisis is headed for resolution. If the norms constrict the flow of intimate feelings, the intimacy crisis will not be resolved. Because few, if any, prior norms for coping with the intimacy were established in the group, the necessity for intimate norms will create a crisis. Thus, a normative crisis created by the sudden need for the development of ways and rules for dealing with intimacy are fundamental to the intimacy crisis. The theory of Whitaker and Lieberman (1964) most profoundly brings out the progression of norm development in therapy groups with particular clarity on the norms effecting sharing of affect.

Resolution of the normative crisis determines the nature and degree of intimacy possible in the group at that stage. The first intimacy crisis is usually the most difficult to resolve. However, the first resolution of an intimacy crisis does not open the group to any and all intimate feelings or all feelings of any kind. Subsequent intimacy crises are essential for the progressive unfolding of more and deeper levels of feelings. Successive intimacy crises during the mutuality phase are concerned with continued testing and re-examination of the previous norms toward the fuller and deeper expression of feelings.

It is neither possible nor advisable for the group to settle all intimacy issues during the first resolution of an intimacy crisis. The group needs only to establish sufficient modes of expression and response to intimate feelings to allow the level of affect available to the members at the time. If the group is pushed, either by the therapist or by the members, toward too much intimacy too soon, the result will be heightening of the intimacy fears, which will cause the group to develop unrealistic norms. Groups with unrealistically high expectations for expression of intimacy tend either to frankly regress into inclusion battles or to press forward into an intellectualized sharing of affect.

Although an intellectual sharing of affect has the appearance of real sharing, the members are not really expressing their emotions. Members will say how they think they and the others should feel, but they do not fully experience their feelings. Each member realizes that he or she is not experiencing the feelings being discussed but thinks that the other members are experiencing these feelings. This process makes each member feel less capable than the others with regard to experiencing and expressing his feelings. One of the manifestations of the intellectualized affective process is that a small range of feelings will be tolerated by the group. Members must have the right feelings; they are not allowed to have feelings that differ from those of the other members.

Time Spheres for Focus

The normative crisis may take place in the discussion of the here-and-now experiences of the group or in the then-and-there experiences of the members. The initial sharing of the affect that touches off the intimacy and concomitant normative crises is a here-and-now experience. Discussion of then-and-there situations in which intimacy is manifest may be extremely important for the unfolding of member's past experiences, fears, and means of coping with intimacy. Even when the discussion of the intimacy crisis occurs entirely in the then-and-there sphere, ideas for the ways in which intimacy can be expressed, responded to, and tolerated can be suggested through the material discussed. For example, when a member comments, "When I tell my friend how I feel, she gets upset and I didn't feel like telling her anymore," the statement can serve as a springboard to further discussion. It is important for the group to discuss the feelings encountered by the then-and-there experiences as well as for all the members to consider the similar feelings in themselves.

Although many groups experience and resolve intimacy crises through then-and-there discussion, particularly when the therapist is unaware of the crisis, there is much to be said in favor of here-and-now resolution of the intimacy crisis. A here-and-now resolution of the intimacy crisis might consist of members expressing their wishes for intimacy and exploring both their fears of intimacy and the ways in which they might be able to tolerate their own and other members' expressions of intimacy. The underlying feelings might be expressed thus: "Will you be hurt if I tell you how I feel?" "Will you understand when I tell you how I feel about you?" "Will you hurt me if I share my feelings with you?"

Assuming the therapist's awareness of his own propensities for intimacy or distance, the decision as to here-and-now or then-and-there focus is based on the readiness of the group. A group with a low capacity for intimacy might best resolve the intimacy crisis in the then-and-there. A group with a high capacity for intimacy might be able to resolve the intimacy crisis in the here-and-now. Most groups fall somewhere in between, and a combination of here-and-now and then-and-there focuses might be appropriate.

Self Issues for the Therapist

The job of the therapist during the normative crisis within the intimacy crisis is to help the group negotiate a level of expression and response to intimate feelings that is appropriate to the capacity of the group at the time. The therapist should be aware of his own comfort and discomfort with intimate feelings from two standpoints. First, the therapist must appreciate his own capacity for tolerating intimate feelings in personal relationships as well as in the professional situation. Second, the therapist must be aware of his feelings about the group members' becoming intimate with each other in ways that the therapist, because of the therapeutic role, may not be able to share. In other words, feelings of discomfort and envy may cause the therapist to interfere with the development of group modes for the flow of intimacy appropriate to their level of readiness.

Manifestations of the therapist's interference with the development of high intimacy arise when the therapist presses the group for too high a level ("Tell us how you *really really* feel."), the therapist forcing himself in the middle and thus keeping members from direct intimate contact, or when the therapist does not give overt and covert permission for members to become intimate with each other. Forcing intimacy through laboratory experiences is very difficult to accomplish without some of the negative results suggested above. Forcing the group to become intimate is closely connected to pushing the group for too high a level of intimacy. Intimate experiences without the development of norms to support the nature and degree of that intimacy create panic in the members and necessitate the regressive or intellectualized outcomes. Most important, the members do not get a chance to deal with the very reason they fear intimacy and the opportunity to develop ways of handling intimacy that might help them not only in the group but in relationships outside the group. In other words, intimacy exercises may help those who have less difficulty with intimacy to become intimate but probably will not help those who have more difficulty to grow in the capacity for intimacy (Tucker, 1973; Gibbard and Hartman, 1973).

Since most intimacy crises occur and are resolved with little awareness on the part of the therapist beyond his noticing the coming together and backing off of the group, the selection of focus is not as crucial as it might appear. The normative crisis is the major process occurring in the group during the period of backing off after initial affective contact. Unless the therapist seriously interferes, groups naturally experiment with progressive attempts at recontacting each other. The members naturally act out their wishes for and fears of intimacy and through trial and error test out the possible ways in which they can express and respond to intimate feelings.

The first resolution of an intimacy crisis increases the probability that subsequent intimacy crises will be resolved. If the early resolutions do not reach the depth desired, subsequent crises during the mutuality phase may progressively reach the desired depth. The group's failure to resolve early intimacy crises does not mean that subsequent crises cannot be resolved. Instead, gains toward intimacy can be made through each attempt at resolution, after an ultimate first resolution. More important than the fact of failure are the reasons the group failed to resolve the intimacy crises.

GOALS: FROM INDIVIDUAL TO GROUP

A major feature of intimacy crises is the synthesis of individual goals into group goals. This synthesis, which results from overt and covert goal deliberations during the inclusion phase, helps to lay a foundation for feelings of acceptance and inclusion for members. When members feel basically accepted and included, the stage is set for risking more intimate feelings. Just as the synthesis of goals serves as a catalyst for expression of intimacy, the first resolution of an intimacy crisis serves as a catalyst for the synthesis of goals. The affective contact resulting from resolution of an intimacy crisis reduces the emphasis on goals as an indicator of acceptance and inclusion. Beginning with the resolution of early intimacy crises, the affective contact progressively replaces the power and influence found in the inclusion phase as indicators of acceptance and inclusion. Members feel more a part of the group and its destiny and feel less need to influence the group toward their own ends. In addition, because of increasing cohesion there is increased feeling that the group will accept almost any and all goals that the individual has for himself and the group.

Some members hold back their wishes for themselves and the group because of their primary concern to be accepted and included under any circumstances. With the advent of intimate contact, these members feel freer to assert their goals; because their feelings of acceptance and inclusion are more assured, they are now freer to risk other desires.

Depending on the nature and composition of the group, the group's accord on goals will be either a synthesis or a confluence. Synthesis represents a full coming together on goals for everyone in the group. A synthesis incorporates the goals of all the members, and few, if any, divergent individual goals remain. A synthesis, however, is possible only when the group members are homogeneous in their needs and desires. The more homogeneous the group, the more likely the synthesis of goals can be attained.

In most long-term groups, where depth of interpersonal and/or intrapsychic insight is the overriding goal, a confluence of goals is more likely during early intimacy crises. Confluence of goals represents a phenomenon in which some group goals are common to all members and other goals, although somewhat different, run parallel to the group goals. A confluence of goals allows diverse individual goals within the group. Whether or not goals are confluent is determined less by the objective matching of the individual goals vis-a-vis group goals than by the feelings of the members toward each other. In other words, with full acceptance, inclusion, and intimate contact, an individual member's goals are perceived as valid for the group because the member is an integral part of the group. Thus, at any given moment in group life any individual member who is in affective contact with the other members can ask the group to pursue his individual goals and the group will respond.

If we can assume that most people have similar strivings in their social-emotional life, though they may differ in the relative strength of these strivings, then conceivably most human beings can find some common concern in the social-emotional experiences of any other human being. Thus, given sufficient mutual acceptance and sufficient time to pursue any and all strivings, any two individuals will find some common concern in whatever each other's strivings may be. Thus, with sufficient affective contact and sufficient time to explore everyone's strivings, strivings of every group member can become integrated into the group. However, no matter how deep the affective contact, if time is actually or is deemed to be insufficient, as it is in short-term groups, then a process of priorities will necessarily be overtly or covertly assigned to the various strivings suggested to the group for its attention.

With the first resolution of an intimacy crisis, the group starts to feel a confluence of goals. They feel, "We are all here for similar reasons," or "We all want similar things from the group." Disagreements over focus, however, will continue to take place since time is not infinite in a given meeting or in the period a member might reasonably want to spend in a group therapeutic process. These disagreements about goals and about the focus of meetings as a manifestation of goals will not indicate possible rejection of individual goals and possible concomitant rejection of the person whose goal is rejected but rather they will indicate an ordering of priorities at the time. The basic acceptance and inclusion of the individual will assure the group's work toward that individual's major goals at some time in the group's life, but less consequential goals may fall by the wayside without the individual's falling with them. The strength of the individual's need is a major factor in the group's working on his individual goals. Communication of that need rather than persistence and dominance will bring the group to focus on the individual's goal after the resolutions of early intimacy crises. Thus, the affective communication replaces domination and influence as the vehicle for asking and receiving help.

Although the negotiation of goals may never come up for direct discussion except in disputes over focus and individuals' gaining time in meetings to pursue an expressed subject, the process of goal deliberation and synthesis is omnipresent. More articulate group members, if asked during the parallel and inclusion phases, will talk about goals mostly in first-person terms, or "what I want." After the first resolution of an intimacy crisis, group members will more likely refer to "what we want" or differentiate between "what we want" and "what I want."

Self-awareness Issues for the Therapist

The therapist's own goals for the group and individual members are a highly controversial subject in group therapy circles. Many group therapists suggest that they have no goals for the group and that the group must determine its own goals. If the therapist brought the group together, then most likely he had reason for doing so. The synthesis or confluence of goals is very dependent on the therapist's awareness of his overt and covert goals for the group. A group synthesis of goals that essentially excluded the therapist's goals would severely impair the therapist's motivation to help the group toward its goals, unless the therapist were truly convinced of the efficacy of the group's goals over his own. If the therapist is unaware of his own goals for the group, he or she is less likely to have worked through the loss of his own goals and may then be in position not only to be unhelpful but also to sabotage the group's work toward its own goals.

The process of negotiating therapist goals with those of the members is best begun during the authority crises and may indeed be one of the issues over which the first or subsequent authority crises arise. If the therapist's goals are made overt and negotiated, the therapist's goals are more likely to be incorporated into the ultimate group goals.

On the other hand, if the therapist persists in his own goals for the group, the resolution of the authority crises is precluded as is successful resolution of inclusion and power struggles during the inclusion phase. Leaving no room for those goals of group members that do not coincide with those of the therapist will intensify the inclusion struggles and make the intimacy crisis almost impossible to resolve. At best, the group could achieve some degree of intimacy by rebelling against the therapist's authority and establishing its own goals in opposition to those of the therapist, thus making the therapist a common enemy. Intimacy formed around a common enemy will not allow for much latitude in relationships among the group members, will require absolute conformity to the group norms, and will submerge conflicts among the members.

The political authority of the therapist and the authority of his expertise are both at stake as he negotiates his goals with the group members. If the therapist links his professional self-esteem to the group's acceptance of his goals for the group and does not look at the reason the group can or cannot accept his goals, the therapist's capacity to help the group will be seriously impaired. A constant struggle rather than a rapport in the therapeutic relationship will result. The significance of the therapist's need to control the group and maintain political authority over the group have already been discussed under the authority crisis.

ROLES: MORE FLEXIBLE

The intimacy crisis represents a watershed for roles. Tentative roles of the parallel phase give way to status and role struggles of the inclusion phase. Roles become solidified over time, and members become more consistent in role expectations for themselves and for other group members during the inclusion phase. The group comes to rely on each member to occupy the roles assigned to him during the inclusion phase. However, part of each member's feeling of acceptance and inclusion during the inclusion phase is closely associated with the roles he occupies. Particularly important in the acceptance of the person in the role is the degree of power accorded to each role and, consequently, to each person in the group.

Affective contact in the first resolution of an intimacy crisis begins to replace other bases for acceptance in the group. As individual members deepen their affective contact with other group members, they have increasingly less need to remain in their assumed and assigned roles. In addition, they have less need to keep other group members in their assigned roles as the intimacy in the group deepens. As subsequent intimacy crises deepen the affective contact and bonds among the members, they have less need to anticipate each other's behavior; hence, stepping out of roles becomes progressively easier.

The duties assigned to each role are also shared by other group members when they have less need for specific roles. Members can begin to perform functions of other roles if they desire, although they may stick to performing role functions primarily associated with their initial roles.

The phenomenon of increased fluidity and interchangeability of roles is extremely important for the growth of all group members. During the inclusion and parallel stages, the members may well have brought past roles into the group. Some, because of the composition of the group, may have readily been able to assume roles that they had long desired but never could assume before. That others were less willing to assume these roles in the group have provided them the opportunity.

However, for most members the roles they assume in the group are characteristic of roles they usually assume with other people. With a basis of acceptance, inclusion, and affective contact, group members can begin to experiment with roles and interpersonal behavior they have long desired but have been unable to assume. Thus, the affective contact of the intimacy crisis begins the freeing of members from their characteristic roles and behavior and allows them opportunities to change their characteristic roles and relationships with other people. As these changes begin within the group, manifestations of these changes can soon be seen in relationships outside the group.

Members who share the therapist's role functions change in a particularly interesting way as the intimacy in the group deepens. During the parallel phase, members who attempt to perform some of the therapist's functions either attempt to help other members counterdependently or they question and make suggestions directly to the therapist about other members. During the inclusion phase, members who attempt to be therapist to others in the group may directly address the other members but still look to the therapist for confirmation of their help. Beginning with the first resolution of an intimacy crisis and because he or she feels acceptance by other members, the therapeutic help from one member to another becomes increasingly direct, with the individual less concerned for permission, validation, or even agreement from the therapist. Thus, the members even have freedom to share fully in the role of the therapist along with sharing the roles of other group members.

6

Mutuality
Phase

A time of dawn, now,
of laughter and loving, the warmth
and a mist of words.
　　　—Jerilyn Elise Miripol

Mutuality is the middle and mature phase of group development. A long-term adult outpatient group will spend most of its life in the mutuality phase. While this phase may be punctured by recurrent authority, intimacy, and separation crises, the resiliency of the group helps it recover at least the level of maturity achieved prior to each crisis. In fact, each resolution of the recurrent authority, intimacy, and separation crises is usually marked by group growth to new levels of autonomy, intimacy, and differentiation. Sometimes the group will regress, exhibiting some inclusion and even parallel phenomena, but it will quickly return to the mutuality phase once the issues that precipitated the regression are dealt with. Major causes of group regression during the mutuality phase are changes in leadership or membership, buildup of new authority, and intimacy issues that the group had not confronted before. The recurrent crises do not necessarily cause regression and they may be considered a part of mutuality phase phenomena. Crises during the mutuality phase can be considered more as points of growth than as regression, unless the group has major unfinished work from the parallel and inclusion phases. Such work must be cleared up before the group can deal with authority, intimacy, and separation crises without regression.

Almost all authors on therapy group development subscribe to the existence of the mature group phase. All support the close feelings, increased capacity for work, and the continued development of intimacy during the mature phase of the group; see, for example: Bion's (1961) work group; Mann's (1967) mature work; Bennis and Shepard's (1974) sub-phase of member-member understanding and acceptance; Northen's (1969) problem-solving medium group. Some authors lend considerable support for the process of differentiation reaching its peak during the mutuality phase. Bion (1961: 26), suggests that each member becomes valued for his or her uniqueness in the work group. Schroder and Harvey (1963) provide the basis for the process of differentiation throughout the group's development and its reaching a peak in the mature group. Garland et al. (1965) emphasize the differentiation process in their theory of group development and even call the mature phase of group development *differentiation.*

Depending upon how well or how fully the group has accomplished its developmental tasks in the parallel and inclusion phases and on how the group has resolved early authority and intimacy crises, the group in the mutuality phase can present an idyllic picture of human relationships. Members feel generally accepted and included in the group, affect flows progressively more freely among members, attendance becomes regularized, tensions arising from the group itself become minimal, and an air of familial comfort pervades the meetings and relationships. This is not to say that hostilities and anxieties are absent, but members are increasingly more comfortable with their own feelings and those of others and they find it progressively easier to share feelings in the group. It matters little whether the feelings are about someone else in the group or about someone outside the group.

Differences Between Mutuality and Other Phases

The fundamental differences between the mutuality phase and other phases are the levels of empathy and differentiation among the members. Empathy represents the epitome of intimacy and increasingly serves as the core of relationships among the members. Empathy begins with the first resolution of an intimacy crisis and deepens with each successive intimacy crisis during the mutuality phase. The bond of empathy changes the basic ways in which the group members view, communicate, conflict, and identify with each other. During the parallel phase, members view others in the group either as objects for potential use by the individual or as competitors for the therapist's attention. During the inclusion phase, they view other members either as allies or enemies. During the mutuality phase, they view other members as people who will deeply understand their own emotions and share in the basic feeling they have at the moment. Differences among group members become not only tolerable but important and useful because of a basic empathy for what the individual members feel (Bion, 1961: 29). Each member no longer has to defend against the thoughts and opinions of others, provided he experiences the feelings of the other members. Thus, a basic feeling of acceptance and inclusion for all members is omnipresent because of the empathic contact and levels of differentiation.

The Empathic Bond

The empathic bond of the mutuality phase is also the major source of individual growth in group therapy. Through the empathic bond there is a deep universalization of each member's feelings, which causes them to become more accepting of themselves, raises their self-esteem, and allows them to be more comfortable with who and what they are.

Because of past familial and peer-group experiences, many individuals see groups as requiring strict uniformity and conformity and they fear loss of identity. What these individuals have experienced are primary and secondary groups that were not fully differentiated as groups. The groups had not developed to the point of mutuality in which there was sufficient differentiation of members from therapist. Individual autonomy was suppressed in favor of appearances of more overt similarities in thought and behavior, which substituted for feelings of intimacy. When people experience the therapy group in a state of deep mutuality, basic acceptance—with full room for autonomy, individuality, inititiative, and empathy—supports the person's self-acceptance or identity and the acceptance of others with their unique identities.

Give-and-take among group members is facilitated as each member feels assured that sufficient acceptance is available in the group to provide emotional support for all. The counterdependent giving that characterized earlier phases of group is supplanted by free giving of one's self and free asking and accepting from others. Both those who developed giving roles and those who developed receiver roles in their past lives find it easier to reverse these roles. Thus, the dependency-counterdependency dilemma of the inclusion phase gives way to the interdependence of the mutuality phase.

Problem with Mutuality

The major problem with the mutuality phase arises from its very idyllic nature. Most people who come to therapy groups have seldom if ever experienced relationships like those in a therapy group during mutuality. Group members experience longings for permanent relationships and particularly for constant relationships based on the same empathic bonds they experience during mutuality. While work in the group may help the members to develop empathic relationships, the expectation that any relationship can be the same consistent source of support and empathy as a periodic and limited-time contact with other people should be tempered. A major part of the help provided during the mutuality phase must aim toward helping the individual experience the empathic relationships of the group while the individual is building outside relationships within realistic limits toward the time when the individual can leave the group for these major permanent relationships.

Role of the Therapist

The role of the therapist during the mutuality phase is varied. Once the group has developed solid mutuality, little anyone can do will inhibit the group's progress. If the group has progressed to the point of mutuality the therapist, most likely, was reasonably comfortable with his or her own needs for authority, control, and inclusion or was at least able to professionally discipline his use of his feelings so that difficulties in these areas did not interfere with the progress of the group. However, the major problems for therapists during the mutality phase have more to do with the therapist's needs to be the primary helper and to be viewed as the person with expertise. The therapist can no longer gain political control of the group or offer professional opinions that will not be questioned and countered by the group members. At this phase, group members also begin to feel some competence over their own lives, and they have knowledge, based on their own coping efforts, to contribute to the coping efforts of others. Each member now has a range of opinions about the origin, nature, and solutions of problems presented. While the therapist is usually seen as having the most expertise in the group, the help provided by other members can be just as potent as that of the therapist and, on occasion, even more so. While the therapist needs to continue providing insight and opinion as well as empathy, the danger of competition with group members is high. This competition by the therapist may take the form of topping the contributions of members or he may begin to question his own abilities for helping. The therapist who is reasonably secure in his professional identity will be able to value the mutual helping of the group members while still providing professional input to the discussions.

The major role of the therapist during the mutuality phase is to facilitate the mutual helping process and to lend further knowledge and insight to the process. *A here-and-now focus during the mutuality phase provides the major source of growth and change for members.* The empathic bond, along with the protection of therapist and the group as a protected social microcosm, facilitates ready change in behavior for individuals. Thus, the value and potential for change in the here-and-now focus during the mutuality phase are underscored. However, each time the group members resolve a here-and-now issue within the group, the group becomes that much more womblike for all the members. If all of the focus remains in the here-and-now, most members will experience increased difficulty in even considering ultimate termination from the group. Some few members can participate in an exclusive here-and-now focus while transferring their learning from the group situation to their outside life. However, most group members either cannot or do not make the direct connections from their group experiences without some direct help. Consequently, a there-and-then focus alternated with a here-and-now focus during the mutuality phase helps members to review and improve their outside relationships. If group members can make gains in their outside relationships, they are helped toward the time when they may have sufficient satisfaction in their outside relationships to relinquish the group.

Almost any group, if it meets long and often enough, will develop some degree of mutuality. However, it will vary considerably with each group; a major underlying variable is the level of psychosocial development of the members.

Effect of Psychosocial Level of Development

Most groups of latency-aged children can achieve a mutual toleration and liking for each other, a strong sense of belonging to the group, some capacity to share feelings, and some degree of acceptance of difference among the members. However, fears of rejection and difference remain important throughout the life of the group and are most evident in the addition of new members. The inclusion process of new members is more likely to cause such a group to regress to inclusion and parallel phenomena for a longer period of time than other groups. For example, if a new member is added to a school-year group after the first few months, the individual might continue to be viewed as the new member for the duration of the school year. It appears that if the new member did not take part in the initial inclusion phenomena, then going back and re-working this phenomena to include the new member is very difficult.

Most groups of chronic schizophrenic adults can attain a degree of tolera-tion and comfort with each other, but the omnipresence of authority, inclusion, and intimacy issues makes any depth of mutuality among all the members of the group extremely difficult. At best, over a two-year period of weekly meet-ings, a group of chronic schizophrenics can become a group with good feelings among the members but with continuing fears of authority, rejection, and differences. The addition of new members can easily cause the group to regress to parallel phenomena.

Many groups of early adolescents can achieve a constricted state of mutuality. Although protracted pseudo-intimacy in a group of early adolescents can be viewed as age-appropriate and indeed a normal step toward intimacy, the therapist must keep room for difference open by himself actively demonstra-ting acceptance of differences among the members.

Most older adolescent and adult groups may begin the mutuality phase with some pseudo-intimacy, but with continued working of authority and intimacy crises develop a depth of differentiation which grows toward the development of members' increasingly feeling acceptance for themselves and accepting others.

AFFECTIVE POLARITIES

Empathic bonds are the foundation of the mutuality phase. The empathy that begins with early resolutions of intimacy crises broadens and deepens during the mutuality phase. Empathy provides the haven, sustenance, and energy for the members to grow in the group.

The two major kinds of empathic responses are positive empathy and negative empathy. Positive empathy results when one member experiences his own feelings in another person. The actual feelings may be positive or negative; the mutuality of the feeling makes it positive empathy.

Negative empathy results when one member experiences his own feelings in another person but finds the experience very threatening or distasteful. The empathizer may or may not be consciously aware that he is empathizing, but he becomes hostile toward the other member. The negative empathizer's expression of the hostility toward the other member generally indicates how the empathizer feels about those same feelings within himself. If the hostility is explored for its meaning to the attacker as well as the attacked, the rejected feelings in the attacker can emerge, bringing about a consequent gratification and growth.

In this way, a sustained empathic process in a therapy group is manifest in an infinite series of immediately gratifying emotional fusions, interspersed with hostile rejections of undesirable feelings in others and self. Thus, the process of differentiation of thoughts and feelings *within* each group member develops and differentiation *between* members develops.

Intimacy and Isolation

The empathic bond among the members is the basis of the deepening intimacy that takes place during the mutuality phase. With each new level of empathic contact there can be a major or minor intimacy crisis. As members reach their limits for toleration of intimacy at each level they often have to isolate themselves from the group to regain or maintain control of themselves. However, as the group deepens in its levels of intimacy it becomes harder to exist in the group without being a part of the intimacy. When members experience isolation during the mutuality phase it is magnified because of the intimate atmosphere among the other members.

Members also more easily experience isolation during the mutuality phase, since small variations in their affective contact with the other members will make them feel excluded from the empathic bond. Although they might very well be in affective contact, they are not in as full contact as others may be at the time. The experience of isolation during the mutuality phase is most often related to lapses in affective contact rather than to the kind of isolation experienced in the parallel or inclusion phases.

Sometimes the individual member seeks isolation from the group because the depth of intimacy or the feelings being discussed are too threatening. The member must deal with the feelings of isolation to gain relief from anxiety and regain affective contact with the group. When all the other members are sharing feelings that are undesired by the isolated individual, the feelings of isolation are especially multiplied. The isolated member feels both threatened by the abhorred feelings and unworthy of being in the group because of his negative reactions to the feelings everyone else seems to share.

Thus, the experience of isolation for the individual member during the mutuality phase is a result of feeling temporarily alienated from the empathic process of the group. It constitutes an intimacy crisis, at least for the individual.

If the isolation occurs because the member has reached the limits of his capacity for intimacy, then the negative feelings can serve to maintain distance and may even become a rationale for leaving the group. Members who survive in the group until mutuality despite severe limitations in their capacity for intimacy cannot proceed much futher. These members must either keep the affective levels within tolerable limits for themselves or become isolated from the group. The empathy and intimacy become too threatening for these individuals and if the situation demands their dealing any further with the intimacy issues, they must drop out (Yalom, 1975: 232-234). It might be well to allow such members to drop out of the group with dignity rather than subject them to further failure. Some of these members, after a course of individual treatment or time away from the group, seem able to re-enter group therapy with increased capacity for intimacy. Allowing them a rest from the crisis seems to give them time to regroup their emotional forces and move forward. However, most of these people cannot proceed further in a group process. Sometimes a group with lesser affective contact can allow such a member to function.

Self-awareness Issues for the Therapist

To help a group with empathy and intimacy, the therapist must be well aware of his own capacities for empathy and intimacy. Negative identification and isolation are phenomena that occur for therapists as well as for group members. Ideally, the therapist shares the bond of empathy with the group members but retains the objectivity essential for helping members deal with each other. When a therapist experiences negative empathy with a member or members of the group, he should seek outside supervision or consultation; the therapist should not depend on the group to help him accept the unacceptable feelings within himself.

Therapy group members come to the group because of pain or dysfunction in their lives. Because the therapist may also be facing the same kind of life stresses at the same time, the empathic bond among the members many times can be beyond that of the therapist-member relationship. At those times when he cannot experience the full depth of the member-to-member empathy, the therapist may well experience feelings of isolation from the group. If these feelings stem from negative empathy, then the therapist needs help to get in touch with the unacceptable part of himself. However, the isolation sometimes arises because the therapist has attained a reasonable degree of mastery over these life experiences and his empathy for those in the immediate situation is thus limited. If the therapist does not fully appreciate the group's capacity to provide more empathy for some feelings or if he is threatened by the group's better ability to join each other in empathy, then the therapist may tend to interfere with the group's empathic process: he may depreciate the feelings, limit the development of the empathy, or undermine the empathic development by forcing the group to experience too much too soon (for example, by saying, "Let's get to the *real* feelings").

Even when the group is dealing with positive empathy and deepening intimacy, the therapist's own capacity for intimacy and his comfort with that capacity might cause him to interfere.

Thus, a therapist can best help a group through the profound affective experiences of the mutuality phase if he is aware of and comfortable with his own capacity for empathy and intimacy and is open to discovery of previously objectionable parts of himself. The role of the therapist at this point is to give permission, support, and help for the development of the empathic bonds among the members. With sensitive support, the therapist can help the isolated and hostile members overcome the barriers to experiencing their deeper feelings in a process from which all members grow with each member's growth.

MAJOR BEHAVIORAL FEATURES: COMMUNITY FEELINGS

Most prominent in the mutuality phase is the emergence of affect in the overt processes of the group. Prior to the mutuality phase, feelings were experienced more covertly and perhaps reflected in the behavior of the members. During the mutuality phase feelings increasingly become part of the direct communication and interaction among the members.

> Variations in member responses to threatening or anxiety-proving material from another member at the several points in group life might be as follows:
>
> Parallel Phase: "I'm not sure I'm in the right group."
>   "What are we supposed to do here?"
>   "I'd like to talk about. . . ."
>   "Do we have to talk about this?"
>   "What you ought to do is. . . ."
> Inclusion Phase: "Let's talk about something else."
>   "Knock it off."
>   "You're full of it."
> Mutuality Phase: "I'm getting angry at what you're saying."
>   "As you were talking I found myself feeling. . . ."
>   "Me too."

The climate of the group becomes increasingly comfortable and relaxed during mutuality. The comfort and relaxation are punctured by recurrent authority and intimacy crises; how often they recur depends on the psychosocial level of the group and how well these issues were resolved prior to mutuality. Inclusion struggles are at a minimum since this time most, if not all, members feel assured of their acceptance.

Fears of partial rejection for certain feelings or actions are omnipresent and serve to reinforce repressive tendencies and temper full catharsis in the group. As group members unearth and experience their feelings, other members simultaneously experience a relief that stems from recognition of the universality of deeper emotions together with increasing pressure to recognize, experience, and express their own similar emotions. Most of the conflicts during the mutuality phase can be traced to negative empathy.

Variations in behavior from one group to another are perhaps wider during mutuality than at any prior phase. Variations arise from the psychosocial levels of the members, the purpose and structure of the group, the degree and manner in which the group resolved earlier formative issues, and the role of the therapist. In short, the nature of the mutuality phase for each group is a product of its resources and early development.

Self-awareness Issues for the Therapist

The role of the therapist in relation to behaviors during the mutuality phase is in many ways the easiest of any of the phases or crises. As the mutuality of the group grows there is less and less the therapist can do to hamper or interfere with the processes since the power and resiliency of the group can counteract most interventions that might either too quickly accelerate or fankly interfere with the group processes. If the group or individual members are not ready or not interested in particular therapist initiatives, they are likely to let the therapist know rather quickly and the initiative will either be pursued on its merit or discarded much like any member initiatives.

The therapist must be fully aware of his own needs to perform helping acts, since the group members by this time have a great many ways in which they can help each other. Generally, the therapist should wait to see if the group can help a member before offering direct help or attempting to facilitate the help the group offers. However, the therapist can also feel free to inject initiatives toward resolution of a particular problem.

The often discussed issue of treatment of the individual in front of others and treatment of the group bears discussion at this juncture. Treatment of the individual is often confused with one-to-one discussions that take place between the therapist and a member during a meeting. Many of the deeper issues likely to emerge during the mutuality phase are, at first, beyond the scope of the group as a whole. Unfolding of these deeper issues often *requires* direct therapist-to-individual help, with the other members temporarily less active. However, when this direct helping takes place, especially during the mutuality phase, the empathic processes among the members ensure that help to an individual remains a group process. Very often the therapist does not even need to engage the other members with the individual after the initial exploratory period. However, if the other members do not engage with the individual after some initial direct help of the therapist, then the therapist can point to the commonalities of the problem, situation, and feelings so that the other members can begin to engage with the individual's problem.

Help to individual members is one of the crucial steps toward deepening the affective level of the group's work. Therapist actions often demonstrate to the other group members possible ways to react to similar future situations. If the group has reached a reasonable resolution of the authority issues, this direct help of the therapist to one member will not re-create a dependency on the therapist but will instead expand the possibilities for what the group can deal with and how it can go about it. A well developed group will be able to pick up the direct helping where the therapist left off and continue helping efforts and empathic responses as they explore the particular meaning of the subject matter for themselves.

More important than the fact of therapist-to-individual helping is the question of how often and how long such helping takes place and how the group responds after the helping efforts have been completed. The affective and behavioral responses of the group will tell more about whether the effort was treatment of one member in front of others or a moment of helping an individual within a group process.

SOURCE OF GRATIFICATION: INTERDEPENDENCE

Most group members increasingly look to themselves for gratification rather than to the therapist or the group. Three major dynamics contribute to this phenomenon: the empathic bond among the members lends emotional strength to the individual for his own coping; the acceptance with autonomy arises from successful resolution of intimacy crises; and the experience in helping others with similar difficulties helps the individual to feel more competent in dealing with his own difficulties.

Interdependence of the members is a hallmark of the mutuality phase. Rather than dependently waiting for others to recognize that one is asking for help, the individual can seek the desired help and selectively use the help offered by the others. The individuals also feel able to help others, especially when asked but even when not directly asked.

Dependency and Counterdependency

Members who during the earlier phases were extremely dependent or extremely counterdependent will tend to lag in the development of interdependency. Extremely dependent members will continue to seek help from the therapist and other members as well as further reassurance that they do not need to seek help. The dependency becomes more of a habitual repetition rather than a continued need.

The extremely counterdependent person will have less difficulty relinquishing the counterdependent helping but more difficulty in asking for and receiving help. Constant reassurance that help is available for the asking is essential. The counterdependent person also needs to have interrupted his pattern of seeking help but being disappointed in the help he gets. This person's growth issue concerns his/her being able to accept the help of others rather than his/her learning about self-reliance. At this phase of group development, other members easily see through counterdependent behavior and resent it.

Self-awareness Issues for the Therapist

The role of the therapist at this phase is to give permission and support for members to rely on themselves for asking for help from others and helping themselves when feasible. Therapists must be aware of their own counterdependent patterns if they are to discourage members from countinuing undue reliance on them. The term *undue reliance* is important; because self-reliance is a growing entity during the mutuality phase, a progressive transfer of responsibility for need gratification in relation to member and group readiness is crucial. The counterdependent therapist may help too little or too much. For most members of the group over- or under-helping by the therapist during mutuality will have little impact, simply because unless the therapist very strongly and repeatedly persists, the group restores the balance. Only very dependent or counterdependent members are held back by a therapist's overindulgence or underindulgence of the group.

RELATIONAL ISSUES

Relationships among the members during the mutuality phase take on an increasingly idyllic nature—one of full acceptance with freedom for individuality. The central question is the degree of intimacy that each member and the group-as-a-whole can and wants to achieve. Each member came to the group with differing capacities for intimacy, differing experiences with intimacy, and differing desires for intimacy. The wishes, potentials, and fears of intimacy for each member interact as the group seeks the ultimate levels of intimacy.

Degree of Intimacy

In all probability, most members of a group will achieve a higher degree of intimacy during mutuality than they have ever experienced before. Ultimate levels of intimacy vary from group to group in accordance with vector forces of the wishes for and the fears of intimacy among the members. In their desires for the group to achieve a high degree of intimacy, therapists often overlook the

nature of the members and their potential for intimate relationships. It is important for the therapist to assess the ultimate capacity of each member for
intimacy and try not to place members in a situation where they are pressured to
go beyond their capacity. The result of such pressure is that the member will not
value what intimacy he has achieved and will see himself as a failure and isolate
in relationships. The degree of intimacy achieved by each member is a differential phenomenon and can become part of the individual's understanding and
acceptance of self rather than a source of low self-esteem. An individual might
decide, "I am a person who needs a lot of intimacy," or "I am a person who
needs some intimacy, but I also like to have my own space."

The group itself, if it achieves a reasonable degree of intimacy, will allow
members to vary in their capacities for intimacy as they will allow differences on
every other matter. However, when a group scorns a member for not achieving as
much intimacy as the rest of the group, the actual level of intimacy achieved
should be questioned. Refusal to accept individual differences is a phenomenon
of the parallel and inclusion phases; when it occurs during mutuality it suggests
that the apparent intimacy is shallower than it seems and the group lacks sufficient member-member differentiation.

Distinguishing between inability for intimacy and fear of intimacy is difficult. After some members or the total group repeatedly fails to resolve some
intimacy crises, the therapist should consider the possibility that members have
reached their limitations. Knowledge of the members' past experiences in
relationships would help the therapist reach an accurate assessment. Yet, almost
every member might increase his capacity for intimacy in the therapy group, the
question is how far he can go.

Increased Give-and-take

Another major relational feature of the mutuality phase is the members'
increasing ability to share their feelings with each other and to respond to each
other's feelings. Even when a member attempts dependent or counterdependent
interaction, the other members generally do not respond in a reciprocal way;
rather, they insist that the member express what he really means or wants.
Group norms and controls develop to demand direct communication and limit
efforts to revert back to old, less productive behavior patterns.

Lack of Factions

Finally, a major phenomenon of the mutuality phase may be seen in the
relative absence of subgroups and factions. Generally subgroups and factions are
totally absent only in groups consisting of fewer than ten to twelve people.
Some groups of eight or nine might still have need for subgroups and factions,

but groups of four to seven people will usually achieve a state of mutuality free from ongoing subgroups or factions. In large groups (more than eight) mutuality often develops within each subgroup and between subgroups, but the members will need to identify with a portion of the group, since intimate relationships on a sustained basis are extremely difficult, if not impossible, with more than six or seven other people at the same time.

Within small groups (eight or fewer people) there may be greater attraction among certain members and more identification and intimacy among certain members, but these relationships involve less exclusion of other members and some degree of empathy occurs among all the members. A major cause of continued subgrouping in small therapy groups is intense negative transference among the members. Especially members who identify with each other in their transference reactions to other members will continue subgroup affiliations until these transference reactions are resolved. The resolution of transference reactions is a major area of therapeutic work during the mutuality phase. If and when the transference reactions become reasonably resolved, the total group can share more evenly in the empathic bond.

Role of the Therapist

The role of the therapist with regard to relational issues in the mutuality phase is to allow and support the deepening of intimacy, empathy, and give-and-take in the group. In the early mutuality phase, the therapist often must help the group tolerate a range of readiness and capacity for intimacy, empathy, and give-and-take. Generally the therapist's acceptance of the differentials among the members with regard to intimacy, empathy, and give-and-take sets an example that the group follows. When the group persists in its intolerance of differences, the therapist needs to help the group unearth the unresolved problems of authority, inclusion, or intimacy that may be standing in the way of the group's achievement of a fully differentiated mutuality.

Helping the group and individual members understand the nature of their deeper transference reactions to each other and to the therapist is a major part of the therapist's functioning during the mutuality phase. Most often these insights initially emanate from the therapist. However, once group members get the drift of transference phenomenon, they can help each other with these issues.

Self-awareness Issues for the Therapist

Crucial for the therapist is his awareness of his countertransference reactions, as well as his own comfort with his own wishes, capacity, and fears of intimacy. Unresolved and repressed feelings of which the therapist is unaware in these areas could cause the therapist to be intolerant of individual differences among the members in their capacity for intimacy. Unawareness of counter-transference reactions could seriously hamper any in-depth work with a member or the total group.

Most productive of change during the mutuality phase is the focus on the relationships in the here-and-now of the group. It is easier for members to change their manner of relating to each other because of the protected nature of the group, the help of the therapist, and the fact that the relationships in the group are less charged than those with people outside the group who are signifi-cant to the members. However, a concomitant there-and-then focus is also essential if members are, on one hand, to understand why they behave with each other as they do and, on the other hand, to begin changing the way they relate to those significant others outside the group. The there-and-then focus during the mutuality phase is an integral part of preparing for self-dependence and termination from the group. It insures that members transfer their relational gains in the group to their relationships outside the group.

The author rejects the assumption that gains in the group will ipso facto be reflected in gains outside the group. Some group members do indeed change in their relationships outside the group because of their gains in the group. How-ever, most group members do not change or transfer their growth from the group to outside situations without direct help through discussion of those out-side relationships.

SELF-OTHER CONCEPT: A REAFFIRMED IDENTITY

The major therapeutic gain resulting from the mutuality phase is the improved or reaffirmed sense of self or identity that members experience. Group members become increasingly comfortable with who and what they are as well as with who and what others in the group are. They value their similarities with other group members but also come to appreciate their differences. Thus, group mem-bers come to value their individuality and the individuality of others.

During the parallel phase, most members were seeking commonalities to reassure themselves of their worth. Some were seeking to validate either their superiority or inferiority to others to maintain a self-other concept consistent with their pattern of adjustment prior to coming to group therapy. During the inclusion phase, members were flocking with people who appeared similar to them in important ways or they were attempting to make others similar to them, while joining in opposition to those who seemed different. With the first resolu-tion of an intimacy crisis and the emergence of the empathic bond, members gain a basic sense of equality with all other members and, consequently, begin to feel more accepting of themselves and others. Because their central core of feelings becomes increasingly acceptable, the rest of them also becomes acceptable. However, when that central core is threatened through negative identification or negative transference, members need to respond with anger and protect their central core of feelings. After becoming comfortable with the new feelings as part of themselves, the members can again feel secure in their self-worth and even value the worth of those people who represented the unwanted feelings. Thus, the resolution of each affective conflict that takes place between members during the mutuality phase contributes to the emotional growth, insight, and self-esteem of the members who are party to the conflict. Most conflicts during the mutuality phase are emotional, as discussed under conflict during the mutuality phase.

The members' common fear of losing their identity by becoming members of a group is not substantiated. Quite the contrary, groups that achieve a reasonable degree of mutuality help each member solidify his identity and become deeply appreciative of the identities of other members. Those whose past relationships were either symbiotic or were ones in which they were fused with other people, like parents, might lag behind the other group members in developing a sense of self in relation to the others. If these members with extreme difficulty in defining their own boundaries can continue in the group through the mutuality phase, they can usually show some improvement toward establishing their identities. However, many such members experience pressures from outside the group as they begin to define their own boundaries; they may even have a series of symbiotic attachments in the group or concurrent with the group as they sever the ties with pre-existing symbiotic or fusion relationships. However, it must be accepted that, because of their emotional limitations, not all members can profit from the mutuality experience. Usually such people, generally schizophrenic, or of very low ego strength, are not in therapy groups that can achieve a full state of mutuality and are thus not threatened with this kind of growth.

The depth of the growth process during the mutuality phase is such that minute fluctuations in growth and regression are greatly amplified. Members progressively encounter increased feelings of mastery as they gain insight and work through to actualization of their changes. However, when members encounter setbacks in their own coping or when they perceive other members making large strides in contrast to their own, they often experience a sense of futility. For the individual member, regressions earlier in their group participation, while they are still new to the growth tasks, are easier to accept. When they experience setbacks in the mutuality phase, members are inclined to wonder whether they are making any progress at all, especially when compared to others who are making steady progress. Thus, feeings of mastery versus feelings of futility are a common dilemma for members, even though feelings of mastery progressively increase for most members.

Self-awareness Issues for the Therapist

One of the most desired yet threatening phenomena for all therapists is the growth of individual members. The most overt manifestation of the growth process is the emerging individuality and mastery achieved by the individual members. The ultimate threat of solidifying identity and mastery lies in that the member will no longer need the therapist or the group. While many therapists may have their mixed feelings about client growth well in hand when dealing with individuals, they may be inclined to lose their objectivity when dealing with a group.

A therapist unaware of these mixed feelings about client growth may be inclined to side with those group members who have to discount the growth of others to protect themselves from feelings of futility. Thus, if he is to remain in a position to mediate interpersonal mastery versus futility conflicts, the therapist must be well aware of his own ambivalence with respect to clients' needing him.

As group members gain or regain their feelings of self-worth and identity, the last shreds of dependence on the therapist begin to disappear. Again, therapists must be aware of their ambivalence about relinquishment of their roles. Most clients who come for psychotherapy have had some mixed reactions, if not all-out prevention, by their parents to their attempts to establish their own identities and self-reliance. Full acceptance of their mastery and identity by the therapist is crucial toward the member's ultimate separation from the group with his sense of well-being intact.

Central to the therapist's acceptance of group member individuality and mastery during the mutuality phase is the therapist's own sense of identity, particularly in the role of therapist. A therapist who is reasonably comfortable with his identity and mastery, in his own life and in the role of group therapist, can allow members to develop their unique identities and ways of mastering their life situations. If the therapist's own identity and life mastery are reasonably in balance, then experience with groups in the mutuality phase will help the therapist allow each member to arrive at his own identity and styles of mastery. The unsupervised therapist whose own life is not in reasonable balance may have to insist that individual members resolve their identity and mastery in ways that the therapist would like for himself. On the other hand, seeing group members resolve their identities and mastery can arouse feelings of futility for the therapist in his own personal coping efforts.

Thus the depth of the process during the mutuality phase requires similar depth awareness on the part of the therapist if he is to provide objective help to the group. Relinquishing the role of therapist during this phase, as many approaches to group therapy advocate, begs the question of the therapist's identity, since as a group member the therapist is no longer as responsible for mastery of self-awareness and countertransference. The group is then limited by the therapist's own degree of resolution of identity and mastery and may be hampered or prevented from resolving issues that the therapist has not resolved.

POWER RELATIONS: SHARED AMONG MEMBERS

Although power becomes fully distributed among the therapist and the group members and is available to anyone who reaches for it, power becomes a relatively inconsequential facet of interpersonal relations during the mutuality phase.

Most important, during the mutuality phase power is vested in the total group; all members gain a sense of personal power from the group. With reasonable resolution of the authority and inclusion struggles, in which power is in major dispute, members feel that the power of the group is behind them in their endeavors, particularly outside the group (Scheidlinger, 1964). The acceptance realized with the end of the inclusion phase and with resolution of intimacy crises is the vehicle through which members feel the backing of the group. Even in conflicts in the group during the mutuality phase, power and acceptance are neither in dispute nor felt to be in short supply.

Self-awareness Issues for the Therapist

If the group has grown through the authority crisis and the inclusion phase, the therapist should have little difficulty in allowing the group to share in the power. As the group continues in the mutuality phase the sharing of power becomes increasingly irreversible; consequently, a therapist who has difficulty in sharing power will become increasingly unable to regain the full power that had been vested in him at the outset of the group. A problem could arise if the therapist feels powerless or impotent because of the relative lack of power. Only deeper understanding and appreciation of the therapist's role during mutuality can counter these feelings.

CONFLICT: ITS RE-EMERGENCE

Conflicts emerge again in the aftermath of a first resolution of an intimacy crisis. However, the nature of conflict is much different then that of the inclusion phase. Survival in the group is no longer at stake in each conflict. During the mutuality phase inclusion and acceptance are assured for each member, questions of status and power are muted, and because members are basically equal, power is shared by all.

While the bases of conflict become much more diverse during the mutuality phase, there are a few recurrent underlying commonalities. Most conflicts involve feelings in some basic or even overt ways and center on each member's self-esteem and sense of well-being. Negative empathy and negative transference reactions are most often the central or underlying issues at stake. The deepening empathic bond is achieved and furthered by positive empathy and transferences, and impediments to the empathic bond come as negative transference and empathy. Each time negative empathy and negative transference conflicts are resolved, the empathic bond is deepened, particularly for the parties to the conflict. Mastery-futility conflicts among members are also common. Many mastery-futility conflicts also involve negative empathy and transference.

The way in which the group deals with conflict is also markedly different during the mutuality phase. During inclusion, members would line up in factions behind the person or persons who either represented their feeling or opinion or who represented someone who had to be appeased. During mutuality, members no longer take sides, but are instead inclined to consider the merits of both sides and experience their own mixed feelings on the matter. Consequently, most members join in the mediating role of the therapist, or even supplant the therapist as mediator. Even if the conflict begins with some polarization among the members on an issue, most members can soon recognize the polarization or ambivalences within themselves and can participate in helping each of the main adversaries understand the mixed feelings in all the members.

Since each member feels basically accepted and included in the group, even during a conflict, an individual member might feel rejected by some of the members but seldom by all the members. Thus, with the threat of rejection minimized, members are free to more fully express their side of conflicts and also free to listen to the other side. Even when members feel that they have lost in a conflict, they feel that only their feeling, behavior, or opinion was rejected; they no longer feel they were rejected.

Ultimately, the experience of disagreement and conflict without fear of rejection is a major vehicle for group members to gain their increased sense of uniqueness and identity. At the same time that members experience acceptance in spite of a difference of opinion, they gain in their capacity to accept others while disagreeing with them. Each agreement to disagree serves as a building block for acceptance of one's own individuality and the individuality of other people. The acceptance of individuality in others is just as important as accepting one's own individuality.

Role of the Therapist

The role of the therapist in supporting both sides of each conflict and helping the parties to the conflict toward resolution remains the same in mutuality as in the inclusion phase, with two major differences. First other members can and will participate in the mediating role; therefore, the therapist does not have to do all the balancing of sides to the conflict nor does he have to play as central a role in conflict resolution. The therapist, however, should consider how to help in the mediation, since all the mediating can gain insight into their own mixed feelings on a subject.

Second is the difference in the depth of the issues overtly or covertly involved in the conflict. Although the therapist may have been able to rationalize support for both sides of the conflicts during the inclusion phase, conflicts during the mutuality phase have far deeper emotional significance. A rationalization in support of one side to balance one's feelings in support of the other could have repercussions that hamper or prevent resolution of the conflict. It helps somewhat that the mediating group members may well have better contact with their mixed feelings on the conflict and may confront the therapist with the imbalance in his feelings. The therapist who is truly open to learning from the group will have many opportunities during the mutuality phase to do so, especially in conflict situations.

Self-awareness Issues for the Therapist

If a conflict between members during the mutuality phase does not seem to get resolved, then the therapist should consider what part his covert feelings might be playing in the process. While there may be other causes or contributing factors, chances are that the failure of group members to resolve conflicts in the mutuality phase in some way reflects the wishes or feelings of the therapist. Unresolved mutuality conflicts do not necessarily prevent the group from moving on nor do they threaten the group's existence in any major ways. However, unresolved mutuality conflicts do preclude some insight and growth that could be important for the parties to the conflict and perhaps for the other group members as well. In fact, it may often not be apparent that a mutuality conflict is unresolved until it reappears in the same or different form.

COHESION: GROUP AS A SOCIAL ENTITY

The cohesion that begins in subgroups during the inclusion phase and engulfs the entire group after the first resolution of an intimacy crisis continues to broaden and deepen through the mutuality phase. On the overt level, group cohesion is manifest in the "we" feeling among the members. They experience the group as a social entity rather than a collection of people who meet at the same time and place on a recurrent basis. The group as a social entity in turn becomes a reference point in each member's identity at the time. Members often report that they take the group with them emotionally when they go about their daily lives (Scheidlinger, 1964). They are inclined to feel and refer to the group as "my group" rather than "the group" or "the therapist's group." On a deeper level, cohesion is affective contact among the members. The epitome of this affective contact is empathy. As the affective communication among the members increases, there are more opportunities for empathy. As the empathy among all the members grows, so does the cohesion of the group.

The depth of the affective bond or cohesion among the members will directly depend on the fullness and depth of the group's resolution of the intimacy crises. Groups will vary in the nature and number of intimacy crises resolutions they require to achieve a depth of cohesion and intimacy, the major factor being the capacity of the members for intimacy. In general, the younger or the more ego deficient the group members, the greater their difficulties reaching and sustaining intimacy.

Thus, some groups may achieve some degree of mutuality with a low level of cohesion and intimacy; other groups will have a high degree of cohesion and intimacy almost as they enter mutuality. If a group enters mutuality with a low degree of cohesion and intimacy, the resolution of further intimacy crises will be needed to deepen the bonds among the members.

The symptoms of low-level intimacy, as opposed to intimacy on a higher level, are generally clear and overt. Foremost is the degree to which the group has to reject people outside the group. Maintenance of the entity of the group is determined by who is excluded more than by who is included. Consequently, groups with a beginning or low level of intimacy will expend considerable effort dealing with their exclusiveness and rejection of outsiders. They will have protracted and intense difficulty in accepting a new member as do latency-aged groups. As the group intimacy deepens, the members will be less concerned with who is excluded. When cohesion and intimacy reach a high level, the members will be more accepting of outsiders as individuals, just as they are more accepting of each other as individuals.

Early in the mutuality phase, every group will to some extent reject outsiders and press to uniformity but it will move toward deeper intimacy and cohesion with requisite reduction in the need for uniformity and rejection of outsiders or deviants.

The protracted absence of conflict among the members may also be a sign of low-level cohesion, since conflicts and their resolve expose and support differences and deviancy. If the hiatus in conflict typically found during and immediately after the resolution of intimacy persists, it may indicate that members fear to differ, preferring a pseudo-intimacy.

Role of the Therapist

The role of the therapist in relation to the growing in the group is to give permission, support, and help to the deepening affective bonds. Realistic assessment of individual member's capacities for intimacy is crucial, since the therapist may expect too much or too little from the group by way of intimacy.

Specific techniques for helping a group develop intimacy begin with the therapist offering empathy to individuals for the feelings they express or imply. Just as in building verbal communication, it may also be important for the therapist to build affective communication by pointing to commonalities of feelings among the members as members express these feelings. In instances of negative empathy, it is important for the therapist to attempt to understand the underlying empathy and help to unearth the empathy from the ensuing conflict or hostility. Thus the therapist builds the base for affective communication.

GROUP AS A ROUTE TO SELF-CONTROL

Group controls are shared by all and all submit to them during the mutuality phase. To the degree that a member has had a share in developing the norms and goals of the group and feels accepted and in affective contact with the other members will that member feel obliged to adhere to group controls.

During the mutuality phase, expressions of implied threats (often found in the inclusion phase) are no longer needed to pressure members to adhere to the group norms. Because they feel they belong to the group, members want to adhere to the norms. When disagreements about norms arise, they are generally negotiated with the group and the behavior either stops or becomes incorporated into the group norms. Thus, the vehicle for group controls in the mutuality phase becomes simple discussion without the necessity of expressed or implied threats.

At the start of the mutuality phase, depending on the depth of cohesion, rejection and possible exclusion may still be an implied vehicle for controls. In groups with low-level cohesion the threat of rejection for deviancy from the norms may at least be considered by the potential deviant and also be expressed or implied by the indigenous leadership. If and as the cohesion deepens, the norms of the group widen and rejection recedes as a vehicle of control.

Role of the Therapist

The role of the therapist is to facilitate discussion of the behavior as the means for resolving deviancy-conformity disputes. However, during the mutuality phase, norms, not controls, are the real issue.

The therapist should vest control in the group as much as possible. Members participating in controlling each other's behavior gain in their capacities to control their own behavior. Particularly with children, adolescents, and acting-out adults, the experiences of exerting controls on the behavior of others helps the person acting out to gain greater capacity for self-control. When the individual member needs more controlling, his attraction to the group motivates him to gain and incorporate controls from the group. In many therapy groups, the development of controls for members is one of the most crucial growth experiences.

In the parallel phase, all members depend on the therapist for controls. The authority crisis begins to vest some responsibility for control in the members. During the inclusion phase the controls are exerted mainly by sub-groups aiming to dominate the group's norms and goals. The first resolution of an intimacy crisis provides the base for members to begin incorporation of group controls. This process parallels the development of the child who, at first, relies on his parents for control, then incorporates the control of his parents, and finally takes responsibility for self-control. Many members have come to therapy groups because of difficulties in their capacity to control themselves and their participation in the evolution of controls in a therapy group can begin to help them gain self-control. Since these people have not been able to gain adequate controls from their incorporations from parents, the peer-group experience of participating in controlling others and being controlled by others helps to develop controls in a way that may not have been available to the individual previously.

TOWARD MORE FREEING NORMS

Norms are the most critical aspect of group processes during the mutuality phase, determining how much growth and development can take place in the group and how much therapeutic work the group can do. Restrictive norms will confine the group to a narrow range of communication and behavior, allowing little opportunity for expression, catharsis, and problem-solving. They will pre-clude the deepening of the empathic bond. The antithesis of restrictive norms lies in freeing norms that will allow the group to grow in its affective communi-cation and experiment with new behavior. Whitaker and Lieberman (1964) base their entire theory of group development on these normative processes.

How restrictive or freeing the group norms are when the group enters the mutuality phase will depend on many factors. Of basic importance is the age and ego level of the group (for example, groups of children or early adolescents and groups of people with low ego capacity will tend to have restrictive norms for most, if not all, their group life). The other major factor is how well the group resolves the normative issues of authority, inclusion, and intimacy. Most critical among these is how the group resolves the normative crisis of intimacy.

Levels of Intimacy

With the early resolutions of intimacy crises the group begins to set a pattern for allowing more or less intimacy to be expressed in the group. If the resolutions are toward narrow ranges of intimacy, then the norms will govern the substance and boundaries of that range. Thus, restrictive norms are developed to control the depth of intimacy reached by the group and further restrictive norms develop to substitute for depth of intimacy.

If group members can achieve a higher degree of intimacy, then successive normative crises as an integral part of successive intimacy crises can result in norms that allow increasing freedom for expression and sharing of affect. In this way, the group may begin the mutuality phase with restrictive norms but progressively develop norms that help to develop and suit deeper levels of empathy.

For Experimental Behaviors

While the issue of the depth of empathy is crucial for the mutuality phase, other behaviors are also important. Individual members each brought their prior modes of relationship and coping to the group. During the parallel phase, they most likely held back their normal patterns of behavior. During the inclusion phase, they tested patterns of behavior and most likely had some patterns accepted as either group norms or as part of their role in the group. In the mutuality phase, members need to experiment with behavior previously forbidden by themselves, parents, or the group and experiment with new modes of behavior that might improve their capacities for relationships and coping. If and as these new or formerly forbidden behaviors emerge, they become immediately incorporated into the group norms by becoming part of the individual's role in the group or by becoming behavior open to everyone in the group (Redl, 1966: 155-96). When these emerging behaviors are rejected by others in the group, deviancy-conformity conflicts arise. As they are resolved, this emerging behavior becomes part of each member's role and uniqueness, or it becomes a norm for some or all of the other members.

Deviancy-Conformity Conflicts

Deviancy-conformity conflicts differ from inclusion conflicts in some basic ways. In both types of conflict, group norms and modes of behavior may be in dispute. However, the basic acceptance and empathic bond of the mutuality phase precludes rejection; therefore, the only issue is the behavior itself. During mutuality the conflict is less likely to be over control of behavior than to be intended for the individual's ultimate growth. The feedback that a member gets about behavior during the mutuality phase is more likely to be particularized or differentiated and more likely to be offered constructively for the individual than as facets of dominance, control, or more totalized rejection. Thus, the deviancy-conformity conflicts serve to free individuals and the entire group to experiment with new behaviors in the group and new ways for coping with relationships and situations outside the group.

Role of the Therapist

The role of the therapist in the group's movement from restrictive to freeing norms in the mutuality phase is to help toward freeing the norms of the group while keeping in mind the levels of ability and readiness of the members for this movement. The therapist must be supportive of pressures toward restrictive as well as freeing norms when deviancy-conformity conflicts arise in the group. If the resistances and reluctances of the members for freer behavior are to be expressed and diminished, the therapist must support those members that represent the restrictive point of view. However, if the therapist does join one side of a normative issue during mutuality, the members opposed to the therapist's point of view are not likely to feel rejected, but will feel free to oppose his position.

Self-awareness Issues for the Therapist

The therapist should recognize those norms he has or would like for the group. Even the most nondirective therapist has norms for a group. The non-directive therapist has at very least the norm that the group should do most or all the work for itself and not rely on the therapist at all. In the author's experience, many supposedly nondirective therapists all too often insist that they have no norms or expectations for the group, yet their groups tend to develop in ways that seem markedly similar to each other. Every therapist has at least some norms, and can best insure that they are not inadvertently imposed on the group by recognizing what they might be. However, the group may need some normative suggestions and modeling from the therapist to allow it to function at its best. If the therapist sees the need for the group to conduct itself in certain ways, it would be least debilitating to the group's self-determination and self-dependence for the therapist to openly share his suggestions and negotiate them with the group. Sometimes he can demonstrate the mode of behavior he advocates, then see if the group would want to continue that mode. He can point out, "Some groups operate this way and other groups operate this other way. Which way does this group think it should function?" If the therapist is honestly prepared for the group to reject his ideas for the norm, there is a greater likelihood that, if accepted, the norm will work for everyone's benefit. If a norm is directly or indirectly forced on a group by a therapist, it might seriously set back the group's self-dependent functioning.

MERGING OF GOALS

The fact of mutuality means that every member still in the group feels that his own goals have been incorporated into the goals of the group or that the nature of the group is such that it will allow the achievement of his goals. As the group moves deeper into mutuality, the covert goals of its members begin to surface, if they have not surfaced previously. Many of the normative struggles of the mutuality phase directly reflect the goals of the members. Since the norms determine how the group functions, inherent in the norms are directions for the group's processes.

The bond of empathy in the mutuality phase is the major universalizer of individual goals. An example can be found in the need to improve relationships. During the parallel phase members might view their work on one kind of relationship as excluding another: romantic relationships rather than parental or child relationships. During the mutuality phase the leveler will be relationships, no matter with whom. While some goals may be excluded by the group, the individual members feel free to insist that the group pursue their goals if they deem it essential.

Another phenomenon contributes to the merging of goals during the mutuality phase. As members experience themselves and other people in the group during the formative stages and into mutuality, they often learn more about what they really want and need from the group. Some of these new ideas are merely the surfacing of covert goals they brought with them but did not raise until someone else said or did something to bring the goals to their awareness. Other new ideas arise from experiencing the needs and strivings of other members and seeing how these might be relevant to one's self.

The central importance of goals from the parallel phase through the first resolution of an intimacy crisis wanes in the mutuality phase for two major reasons. First, the group has worked out any major goal differences to reach mutuality; any serious dissenters would not have survived in the group or the group would not have reached mutuality without reconciling the differences. Second, the empathic bond becomes strong enough for the group to either incorporate new and different goals or even become pluralistic in its endeavors, rather than make or let a member leave.

Role of the Therapist

If the therapist has new or alternate ideas for group or individual member goals, he or she can express and negotiate them with the group. If the goal is meaningful for the members, they will probably incorporate it into their strivings. Here again, it is important that the therapist be free to accept the group's rejection of his goals if the goal suggestions are going to have any dynamic meaning. Failure of the therapist to accept such rejection might lead to a relational gap between the therapist and the group, rather than to any regression on the part of the group.

ROLES: OPEN TO ALL

Two major aspects of roles in the mutuality phase are, first, the role of the member in the group and, second, the manner in which the group member's roles reflect that person's functioning in roles outside the group. Group roles progressively become diluted in the mutuality phase. Any functions that may have been performed primarily by one or more members previously, including many of the therapist's functions, increasingly can and are performed by any member at will. Even indigenous leadership can shift back and forth among members. Who gains leadership at any given moment in the group will depend more on their unique contributions to the focus of discussion than on any innate capacities for leadership. Consequently, the tasks of the various roles in the group are either fully distributed during the mutuality phase or open to anyone who wants to perform them at a given time.

The other important aspect of roles during mutuality lies in the increasing unfolding of the whole person in the group. As trust, autonomy, and intimacy grow in the group, members risk more of themselves and their modes of functioning in the group. Many members, simply due to the climate, progressively develop roles in the group in which they actualize much growth in relationships and coping efforts. Other members, as they venture more of themselves into group roles, encounter the very same difficulties that they have encountered outside the group. While some of these difficulties are manifest and even changed during the formative stages of the group, deeper aspects of their total functioning emerge during mutuality. In the climate of acceptance, intimacy, and differentiation, it is easier for these members to obtain feedback from other group members and to risk new experiments in behavior in the group. Just as group roles become more fluid and interchangeable, so do roles that members bring to the group from the outside. Changes in roles are also accomplished not only from direct feedback but also from incorporation of other group member's behavior. Thus, the concept of increasing fluidity and interchangeability of roles in the group extends not only to group roles but also to those aspects of member's roles in the group that manifest their manner of functioning outside the group. (For example, a member who is passive and dependent in relationships outside the group can become more assertive both in the group and in outside relationships.)

During mutuality, more than at any other time in the group's life, the group becomes a laboratory for experimentation with new roles. The support of the group in these new role ventures reinforces the person's capacity to change his role behavior outside the group. Since each role represents a system of expectations on the part of self and others, the work in the group under favorable risking conditions can bring about basic change in how the member perceives the expectations of self and others in a given role.

While many group members who change roles in the group find that these changes carry over into situations outside the group, most group members need to directly focus on the parallels between their here-and-now changes and the there-and-then situations of their lives outside the group. The differential roles that members occupy in the group are a major factor in the development of increased awareness and comfort with one's own identity.

Role of the Therapist

The fluidity and interchangeability of roles in the mutuality phase calls for the therapist to be self-assured in his role during mutuality and to be able to share many of the therapist functions without becoming unduly threatened. Basic to this security is a philosophical stance in relation to the function of a therapist with a fully developed therapy group. Of course, there is no substitute for experience with groups in this phase to help a therapist develop a sound degree of self-assurance in the role, but the philosophical stance might be useful to aid the therapist in gaining the necessary experience. Role uncertainty during the mutuality phase can cause the therapist to do too much or too little for the group. However, during mutuality the group can counter the therapist's efforts and maintain group integrity in spite of the therapist. The group can also request the therapist's help when needed, since the mature interdependence of the group includes the maturity to ask for and pursue necessary assistance.

7

Separation
Crises

Abandoned, I withdrew
into my child-sphere of loss.
A sun-shell, lost in the night element.
　　—Jerilyn Elise Miripol

Separation crises occur throughout the life of a therapy group, but have a special function as a transition from the mutuality phase to the termination phase. Separation crisis phenomena occur when a member enters a group, during the authority and intimacy crises, around separation from the group and the therapist, and finally as a prelude to the individual and/or group termination. Each successful resolution of a separation crisis helps group members deal with subsequent separation crises and with either their ultimate separation from the group or the group's termination (McGee et al., 1972).

A major source of therapeutic gain is inherent in resolution of separation crises. Since all group members have to confront major or minor separations and losses during their lives, the development of capacity to deal with separations and losses in the group is helpful to all concerned. In addition, for many who come to therapy, unresolved separation and loss issues are either a primary reason for therapy or at least a contributing facet of their difficulties. These past separations and losses become a major determinant of how the member handles separations in the group and the reworking of these past experiences during separation crises becomes a major source of growth.

Most group members experience a progression in the depth and intensity of their separation crises. Early separation crises do not directly call forth the deeper and underlying separation trauma. Most members are inclined to deny early group separations even though they may react to these separations in some overt ways. With subsequent separation crises, deeper issues and affect are unearthed. It is common for members to mourn major losses or the end of significant relationships during later separation crises in the group (Parkes, 1964).

Frank, a young adult man, entered a long-term open-ended therapy group early one summer. A few weeks later, when the therapists announced their August vacation plans, Frank became angry at the other group members saying, "They're (the therapists) entitled to a vacation. I don't understand why you (other group members) are getting so mad at them. I think you're all selfish."

Four months later, the therapists announced their plan for a vacation during the Christmas season. Frank turned to a newer member and jokingly explained, "They (therapists) expect everyone to get mad about their vacations so we humor them. They like to be punished for their guilt about going away."

Six months later in early June, the therapists announced that they would have to be away to conduct a one-week workshop. This time Frank became very anxious and explained, "You're (therapists) leaving at a very bad time for me. I'm just finishing my training and will start my new job when you are away."

From late June through to the therapists' August vacation, Frank withdrew from active participation in the group, sulked a great deal during meetings, refused overtures from members and therapists to talk about how he felt, came late very often, missed a few meetings, and developed a leisure time activity that often conflicted with group meetings.

At the first meeting in September, when the therapists returned from vacation, Frank announced that he was terminating from the group. In the ensuing discussion, Frank was able to express how angry he was at the therapists for being away and not caring, particularly at such a crucial time in his life. Later in the discussion Frank blurted out to the male therapist, "You're just like my father. You let me down when I most needed you." For the first time Frank began to deal with the loss of his father when he was an early adolescent. Frank stayed in the group, completing his mourning process and dealing with other issues in his life more productively.

It is difficult to make a distinction between the final separation crisis and the start of the termination phase. The final separation crisis for an individual (particularly in open-ended groups) serves as the major task of the termination process. With sound resolution of the final separation crisis, the termination phase can be a comparatively uneventful aftermath. However, many group members leave groups during a separation crisis with little resolution.

Reaching the mid-point in a time limited group or setting, a termination date in longer-term groups precipitates separation crises. If there is insufficient time or ability for a full termination process, the separation phenomena may or may not be resolved before the individual leaves or the group ends. However, the reality of a termination date often facilitates the resolution the separation crises before termination (McGee et al., 1972). It is important that the therapist not expect the individual or group to cope with separation crises at a higher level than the group has been able to cope with any other issues.

Many of the authors on therapy group development have little to say about separation or termination. Those that do discuss termination are primarily sequential theorists, who talk mostly about time-limited or closed-ended groups (see, for example: Garland et al., 1965; Northen, 1969; Hartford, 1971; Mills, 1964; Mann, 1967). Long-term and/or open-ended groups do not have a termination phase until perhaps the group comes to an end (Yalom, 1975). Therefore, the concept of separation crises is employed to differentiate between the recurrent separation issues that often pervade therapy groups and the full experience of termination for an entire group.

AFFECTIVE POLARITIES: FEAR OF ABANDONMENT

The underlying affective polarity in separation crises is the striving for autonomy and the fear of abandonment and loss. As in authority crises, separation fears call forth the individual's past experiences with autonomy strivings: the two-year-old, the eight-year-old, the early adolescent, and the young adult. Authority crises and separation crises are both concerned with group members gaining or asserting their autonomy without punishment, rejection, or abandonment. In authority crises, members are concerned with autonomy within ongoing relationships. They ask themselves, for example, "If I assert myself, will I be punished or rejected?" In separation crises members are concerned with autonomy without the relationship: "Will I be rejected or punished if I become independent of the group? Of the therapist? Of my parents?"

Support of each individual's autonomy and self-dependent behavior through the life of a group helps the individual prepare for separation. The member can think, "The therapist and the group have accepted my independence throughout the group; therefore, they can probably accept my independence from the group." Thus, members can take the support and permission of the group with them; they do not have to flee the group to gain or preserve self-dependence.

Actual losses may not be the only losses members experience and re-enact in the group. Virtual loss of parents through actual or felt abandonment for reasons of autonomy or self-dependence may be re-awakened in separation crises. A particularly contemporary problem is the launching of young adults from families. Modern child-centered families may or may not allow a great deal of autonomy within the family; all the same, the family needs to retain the child in the family system to maintain the emotional balance of the system. The child's strivings for self-dependence from such family systems are met with punishment, rejection, possibly even abandonment. This actual or threatened abandonment arises for group members during separation crises. Potential abandonment indeed is a major reason why group members experience separation as a crisis.

Finally, many group members have never drawn close to other people in their lives. Having experienced the closeness of the group, they despair during separation crises of ever again achieving equivalent relationships. Some of these members in an autistic act of self-preservation, will drop out of the group during a separation crisis set off by another member leaving or by the absence of the therapist. Unless the member entertains hope of new relationships in and out of the group, he has to protect himself from further disappointment. These members seem to prefer the safety of their isolation than to have their hopes of relationships raised, then dashed. Many of these members can increase their capacity and readiness for relationships by having the experience of establishing of new relationships in and outside the group.

The question of an individual's ultimate capacity for relationships must be raised in assessing the merits of encouraging a member to remain in the group. Some may have come as far as they ever could; others may have come as far as they could at the time. Given permission from the therapist and group to withdraw, the member who has temporarily reached his capacity for relationship will be more likely to re-enter therapy when ready to further his growth in relationships.

Self-awareness Issues for the Therapist

The self-awareness issues for the therapist during separation crises are profound. Therapists must be aware of their own reactions to separations in their lives as well as reactions to group members during separation crises. Therapists who have not had any major difficulties with autonomy and abandonment in their past lives may not fully appreciate the difficulties group members have with separation crises. The therapist who himself has unresolved separation issues may either insist that members deal too fully and prematurely with their separation reactions or he may join the members in denial of separation phenomena.

In each separation crisis the therapist should be aware of the possible feelings that might cause him to encourage continued dependency of a member on the group or on the therapist. The counterdependent needs of the therapist could cause some miscalculation in assessing the individual member's and group's readiness and need to deal with separation issues. Unresolved reactions to past losses could cause the therapist to discourage, or at least have difficulty dealing with, the mourning process that separation often sets off among members of the group.

The role of the therapist during separation crises is to support the individual and group gains toward autonomy to date while demonstrating continued acceptance for the individual and the group. This role is particularly difficult during a separation crisis since the group members might confuse the therapist's noninvolvement with their renewed dependency pleas as rejection and abandonment.

Because the resolve of current separation crises are closely linked with past and future separation, there is a crucial need for a dual focus on here-and-now and there-and-then spheres during separation crises. Group members need to rework past difficulties arising from separations and abandonments as well as prepare ultimately to leave the group.

BEHAVIORAL FEATURES:
REGRESSION-DEPRESSION AND SUPER-DEPENDENCE

Two major behavioral features serve as hallmarks of separation crises: regression-depression and super self-dependence. Both sets of behavior are based on the denial of the feelings associated with actual or potential loss. Both the regression-depression and super self-dependence carry implicit requests for help and test the therapist and group for signs of permission for autonomy and independence.

Members exhibiting the depressive state may come to the meeting with defeatest there-and-then material. They as much as say, "See how I can't cope even with things I've already mastered," or they withdraw from the process in ways that invite others to engage them. The essential theme of the meeting is regression and inability in both content and process. The relinquishment of autonomy by the group can, if the therapist is not aware, cause the therapist to take over and function in ways that weren't essential since early in the group life. The regressive messages of the members come as pleas: "Please help me," and "Don't be mad at me for being adequate. I'll show you how inadequate I am."

The super self-dependent behavior (Mann, 1967, calls this manic denial) may be exhibited by individuals or the total group. Members exhibit a surge of energy in their coping with each other and their problems. As it develops there is an unreality to the kinds of coping and self-expectations that make obvious the need for help by the therapist. This behavior is exemplified in the attitude of "I can handle anything and everything that comes." The therapist, if not aware, can be drawn into rescuing the members from their unreality, rescuing they may or may not allow. Disallowal of the rescue work is again a way of heightening the call for help without asking for it directly.

Role of the Therapist

It is extremely important that the therapist understand the behavior as a reaction to separation and not a true regression. The therapist needs to temper his helping efforts least he or she, on one hand, abandon the members by not helping or, on the other hand, confirm for the members that they really are as dependent on the therapist as they appear or feel. If the therapist supports the members by pointing to past resolutions and coping efforts and grants permission and support for appropriate self dependence he or she will help the group unearth and deal with underlying feelings. If there are some as yet unresolved mourning issues, these issues may begin to unfold.

Successful resolution of separation crises results in the expression of anger over the actual or threatened loss. Depending on the group, the anger may be expressed directly toward the objects of loss, it may be displaced in interpersonal conflicts in the group, or it may perhaps even be generalized to objects and events outside the group and unrelated to loss per se. The degree to which the group is able to directly express the anger will depend on the group's capacity for expression of any feelings and its point in development as a group. Groups experiencing separation in early phases will be less likely to express anger than groups that are fully developed.

Once the anger is expressed, members can accept the separation and complete the mourning process for that crisis. In closed groups there is generally a progression in capacity to deal more directly with the anger. In open-ended groups newer members are generally less able to deal with the anger. Some new members have the anger expressed vicariously through the other members. Others can become extremely upset over the angry feelings brought out by separation, since they aren't even ready to entertain the feeling that losses engender anger. If possible, it is often more helpful to allow these new members their denial of the angry feelings and sometimes even to support their defenses.

One prominent feature of the denial or expression of hostility during separation crises is the tendency for members to be negative about the group, the therapist, and the experience. The hostility, when it emerges, might tend to be directed at the therapist in the form of depreciation of the help received. The depreciation begins with the depressive-regressive or super self-dependent behavior, which seems to signify to the therapist that the process hasn't helped. If the therapist holds the line on helping the group back to its formerly achieved level of function, the members may express some hostility at the therapist for not providing the quantity and degree of nurture they are calling for by their depression or their super self-dependence.

Self-awareness Issues for the Therapist

Thus, the depressive-regressive behavior and the expression of hostility through depreciation of the therapist can well cause the therapist to feel, first, that he hasn't been as much help as he had hoped to be and, second, that the members know it and are mad about it. When joined with the therapist's own reactions to separation, the impact of the separation crisis on the therapist can be enormous. It is important for therapists to understand the meaning of separation crisis behavior and to be able to sort out the meaning from the manifest content, particularly if the final separation crisis for a group and/or member catches the therapist at a time when he or she might be evaluating the helping process and considering what was and was not accomplished. Since even the best of helping processes often leave some unresolved issues, there is danger that the therapist might dwell on what hasn't been accomplished after the onslaught of the separation crisis. If the therapist isn't in position to withstand the on-slaught and help present a balanced view of the process, there is danger not only that the therapist may feel unfulfilled as a helper but also that the members may leave with a lesser feeling about themselves and where they have come.

In closed-end groups the therapist must carefully evaluate the individual and group growth prior to the final separation crisis. With a firm idea of what has or has not taken place in the group, the therapist can accurately assess the behavior in light of past achievement, then help the group by helping them back to achieved levels of coping.

SOURCE OF GRATIFICATION: MOVING BEYOND THE GROUP

Fundamental to the separation crises is the threatened loss of the therapist and group as sources of gratification. In early separation crises the threatened losses are a source of much anxiety for the group members. As the group experiences and resolves earlier separation crises, the individual members become better prepared to cope with their own final separation crisis. During the mutuality phase most group members work on developing or improving significant relation-ships outside the group. If these outside relationships serve as part of the focus during the mutuality phase, then the members may be less fearful of relinquish-ing their ties to the group and more secure with the potential gratification from outside relationships.

Problems of Extreme Dependency and Counterdependency

Extremely dependent and extremely counterdependent members have a more difficult time relinquishing the group as a source of gratification. Many counterdependent members grow to allow the group to meet their emotional needs and often use the group as their sole source of gratification, becoming increasingly counterdependent in their relationships outside the group. In addition to learning how to receive emotional support from others in the group, it is essential that counterdependent members receive help in opening themselves up to give-and-take with others outside the group.

Very dependent members begin to struggle with loss of gratification right from the first resolution of an authority crisis. First, the dependent members resist the spreading of dependency from the therapist to the other group mem-bers. Group development itself serves as a foil for exteme dependency needs. During separation crises, the dependent member often attempts to regain dependence on the therapist and discounts the possible help of the other group members. Exploration of past insufficiencies in obtaining gratification along with support for growth in giving and getting from other group members and persons outside the group is often essential to help the very dependent member prepare to relinquish dependency on the group.

An important part of the initial depression during separation crises arises from the recollection of unmet dependency needs for all members. Almost all members, whether their patterns are dependent, counterdependent or somewhere inbetween, mourn past deprivations during separation crises and need to recognize, express, and feel comfortable with their anger over the loss of gratification. Counterdependent members often spearhead the denial; dependent members spearhead the depression. In early separation crises the therapeutic objective lies in helping all members to mourn their past disappointments in interpersonal gratification as they prepare to learn both how to take initiative and how to allow others to meet some of their needs.

Self-awareness Issues for the Therapist

Thus, preparation for loss of the therapist and group as sources of gratification in the final separation crisis begins with the resolution of authority crises and continues through successive separation crises during the inclusion and mutuality phases. Fundamental to helping group members prepare for the loss of the therapist and group is the therapist's awareness of his own dependency-counterdependency needs. Therapists generally tend to gratify their own needs through counterdependently helping others and particularly through helping their clients. The therapist needs to be aware of his own past emotional deprivations, possible anger stemming from these deprivations, and his own patterns of either seeking gratification or compensating for these deprivations. It is only through full awareness of his own emotions dealing with basic need gratification that the therapist can be in an objective position both to serve as a source of need gratification for the group members and to help group members become able to meet their own needs and accept gratification from others outside the group. To the extent that the therapist is counterdependently gratifying his own needs through helping the group members will he have difficulty preparing members for self-dependent and interdependent behavior that can serve as the basis for successful termination from the group.

RELATIONAL ISSUES:
BUILDING NEW RELATIONSHIPS AND MOURNING OLD ONES

One of the most difficult aspects of separation crises is the threatened loss of relationships developed in the group. Early sepration crises arouse member's fears of loss and support the reluctances to becoming interpersonally involved.

Later separation crises, particularly during the mutuality phase, raise the spectre of actually losing the new-found relationships. The prospect of relinquishing relationships with other members of the group causes members to despair that they will not be able to have similarly rewarding relationships in the future.

To cope with the loss of the interpersonal relationships in the group, group members should be helped in two major ways. First, members need help to carry their new-found or improved ways of relating over to relationships outside the group. Carryover may take place by itself, but direct discussion of these relationships and help to the members in developing and sustaining these relationships provide the most assurance that each member will not just be relinquishing relationships but will be going on to other satisfying relationships.

Second, group members need help to mourn the loss of the relationships in the group. A major part of the mourning, of necessity, is the member's recognition that he or she cannot expect that extragroup relationships to be sustained in the same way as group relationships. The kind of interaction and close relating that members can sustain in an experience limited in time and frequency cannot serve as a realistic expectation of relationships beyond the group. It is hoped that through the entire life of the group, members come to grips with how much of the idyllic relationships in the group can be attained in extragroup relationships. Certainly, relationships can have moments and periods with the kind of give-and-take, empathy, and openness characteristic of the mutuality phase.

One very positive aspect of the separation anger is that when members get in touch with negative aspects of the group they may tend to idealize the group relationships less. A realistic view of the relationships in the group with their ups and downs even during sessions limited in time and frequency helps greatly toward the members developing realistic expectations of ongoing extragroup relationships. Thus, through support of the member's realistic perception of the relationships in the group and understanding the realities in comparison to sustained extragroup relationships, the member can be helped to cope with the loss of the intragroup relationships as long as the member has reason to believe that reasonably gratifying relationships are possible outside the group.

Self-awareness Issues for the Therapist

The therapist must be fully aware of his own relational situation beyond the group. If the therapist has satisfying relationships outside the group, then he or she is in position to provide full support for the members to sustain or confidently aspire to satisfying relationships beyond the group. However, if the therapist doesn't have sufficient gratification from outside relationships he may, on one hand, not communicate full support for the members to realistically aspire to relationships outside the group and, on the other hand, not give real permission for members to leave the group. Deficiencies in the therapist's personal relationships do not preclude the therapist's giving help to the members; however, they do require full awareness and understanding by the therapist of how his own difficulties might interfere in the helping process.

SELF-OTHER CONCEPT: THE GROUP AS PRIMARY REFERENCE

By the time a group or group members arrive at a full separation crisis, the group becomes a primary reference group for each member (Scheidlinger, 1964). Much of the direct and indirect impact of group therapy on the individual member is the result of reworking prior reference group experiences. The family of origin and peer group experiences, particularly adolescent peer experiences, are primary determinants of each member's concept of self in relation to other people. As these prior familial and peer experiences are re-enacted in the group the member, it is hoped, receives support for those experiences that have led to growth and opportunities to change problematic experiences. The critical question for each member in the separation crisis is whether they can sustain the sense of increased self-worth and identity derived from the group experiences without the actual ongoing support and re-experience of this identity in the group.

Another aspect of the separation crisis is the there-and-then content of the meeting. Support of the there-and-then accomplishments in feelings of equality with people and relationships outside the group help to sustain members in their hopes for maintaining their improved self-concept without the ongoing support of the group.

Role of the Therapist

The therapist's role takes on two major aspects during separation crises. One concerns the here-and-now experiences of the members in the meetings. Because the separation crisis stirs up deep hostility in the members, the therapist is needed to help the members express and accept that hostility where and when the members are capable of such expression. Harboring of separation anger itself contributes to the separation crisis in that members once more feel that they have vile feelings others do not have. Expression, empathy, and universalization of the separation angers contribute to the re-affirmation of the equality feelings and members once again do not have to feel inferior for having what they often consider illogical and undeserved angry feelings about separation. Or, as they might phrase it, "How can you be angry at someone for leaving? Being sick? Taking a vacation? Dying?"

Self-awareness Issues for the Therapist

The major issues for the therapist's self-awareness are his own feelings about emotional equality with other people and comfort with separation anger.

Unawareness could lead to the members' feeling bad about themselves, no matter what the therapist overtly expresses to them.

POWER RELATIONS: THE POWER TO LEAVE

Anticipation of separation is made doubly difficult because the power members derive from the group helps sustain them in extragroup life, yet they also need power to accomplish the separation from the group. Even when all the other members of the group agree with the individual's decision to leave they still are angry about the possible separation. The member leaving must be able to deal with the power exerted by the other group members to keep him in the group.

Most group members have had a difficult time separating from their family of origin. Many of the difficulties that bring them to group therapy relate to families that would not let them go. Other group members have come to group therapy either because the family of origin was too weak or because, although they chose flight as a way of getting out, they never dealt with separation from the family. Thus, in separation crises unfinished issues with families of origin permeate the emotions of all members. For many older group members, other members' leaving reminds them of the potential or actual separation of their children.

Through the resolution of successive separation crises, members rework their separations from families of origin and prepare for their own separation from the group. In open-ended groups, members experience each of the other members' dealing with a final separation and vicariously gain capacity to deal with their own ultimate separation.

Just as in the authority and inclusion power struggles, there is a high potential for members to flee the power struggles of the final separation crisis. The member flees because he fears he will not be able to deal successfully with the group and accomplish the separation. If a member has chosen flight from the family of origin as the way to establish independence he may also attempt to accomplish separation from the group in the same way. Moreover, members who have not yet been able to accomplish a healthy separation from the family, if and when they attempt to separate from the group, might also flee in an attempt to maintain their dependence on family and not have it further threatened by the group.

When members are facing a final separation crisis, it is usually best if they can come to at least one more session to deal with the group. Usually both the member and the rest of the group gain from the experience. In particular, the member separating from the group often feels better about the experience and the decision to leave, even if the therapist and all other members oppose the decision. Members are more likely to work out a suitable termination process if they resolve the final separation crisis. Having stood up to the power of the group, the member feels better able to exert power outside the group.

In a closed group, all members will be dealing with the final separation crisis at similar times. In many ways this is easier: there is less threatened opposition from other members and more support of other having the same experience. However, some of the depth of the experience is lost to the individual members since they are not leaving a going concern and do not have to make and uphold any decisions about leaving. In closed groups the decision is often forced because the time runs out.

Role of the Therapist

The role of the therapist requires support for both individuals and the group during the final separation crises. The therapist in particular must be in position to deal with the authority side of the authority-autonomy issue inherent in separation from the therapist. He or she must consider objectively the pros and cons of the individuals' leaving, since this is the last vestige of authoritative power he or she holds for the individual member. The therapists must understand their own feelings about loss of members. To the degree that therapists serve counterdependent needs through therapy it is difficult for them to relinquish the objects of counterdependent need gratification. Affectional and countertransference ties to offspring might also be involved in difficulties of allowing members to leave. On the other hand, unmitigated negative feelings toward the member might either cause the therapist to hang on to the member defensively or to banish the member through separation.

CONFLICT: STAYING vs. LEAVING

The central conflict in separation crises is staying in the group versus leaving the group. One major factor that fuels the conflict is the ambivalent feelings of all concerned about the separation. Whether a closed or open-ended structure, all the members share mixed feelings about separating from the group. The intensity of the ambivalences contribute to the group's regression in their modes of dealing with conflict (Zimmerman, 1968).

During the inclusion phase stronger members tend to take sides and to feel and express one side of their ambivalence in a conflict situation. In the mutuality phase most members—except perhaps the immediate adversaries—are inclined to be in touch with both sides of their conflictual feelings and, as a result, supportive to both sides of the conflict. In closed-end groups, all the members are equally involved in the final separation crisis and might, therefore, polarize and develop factions around the separation issues. In open-ended groups, however, everyone except the member leaving may oppose the leaving, since the member leaving often carries the total burden of the other side of everyone's ambivalence.

How temporary the polarization and factioning around separation crises are depends on how well the group has developed in its ability to conflict. A group that has achieved a high degree of intimacy and mutuality will have less difficulty in fully dealing with both sides of everyone's ambivalence. A group that is still in the parallel or inclusion phases will have a great deal of difficulty dealing with their mixed feelings about separation. Chances are that a group in the parallel phase will hardly deal with the final separation of a member, except to the degree that it either represents a threat to the existence of the group and gives cause for holding back from involvement or causes many members to feel that participation will be easier with fewer members to share the therapist. These latter feelings often raise considerable guilt in the members.

During the inclusion phase, a final separation crisis would cause the factions that had developed to take sides or even become a faction of the whole and join in opposition to the member who is separating.

Role of the Therapist

The role of the therapist in relation to conflict during separation crises is to help and allow full expression of the facts and feelings on each side and, ultimately, to help the opposing factions experience the other side of their respective ambivalences. The therapist should be aware of his own ambivalences so that he can truly be in position to support both sides of the conflict.

COHESION: UNDER STRAIN

Separation crises create the ultimate strain on group cohesion. The primary threat of separation—that interpersonal bonds will be broken—evokes the many fears of loss that threaten group members when they even consider getting closer to other people. Separation crises during the parallel phase are particularly threatening since they "prove" to the members that they shouldn't become involved with the group because they might be abandoned. During the inclusion phase, separation crises also are inclined to counterpoise the threat of abandonment over the desires for closeness. Members who were becoming close to the member separating get confirmation that their fears of getting closer to other people opens them to abandonment as they might put it, "See, every time I get close to someone they go away." Members of opposing factions tend to feel guilty about a member of the opposite faction leaving since it confirms that their anger and aggression drives people away and therefore shouldn't be expressed. Or, in their words, "See, it goes to show you that if you tell people how you really feel, they go away."

During the mutuality phase, if the intimacy crises have been well resolved, separation signifies mostly loss for both the one leaving and those remaining in the group. While the anticipation and aftermath of separation might cause some pulling back from interpersonal bonds, a group in mutuality tends to close ranks after a separation and go on with its work. However, the group does need to mourn the loss of the member if it is going to cohere once more as a group. Unresolved mourning issues often cause a group to sustain the lost member as a ghost and either reject new members or simply not allow new members to become included.

Role of the Therapist

The role of the therapist is to help the group mourn the loss of the member by helping the members express their grief and anger, then reaffirm their commitment to going on with their work and relationships in the group. Therapists also need to mourn the loss of a member and accept that the group will be different than it was. The nature and climate of each group undergoes change with each member leaving; acceptance of its new nature and climate by the therapist is extremely important to helping the members accept the new form of the group.

RELINQUISHMENT OF CONTROLS

There are few ways in which a group can exert controls over a member who is separating. Consequently, the threat of rejection returns as a major potential source of control. The possibility of exclusion holds no threat to the separating member, but the possibility of abandonment does. Both the member leaving and the members staying are threatened by their fears of abandonment. Resolution of the separation conflict alleviates the fears of abandonment and allows the separating and remaining members to experience the ultimate expression of autonomy without rejection and abandonment. Thus, relinquishment of the ultimate control (exclusion) by the group lets the separating member leave the group and neither feel he has abandoned the group members nor feel abandoned by them.

Exclusion is also the ultimate control of the therapist; therefore, it is equally important, if not more important, for the therapist to relinquish control of the member who is leaving. Each time the therapist allows a member to leave the group without feeling abandoned by the therapist, other members gain hope that they too will be able to leave without feeling abandoned.

Self-awareness Issues for the Therapist

Again, it is essential that the therapist sift through his own feelings about the group member separating since, overtly or covertly, the therapist may exert the final control that would cause the separating member to feel abandoned, rather than free to leave with a full sense of autonomy. The key to leaving with autonomy lies in the full expression of feelings about the separation by the therapist and all the group members. No matter what the feelings are, the affective contact between the member leaving and everyone else in the group helps all to feel a continuity in the relationships despite the ending of the actual contact. However, full expression means dealing with both sides of the therapist's and group members' ambivalences, not just the postive or negative sides.

NORMS

Norms for dealing with separation crises develop as each successive separation crisis is resolved. These norms will be strongly influenced by the group's state when crisis occurs as well as by their experiences with prior separation crises. In the parallel phase groups will tend to deny the separation overtly but will tend to reinforce their feelings about holding back from engaging in relationships with each other. In the inclusion phase, there is a danger of other members expressing only their positive or negative feelings about the separation without experiencing and expressing both sides of their ambivalence. Depending on the degree of freedom of affective expression attained during the mutuality phase, the group will be able to express its full range of feeling about the separation and its meaning for everyone.

Self-awareness Issues for the Therapist

A problem for therapists arises in the expectations of the group to deal fully with a separation crisis, no matter what the group's norms for expression of any feelings have been. Therapists, particularly with groups that are not fully developed or in which there are restrictive norms for affective expression, need more than ever to be aware of the full range of their own reaction so that they don't force the group to do more about separation than it can.

With groups that are less able to express fully their own feelings it may be more important for the therapist at least to express all of his feelings so as to keep therapist-member affective contact open through the separation. However, the individual member's ability to tolerate the full expression of the therapist's affect must be a prime consideration. In groups with little ability for dealing with separation and a separating member who cannot tolerate the expression, it may be well for the therapist to allow the usual denial of the feeling surrounding separation to operate.

Soon after the start of a group of severely depressed people, the therapist decided to leave the agency. The group was still in the mourning phase that depressive groups often start in. Almost by definition it meant that the group could in no way experience and express their anger at the therapist. It was decided that the group be allowed to handle the termination of the therapist in whatever way they decided. The group planned a party, gave the therapist a little present, and never discussed their anger. After the new therapist developed a relationship with the group, the members began to express their hostility at the former therapist.

GOALS: ACHIEVEMENT

The major reason a final separation crisis develops is because individual and/or group goals are reasonably achieved. Separation crises during the parallel and inclusion phases may be precipitated by members' feelings that their major goals are not achievable in the group. In premature separation crises it is important that the therapist and other members understand what the member was seeking and whether those goals were indeed possible within the group.

If a member has reasonably achieved his goals, then it is important that he consider the process by which he did so and learn how the therapist and other members evaluate his goal attainment. Support for the achieving of major goals contribute to a member's feeling of autonomy as he leaves the group. If everyone is agreed that major goals have been achieved, then all that needs to be done is to work out a termination process suited to the member's particular inclinations. Some members need to terminate immediately; others want to taper off in attendance. Still others will choose a definite time or outside event in order to test the solidity of their achievements apart from the group. A period of mastery in the form of a termination phase is helpful to most members, but a termination phase precipitates a regression for some members that can ultimately undermine their termination.

In any sound course of therapy many more questions than resolutions arise. Whenever a group member achieves his or her major goals, the therapist and other members tend to raise unresolved issues that they think need to be resolved or mastered before the member leaves. It is vital that all consider how important these remaining issues really are before prevailing on a member to stay. More to the point are the possibilities that the new goals are motivated by unresolved separation issues rather than real need for the member to achieve them before separating.

At times, although others may feel a member really has much further to go by their standards, the individual may have achieved all he or she can for the moment. In the author's opinion it is well to let a person leave the group with a reasonably accurate perception of where he is but with permission to either remain on a plateau or attempt to go the rest of the distance on his own. The author has found that if individuals are allowed autonomy with respect to separation, they find it easier to return for help either with the same therapist or with another therapist. When members are pressed with unfinished work and forced to stay when not really committed to it, their feelings of autonomy tend to be undermined, resulting in regression both in their achieved levels of functioning and their use of the group. Members who separate loaded with all they haven't done do so with less certainty and with feelings of abandonment by the group because of the inherent rejection of their autonomous strivings.

In goals achievement discussions the therapist and other members must fully appreciate both what business the member leaves unfinished and why the member feels the need to separate with what he has achieved. With full understanding of the motives for leaving, the member is more likely to stay if it is really essential; moreover, if the member does leave, he is more likely to leave feeling understood, not abandoned, and readier to return to therapy if and when he feels the need.

RETURN TO EARLIER ROLES

During the period of depression in separation crises, members tend to revert back to roles they occupied earlier in the group's life, especially if the group has not achieved a high degree of intimacy and mutuality. The return to earlier roles protects against feelings of exclusion and against reactivation of fears of rejection. The reversal to earlier roles is important only as a way of understanding the general regression in the group.

Self-awareness Issues for the Therapist

The therapist must not get caught up in the regression to the degree of feeling either that all the growth was for naught or that the group needs the kind of help it did when people occupied these same roles earlier. As the group resolves the separation crisis by accepting the fact of separation and dealing with both sides of their ambivalent feelings about the regression with particular emphasis on the expression of the separation anger, then members readily relinquish these early roles and return to their achieved levels of interaction. Most important, the therapist shouldn't return to early roles that he performed in the groups. This is particularly true if the group has achieved a high degree of mutuality and the therapist has relinquished most of the political power and authority for the group. It would undermine the group for the therapist to take over for the group again as he did in the parallel phase.

8

Termination Phase: Self-dependency

Death is but crossing the
world, as friends do the seas;
they live in one another still.
—William Penn

The termination phase begins with the final separation crisis and lasts either through the end of the group or until the mourning of the lost member is completed and the group accepts the new composition of members. Termination phases are a phenomenon of closed groups and occur less frequently, if at all, in open-ended groups. Most often in open-ended groups, members terminate instead of, during, or after experiencing a final separation crisis. However, closed groups undergo an inevitable termination phase as everyone in the group grows in awareness that the end of the group is approaching. In most short-term groups, those of less than six months' duration, a separation crisis ensues with the advent of the mid-point in the group's life.

The midpoint separation crisis is very often the beginning of the termination phase in short-term groups. As the members experience the possibility of the group ending they being to despair of achieving their goals before the end. Members also begin to be concerned with the inevitable loss of the other members and the therapist at the end of the group and develop some degree of hesitancy in further investment in relationships. The goal issues are more easily resolved than the relationship issues since the goals can be renegotiated or redefined and the effort to accomplish the goals before the end of the group can be maximized. The relational issues, however, are considerably harder to settle because they represent the worst fears of the members, those that serve as the reason in the early phases to not be involved with each other. As loss becomes a more tangible reality at the midpoint crisis, the threat of rejection and loss is reinforced.

In groups of fewer than eight sessions, the midpoint crisis might arise in the second, third, or fourth session. Thus, the midpoint separation crisis arises right when members may be experiencing some fight-flight dilemmas and, consequently, most members will resolve the issue in favor of flight. This flight may not mean that members actually leave the group; it might mean that they do not press their demands for norms and goals and prepare to accept whatever they get from the group.

In groups of twelve or more sessions members have sufficient time to resolve fight-flight issues by deciding to fight and resolve; therefore, there is greater probability that the group will have more cohesion and sounder formation by the time it reaches the midpoint separation crisis. In groups of between eight to twelve sessions, the nature, structure, and composition of the group determines whether they can develop sufficient cohesion and direction to have a reasonably profitable experience.

Final separation crises begin either with the reaching of the midpoint crisis in closed short-term groups or by the therapist's or member's recognizing that the end is in sight. The dynamics of the termination phase for short-term and long-term groups is similar but the depth of those dynamics differs with the length and depth of the process.

A typical termination phase may begin five sessions prior to the end of the group. If group members have not overtly recognized the fact of termination the therapist might well announce the fact and set in motion the final separation crisis. Some factual questions relating to termination may arise during the following meeting, but the reality of termination will be flatly denied by most, if not all, the members. The next few meetings will be rife with the separation crisis phenomenon of repressing the inevitablility of termination through super self-dependent behavior or frankly regressive and depressive behavior. Whether manifested by the hyperactivity of super self-dependence or the doldrums of frank depression, the underlying affective issue is the experiencing and expression of hostility as opposed to the guilt over having and expressing these feelings.

Depending on the nature, structure, and duration of the group, the therapist should consider whether and how to he'p the group experience and express termination anger. It may not be realistic to expect the group to deal any more overtly with their angry feelings about termination than they have dealt with any other feelings during the course of the group. Basic to the help with experiencing and expressing the anger is legitimating angry feelings about termination in the group. Most people feel that separation and termination anger is unjustified and unfounded since most often no one can be blamed. It often helps to explain that most people feel unjustified in experiencing these angry feelings, but that the feelings are, nevertheless, omnipresent in separations and are neither good nor bad, but human and universal.

The unfolding of the anger as a process often begins with indirect expression. The depressive or super self-dependent mood of the second or third meetings after the formal recognition of termination often gives way to the there-and-then discussion of angry or morbid subjects—for example, war, crime, mutilation. Members may even begin to talk of anger at past but disappointing sources of gratification—their bad parents, bad teachers, bad bosses, bad lovers. In a group whose members have not been able to deal with any depth of feelings, it might be well to allow the expression of the separation anger in the there-and-then sphere. However, in groups who have been able to experience and express a wide range of affect, it would be useful to connect the there-and-then expression of hostilities to the here-and-now. A group that has been well able to express their feelings about most other issues and has resolved several separation crises in the past may not even need the therapist's help to bring the focus of hostility into the here-and-now. In any event, the initial here-and-now expression of hostility will be directed at the therapist and the group from the stand point of what the therapist was supposed to have provided by way of group experience but didn't provide. In a five-session termination process the full brunt of the hostility is often expressed in the third or fourth session.

If the therapist accepts the hostility without becoming unduly alarmed, dejected, or defensive, then the members can complete their catharsis and begin to deal in a balanced way with the fact of termination. Focus of a balanced process in the last meeting or two generally is on a recapitulation or positive and negative evaluation of the group experience and/or a discussion of where the individual members are going in their lives after the group is over. The here-and-now recapitulation often includes the historical development of the group and its meaning to the individuals, as well as the meaning of the individual's relationships to other members of the group both historically and currently. The balanced discussion often includes how the meaning of ingroup relationships and development can be carried on in life after the group.

Affective contact (positive and negative) among all the members and the therapist helps members leave the group without feelings of abandonment. To the degree that this expression is unrealized for each member will each member feel unfinished and possibly abandoned or rejected by the group. What is said in final affective exchanges seems less important than the fact of final affective contact.

> In the second to last meeting of a closed-end, school year group of early adolescent boys, the therapist asked the boys how each felt about rejoining the group in the fall. Rich, who consistently came an hour early for most meetings, responded, "Come to this stupid group again? As far as I'm concerned its been a total waste and I've been bored all year."
>
> The other boys joined in a heated depreciation of the whole experience. In the course of the meeting the anger gave way to joking about incidents that occurred during the life of the group. When the boys left the meeting they unscrewed the light bulbs in the hallway chandelier outside the therapist's office.
>
> In the final meeting, Rich was apologetic for what he had said in the previous meeting, saying, "I went a little overboard last week; so, just in case you got the wrong idea, I think I might want to be in next year's group.
>
> In the ensuing discussion, the boys talked both about their summer plans and whether or not they felt further need for the group.

If a group has been unable to achieve any degree of affective contact in its life, then the separation and termination process will be no more disappointing than the lack of affective contact itself. Attempting to make up for the lack of affective contact during the life of the group in the termination phase can create greater feelings of abandonment by stirring up hostile feelings that cannot be fully released and that perhaps leave members feeling even more unworthy after the group is over.

The individual member who terminates from an open-ended group after experiencing a final separation crisis most often doesn't stay through a termination phase. However, when members do stay for a period of termination after undergoing a final separation crisis, they go through a gradual disengagement from the group processes while focusing most of their energies on their outside lives with particular emphasis on mastery of there-and-then situations. The member needs to experience as an individual what was described above for the whole closed group by way of a final separation crisis and full, final, affective interaction with the therapist and other members. From the evaluation of the individual's readiness to leave the group, other members begin to get ideas about what it might take ultimately for them to terminate. From the individual's final affective interaction other members prepare for their own affective termination from the group.

No matter how long a member has been in a group, if he or she attends at least one final meeting to deal with the decision to terminate, he or she almost always seem to feel better about the decision. Very often, the other members can contact the member who is leaving prematurely and help the member stay in the group, especially if the reason for leaving is because of fight-flight or intimacy fears. The affective contact afforded by a full discussion with the group will often relieve the fears that were causing the member to flee. In fact, for new members of an open-ended group the fight-flight and intimacy fears quite frequently are reduced or resolved by a member's reaching a point of wanting to terminate but returning to deal with the group and finding that the group will bend to their wishes and include them.

Role of the Therapist

The role of the therapist in the termination phase is crucial, since a great deal of how and whether the group handles termination can be traced to the therapist's comfort and skill with the process. The therapist's role begins with initial contact with each member. The therapist should come away from that first contact with some idea of the member's therapeutic needs and the member's potential for meeting those needs in the group. In addition, the therapist should try to determine the degree to which the member might become dependent on the group or on the therapist because of the member's personality structure and the requirements of accomplishing the therapeutic task. In other words, at the outset of therapy the therapist must begin to develop ideas about how the individual can reach a point of doing without therapy.

From the mutuality phase a balance in the focus on the here-and-now and there-and-then time spheres supports the transfer of here-and-now growth to the there-and-then. The author feels that the here-and-now focus is the most powerful way to produce growth in the group but that most group members need direct help to transfer this growth to outside situations. Children and adolescents are more likely to make the transfer than adults. People with a high degree of anxiety or an overt or underlying schizophrenic process will have more difficulty transferring here-and-now learning to their outside lives. Thus, most clients must be prepared for termination long before the actual termination process and must be helped to make there-and-then connections with their here-and-now growth. Increasing confidence in coping with the there-and-then tends to facilitate members' consideration of being able to do without the group.

Long before the actual termination phase, it is crucial for the therapist to assess where the individual members in the group are and what they hope to accomplish. Several authors have considered criteria for determining readiness to leave psychotherapy groups (see, for example: Nacht et al., 1954; Weiner, 1973; Bross, 1959). Ultimately, the criteria should reflect the individual members' reasons for coming and their progress to those ends. In supervision, the author has often required therapists to summarize each member's progress a month or two before termination was formally introduced to closed groups. The idea of the summary was to assess the gains and the continuing needs of the individual members with an eye toward the feasibility of termination. In a closed-end group that assessment has to be made in light of the projected ending date. Members who have reasonably benefited from the process need to be helped to terminate. Appropriate dispositions must be considered for those with whom continuing need is anticipated.

Self-awareness Issues for the Therapist

Most important is that the therapist gain a sound position with respect to his thoughts and feelings about each member considered for termination from the group. In other words, the most important pretermination function of the therapist is to come to realistic terms with himself about his work and relationships with the group to be able to help the individuals and/or group with the termination process.

In addition to his own feelings about terminations based on past experiences in his personal life and prior therapeutic endeavors, the therapist faces many very difficult self-awareness and countertransference issues in the termination process. The first difficult phenomenon is the regression or super self-dependent behavior of the group during the final separation crisis. With a firm grasp of the achieved level of the group prior to the separation crisis, the therapist is less vulnerable to perceiving the group and individual as needing the kind of help they received in earlier phases. Unless the therapist comes to grips with what has and has not developed in the group, the therapist may be subject to feelings of failure, guilt, and anger at the members for regressing. These feelings may cause the therapist either to miscalculate the situation and contribute to the regression by providing the earlier forms of helping or to become too demanding of the group and not allow the regression to run its course. Not allowing the regression to run its course might force the premature experiencing of separation anger, causing the group either to repress the anger more firmly or perhaps move toward expression before they have completed the mourning of the group's loss.

The next critical point in the termination process is the unfolding and expression of the anger toward the therapist. If the therapist understands the meaning of the experience to the members, he or she will be able to withstand the hostility with less feeling of failure, rejection, or unappreciation. If the therapist has not reconciled personal feelings about the group prior to the termination process, he or she is in danger of becoming either punitively hostile or defensive. Either behavior causes the members to feel guilty about their separation hostility and interferes with the full expression of hostility and, subsequently, with the full affective contact essential for members to terminate without feeling abandoned.

Finally, the therapist must have his own assessment well in hand for the final one or two sessions when members are fully evaluating their experiences. The therapist's contributions to these evaluations are crucial in shaping the members' future concept of the experience. A member leaving a group feeling good about what has been accomplished will more likely return to a group when he has need than a member who leaves feeling the therapist saw no gains in him. Even if a member hasn't completed the work he came for, he is more likely to return to the group or seek another therapeutic situation if he feels understood in his reasons for leaving. A therapist who feels insecure about unfinished help might undercut the individual's attempt to be self-dependent, setting up a self-fulfilling prophecy about his return. A member who learns the opinion of the therapist and the other members about his unfinished work but also receives their understanding about the desire to leave is more inclined to stay or return if and as they experience the need for further help. In the author's experience, many members who leave prematurely with full affective understanding return for help with a new and fuller commitment to the therapeutic process.

> In an open-ended couple's group, Walt and Jane announced at one meeting that they had been getting along very well for the past few months despite some major pressures and upheavals. As they described how they had handled some of the upheavals, it appeared that they not only had developed viable ways of coping with their conflicts but also were able to enjoy their intimate periods as well. The other group members and the therapist each gave their feelings and reactions to the prospect of Walt and Jane leaving the group. Walt and Jane then decided that they would come to three more sessions "just to make sure that we are not overlooking anything since we have made a big investment in our therapy and don't want to take any chances."

When they returned for the next meeting it was apparent that they had not had a good week. As the events of the week unfolded, it seemed that Walt and Jane had regressed to a point very close to that which brought them to the group two years earlier. The other members began to question whether Walt and Jane were really ready to leave the group, pointing out how they seemed not to have mastered even some of the basic communication problems in their relationship. The therapist focused on what seemed like the major problem besetting them that week and recalled with them their prior experiences with a very similar problem. In the ensuing discussion they were able to cope with the problem with a minimum of help from the therapist and other members.

The therapist then suggested that in the previous session they and the group had only evaluated their readiness to leave but had not really dealt with their mixed feelings about the group, what it had meant to them and how they would miss not only the help and support but mostly the people. They came to group for two more rather uneventful (for them) meetings, then left.

AFFECTIVE POLARITIES:
GUILT OVER TERMINATION HOSTILITY

Guilt over the hostile feelings about termination and fears of abandonment are the major affective issues of the termination phase. The basic feeling that hostility is unfounded or undeserved creates guilt, which is the major cause of people being unable to express the hostility. For those with difficulty experiencing feelings in general and particularly for those with difficulty expressing hostile feelings, unalleviated guilt over termination hostility often causes them to feel abandoned.

Members who are able to experience and express their hostile feelings about termination and gain some comfort with them find relief from the remnants of unfinished mourning in past losses and are better prepared to deal with future losses and separations. Ideally, the resolution of the hostility-versus-guilt dilemma is a progressive process through the resolution of separation crises throughout the life of the group and the final separation and termination represent mastery of this growth.

MAJOR BEHAVIORAL FEATURES:
REGRESSION AND RECAPITULATION

Many needs are served by the regression and recapitulation of the termination phase (Garland et al., 1965; Mann, 1967). The regression is a means of re-immersing oneself into the group to avoid the inevitablility of termination. Regression in the face of termination is fueled by the underlying hostility and guilt over termination: for many members feelings of low self-worth recur and are directly due to their feelings about the hostility.

As the guilt and negative self-concept feelings about hostility are eased, the full affective interaction among the members facilitates the decathexis. To the extent that expression of termination hostility is blocked or inhibited the decathexis will be incomplete and either will never be worked out or will be worked out only in time after the member leaves the group. The full affective interaction of the termination phase allows all parties to the interaction to separate with a sense of completeness in the relationship.

SOURCES OF GRATIFICATION: TRANSITION

The major dynamic around sources of gratification in the termination phase is the transition from dependency on the group to dependence on self and people outside the group. The depression, regression, and super self-dependence of the separation crisis and termination phase are ways in which the members can deny their dependence on the therapist and group while indirectly continuing to ask for help. Support for the member's self dependence and dependence on people outside the group help the member gain reassurance for their capacities and permission for reliance on self and others outside the group.

RELATIONAL ISSUES: RELINQUISHMENT

Relinquishment of the group relationships is the key issue in the termination phase. The relational issues arise in the breaking of ingroup ties and the transfer of these ties to relationships outside the group. Full affective resolution of the termination process helps the individual member to carry the relationship achievements into other relationships outside the group. Less than full affective resolution of the termination processes leaves the terminating individual and the group with unresolved relational issues. Because most people come to group therapy with a history of difficulty with losses and separations in their familial and peer group, failure to resolve the termination from the group leaves them in doubt as to whether these other terminations were resolved during the course of group therapy.

Because the idyllic nature of relationships among members of a group in the depth of mutuality is difficult to achieve in relationships outside the group, members need to mourn the loss of these relationships and develop realistic expectations for marital and other relationships outside the group both while they are in the group and after termination.

SELF-OTHER CONCEPT: AFFECTIVE EQUIVALENCY

One of the most important vestiges that people take with them from a therapy group is the concept of self in relation to other group members and perhaps other people in general. While the feeling of equality that grows for members during the mutuality phase provides the basis for the self-other concept that members take from a group, the final test of that concept in the group arises separation and termination process can, if unrelieved, cause members once again to feel inferior to other people unless they leave the group with at least intellectual understanding of the universality of this anger and unless they experience and express this anger under optimal circumstances prior to termination. Empathy over separation anger is the final proof for the individual that he or she is indeed the affective equivalent of most other people.

> Martha, one of the author's individual clients, attended a three-day marathon conducted by a local sensitivity organization. She reported that she felt pretty good during the marathon until the grand finale. At this time each member was encouraged to give their final expression to the assemblage. Each member in turn got up and professed their *love* for everyone in the room including the trainers and other members. Martha at first balked but then did the same as all the others. After the marathon was over she became immediately despondent and felt there was something seriously wrong with her. At best she got to like two other people in the marathon and she did not feel the *love* for all the others that everyone else seemed to feel. In addition, she felt anger and even hatred for some of the people, something that no one else seemed to feel. Consequently, she felt so far inferior to others in the marathon that she was fearful that she would never be able to establish meaningful relationships. It took a great deal of reality-testing and universalizing to help Martha see the sham and to help her recognize that others probably left the marathon feeling as she did.
>
> What had apparently happened is that the trainers developed some *positive feelings only* norms for the group and enforced repression of anger and any other disagreeable feelings. In the grand finale the trainers set the tone by first expressing their *love* for everyone, which built on the guilt of the participants and forced them to express only their *love* feelings. In some subsequent contacts with others who attended the marathon, Martha was reassured that others indeed played the game in the group and also had some unexpressed anger.

POWER RELATIONS: NO LONGER AT ISSUE

In the face of termination, power is no longer a major issue for group members. Generally, if termination is occurring after the group has been in a solid state of mutuality, then power would have been well distributed among the therapist and group members. The only remaining need for power is for leaving the group. Members who consider leaving the group against the feelings and opinions of the therapist and or other group members need a surge of personal power for the conflict that results from the attempt to leave. If the member reasonably shared in the mutuality power, then getting the power to leave presents no major problem. If the member did not reasonably share in the mutuality power or if the member is leaving the group prior to mutuality, then getting the power necessary for leaving would depend more on the individual's capacity. Members who do not feel they have sufficient power to deal with the group about termination very often leave without confronting the issue in the group. Sometimes members who do not feel sufficiently powerful to deal with the group but who attempt to deal with the group anyway most often feel more powerful as a result of the confrontation with the group. Of course, the therapist's support during such a confrontation often makes the difference.

CONFLICT: FREE AND OPEN

The nature of conflict during the termination phase basically remains as free and open as in the mutuality phase. The tendencies to take sides and form factions prominent in the inclusion phase and reduced during the mutuality phase remain basically reduced. However, since many of the termination conflicts are concerned with potential loss of members, there is some reactivation of the ultimate fears of rejection that make conflict during the inclusion phase so highly charged and bombastic. The fear in the termination phase of the group or in the termination of an individual from the group for both sides of the conflict is abandonment. Thus, the resolution of the termination conflict means the resolution of everyone's ambivalent feelings about leaving and being left. As described earlier, resolution of the termination conflict results in affective contact through empathy around the termination hostilities. With empathy around the termination hostilities the important foundation is laid for all the members to deal with both sides of their termination ambivalence.

COHESION

During the termination phase members of closed groups progressively back away from deepening their ties. They also begin to insulate themselves from each other by lessening the degree to which they empathize. However, the affective bond can be sustained around the common feelings about termination itself. An inverse cohesion also occurs around the sharing of common feelings about needing to gain more distance from each other. Many groups that have achieved a depth of mutuality prior to the final separation and termination phase continue the empathic bond around the feelings of needing distance, separation, anger, and ambivalence about leaving. They also share feelings of nostalgia for their common experiences in group. Thus, a well-developed group maintains affective contact even through the termination phase.

In short-term groups or groups without sufficiently developed cohesion, group members begin to withhold themselves from any further depth in closeness during the termination phase. In very short-term groups (those of eight to twelve sessions) development of empathic bonds, other than termination feelings, begins to wane if not disappear. In groups of fewer than six sessions, apart from those special instances where a group faces an overriding common fate, members are inclined to hold back from developing closeness because the fear of loss or futility in developing close relationships for too short a period of time precludes reaching out for each other affectively.

In open-ended groups, terminating members have a little more difficulty with cohesion toward the end of their membership. There is a greater tendency for other members to polarize against the terminating member with respect to the termination ambivalences. Again, depending on the state of the group's development, this polarization can be resolved with a sharing of the termination fears, anger, and ambivalence. During and after the terminating members leaves, the remaining members need to reconcile their own fears of loss so as to re-establish and/or continue the former level of cohesion and continue on from there.

It is crucial to the terminating members that out-group ties have been developed and sanctioned during the mutuality phase so that greater emotional investment in these outside bonds can facilitate the movement out of the group.

CONTROLS: REVERSION TO PUNISHMENT AND REJECTION

Since the ultimate control of exclusion from the group can no longer serve as threat to terminating members, the ultimate controls revert back to punishment and rejection. The major fear of rejection during the termination phase is the feeling of abandonment for both the members leaving and the members remaining in the group. However, acceptance by the group for termination serves as the major hold that the group has over the departing individuals.

If termination is occurring after the group has achieved a depth of mutuality then controls are shared by all the members and are mostly likely incorporated by the individuals as personal controls. Full affective contact among the terminating and remaining members, even if that contact involves the full sharing of mutual ambivalence and not acceptance of the termination per se, insures the preservation of the positive feelings about the group experience and the continued incorporation of group controls.

NORMS: SPECIFIC TO TERMINATION

The terminating individual will incorporate the norms for affect and behavior developed in the group to the same degree that he was involved in normative development and the empathic bond of the group. Depending on the depth of mutuality, the freedom to differ comfortably in affect and behavior with others in and outside of the group is also firmly implanted.

During termination itself, however, the group develops specific norms that determine the manner in which termination is accomplished in the group. Termination norms are developed through the progressive dealing with separation crises and by the way in which normative crises are resolved with each intimacy crisis faced by the group through the mutuality phase. If restrictive norms for expression develop, then the final separation and termination phase will not be likely to contain the essential expression of affect. If the norms of the group grow progressively more freeing, then a full termination process will most likely be completed. Although normative growth is always possible during the termination process itself, norms developed during the earlier life of the group are more likely to govern the termination phase.

GOALS: THE ACCOUNTING

A full termination process includes an accounting of how the members and the group achieved their goals with a realistic appraisal of whether and to what degree their individual and group goals were achieved. In open groups, where the members most likely are leaving after having achieved significant goals, this assessment helps the departing member gain closure on the experience. Remaining members gain in their capacity to assess their current position with respect to goals and develop increasingly realistic ideas of when they will have achieved what they want from the group.

Very often, the termination of one member infects others with the thoughts of termination. Sometimes, this contagion is useful, encouraging members who are actually ready to leave but have not been able to begin termination. However, other members consider termination or actually terminate out of fear; they are reluctant to reinvest in newer members and feel the group will never be the same. Some members consider termination because the member leaving was the most meaningful to them and they fear, are reluctant, or are not hopeful about establishing similar ties to other members of the group. In any event, the assessment of goal achievement for each terminating member facilitates the process of assessment for the remaining members and may help the members, more than anything else, to see reasons of their own for going through the process of reinvesting in the group rather than leaving with the terminating member.

In closed groups, where the group may end before some individuals are truly finished, and in open-ended groups where a member terminates prematurely, the members should be helped to think about what is left undone and how these wants and needs might be served in other groups or other services. It is important for all members to share their goals beyond the group with the group. Sharing of external life goals helps to make the termination more of a commencement of life without the group rather than only a termination from the group.

ROLES: LOSS TO THE GROUP

The progressive disengagement of members from the group during the termination phase results in a relinquishment of roles occupied in the group. In groups that have achieved a depth of mutuality there is less difficulty when a member relinquishes a role because others may have shared that role and functions. If a member is terminating before the group has achieved some depth of mutuality, then the loss of that member's role may become a major problem for the group. On one hand, a struggle for the role may erupt among several of the members. On the other hand, there may not be a ready replacement to fill the role of the person terminating and a gap in the performance of that role may result.

The real test of whether a termination will leave a gap or whether someone will move into the role occurs after the terminating member actually leaves. If there has been a full mourning and termination, then others find it easier to step into the role. However, if the group has unresolved feelings about the person leaving, then the role is less likely to be occupied immediately and a ghost chair haunts the process.

While every person's role relinquishment has an impact on the group, some role relinquishments are more obvious to everyone than others. Indigenous leadership roles are generally more obvious to the members. Members whose roles were a part of the overt activity of the group—stimulators of discussion or injectors of anxiety, even group thermostats who cut off rising anxiety—are more directly missed. Most dramatic is the loss of the group thermostat. Although it might be expected that in the absence of the thermostat the group will forge ahead, instead, the group becomes more frightened of risking anxiety-laden subjects without the thermostat there to control the level of anxiety.

Less dramatic but nonetheless significant are the terminations of more passive and withdrawn members. To the degree that these members become objects of group pity or uncertainty they often inhibit discussion, simply because the other members don't want to make them feel bad. Termination of a more passive member often lightens the emotional climate of the group and frees the members for more open interaction.

In sum, whether the role of a member is more or less obvious, his leaving always has an impact on the group and necessitates a major or minor reorganization of the roles of the remaining members. The earlier in the development of the group the termination occurs, the more it disrupts the role organization of the group. The later in the group development that the termination occurs, the more likely that the resiliency and fluidity of roles will fill the gap it creates.

PART THREE

1

Emotional
Dynamics

The interaction of individual emotions in groups has been the subject of much theoretical speculation and research. At present, no one theory consistently and completely accounts for the interaction of individual emotions among the members of a group. The following discussion attempts to describe the ebb and flow of emotions within and among individuals in a therapy group. Emotions that recur most often in group therapy are anxiety, empathy, hostility, transference, and identification. Conflict is a major way in which individual emotions interact.

ANXIETY IN GROUPS

Individual anxiety—apprehension and uneasiness—comes from many sources. Members of therapy groups bring anxieties from their past lives, anxieties about their current and future life situations, and anxieties arising from the group experience itself. Anxiety is both the boon and bane of group experience and its management by the therapist and members is perhaps one of the most crucial aspects of group therapy. Some anxiety helps individuals and groups to mobilize their resources in order to cope with the causes. An overabundance of anxiety tends to interfere with a person's or group's coping capacities. Absence of anxiety can render the group useless. A recent study by Moxnes (1974) clearly demonstrates the rise of anxiety when members are on the brink of sharing private or previously undisclosed personal material. Anxiety levels receded when either the material was shared or the pressure for revelation receded.

Individual anxiety about current life and group situations serves as a major early source for group processes and particularly for the interaction of emotions among members. One member's anxiety can be the stimulus that causes other members to become anxious about the same or similar phenomenon that provoked the initial member's anxiety. Redl's (1942) theory about emotional and behavioral contagion is based on the diffusion of anxiety in groups. A group is working at maximum emotional effectiveness when the anxiety of one member contages the anxiety of other members and leads to the other members experiencing the meaning of that anxiety for themselves. *The group is providing a simultaneous emotional growth experience for all the members to the degree that other members of the group experience their own anxieties about the subject at hand. To the degree that other group members do not experience their own anxieties about the subject at hand, to that same degree the group is treating one member in front of the others.* Much of the process of therapy groups centers on the ways in which anxiety is allowed to spread from one member to other members and how much it is stopped at the source, diverted from group processes, or shut out by other members. When anxiety flows among members, then empathy, identification, and transference can also flow. Stemming the tide of anxiety can at best give rise to helping one person in front of the others or at worst provide no help or growth for anyone in the situation. Empathy, hostility, and conflict are the major phenomena which can either open or close the flow of anxiety among group members (Flescher, 1957).

The first line of protection against the anxiety contagion among group members is the personal patterns or defense mechanisms of each member. Each member employs his own defense mechanisms to shut out the possible impact of the anxiety upon himself. Although each member, especially during the parallel phase, may experience discomfort with another's anxiety, each handles the discomfort in his own characteristic way.

A second line of defense against the flow of anxiety, a parallel phenomenon, but one that may appear whenever the source of anxiety is too threatening, is to stop the anxiety at the source. Group members are likely to try stopping anxiety at the source in one of two major ways. In the first, everyone helps the person with anxiety but remains detached from the subject. Particularly characteristic of stopping the anxiety through helping are suggestions from the other members on handling the problem before the full unfolding of the nature of the problem and how the person feels about it. Also missing in such a discussion is how other members feel about the problem, the person having the problem, and particularly about the person's bringing the problem to the group. The other members providing the intellectual and distant helping do so in the hope that the problem will be solved, the individual's anxiety will be diminished, and the anxiety will all go away. Very often the advice of other members will help solve the particular problem and, consequently lower the individual's anxiety but the individual will miss the possible universalization of the problem and the empathy of the other members. The other members miss dealing with similar problems and feelings in themselves and also the empathic experience.

The second major way that group members try to stop anxiety at the source is by getting angry at the person, changing the subject to less anxiety-provoking issues, or overtly discounting the problem. For example, the members might begin to talk about other matters, joking, acting out, and creating diversion. In children's groups these diversions are usually behavioral disruptions.

The process of moving from shutting out anxieties aroused by others to experiencing the anxiety and its full significance for oneself is basic to emotional interaction in therapy groups. Members actively engaged in detached helping or in other anxiety stopping behavior at the source are less able to shut out the anxiety. The need for other members to actively help or divert the anxiety of others means that their anxiety is making them uncomfortable to the point where their personal defensive structure is not shutting out the anxiety and they need to do something more direct about it. Their interest in stemming the anxiety in the other person is to stem the growing anxiety in themselves.

Inviting the detached helpers to consider the meaning of the issue for themselves begins the process of helping them and the group toward emotional interaction. Asking members who discount, divert, or get angry at the anxiety-provoking member or issue to discover its significance for themselves also helps toward emotional interaction. However, the therapist must be aware of and must respect the reasons members need either to shut out anxiety or to stem the tide, for it is only through overcoming these reactions that the individual can be open to deeper emotional sharing (Whitman et al., 1960). Emotional sharing is both a means and an end of group therapy. Emotional sharing is a product of group development through the parallel and inclusion phases and requires adequate resolutions of authority and intimacy crises for most groups. Once the long-term group is fully developed, then emotional sharing becomes the basic vehicle for group therapeutic processes.

When too much anxiety leads too quickly to emotional sharing, it often leads to intellectualized or sharply delimited emotional sharing. The basic reaction of the members to too much anxiety too soon is to actually or virtually disassociate themselves from the group. This disassociation may take the form of actually dropping out, attending sporadically, or arriving late at each meeting. However, basic disassociation from a group may also appear as withdrawal at meetings or intellectualized participation. Members who participate in intellectualized ways come to know what feelings and reactions are expected in the situation and they behave *as if* they have these feelings and reactions but they aren't really sure what they experience. In a negative way, these members can become increasingly aware of other feelings and, if they perceive these feelings as unacceptable to the others, they are inclined to feel worse about themselves since they don't gain any feeling of universality. The ultimate defense from too much anxiety is the pseudo-intimate group, in which everyone has to look, feel, and act alike. Hostility and conflict are often ruled out in such groups since difference and disagreement are threatening to the facade of togetherness.

> George, a young adult man, entered a long-term open-ended therapy group mainly because he felt unable to attract young women and establish relationships with them. He was very active in his pursuit of women but seldom got dates and what dates he did manage to get were generally one-time events. The group George entered consisted of young to middle-aged adults of both sexes and, among other things, all were concerned with relationships, particularly with the opposite sex.
>
> At first George would go into long and often poetic exhortations of his anguish over not being able to realize his "god-given right for sex." The other members would respond to George with a mixture of joking and specific suggestions about his appearance and demeanor. Although George's appearance very slowly improved, his exhortations and relaying

of failures to get dates continued. He was almost totally unresponsive to other group members and their plight but would patiently wait for a "turn" to air his weekly plea.

Finally, one of the young women in the group became very angry with George for only being interested in sex and not in totality of a relationship. The young woman also shared her concern about a new relationship. She was becoming interested and was afraid that sex was all the new boyfriend was interested in. Other group members tied into the experience of this young woman then angrily questioned George about his sexual interest in the other members of the group. A direct dealing with the reactions of others to George's exhortations about sex and how they are put off by him in the group began to help George deal with his fears of relationships both within and outside the group. George's exhortations gradually diminished and were progressively replaced with his attempts to make emotional contact with other people both within the group and outside it.

Although George had many similar interactions in the group, the one described above was the first in the series and exemplary of the continuing process. George's anxiety about his situation was partially masked by his intellectual exhortations. However, the other group members were upset by his plight. Although the other members recognized that it represented a more serious relational problem than their own, they often felt that their relational problems were as hopeless as George's seemed to be. George's anxiety about his plight would touch off the anxieties of the other members who feared similarities in their plight. By keeping George's plight humorous and comfortably distant from their own, other members didn't have to experience their own similar anxieties.

The reaction of the first young woman to George helped to punch through George's employing his preoccupation with sex to stave off relationships in the group in much the same way he used his preoccupation with sex to stave off relationships outside the group. The result was that George became able to experience and share his many other concerns about relationships as well as tie in to similar concerns of others.

TRANSFERENCE AND IDENTIFICATION

Two major emotional phenomena that are an integral part of every group psychotherapeutic process are transference and identification.

Transference

Transference is an overused and abused word in mental health literature. Some definitions seem to incorporate the entire therapeutic process into transference, while others are more circumscribed. In this discussion *transference* is taken to mean the attribution of feelings and desires stemming from other relationships to the therapist and other members in the therapy group. Basic transferences derive from unconsciously retained early childhood experiences, but subsequent and particularly current relationships often influence the individual's perception, feelings, and reactions to other people in the group whom they invest with qualities from relationships outside the group (Kadis et al., 1974:75-78).

Two basic forms of transference occur in therapy groups: first are transferences deriving from relationships with parents or parent surrogates and further developing in relationships with such authority figures as teachers, employers, and doctors. Second are transferences deriving from relationships with siblings and further developed in relationships with peer groups, fellow students, and fellow employees. (A myriad of literature is available on various transference in groups. See, for example: Glatzer, 1965; Battegay, 1966; Durkin, 1964: 140-143.) Relationships with love objects represent another possibility for transferences in the group and these transferences derive from a combination of relationships with parents and siblings. Finally, for group members who are parents, transferences derived from relationships with children may emerge (Slavson, 1950:17-20).

In the initial phase of group development, transferences generally develop in the classic manner: the therapist is invested with qualities basically derived from feeling about parents and authority figures and the other members are vested with qualities derived from sibling, peer, and love relationships. However, wide age differences between members (more than fifteen or twenty years) often awaken parental and parent-child transference reactions in the respective members during the early phases of group development (Slavson, 1950:16-19). As the group develops, parental and authority transferences develop among the group members even when they are similar in age (Durkin, 1964:148).

Positive transference reactions help members enter relationships with the therapist; negative transference can inhibit the development of relationship with the therapist (Yalom, 1975:200-201). Just as in individual therapy, in group therapy many aspects of the transference to the therapist are beneficial. Endowing the therapist with parental functions allows corrective emotional experiences or reparenting. Experiences of nurture, acceptance, support, and freedom to develop autonomy within an empathic relationship with the therapist can provide some compensatory experiences to substitute for past lacks or distortions stemming back to early childhood.

It is extremely important that over time the member come to understand the nature of the transference in the relationship with the therapist and that he progressively come to perceive the therapist as another human being, not necessarily like a parent. Understanding and change gleaned from reducing the transference in the relationship with the therapist help the member understand and change relationships with parents and authority figures (Hulse, 1961). One added factor that therapy groups provide is a re-experience of triadic relationships among siblings and parents. Familial transference reactions based on relationships with other group members as siblings and the therapist as parent provide opportunities for the group member to understand his reactions to peers in the presence of authority and the archaic origins in the family. Gaining a different experience within the therapy group can help the member understand and change the nature of his role in the family with respect to siblings and parents as well as in other life situations where the influence of the archaic family role are manifest.

Perhaps more important in the long-term therapy group are the transference phenomena that arise among the members. Because they can include multiple transferences among members as well as mutual transferences, these phenomena become very complex as the group develops. Multiple transferences arise when one member endows another with parental transferences and at other times endows this same member with qualities reminiscent of a sibling or lover. (Slavson, 1950: 25-26; Durkin, 1964: 149-152).

In an open-ended therapy group of five members there were two young women in their mid-twenties, one older woman in her late forties, one older man in his early forties, and one young man of about thirty. The first young woman came to the group after obtaining a divorce from someone she married very quickly after her mother broke up her relationship with another young man because of religious differences. Since her divorce, the young woman was living at home with her mother. She wanted to leave home but couldn't cope with her mother's manipulations to keep her at home.

The older woman came to the group with many relational, vocational, and emotional complaints and, in particular, was feeling the anticipated loss of her son, who was graduating from high school and leaving for college within a few months.

A second young woman had left home and was living with a roommate and, among many other difficulties, was closely tied to her mother's directions for her.

The older man had come to the group primarily because the balance in his marriage, which has been an overadequate-underadequate relationship, had shifted and his wife, in a surge of independence, was threatening to leave him and refusing to participate in therapy.

The young man had come to therapy primarily because he was having trouble in his career and his relationships with women.

When the first young woman talked about her situation with her mother, particularly when she talked about moving out of her home, she would gain support from the other two young people but the two older people would directly and indirectly advise and caution her against rash action. The manner in which the younger woman presented herself tended to invite advice and parenting by all the other group members.

When the older woman talked about her situation with her son she would tend to get support from the older man; the young people in the group tended to see things from her son's point of view.

In the course of here-and-now discussion the younger woman was increasingly made aware of her tendency to play the helpless child, not only for her mother but also in the group and in other relationships. The older woman was also becoming aware of her tendency to mother everyone in the group and outside the group as she mothered her son and several recent bosses who ended up firing her. The only people who ever confronted the older woman directly were the two men. The two young women would go only so far with the older woman as usually the young man would express his hostility. One day one of the young women got extremely angry at the older woman and confronted her with her feeling that the older woman was smothering her. A heated discussion took place and the two men tried to help both see how they set each other up for their mother-daughter interaction. As the conflict developed the young woman experienced her anger at her mother for keeping her down, the older woman experienced her fears of losing her son when he leaves home, the second young woman experienced her fears of expressing anger at her mother, the older man got in touch with how he might be smothering his wife.

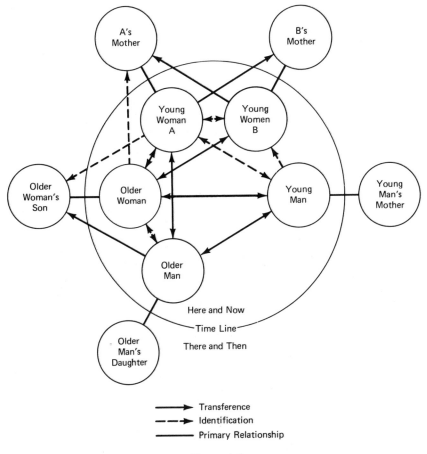

Figure 1.2

A few weeks later, after some similar but decreasingly bombastic confrontations in the group, the first young woman found an apartment and moved out of her mother's home after several heated conflicts. The older woman had a long talk with her son and shared her feelings about wanting him to stay home but also gave him a clear message that the best thing for both of them was for him to go. The second young woman soon after became able to disagree with her mother for the first time.

In this example, mutual transference arises when the older woman endows the younger woman with qualities derived from her relationship with her son while the younger woman endows the older woman with qualities derived from her relationship with her mother. The older man sometimes endows the older woman with qualities derived from relationships with his wife and at other times endows the older woman with qualities derived from relationships with his mother.

Identification

Identification (seeing some of oneself in another person) as an emotional process in group therapy is perhaps as important if not more important, than transference but has received surprisingly little attention in the literature. (Jeske, 1973, found a direct relationship between incidence of identification among group members and change in adult therapy groups.) Particularly in short-term groups, identification in its several forms may be the major factor in support and help. In long-term groups as well, identification plays a major role in both individual and group development.

Different levels and forms of identification operate in therapy groups. In a fundamental way identification arises from one person's perceiving others as having qualities that are similar to oneself or perceiving oneself as having qualities similar to others. Identification among members in overt ways is the first building block of group cohesion. This form of identification through perceived similarities begins to take place in the parallel phase and continues throughout the life of a group. Early and ready identification with another in the group often makes the difference between a person's staying in a group or dropping out early. It is important when forming groups to insure that, even in heterogenous groups, each member has at least one other member with whom he can easily and readily identify (Redl, 1966:236-253). Early identification among members provides the basis for initial pair and subgroup formation. In the previous example, the two young women and the young man identify with each other because of overt similarities in age, familial situations, and their attributing (transference) similar maternal qualities to the other woman in the group.

A second form of identification arises from vicariously experiencing another group member's act, almost as if one had done it himself (Redl, 1942). The vicarious experience through identification with other group member is a major source of therapeutic gain in groups. When thoughts, feelings, and acts that were taboo for the individual are expressed in the group by other members, the individual can gain relief through the other person's expression, can achieve vicarious satisfaction from results, and often, can have an opportunity to see that the feared consequences of those taboo thoughts, feelings, and actions either do not occur or aren't as horrendous as anticipated.

Each time a group member ventures into new expressive territory the other group members either join in or watchfully and anxiously wait to see the results (Redl, 1942). If those results are favorable, then that expression or action becomes open to any and all in the group. Unfavorable results can, of course, work to the continued repression of those thoughts or feelings. The prime example that occurs in every group is the first time any member disagrees with, expresses hostility toward, or is in any way negative toward the therapist. How the therapist reacts to the first negative actions by a member determines whether the other members will feel free to do likewise or will back down. Some members in some groups (for example, groups of chronic schizophrenics) may never confront the therapist themselves but can gain vicarious expression as other members confront the therapist. In the previous example, both young women gained vicarious satisfaction from the young man confronting the older woman, even though they were unable to confront her directly themselves. A therapist must also bear in mind that the vicarious identification can make the nonacting members feel anxious or guilty over their feelings and wishes to do the same. This phenomenon will be further elaborated under hostility.

A third form of identification arises from a member's wish to be like another person in the group, either the therapist or one of the other group members. This form of identification most often leads to incorporating or introjecting the other person into the self and becoming like the other person (Masler, 1969). A member may identify with an entire person or with parts of the other people in the group; their thoughts, feelings, or actions. A great deal of growth in group therapy stems from a member's wishing to be like another person and progressively growing to think, feel, or act, in whole or in part, like the other person.

If this kind of identification is to provide maximum benefit to all members, the group should have a variety of people who will think, feel, and act in different ways in response to similar problems. In such a group each member derives a wider range of reactions and coping potentials.

In the group previously described the first young woman identified with the young man when he would confront the older woman. As she vicariously experienced his confronting the older woman, at first she was anxious about his actions but also gained gratification from his expression. As time went on it was apparent that the young woman began to incorporate the young man's feelings and actions and finally was able to confront the older woman herself. The strength of the incorporation was evidenced in her going on to be able to confront the older man in the group, her mother, and eventually, bosses and almost anyone else when necessary.

A fourth form of identification concerns a person's feelings and reactions to the group as a whole and has two major aspects. First, one ascribes an emotional meaning to the group as a source of need satisfaction and nurture. Second, one gives up a part of one's identity to the group and views oneself from the self concept one develops as a group member. The nature and development of this phenomenon is discussed in the dynamics of group development under the self-other concept (Scheidlinger, 1964). Essentially, as the individual's identification with the group as a whole grows, the individual comes to feel a "sense of belonging" and a primary attachment similar to what one experiences in a family. The deeper the sense of belonging, the more the individual incorporates the group as a part of self. After leaving the group, the individual who has experienced a deep identification with the group has a new framework for viewing self in relation to others. This new framework stems from the emotional attachments developed with the group.

Transference and identification are not limited to members of the group during group discussions. In the group described previously, when the older woman talks about her son and how she attempts to prevent him from leaving home, the three young people in the group identify with the son. When one young woman talks about her mother, the other young woman endows that mother with qualities derived from her experience with her own mother and thus transference enters the reaction.

The basic sense of belonging develops from the three preceding forms of identification among individuals in the group. As members increasingly develop identifications with each other's thoughts, feelings, and actions, the bonds among them progressively extend to the entire group. The affinities that individuals have for each other start with the overt similarities in age, sex, and appearance, then deepen to include ideas and behavior and finally, extend to feelings. As the shared feelings progress, a basic bond of empathy develops among the group members and between the member and the group as a whole.

In the previous example, the two young women developed an identification with each other based at first on their both being women similar in age. As they progressed they found that they had similar feelings and difficulties in relating to mothers and other authority figures. As they became able to make affective contact with the older woman and older man in the group, they at first experienced the overt and ascribed (transference) differences. As the transference diminished, the two young women were able to identify with the older woman on the basis of the older woman's feelings about her own mother. What the young women essentially found was that the older woman basically identified herself with her own mother, with whom she had a hostile dependent relationship, and that she compensated for what she felt she didn't get from her mother by counterdependently mothering everyone she came in contact with.

Similarly, the women and men came together around their deepening mutual identifications and resulting empathy.

Many members who have been in a group for a long time report that after leaving the group they found themselves thinking about how the group would feel about the way they had met situations and had done. Such feelings are often sources of support or control. At first glance one might suggest that these are manifestations of the group's becoming the person's superego or conscience. However, since the individual has usually had some part in developing the group feeling or view and since a well-developed group has diverse feelings and points of view, it is more likely that this phenomenon of thinking about how the group might feel is more a result of the person's own expanded sense of self.

Classically, persons who have terminated from a group carry with them the sense of equality with all human beings that they grew to experience in the group. Whereas prior to coming to a group some individuals may have seen themselves as a child in a world of adults, a little sister, a big brother, or any other location in their basic identity, after being in the group they carry a greater sense of equality with other adults. Thus, identification with individuals in the group and with the group as a whole provides a new basis upon which members who were deeply involved view themselves in relation to other people (Scheidlinger, 1964). Especially since the group that has achieved a depth of mutuality values similarities and uniqueness, the process of identification in groups contributes in a major way toward development and/or affirmation of each member's basic identity.

THE EMPATHIC PROCESS

Empathy is the process of feeling some of oneself in another person. The life of a group can be divided into two parts: the search for empathy and the achievement and deepening of empathy. The search for empathy or deep human contact underlies the process of group formation from the parallel phase to the end of the inclusion phase. Beginning with the first affective contact and the resulting intimacy crises, progressive and deepening empathy serves as the basis of nurture, communication, and insight, particularly for working through from intellectual to emotional insight (Scheidlinger, 1966; Dymond, 1948; Stewart, 1954; Chessick, 1965; Cottrell, 1949). Participation in the empathic processes of the group itself goes further in developing or enhancing group members' capacities for relationships outside the group.

It is easier to experience empathy than describe it. Robert L. Katz has gone as far or further than anyone in attempting to set down the nature and development of empathic processes. Katz described four sequential phases of the empathic processes: Identification, incorporation, reverberation, and detachment (1963:41-47).

Identification

In Katz's formulation the individual is first absorbed in contemplating the other person and his experiences. This process of identification can take place on many levels and is limited mainly by the capacity of the person to allow feelings to be evoked and activated.

Incorporation

Incorporation is the act of taking another person's experience into oneself. Katz distinguishes incorporation from identification in that when one incorporates he takes other's feelings into himself and when one identifies he attributes his own feelings to someone else. Katz sums up by suggesting that when one incorporates another's feeling he takes it in as if it were his own.

Reverberation

In reverberation the feelings of others that have been incorporated begin to awaken feelings from the self. Katz suggests that the interaction between the incorporated feelings and the awakened feelings in oneself give rise to new appreciation and insights into oneself. Part of the person is infused in the identity of the other while another part of the person's feeling and thinking responds to the experience as external to the self.

Detachment

In detachment, reason and scrutiny are employed to help withdraw from the subjective involvement in another so as to reaffirm one's own integrity and establish the commonness and uniqueness with respect to others.

During the parallel phase, empathic levels are generally limited to identification on the basis of perceived similarities. The major, if not only source of empathy for individual members during the parallel phase is the therapist. During the inclusion phase, pairs and subgroups may begin to incorporate each other's experiences with reverberation or awakening of their own feelings. As group members experience the awakening of their own feelings through the incorporation and reverberation processes, their fears of intimate contact are also aroused. Central to these fears is the vulnerability of being open to the feelings of others. While each person experiences their own particular fears of vulnerability, the range runs from fears of rejection to fear of engulfment by the person with whom empathy is developing (classic fears at the intimacy crisis). Thus, as feelings in each member are awakened by the feelings of other members a critical situation develops in which members must either risk joining each other in empathic experiences or protect themselves through isolation from the feelings of others.

During the intimacy crisis, group members are negotiating with themselves and each other to insure that further empathic contact will not result in rejection, engulfment, and many other dangers in between. Depending upon the individual's past experiences with empathy, each member will sooner or later achieve the limits of their capacity to allow the feelings of others to evoke their own feelings. In this way, the group builds the safeguards for detachment in which members can sort out their subjective involvement with one another to arrive at a sense of their sameness and uniqueness. With each successive intimacy crisis, members become less fearful that empathy will lead to vulnerability. Each subsequent empathic experience reduces fears of rejection and successive experiences of detachment reduce fears of engulfment.

During the mutuality phase, the group members increasingly draw closer to each other and, at the same time they increasingly experience and value their uniqueness. (Schafer, 1959, calls this process generative empathy.) In other words, the empathic process is a major contributor to affirming or reaffirming each member's identity while helping him realize his capacity for empathic relationships. For the author, the major difference between identification and empathy is that in identification a person sees oneself in another person; in empathy, a person feels oneself in another person.

Empathic Experiences

Some of the classic examples of empathy in groups arise when all the members experience the overt or covert feelings of other members. When a group has been together for a long time, one member's expressing feelings of hopelessness awakens feelings of hopelessness in everyone. However, as some members experience the hopelessness, they become depressed along with the depressed member and consider the hopeless aspects of their own situations. As other members experience the hopelessness, they get drawn into experiencing the same feelings about their own situations, but then they begin to defend against those feelings either by attempting to get the other person to cope or by rallying their own coping efforts. The later phenomena will be further elaborated upon in the discussion of hostility and negative empathy.

Some of the most profound empathic experiences in groups have occurred in groups of depressives. In a series of groups led by the author for women who were suffering from protracted postpartum depression, the point where members become able to experience and express their feelings of resentment and hostility toward the babies are very dramatic moments. After twelve sessions of depressive incantations in one group, one mother blurted out that she sometimes gets so angry at the baby she could kill it. The other mothers in both horror and relief unanimously responded with reactions of "You too!" "I thought I was the only one," and "What kind of mothers are we?" The initial impact on the group was a feeling of relief that others shared their feelings coupled with a tendency to view themselves as bad people and bad mothers. However, the universal support through empathy led them to appreciate the probability that every mother harbored some rejection of the newborn and such rejection neither made them bad mothers nor meant that they didn't have other, more positive feelings about the baby. Over the ensuing sessions each was able to more fully explore the common meaning of motherhood and the baby for them as well as the meaning for each individual in her unique situation.

> Another example of the empathic process: One young man was constantly bemoaning his difficulty in establishing relationships with women while keeping the group at bay by persevering in his ineptness and unattractiveness. He kept rejecting the empathy of another young man in the group who was having almost as much difficulty in relationships. Finally, a young woman in the group angrily confessed that, even though she had many male friends, she was every bit as lonely and fearful of relationships as this young man. At this point the young man, almost in tears, asked, "You really feel as lonely as me?" This led to a discussion of how this young man put off everyone in the group and how other members grew to keep him at a distance because he overtly manifested what they experienced more privately, despite their seeming success with other people. From this point forward this young man began to establish more meaningful relationships with men and women in the group and outside the group.

Empathy is the core of the mutuality phase of group development. It is the empathic bond and processes that determine whether a group therapeutic situation involves treatment of one person in front of others or simultaneous treatment for the entire group. With empathic contact it matters very little whose situations are being discussed or whether discussion focuses on the here-and-now or there-and-then. Experiencing the parts of oneself in each situation that the group focuses upon is the way the entire group derives simultaneous help. Going back and forth between one's own feelings and the feelings of others serves both the person and situation in focus as well as all other members and their situations.

ACCEPTANCE AND EXPRESSION OF HOSTILITY

Hostility is an extremely important and often dreaded aspect of therapy groups. Many prospective members have visions of sitting in a "hot seat," with the therapist and all the group members yelling at them. Before coming into a group, hostility with its implications for punishment and rejection is often the biggest fear expressed by many people. It is interesting to note that, after being in groups for awhile, members come to terms with hostility but their fears of closeness with other group members loom as a larger danger than hostility ever did.

There are two major aspects of hostility in therapy groups. First is the function of the group to help people experience, become comfortable with, and express their hostility. For many groups, the function of becoming comfortable with experiencing and expressing hostility might occupy the entire process. Such groups might spend their entire existence in parallel and inclusion phases, with perhaps a few poorly resolved authority crises. In groups of chronic schizophrenics and groups of withdrawn children or adults, the major treatment objective may be encompassed by helping members to develop the capacity to express their hostilities and reduce their fears of hostility and its expression. Many of the nihilistic fantasies that such people associate with hostility are disconfirmed by the group process and the disconfirmation more than anything else helps to reduce the fears of hosility, free the expression of hostility, and diminish the dammed up or volcanic fears that overly repressed hostility can cause.

The other side of increased comfort with expression of hostility is the development of capacity to receive hostility from others. Many people, because of either past trauma or training, confuse hostility with punishment and rejection. Very often, the same people who have difficulty experiencing and expressing hostility also have difficulty accepting hostility from others. As individuals in the group experience hostility from others and find that they can still be accepted by the others they learn to cope with hostile expressions outside the group as well.

Although learning to express and accept hostility may be one of the major goals of treatment for many people, almost everyone in group therapy needs some help in feeling comfortable with their own and other people's hostilities. In most adult outpatient groups, hostility is the first major feeling that requires help yet the free flow of hostility serves as a means rather than an end in itself.

As group members become comfortable with their own and other people's hostility, then hostility becomes an important interpersonal emotional dynamic, highly productive of therapeutic gain and particularly insight. Hostility is very often a factor in unearthing the flow of anxiety, transference, identification, and empathy.

When an anxious member overtly or covertly expresses anxiety, other members can react by experiencing and sharing their own or similar anxiety or by defending against the anxiety. In the early phases of group therapy, members who do not experience the anxiety aroused by one member may defend themselves by stopping the member arousing anxiety, diverting the focus to safer areas, or denying the implications for themselves. As efforts to stop, divert, or deny the anxiety begin to fail, members can either accept and deal with the anxiety or become angry over the discomfort that the anxiety is creating for them. Again, this anger may be an attempt to stop or divert the anxiety but at this point the angry person's defenses are beginning to wane. Expression and exploration of the anger can now be productive in helping the angry person discover in himself the growing anxiety that is causing the discomfort and anger. Thus, the first sign of contagion of anxiety in a way that might be productive of insight may be hostility toward the person exciting the anxiety. Two common forms of hostility resulting from waning defenses against anxiety are feelings of boredom or detachment during the meeting. After direct experiencing and expressing of anger toward the anxiety-provoking member, boredom with and detachment from the discussion are most often manifest signs of growing hostility. When members express or demonstrate boredom or detachment, an attempt to explore their feelings will usually lead to their discomfort with the subject and its significance for them. Boredom and detachment are often the first signs that other active and passive defenses against the anxiety are waning.

Transference anger is often the easiest to detect in group processes. When one member expresses untoward anger at another, it is often because of transference (Slavson, 1950: 106). Untoward anger is anger that goes well beyond what seems appropriate for the situation. Exploration of this anger often shows that the angry individual was reacting not so much to the other person or what the other person expressed, but rather he was reacting to what he attributed the other person's actions to. Exploration of those experiences that contribute to the anger at the moment can produce insight for the individual and help resolve the immediate situation. More important is the function of anger as an expression of *negative identification* and *negative empathy*. Especially during the middle or mutuality phase of group development when resistances and defenses in the group recede to relatively low levels, most hostility in the group results from negative identification and negative empathy. Just as the anger evoked by anxiety functions and perhaps intertwines with anxiety, mutuality hostilities result from the basic bond of empathy and identification interfering with individual's being able to defend themselves from common feelings. The only difference between positive and negative identification and empathy is that the positive feelings are more directly and easily experienced where as the negative feelings result from fears of experiencing the identification and empathy. The essential ingredient in negative identification and empathy is experiencing some part of the other people that group members reject in themselves. The major difference between negative identification or empathy with projection is that, in negative identification or empathy, both people have the same feelings, whereas in projection the projector is attributing their own feelings to others who may or may not have them (Cowden, 1955).

As in anger over unwanted anxiety, the defenses of group members against the feelings of the other person reminding them of similar feelings in themselves are lowered or nonexistent in the middle phase of the group. As a last-ditch stand against getting in touch with a rejected part of oneself, a member becomes angry with the other person for exhibiting the rejected part. Thus, the angry member attempts to protect himself from experiencing that rejected part of himself by rejecting that part of the other person. If it wasn't for the empathic bond among the group members, each member could better defend himself against parts of other people that remind him of rejected parts of himself. However, because of the empathic bond, the only alternatives become active rejection of the same feelings in the other person. Other precursers or substitutes for the experiencing and expressing of the anger itself are the feelings of boredom, detachment, and preoccupation. Exploration of the anger, boredom, detachment, and preoccupation will often lead to the angry person's discovering the inner conflict over experiencing similar feelings. However, the angry person might first have to express fully his feelings toward the person manifesting the rejected parts of feelings.

An example of hostility as a reaction to anxiety, identification, and empathy kept recurring in a long-term adult group.

> Jack was a thirty-year-old man who kept making excellent progress in the group but following each pinnacle of progress he would lapse into a regression and depression. In such periods, Jack would come to group meetings with long lists of failures, and feelings of helplessness, hopelessess, and despair. Other group members who prior to these episodes were dragging in their own coping efforts would get very angry with Jack and often brutally deride him. In each case, the person most incensed with Jack's outpourings would, after full expression and derision of Jack, get in touch with his or her own similar feeings as well as feelings of wanting to get going. In every case the member expressing the most anger at Jack would begin to make major progress both in therapy and in their lives outside the group.
>
> It appeared that Jack was representing the feelings of other people when they were at a point of ambivalence: the dilemma of mastery over their situations versus despair. Because Jack for many reasons was stuck at that dilemma, he represented the rejected side of the ambivalence for the other members. Members beginning to experience wishes for mastery apparently were attempting to repress or deny feelings of despair and helplessness, feelings that Jack's exhortations reminded them of. Of course, the result of fully dealing with their ambivalences in each case helped to remove obstacles to progress for Jack and for the attackers.

The group's capacity to develop is directly related to its capacity to accept and express hostility (Slavson, 1950: 107; Theodorson, 1962). Without norms or room to accept and express hostility, it is doubtful that authority crises and inclusion phenomena can be resolved. If the authority and inclusion issues cannot be resolved, then the crucial process of differentiation is impossible and the best that can happen is that the group will develop an engulfing, undifferentiated pseudo-intimacy.

CONFLICT AS A SOURCE OF GROWTH AND CHANGE

In a group with a warm empathic atmosphere, interpersonal conflict becomes a a major source of growth and change. Basically, two kinds of conflicts concern therapy groups. The first are conflicts arising from actual or feared scarcity; the second, conflicts that represent an externalization among members of conflicts that reside within each member, or at least within each member who is party to the conflict. The two kinds of conflicts frequently overlap, since there is often something actually scarce or perceived as scarce in externalized internal conflicts and there are usually internal components of conflict arising from actual or perceived scarcity. Conflicts where the core is scarcity are *undifferentiated conflicts.* Conflicts where the core is externalization of internal conflicts are *differentiated conflicts.*.

Undifferentiated conflicts are the more primitive kind of interpersonal conflicts and their resolution is the major vehicle of developing mutual accep- tance and differentiation among members in therapy groups. Differentiated conflicts are a more advanced kind and their resolution, a major vehicle of self- acceptance, internal conflict resolution, insight, and development of identity in therapy groups. The major difference between undifferentiated conflict and differentiated conflict is the acceptance felt by the parties to the conflict. In undifferentiated conflict, one or both parties fear rejection from the other side; in differentiated conflict both parties feel basic acceptance from the other side and feel rejection or disagreement only for the feelings or issues inherent in the conflict. The discussion and examples to follow will elaborate and demonstrate the two types of conflicts.

The relationship between internal conflicts and interpersonal conflicts has been the subject of much inquiry and theorizing in social psychology and clinical literature. The basic conflict or love-hate ambivalence was posited by Freud (1935: 212-217) for sustained and intimate relationships. Coser points out how development of closeness or intimacy intensifies affectionate feelings but also intensifies feelings of hostility with the requisite intensification of fears of rejection (Coser, 1964: 67-72). Both sides to a relationship are afraid to express hostile feelings lest it result in rejection. Thus, as members come to accept their own and other group members' hostility and differentiate between hostility and rejection, groundwork is laid for toleration and expression of hostility in close relationships with decreasing fear of rejection.

The connections between internal and interpersonal conflicts is brought out by the works of Lewin (1951) and French (1952). From slightly different perspectives, they pose the forces and counterforces within and between people's emotions. Lewin's notions of force-counterforce and French's notion of disturbing and reactive motives within and between two people help to establish the relationship between internal and external conflicts. Whitaker and Lieber- man (1964) developed a whole theory of group development based on French's diadic concepts of internal and external conflicts. The essential assumptions in all of these theories are: (1) all parties to a conflict harbor both sides of the conflict within themselves and in their interaction, (2) parties to a conflict can either collude on one side of the conflict or polarize a conflict by representing opposite sides. In the Whitaker and Lieberman theory whole groups can collude on one side or polarize among individuals or subgroups. Whether through progressive recognition by a group in collusion or polarization among members or subgroups, the group resolves the conflict by recognizing and reducing the counterforces or reactive motives (which are usually fears) and by realizing and expressing the forces or disturbing motives (which are usually wishes).

Undifferentiated Conflicts

Undifferentiated conflicts are conflicts that arise from actual or perceived scarcity and in which both sides fear rejection for their feelings, thoughts, or behavior. The term *undifferentiated* applies since the parties to the conflict fear that it is not just their thoughts, feelings, or behaviors but their very acceptance or rejection that is at stake.

Undifferentiated conflicts arise in the early phases of group development from the parallel phase through the inclusion phase. The conflicts arising in the early authority crises are the first undifferentiated conflicts. Members who conflict with the therapist fear that they will be rejected by the therapist for what they perceive as their differences with the therapist. (Heider, 1958, elaborates on the pressure for mutual rejection arising from interpersonal disagreement.) As the member experiences acceptance from the therapist, particularly acceptance in spite of disagreement, then the member-therapist conflicts become more differentiated and particularized to the issues. Consequently, as much acceptance as possible of the member's thought, feelings, and actions can lay a foundation for the member to feel more secure in conflict with the therapist.

Conflicts over Norms and Goals. In adult groups, the early conflicts with the therapist center around group norms and goals and are reflected in such thoughts or questions in the group as: "Do we have to talk about ourselves." "Why don't you tell us what to do?" "Why don't you make some suggestions for us to talk about?" Through sympathizing and empathizing with the "resistances" in a way that allows group exploration, the therapist is both accepting the conflict with authority and accepting the members who are conflicting with what they perceive as the therapist's wishes for the members to talk themselves and initiate their own discussion. In groups with lower psychosocial capacity, chronic schizophrenics and young children, sympathizing may not be enough. In such cases the members may be asking for help and structure that is essential to their level and capacity to function as a group. Thus, the therapist can communicate his acceptance of members who are less able to function as a group only by acting on the expressed or implied wishes of the members.

Early behavior problems pose a difficult challenge to the therapist's authority. If he limits behavior he runs the risk of communicating rejection to the member or members who are acting out; on the other hand, if he condones or allows disruptive behavior he might threaten both the acting-out member and the other members. Members who are used to incurring rejection as a means of establishing contact with others might feel rejected in the absence of limits. With groups of children, limiting the behavior while empathizing with the possible feelings expressed in the behavior offers acceptance of the child with rejection of the behavior. What the therapist communicates is "You can't hit him, but I understand why you are mad at him," or "You can't hit Jimmy, but you can tell him why you are mad at him," or "You can't run out of the room but if you don't want to talk about what happened in school, you don't have to." Thus, in authority conflicts, the therapist can defuse the conflict by empathizing with the underlying feelings of the member, then negotiating the overt issues. For example, the therapist might say, "I understand that you are angry at Jimmy because he used your crayons but is there another way we can settle this without hitting each other?"

Empathizing with the feelings of the member, particularly with negative feelings about the therapist, provides the basis of acceptance and opens the possibility for authority conflicts to become differentiated in that rejection for difference or assertion of autonomy becomes less of a fear for the member. The implications for the development of autonomy through the process of the therapist accepting the differing member are basic for the therapist-member relationship as well as for the individual's development in the group and for the group's development.

Inclusion Conflicts. The next set of conflicts that become important are the inclusion conflicts. Inclusion conflicts are undifferentiated in that the group member experiences difference or disagreement among group members as threatening, if not tantamount, to utter and total rejection. The group member thinks. "If other members don't accept my ideas, behavior, or feelings, they don't accept me. If other members do accept my ideas, behaviors, or feelings, then they accept me." The basis of inclusion conflicts stems from sibling experiences. The feared scarcity of acceptance of the members by the therapist serves as the here-and-now counterpart of the members' past experiences with siblings in their families. Group members, young and old, bring their experiences as siblings experiences into the early group meetings with their accrued feelings of acceptance and/or rejection from these experiences. Thus, early inclusion conflicts among members are mostly for the benefit of the therapist. These conflicts are based in concern over which side the therapist is going to favor. If the therapist is truly supportive of both sides, then the members must deal with their own mixed feelings. However, the wish for inclusion and acceptance in the group and the fear of rejection by the other members remains the basis of inclusion conflicts among members. If and as the therapist demonstrates support for both sides, then both sides feel acceptance from the therapist and can hope for acceptance from the other members. Inclusion conflicts are resolved when the members feel either sufficient acceptance from the therapist and the other members or when empathy develops. Interestingly, the feeling of acceptance necessary to resolve inclusion conflicts often results from members sharing and empathizing around their wishes for acceptance or fear of rejection.

> The inclusion struggle of the nine- and ten-year-old group of boys described in Chapter 4, Part II demonstrates how therapist support for both sides of the conflict is crucial to the resolving of conflicts through the emergence of bipolar identification. The issue concerns the disruptive behavior of the boys acting out as opposed to the conforming behavior of the constricted boys.
>
> Both sides to this conflict were uneasy abut the therapists' not taking a stand but, instead, being supportive to both subgroups. The therapists refused to split up the group but suggested that the group could divide the meeting room and each have their own side. Both sides took to this idea readily and two meetings ensued where the room was physically divided. Because the therapists refused to reject either side and because of the physical safety provided by the divided room, the constricted children began to express their hostilities toward the actor-outers. In the third meeting after the initial room division, the boys forgot to divide the room. A meeting later one of the actor-outers made an airplane of Lego blocks and asked permission to land in an airport project that the constricted subgroup had made together. The constricted subgroup disagreed over whether the other boy could land but finally permission was granted. The fifth child started working next to the indigenous leader of the constricted subgroups and subsequently they collaborated on making something.
>
> There were several discussions within each subgroup and among all the boys about wanting friends and about the fact that all of the boys had had some experiences where they were rejected. The long-term result of this group was that the constricted boys were better able to express their hostile and aggressive feelings and the actor-outers developed considerable improvement in controlling their behaviors and seeking acceptance rather than settling for rejection as the form of human contact available to them.

Most important, the constricted children didn't curry favor with the therapists for their "goody goody" behavior and the acting out children didn't curry rejection for their behavior. In the absence of rejection from the therapists, they rejected each other totally or undifferentiatedly. In the process of existing next to each other in the subsequent group meetings both sides were able to see and experience some advantages in the modes of behavior of the other side. The constricted children were able to experience acceptance with expression of their hostile and aggressive impulses. The acting-out children were able to find acceptance by other children and less need to protect themselves with their hostile acting-out. In other words, as the boys found acceptance of themselves and each other, they were better able to accept parts of themselves that they had rejected in themselves and the other boys.

To phrase it in terms of the discussion of emotional dynamics in this chapter, the constricted children had a positive identification with each other and a negative identification with the acting-out boys. The reverse was true for the acting-out boys; they had a negative identification with the constricted boys and a positive identification with each other. Both sides had mixed feelings about the acting out-control issues. As they experienced the other side of the mixed feelings respectively, they developed *bi-polar identification.*

Differentiated Conflict

Once a group has developed some mutual acceptance and intimacy, conflicts become much more particularized to specific issues and feelings and fears of total rejection become gradually reduced with each successive and successful conflict resolution. In addition, during the inclusion phase, group members tend to choose sides in any conflict through positive identification or empathy with members of their chosen subgroup and negative identificaion or empathy with the opposing faction. Once members are more secure in their feelings of acceptance, they are less likely to form subgroups tied to their identifications and empathies and more likely to experience bipolar identification or empathy in a conflict. During the inclusion phase, the bipolar identification or empathy resolves the emotional base of conflicts and serves as the force that draws opposing factions into a cohesive group. During the mutuality phase, any two or more members might polarize in their feelings about common issues but the rest of the members would probably be able to identify with both sides and help resolve the conflict through direct emotional support of both sides. Thus, conflict differentiation occurs both within each member and among members of a group.

> During a meeting of a long-term adult therapy group, Frank was presenting himself in his customary depressed and helpless way. Bill, an alcoholic who a few months previously had made a miraculous comeback from his "inertia," lost his temper at Frank's petulance. He insisted angrily that the group had helped Frank to understand himself and shown him what he should do, that Frank was making no effort to do it, and that he, Bill, wanted no more of this kind of talk from Frank. Frank refused even to listen: he had heard similar explosions from Bill before. Other members variously pointed out that they sometimes had periods of energy and periods of inertia and that, on one hand, it wasn't easy for Frank to mobilize himself but, on the other hand, Bill was again asking too much of himself in never allowing himself to rest his efforts. During this discussion Bill admitted for the first time that he was pushing himself to keep going and relying on the support of the group to do so, and therefore was unnerved when Frank presented himself in this helpless fashion. Hearing Bill's admission to his own fears of helplessness enabled Frank to empathize with Bill for the first time and to express his desires for taking initiative for himself. In ensuing meetings Frank, Bill, and other group members were able to share bipolar feelings about taking initiative and getting tired and discouraged.

The issue in this meeting was trying versus resting or giving up. Underlying the issue are all the emotional conflicts that have resulted in Frank's and Bill's fearing their own aggressiveness. However, during mutuality these conflicts converge on the dilemma of mastery versus futility. Neither member experienced rejection of their feelings and ideas by the group, only by the other party to the conflict. The other group members and the therapist supported both sides of the conflict with empathy for each extreme feelings. Within the climate of full affective support for both sides of the conflict, the respective parties were able to develop bipolar empathy and each became more comfortable with the other side of his respective feelings. Frank did begin to take more initiative both in and outside the group; Bill did soften his harsh demands of himself.

Scapegoating

Scapegoating is a special instance of group conflict. If one assumes that both the persecutor and the scapegoat have a hand in obtaining their roles, then both are parties to a form of group conflict. As with any other role in any group, the role of scapegoat is both assumed by the scapegoat and assigned by the other members. The role is assumed by the member who most needs it and it is assigned by the other members, particularly by the person who most needs a scapegoat at the time. If the therapist, as he sets out to resolve the situation, identifies only with the scapegoat as a poor, downtrodden person, he had little hope of succeeding. If, however, he looks to the reason why both the persecutor and the scapegoat has assumed their roles, then he is in position to help resolve the conflict.

In a classroom of eight perceptually handicapped children of normal or above normal intelligence, six of the children, three boys and three girls, had been together the previous year. Two new children, Tom and Beverly, were added in September. Tom became the leader of a scapegoating movement aimed at Beverly. All the children took to picking on Beverly. As the teacher and therapist discussed the situation with the children over a period of time, it became apparent that Beverly was intentionally provoking the others, even during the discussions. It further became evident that Tom was also setting up situations that led her to provocation, which he and the others would then seize upon to torment her.

The situations that led to scapegoating were many: a ball on the playground, movement of a desk during class, one child's making noise while the other was working, and so on. The underlying emotional conflict within and between the two major opponents was acceptance-rejection. Tom came from a highly demanding family and, although he was very bright, he couldn't learn and was rejecting himself and feeling rejected by his family for his "stupidity." His strategy was to constantly point out how stupid Beverly was and punish Beverly for being stupid. Beverly's father had recently left home and her mother had told Beverly that the father left because of her. In addition, Beverly had received much rejection in another school over her learning difficulties, both by the teachers and other students. Consequently, Beverly was not feeling very good about herself and was expecting nothing more than rejection from others.

It was easy for these perceptually handicapped children to identify with desires for acceptance and fears of being rejected because of their own experiences in other schools before coming to this special school. They could identify with Beverly's feeling that no one was going to accept her anyhow. They could also identify with Tom's fear of being rejected by the others and fear of being stupid. As empathy for both sides grew among the other children in the classroom, all withdrew from the scapegoating except Tom, Beverly, and one other boy: the three continued the scapegoating, but more sporadically. As Tom made academic headway, he was able to give up his scapegoating altogether. Two simultaneous events finally prompted Beverly to cease provoking other children to torment her. One, she received a better prescription for glasses which helped clear up some multiple eye problems that were interfering with her academic progress. The other was a private session with the therapist wherein she began to recognize, from facts she was already aware of, that her father was indeed very much interested in her and that she was not the cause of his leaving home. She was finally able to give up the provocative behavior and establish friendships with the other girls in the class.

Interpersonal conflict can serve as a propellant and vehicle for unearthing, change, and exchange of ideas, feelings, and behavior leading to differentiation. Suppressed or poorly handled conflict can destroy a group. Absence of group conflict will allow a group at best to achieve a state of pseudo-intimacy. To be helpful to a group in resolving conflict, a therapist must empathize with both sides of the emotional polarity. If a therapist actively identifies or empathizes with one side and not the other, the conflict will not be resolved. Parties on the side opposing the therapist may passively accept the "resolution" but they will not feel that the conflict is over nor will they be able to grow from the experience.

In assessing conflict it is also important for the therapist to determine when conflicts are being perpetuated so as to avoid the intimacy that could result from bipolar empathy. During the inclusion phase many conflicts are continued or replaced with new issues in order to preclude feelings of closeness. In such instances it is important that the therapist focus on the fears of resolving the conflict since the real emotional issue is not conflict but intimacy.

Full resolution of conflict requires reasonable gratification of felt needs, resolution of the issues, and finally bipolar empathic convergence of underlying feelings. Only with the bipolar empathic convergence of underlying feelings can conflict resolution have any permanence. In the process itself, it is best to first allow the full expression of the hostilities, then to tackle them, issue by issue, until the underlying emotional polarizations become apparent to all concerned. Premature pointing to the underlying emotional issues will often defuse the hostilities but may not help the parties to the conflict learn how to experience, express, and resolve conflicts.

2

Role
of the
Therapist

The role of the therapist must vary in relation to the needs of the group and the needs of the group vary from one group to another, within the same group at different times, and within the same group at the same time. It is important that the role of the therapist is appropriate to the status of the particular group at the particular time.

Group needs will also vary with the purpose, structure, membership, and duration of a group. A short-term group for a specific purpose may need to have the therapist take a very active and central role, maintaining that role throughout the life of the group. Groups of children or adult schizophrenics will need to have the therapist assume and maintain a central and powerful role most of the time, regardless of how long they meet. A group of relatively normal adults who are all undergoing a similar crisis may not need much direction or structure from the therapist and might proceed quite independently from the outset.

Although the therapist may need to play a central role at the start of a long-term adult outpatient group, as the group progresses the therapist may be able to transfer responsibility and power to the members as they become ready and willing to accept and use their power. Thus, the role of the therapist varies over time and in relation to the developmental level of the group.

Uneven development for the individuals within a group and for subgroups within a larger group is sometimes seen. While some members may reach a full degree of mutuality, others may languish in a more dependent mode on the therapist. Newer members in a long-term open-ended group may need more direct support from the therapist than older members, who can take more initiative and responsibility for themselves and each other. In both instances the therapist may have to differentially relate to those members and subgroups that are well developed as well as those members and/or subgroups that seem less developed.

In the author's experience, many therapists are introduced to group therapy with monolithic models of therapist roles. These models are often attuned to a particular kind of group in a particular setting within a given structure and philosophy. Although the particular model may suffice for the group in question, it often doesn't provide a basis for differential assessment of need for other kinds of groups in other settings, for other purposes, with different kinds of people, or even with the same people over time. These models are often preserved in the face of repeated failure by more carefully selecting members who are suitable to the model instead of varying the model, the groups, and the styles of leadership to suit different needs, purposes, and members.

OVERVIEW OF THE THERAPIST'S ROLE

The ensuing discussion attempts to present a way of viewing the therapist's role that provides for starting at the level of the group's initial capacity and modifying the role if and as the group develops. This model is closely tied to the group developmental theory presented in Part 2 as well as to the individual developmental theory which also underlies the model of group development (Werner, 1948; Erikson, 1968).

The therapist's role begins as an empathic-nuturer and moves toward an empathic-facilitator. Movement from empathic-nuturer to empathic-facilitator requires that the group develop from the dependence of the parallel phase to the interdependence of the mutality phase and that the therapist allow and help the group toward this development.

One of the most controversial issues among group therapists is whether or not they should meet initial dependency needs of the group. The major argument of those opposed to meeting initial dependency needs of the group through nurture is that the group will remain dependent and never achieve self-sufficiency. In a study of several different leadership types in a wide variety of groups, Lieberman et al. (1973: 226-67) found that when the therapist provided a warm supportive atmosphere for their groups, members experienced more lasting growth and the least casualty from the group experience. Groups in which the initial needs for nurture from the therapist are met can indeed develop toward self-dependency, providing the members are capable of self-dependency and the therapist can allow and help the group to achieve it.

The anxiety aroused from nondirective leadership can often propel a group into rapid development if the members are capable of such development. However, if a group is not capable of such development, then not meeting early dependency needs can result in overwhelming hostility leading to hostile silences. Several recent studies have shown that even when a group develops in which some of the members are not up to the social capacity of the others for achieving and sustaining self-dependent group process, the less able members neither participate in nor benefit from the early developmental phenomena (Tucker, 1973; Gibbard and Hartman, 1973). Rather, the less able members tend to continue to relate to the other group members in their fixed ways.

The Emphatic Nurturer

The empathic nurturer meets the immediate dependency needs of the members and establishes warm, supportive, and accepting relationships with the members and builds toward interaction and relationships among them. The empathic facilitator helps the members to interact, relate to each other, give help to and receive help from each other, at times provides direct help to members, adds to individual and group understanding, stimulates emotional experience and expression, and helps to guide the focus of the group. To move from the nurturing to the facilitative role the therapist needs to sow the seeds of self-dependence from the outset of the group. The first major steps toward helping the group to build its autonomy are (1) for the therapist to provide acceptance and empathy for the individual members and (2) for the therapist to support any and all supportable initiatives by the members, particularly if they disagree with the therapist. By the demonstration of acceptance and empathy even for initiatives (ideas, feelings, behaviors) that run counter to the wishes (overt, covert, real, or imagined) of the therapist, the therapist demonstrates acceptance of the individual members while granting individual autonomy. As the members are or become capable of exerting their autonomy the resolution of authority and inclusion issues can be addressed by the members.

Pointing to commonalities in thoughts, feelings, and behaviors can lay a base for members to begin to identify and empathize with each other and can facilitate the development of interpersonal ties and subgroup formation. Pointing to and clarifying differences in thoughts, feelings, and actions can begin to focus the group's attention on emerging conflicts among the members. Full empathic support for both sides of inclusion conflicts can pave the way for conflict resolution and the resulting empathy that can bind the factions into a group as a whole.

The Empathic Facilitator

Once the group has attained its empathic bond the therapist can become the empathic facilitator. The range of possible helping techniques in a group that has achieved some degree of intimacy and mutuality is boundless. On a base of continued interpersonal and intrapsychic empathy, interpretations and confrontations can help members in both the here-and-now and there-and-then spheres of group focus and experience.

In groups capable of high degrees of self-sufficiency, the major problem in the shift from the nurturing to the facilitative role lies within the therapist. A therapist with excessive needs for counterdependence, control, or acceptance will have difficulty in both technically helping and allowing a group to become self-dependent and will also communicate covert prohibitions to the members against self-dependence.

RELATIONSHIPS WITH MEMBERS AND GROUP

In any group formed by the therapist, all relationships are initially between the individual member and the therapist. This relationship represents an island of safety in the group situation that the members can both back on for support and use as a base of entry into the situation.

The question of dual relationships between the therapist and individual members and the therapist and group as a whole becomes more controversial when the group being considered has developed some degree of intimacy and mutuality. Much in group dynamics theory supports the notion that individual relationships between group members and the therapist will inhibit group development. In speaking strictly about group development, the author tends to agree that individual relationships with the therapist can inhibit the "group process." However, the question is whether individual relationships inhibit the group therapeutic process. If one accepts that part of the group therapeutic process is the recapitulation of the social development process, than the question of group process per se becomes moot.

Those philosophies which suggest that member-to-member relationships are the only important factor in group development discount the dynamics and potentials of members reexperiencing the natural developmental process of children first relating to parents and then, with sufficient levels of satisfaction in these relationships, growing toward the outside world of parent substitutes and peers. The assumption underlying this book is that it during the group development it is just as important for individuals to experience their relationship to the therapist and to grow within that relationship as it is for them to move out to peers. If the early experiences tended to inhibit individuals' capacities to move out into intimate relationships beyond their families, then the experience of moving from the relationship with the therapist to a peer relationship can be corrective.

If one assumes from the outset of the group that if the therapist consistently forces member-to-member interaction and denies the significance of therapist-member interaction and relationship, then the group might very well develop, but what may be lost to the members is the realization and overcoming of difficulties in becoming launched from the primary family.

Julia was a young woman in her middle twenties who had never been away from her mother for more than three weeks in her whole life before she entered a long-term open-ended adult group. Her mother had successfully drawn a moat around their relationship by painting father and everyone else as ill-intentioned toward her. For months Julia sat quietly during meetings and when an opening came she would address herself directly and exclusively to the theapist, almost oblivious to the fact that others were reacting to what she was saying and attempting to interact with her. Her behavior often caused the other members to seek out the therapist in the same way and discuss both their lacks from their own relationships with parents and their wishes for exclusive relationships with the therapist. The other group members came to terms with their felt losses in relationships with parents and moved into close relationships with each other in the group and with people outside the group. However, Julia lagged behind because her past parental mandates against any other relationships were more severe than were those of the other group members. Many of the other members went through periods of negative identification with Julia and would become angry with her for not responding to them and for continuing to seek the safety of an exclusive relationship with the therapist. Finally, as the other members became more comfortable with their mixed feelings about relationships with the therapist and with each other, and with significant people outside the group, they were able to be more fully empathetic to Julia's strong needs for remaining the dependent child. The result over time was that Julia was finally able to relinquish her attempts to nestle into an exclusive relationship with the therapist and began to relate to other group members and establish romantic relationships outside the group.

Julia's previous way of handling peer relationships had been to start by counterdependently looking after other people until she experienced her overwhelming needs for nurture. Then she would have her mother's prediction confirmed because other people would indeed let her down. Had she been forced to relate to the other members prematurely, she would have brought her pattern of handling relationships and, after counterdependently helping everyone else, would have then descended on the group with her overwhelming needs for nurturance; she would become disappointed and probably would have left the group. Instead, Julia's shelter in the relationship with the therapist provided her the opportunity to see what happened to other group members in moving out to each other and ultimately to find that the resulting relationships looked inviting rather than formidable.

Although Julia's example is an extreme one, none the less, it is symbolic of what can happen to any group member. Members with less difficulty in moving out to other people in the group will relinquish their efforts toward exclusive relationships with the therapist more easily, but still, they will do so only after they have satisfied themselves to some degree. Thus, by starting with and maintaining individual relationships in addition to the group as a whole relationships, individual members can re-experience the process of initial relationships with parents and grow toward autonomy and relationships with peers. If, by influencing group norms, the therapist forces members away from relationships with himself and toward relationships exclusively among the members, it awakens anxiety and hostility over the loss of parents and unmet dependency needs. Many members like Julia need the haven of the relationship with the therapist until they can assert their autonomy and move out into relationships with the other members.

By granting individual interviews to a group member, the therapist can detract from the group process because the member will have less impetus toward dealing with the problem in the group. However, if the therapist refuses requests for individual interviews, while it might be better for group development, it might also result in the unnecessary loss of a member from the group. Although the reasons for individual interviews often seem remote from group issues, they are most often a direct result of the individual's difficulty in the group. It is useful to use individual interviews whenever possible, no matter what the overt reasons for the request, to discover what difficulty the member is having with the group. If the individual interview is used to help the member back to the group both to deal with the problem presented in the interview and to deal with the group-related problem, then the dangers of exclusive or special relationships can be reduced. Sometimes granting the request for an individual interview is essential because the group may not be ready to cope with the particular problem or crisis at hand for the member. However, most requests for individual interviews center around inclusion and intimacy issues— for example, a member's growing hostility toward another member and inability to express it, feelings of being rejected by the other members, or fears of growing intimacy. Thus, helping the member to feel better about the group issue and preparing him to go back to the group and deal with the other member or members can make the difference between keeping or losing a member. While granting individual interviews might be at some temporary expense to group development, so too is losing a member.

POWER AND AUTHORITY IN THE ROLE OF THERAPIST

Perhaps no aspect of the role of therapist is more confusing than that of power and authority. This is primarily because both therapists and members confuse political power with the authority of expertise. The matter is further confused because most people see expert opinion as having some commanding or irrefutable overtones. Indeed many statements therapists make based on their expertise really have the implication of a command or the definitive statement on the matter at hand. At one extreme those group therapists whose model of therapy consists of a powerful central person in the therapist often want their authoritative statements to be taken as commands. At the other extreme, those therapists who take a more passive or lassez-faire role consider any authoritative statement as possibly exerting power. The following discussion makes some distinctions between political power and expert opinions of group therapists and shows how they can be differentially applied in the therapeutic role.

At the outset of any group the therapist is vested with all the power, both political and professional. However, the political power vested in the therapist mostly concerns the goals and direction of the group and how the group can go about achieving those ends. In other words, the therapist is vested with the political power to decide what the goals for the group will be and what means or norms the group will abide by to reach those ends. The therapist is also vested with having all the important knowledge required for the growth and development of the group and its individual members. The initial expectation is that the therapist will provide all the essential knowledge to help the members and that the members have little or no professional knowledge to contribute. The problem facing the therapist in most groups is how to distribute the power both for making means and ends decisions and for engaging the members in the diagnostic and treatment process for themselves and each other.

The problem for many therapists is that they have an *"either or"* notion about power and its distribution. They feel that either the members decide or the therapist decides; there are no inbetweens. Yet, there are a wide range of possibilities between the therapist's making all the decisions for the group and the group's deciding for itself. The task of the therapist with respect to group development is to help the group develop the capacity to make its own decisions and to turn progressively increasing responsibility over to the group as they demonstrate their readiness to handle decisions.

Building the group's capacity to become self-determining begins in the first meeting of the parallel phase, regardless of group capacity. The capacity of the group will make a difference only in the manner in which the therapist approaches the group's own decisions. Even in a very dependent group the members directly or indirectly let the therapist know what they would like. They might do it through their behavior, indirect messages, or direct requests.

If the therapist asks, "Would you like to introduce yourself to each other?" in a first meeting, he is opening the options for people to say *no*. However, many group members will view a question or suggestion by the therapist as a command. If a member directly opposes the idea and the therapist responds by saying that those who don't want to introduce themselves don't have to, then that member and all the others can begin to see that the therapist will respond to their wishes. Some members will indirectly oppose the therapist's suggestion by looking uncomfortable or showing some other sign of dissent. If the therapist turns his observation of disagreement into permission to do other than introduce oneself, then again members can begin to feel that their wishes will be honored.

As discussion begins during the early meetings, there will be many more instances where members will perceive commands by the therapist and or other members. It is important in each of these instances that the therapist recognize the overt or covert "vote" of each member and respond accordingly. A major problem in early meetings is that the overt subject matter becomes disjointed as each member tries to pull the focus in his or her own direction and many members are inclined to shift the focus so as to prevent risking too much too soon. Many a group has been stymied in early meetings by the therapist's insisting, directly or indirectly, that members bring up "more appropriate" or relevant subject matter, meaning, of course, subject matter that the therapist feels should be discussed. Allowing a member to flee by allowing him to change the subject to an irrelevant issue in early meetings is, once again, a statement of the therapist's intent; it shows members he will allow them to determine the focus themselves. It also shows members that they can take refuge in the group when they feel the need. Valuing early contributions of each member—no matter what they are—demonstrates to the members tht they can take the responsibility for determining focus. Disallowing or rejecting any initial offering will, in effect, tell the group that the therapist intends to govern the focus of the meetings. In addition, a member will usually take the disallowal or rejection of his initial offering to mean rejection, and consequently, he feels less adequate as a potential group member.

As the therapist detects a variety of opinions in the group about what should happen or what should be discussed during the parallel phase, the therapist needs to become the integrator of wishes and the maker of decisions based on the available information. At first the therapist may make some judicious decisions about the different wishes, but as the group progresses, he will more and more ask the group which course the group might take and thus invite the members to deal directly with each other.

The final step in the therapist's helping the group develop its capacity to govern itself is simply allowing members to resolve the issues in whatever way they happen to resolve. When a member's point of view gets lost in the shuffle the therapist should decide if that member is capable of representing his own views and if getting overlooked by the group will make the member angry enough to take initiative or if the member needs the support of the therapist to make demands on the other members. Of course, when the individual and/or group demonstrates the capacity to take direct initiative with each other, the therapist's allowing and supporting this direct initiative—and serving as mediator if necessary—is all that's required.

Group members coming to a professionally led group have the right to expect professional opinion throughout the life of the group. The only question is when and how that professional opinion is offered and how much responsibility the group members have for professional assessment and reaction. The therapist's objective for groups members most often is that they learn to experience and understand their own feelings and reactions. As members progressively come to understand themselves and others in the group, they are able to contribute much the same kind of information as the therapist. However, the members always expect that the therapist might either concur with their opinions or add another dimension to opinions expressed by members. If the question of political authority and power is well resolved in a group, members are less confused about what constitutes an authoritative professional opinion and what is either a command or an irrefutable statement to members. With political authority shared among the therapist and members the therapist's opinions are more likely to be challenged and questioned along with everyone else's. In the long run, professional opinions that are questioned and challenged tend to have more lasting value for members. When the opinions don't quite apply or miss the mark, it is through the questioning that the member are able to take from the opinion that which is significant for them and pass up the rest. In advanced groups, therapists can freely offer professional opinions and run less risk of fostering dependency as a result of giving their opinions. Of course, unlike the therapist for an individual, a group therapist must be able to accept both that his opinion may not always be the best opinion available in the group and that group members, although they generally value professional opinions, will not accept an opinion just because it came from the therapist.

FOCUS AND THE ROLE OF THE THERAPIST

Two major aspects of the focus of therapy groups are, first, the dilemma between the individual and group focus, and second, the time sphere to serve as direct discussion in sessions.

Individual vs. Group Focus

There is much controversy among group therapists about whether the focus can be on individuals or whether it should always be on interactive phenomenon in the group. Some forms of group therapy make the major focus treatment of the individual in front of the others. Other members are perhaps called upon to react to a given member's problem, but the interaction among the members is considered either unimportant or only important insofar as it reflects the immediate problem being discussed by the individual. Other forms of group therapy call for discussion of only group process phenonomenon. Those that support the "process only" focus propose that the only real growth that takes place in groups results from immediate experiences and realization arising from group interaction.

Any decisions about individual versus group focus must be considered within the framework of the particular individual and the particular group: its purpose, structure, membership, duration, and level of development. Most therapy groups start with individuals presenting their own problems in the parallel phase. The early riskers are usually seeking something for themselves from the other members and particularly from the therapist. Unless the members have been assessed as having a high level of and capacity for social functioning, getting them to focus on their immediate relationships with each other from the outset would be difficult. Most members move into a group by first presenting themselves and the concerns they feel are most presentable. Thus, the early subject matter is likely to be highly individual and connected to life and events outside the group. Some process issues might usefully be introduced—perhaps the fact that everyone wants the therapist to help him first, or the initial difficulties in risking, or the initial anxieties of early meetings. However, for most groups, a group focus at the outset is often premature and more frightening than relieving.

Building toward a group focus begins as the therapist interacts with individual members and offers his own recognition, understanding, and empathy for what is expressed. Next the therapist points to the commonalities in what members are expressing. Pointing to commonalities universalizes the experiences of each member and puts members in position to begin the process of identification with each other. Consequently, most members become more relieved about possible similarities with others in the group and become interested in other members of their own accord. The exceptions to this process (as discussed in Part 2, Chapter 2, The Parallel Phase) are very depressed people, who must see themselves as worse than others, and paranoid people, who must see themselves as better than others.

Although there is little question that as the group develops the process experiences and their direct discussions are the most potent force for member growth and change, there is still value in pursuing individual issues as well. The emotional dynamics discussed in the preceeding chapter demonstrate how, on the deeper affective level, group members in a developed group share an underlying emotional process. This underlying emotional process provides deeper levels of interaction that, while they are manifest in the overt interactive processes of the group, also far exceed the overt processes. Thus, exploration of one member's problem in depth by the therapist and group can open up some new areas for all to deal with.

> Margaret began to talk about her fear of getting too close to her boyfriend. She related a recent experience in which she and her boyfriend shared a great deal about themselves and how they felt. Soon after Margaret had second thoughts about this boyfriend and began to consider his many faults. Others began to share similar experiences with close relationships, discussing both the dangers and benefits of getting too close. The therapist reminded the group that at the last session and even now Margaret had shared a great deal with the group and was perhaps wondering how others were feeling about her. Margaret readily agreed and other members began to react both to Margaret and to what she had shared about herself. Some of the other members also began to empathize with Margaret's quest for a realtionship with others in the group and their fears of sharing deeply in the group.

> Previous discussions in this particular group centered mostly on discussing individual experiences of the kind Margaret related. They were inclined to take turns and relate to similar outside experiences and feelings about these experiences. Past efforts on the part of the therapist to focus this intimacy crisis onto the relationships among the members themselves had not been as productive. However, this time the group seemed readier to deal with their mixed feelings about sharing with each other.

The process issue of intimacy was present during the meetings when members discussed their individual situations outside the group. These discussions gave them consensual validation and reassurances that others in the group were also frightened of intimacy. Members of this group apparently needed sufficient reassurance that others shared their fears before they could risk dealing directly with their fears about intimacy within the group. They got this reassurance through the discussion of individual situations in tandem. The subsequent experiences they all had with intimacy in the group were instrumental in helping them grow in their capacities for intimacy in outside relationships.

The important point here is that, although discussing the process is generally more potent for growth and change, allowing and supporting individual focus is often essential. In the early phases of group development the individual focus provides a base for people to introduce themselves in full and offers a safe vehicle for interaction. In the middle phases of group development, individual focus must be evaluated for its possible significance to the underlying affective processes. A series of individual focuses in which the members are all helping one individual will usually have the underlying affective processes. It is often important to explore these focuses to understand the underlying affective processes, then help these processes surface for direct group interaction and discussion.

Early focus on individuals might very well constitute treatment of one person in front of the others. However, as an underlying affective process develops in the group most, if not all, individual focuses have their group implications; the question is when and how to connect them to the immediate process. The discussion of time spheres that follows might provide some further help with connecting individual and group focuses. Suffice to say that very often in middle phases of group therapy new depths of affect are achieved through the examination of an individual situation in depth even when it seems to be the therapist and the individual member doing the overt work. It is, of course, extremely important to engage the other members in both exploring the individual issue and reacting to the individual issue. The affective connection (empathy) or even revulsion (negative empathy) of the other members is more an indicator of whether it was treatment of one person in front of others or group therapy. The only sure way to find out is to ask the others what meaning it had for them.

Time Sphere Focus

Another aspect of focus is the here-and-now as opposed to the there-and-then time sphere in group discussion. Past events can refer to the recent past or to the past so the far distant as to be relegated to the individual member's unconscious. There is much controversy among group therapists as to which time sphere is most important and appropriate for group therapy.

The determination of which time sphere to focus on in group therapy must be related to the purpose, structure, memberships, duration, and level of group development. It would be folly to engage a short-term crisis group in exclusive exploration of here-and-now phenomenon when their concern is the crisis at hand. Those aspects of the crisis that parallel the here-and-now situation might be worth dealing with but most of the group's concern and effort needs to go into resolving a crisis that the members have in common. At the other extreme, if a long-term open-ended group of outpatient neurotics did not deal with the here-and-now of their process they would miss major opportunities for growth and change.

There is always a connection between the here-and-now and the there-and-then. When individuals choose to discuss an individual there-and-then situation in the group, the situation is always connected to the here-and-now. In the above example Margaret chose to talk about her intimacy dilemma with her boyfriend, which was connected to the impending intimacy in the group. When intimacy is growing in a group, members often begin to talk about relationships outside the group. Discussion of an intimate relationship outside the group will stimulate members to experience their thoughts and feelings about intimacy in the group.

Here-and-now issues stimulate thoughts and feelings about there-and-then issues and there-and-then issues in focus stimulate thoughts and feelings about here-and-now issues. When people come to a group meeting with some there-and-then event on their minds they tend to experience that same issue with the others in the group. In the same way, when members discuss a here-and-now issue in the group it causes them to ponder or react to the here-and-now issue on the basis of their there-and-then experiences.

The connection and the interaction of the hear-and-now and there-and-then makes the decision of which to focus on more complex. The decisions at any given moment in the group must rest on which particular time sphere both the therapist and the members deem appropriate. The discussion of individual versus group focus has already shown that there-and-then discussion serves the function of introducing the person and his situation to the group and often of opening new depths for everyone in the group.

On the other end of the process is the ultimate goal of group therapy: the improved future life of each individual member independent from the group. If the gains from the here-and-now growth are to be useful to the individual in current and future life, it is most often essential that the connection be made between gains in the group and life outside the group. A sole focus on the here-and-now of group process assumes that gains made in the group will automatically be reflected in relationships and situations outside the group. In the author's experience some members do indeed make gains in other aspects of their lives mostly by changes they undergo in the here-and-now of group process. However, most people do not make the direct transference of their group gains to their outside lives. In particular, people with schizophrenia, hysteria, high degrees of anxiety, or lower levels of intelligence have more difficulty translating their group experiences to other experience without direct help. This is not to say that other people will not also experience difficulty; however, the difficulties of these four types of persons have been particularly noted in the author's experience. Consequently, for these people who cannot easily connect the growth and change they gain in the group to their outside lives, a balance of here-and-now and there-and-then focus is essential before termination.

THERAPIST ROLE AND SELF-REVELATION

There is growing controversy among group thereapists about the appropriateness and usefulness of self-revelation on the part of the therapist. Learning more about the therapist as another human being can help most group members if the revelations are timed to the needs and readiness of the members.

The therapist's early revelations of sympathy and empathy are absolutely essential toward helping a group initially form and develop. "As if" revelations by the therapist are also very helpful as expressions of sympathy, empathy, and understanding. For example, the therapist can mention, "I would feel that way if I were in the same situation." Another useful form of early revelation is the allusion to a similar experience in the therapist's past life. However, elaboration on therapist's past experiences early in group life often becomes more burdensome and uncomfortable for group members than helpful. At this point it is usually more appropriate and helpful to let the members know that the therapist has also had the same or a similar experience but, at least in the early phases, members usually don't want to know more than that.

Early revelations of strong feelings in reaction to the group members and the process more often hinder than facilitate process. Expression of strong feelings by the therapist, particularly feelings of anger, is most often perceived as rejection by group members in the early phases of group development and is best saved for a time when and if the group develops some strong degree of cohesion. After group cohesion develops members are less likely to perceive the strong feelings expressed by the therapist as total rejection. If these feelings are expressed, members are less likely to take them as rejection; moreover, with cohesion, at least the members can feel support and acceptance by other members. Strong positive feelings can also make members as uncomfortable as or even more uncomfortable than strong negative feelings but are less likely to result in the members dropping out.

In the long run, the therapist's progressive sharing of himself as a human being serves to help the members feel equal with the therapist and helps to reduce and legitimatize their own feelings. Also important, the transparency of the therapist tends to reduce transference, helping members deal with the therapist and other authority figures more realistically. However, in the early phases of group development many members need to attribute some powers and functions to the therapist if they are to feel comfortable in the group therapeutic situation. If the therapist descends from the omnipotent role too soon —that is, before individuals and groups feel sufficient power and comfort in the situation—some of the essential aspects of initial reliance on the therapist as a helper may be prohibited, causing the members to maintain their usual defenses against entering into treatment relationships with both the therapist and the group.

STIMULATION OF STRONG OR DEEP FEELINGS

Timing is the byword for the therapist's role in the stimulation of strong feelings in group members. Stimulation of strong feelings about here-and-now or there-and-then situations can be one of the most potent tools for helping in group therapy, however, if such feelings are elicited too soon—that is, before the individual or group is ready to handle them—an immediate consequence may be drop-outs. Premature hostility among group members as well as premature intimacy can frighten members and often, if members don't drop out, they bring to bear their defenses either by avoiding the difficult affective areas or by developing intellectualized emotional processes by which they are not really cathected. For example, if members are stimulated or pushed to express their hostility too soon, they intellectually recognize that they are supposed to be angry in certain situations and will comply with simulated expressions of anger to please the therapist.

On the other hand, stimulating accelerated intimacy will cause members either to drop out or, again, to develop constricted forms of intimacy that will inhibit the full experience of intimate relationships and fixate group development at a low level of intimacy until or unless some later intimacy crises are more fully resolved.

Gestalt psychodramatic, and other techniques for accelerating affect can be very useful in a therapy group, but only after the group has developed some degree of cohesion and comfort. Otherwise, the degree of therapist direction as well as the potential expression can be too threatening to the individual and group and cause others to fear and protect themselves from being placed in the situation. Once members are comfortable with each other and have already shared many feelings, then stimulation of more intense feelings is useful and often essential for the treatment process.

> Jane, a new member in an open-ended group, was a middle-aged woman widowed six months prior to entering the group. She had had some individual treatment and joined the group to help herself deal with her new experience in the singles world. In her second group meeting, Francis, a member who had been in the group for some time, began to push the new member to express her feelings about her deceased husband and how they might be interfering with her dating life. Francis had recently been experiencing her anger at her former husband and was attempting to validate her own anger through Jane.
>
> Jane plunged headlong into a full defense of her husband and his memory. As the group confronted her with the other side of her feelings, which were manifest in her defense, she began to experience some of her anger at her husband. The therapists efforts to moderate the impact were of little avail. Jane expressed her deep gratitude to the group but never returned.

Perhaps, if Jane had been allowed time to gain comfort in the group and if this expression had built up after developing some degree of intimacy with the others, she might have been able to resolve her feelings about her husband, as Francis ultimately did. However, the initial hostility of the other members, particularly Francis, toward Jane was inherent in the supposed help that Jane was receiving. Moreover, these very negative feelings, still new to Jane, occurred as she was also experiencing the initial covert hostility of the group. She lumped the group hostility with her own rejection of her own feelings and felt basically rejected by the group. Examination of the process and expressions of empathy from other members did not seem to allay Jane's reaction to this experience.

SUMMARY OF ROLE OF THE GROUP THERAPIST

At the outset the group therapist accepts the parallel and dependent nature of the group, provides nurture through support and unqualified acceptance to individuals, and lays the base for individuals to gain initial contact with each other through growing awareness of commonalities. The therapist allows or helps the group to develop by supporting all the members' overt and covert, expressed and implied wishes for the group. The therapist facilitates group development by directly actualizing each and every member's wishes through his own efforts or allowing and supporting the self-initiative of members who take early risks. To the degree that the group is ready for and demonstrates its own initiative, the therapist needs to modify his role from empathic nurturer to empathic facilitator. To the degree that the group is incapable of development the therapist must continue to serve as both nurturer and facilitator. Whether the therapist assumes the role of nurturer or facilitator, the touchstone of the therapist's role is empathic relationship with each individual and the group.

3

Co-therapy

by Virginia Gallogly and Baruch Levine

Two heads are better than one—as long as both are working. If both therapists are contributing to the diagnostic and treatment process, co-therapists can provide clients with a greater range of clinical thoughts, perceptions, and actions. If only one of them is functioning, the disadvantages far outweigh the advantages (Rabin, 1967).

PROS AND CONS OF CO-THERAPY

The pros and cons of co-therapy are numerous. The first major advantage is that the presence of two therapists helps to re-create the two-parent family, particularly if one therapist is male and the other female. The full re-creation of a primary family gives clients greater potential for a corrective emotional experience (Lundin and Aronov, 1952; Hulse et al., 1956; Schonbar, 1973; Mintz, 1963). Also, the potential for the perpetuation of a transference resistance is less likely with two therapists than with one (Pine et al., 1963). For example, the re-creation of an oedipal transference toward a therapist of the opposite sex is both facilitated and limited by the presence of another therapist. Likewise, oedipal struggles between a client and a therapist of the same sex can often be more easily worked through with the presence and support of another therapist. This is not to say that the group cannot serve the same functions as a second therapist, but a second therapist can often more easily facilitate and insure the resolution of these issues.

The relationship between co-therapists can provide a model of relationships for clients and can also be a catalyst for the development of relationships among the members in a group (Solomon and Solomon, 1963). For example, if the group members can see that the therapists can and do disagree or conflict without rejecting each other, then group members come to understand that it is possible to assert one's individuality in a relationship without being rejected (Block, 1961).

The dilution of authority between two therapists can help clients resolve the authority-autonomy issues. If co-therapists do indeed share authority and neither strives for autocratic control of the relationship or the group, then their sharing makes it easier for group members to share in group decisions. The very existence of two relatively equal authoritative opinions in a group can provide the group members with the opportunity to select the opinion most helpful to them or to come up with an opinion of their own. At the very least, with two authoritative opinions, the members may find it easier to oppose the therapists and express their own opinion or resistance. In a very practical way, the seating of the co-therapists can serve to defocus the authority. When co-therapists sit apart from each other, attention is no longer focused in one direction; instead, group members must turn from one therapist to the other, increasing the likelihood of directly communicating with other group members in the process.

Co-therapy also offers the potential of providing a wider array of therapeutic interactions. With two therapists present, each can assume different roles when appropriate. For example, if one therapist is supportive and one confrontive with a member or a group that is difficult to confront, it is often easier for the group or member to accept and gain from the confrontation.

Finally, the various strengths of each therapist can often complement the other's weaknesses; the group profits from the best of each therapist; it is not deprived by the limitations of one therapist.

The disadvantages of co-therapy primarily arise from situations where the co-therapists fail to develop a good relationship with each other (Lundin and Aronov, 1952; Gans, 1962; Davis and Lohr, 1971). The first danger is that the therapists may act out their respective or mutual difficulties, or both, in or through the group. The classic example is when one therapist is angry at the other and, consequently, interferes with or subverts the other's efforts in the group.

A second danger arising from a malformed co-therapy relationship is poor modeling of relationships. Since most members of a therapy group have already experienced poor relationships, it behooves the co-therapists to provide a healthier model for relationships not only to provide a corrective emotional experience for the group members, but also to set a healthier relational atmosphere through their own interactions. For example, co-therapists in a dominant-submissive relational pattern may inadvertently lend support for group members to identify with the dominant or submissive pattern in their own relationships.

Third, a malformed co-therapy relationship can hamper group development. Although many groups can develop in spite of problems between co-therapists, other groups may falter or fail as a direct consequence of the co-therapy relational difficulties. For example, if one therapist has untoward needs for power and successfully dominates the other, that very same domination can extend to the group. A more common example occurs when the co-therapists are involved in an unending power struggle and, consciously or unconsciously, enlist the group members to carry on the struggle. This type of struggle can result in the group's possibly never achieving intimacy or mutuality.

Finally, a malformed co-therapy relationship can deprive the group of the combined complementary therapeutic skills of the co-therapists and can even leave the group with less than the level of skill either therapist individually could have provided. For example, a group may be deprived of well conceived therapetuic initiative if one therapist subverts that initiative or supplants it with a hastily or ill-conceived countermeasure. In other words, the group members are doubly deprived: first, they do not receive the well conceived therapeutic initiative and, second, they probably do not receive the best initiative of the other therapist.

CO-THERAPY: WHEN AND WHO

By and large, co-therapy can be used in any group. However, in some situations it can be extremely important. In children's groups, for example, there are both practical and therapeutic reasons for using co-therapists (Kassoff, 1958; Kluckmann et al., 1967). From the practical standpoint, the mere presence of two adults can help maintain control with less need for limits and also can allow one therapist to cope with an individual problematic situation while the other therapist continues with the rest of the group. From the therapeutic standpoint, the presence of both male and female therapists provides potentiality for the recreation of the two-parent family and a subsequent corrective emotional experience.

In couples' groups, it is important that co-therapists be of opposite sexes to provide a balance of masculine and feminine support (Low and Low, 1975). As nonsexist as any therapist might be, there can always be incipient sexist elements in the countertransference of a single therapist. Hence, if therapists are of opposite sexes, they are more likely to be able to counter each other and serve as relational models.

In groups of depressives, two therapists can share the heavy emotional burden by providing mutual support during and after sessions. In groups of depressed persons, as well as other groups of very dependent persons, a well developed co-therapy relationship can serve the function of spreading both the dependency and authority, thus decreasing the dangers of perpetuating conformity and dependency. However, a poor co-therapy relationship can increase the dependency on authority to a greater extent than a therapist working alone.

Although co-therapists of the opposite sex are preferable, therapists of the same sex can often function as well and serve some of the purposes as therapists of the opposite sex (Block, 1961; Davis and Lohr, 1971). In groups of adolescents, particularly early adolescents, a therapist of the opposite sex often creates many transferential issues. Consequently, in short-term groups of adolescents (groups with fewer than twenty-four sessions), it is best to have one or both therapists of the same sex as the group members, since there is insufficient time for the transferential issues to be resolved. In longer-term early adolescent groups, one therapist of the opposite sex can serve as a catalyst for the stimulation and resolution of these transferential issues.

THE DEVELOPMENT OF THE CO-THERAPY RELATIONSHIP

Co-therapy relationships are similar to therapy groups in their developmental patterns. Somewhat as groups must, co-therapists must work through several phases and crises before they develop a mature relationship. The phases and crises the authors believe occur in the development of a co-therapy relationship are: (1) It's nice working with you; (2) One of us is no good; (3) We may make it; (4) We're a good team; (5) It's too bad we have to give this up. The full dynamics of these phenomena parallel the phases and crises of therapy group development explored in Part 2 of this book. Below we will focus only on some of the more common feelings co-therapists experience in each phase and crisis so that they may assess the developmental level of their relationship.

It's Nice Working with You (Parallel Phase)

Each therapist most often brings his or her respective and previous status and roles to the new co-therapy relationship. In spite of negotiation, each will tend to view the other from the perspective of his or her prior status and roles (Heifron, 1969). A number of stereotypic patterns occur in early co-therapy relationships. One is the "separate but equal" pattern. Initially, the "separate but equal" co-therapists are inclined to be extremely polite, to respect each other's opinions, to religiously take turns at therapeutic interventions, to be exceedingly careful not to step on each others toes, and not to risk the full extent of their therapeutic skills. This co-therapy team usually views themselves as fairly equal in knowledge and skills.

Another stereotype is the "expert-novice" team. On this team the co-therapists initially, overtly or covertly, agree that one or the other is more expert. Some teams develop an overt contract of equality in spite of a gap in expertise; others develop an overt contract of inequality whereby the expert will continue to be the expert and the novice will look on without any real power of therapeutic decision.

A third stereotype is the "dominant-submissive" team. The dominant member can gain the dominance from several sources: personality differences, mutual sex-role expectations, prior status as a supervisor, group therapy expert, continuing therapist in a group taking on a new co-therapist, or simply being the co-therapist with greater needs for authority and control.

Of course, there are a myriad of other possibilities, but these are some of the more common ways co-therapy teams begin their relationship. Although the authors feel that a fully developed, mature co-therapy relationship is egalitarian in nature, the relationship could well start in any one of these modes (Getty and Shannon, 1969). The problem arises not with starting in these modes, but with perpetuating them.

Co-therapists must contend with both feelings and behavior if they are to develop a mature egalitarian relationship. While the feelings, of necessity, take time to be resolved, co-therapists can readily identify and structure egalitarian behavior in several overt ways in the therapy group.

A most overt feature of nonegalitarian or highly competitive co-therapy relationships is tandoming. Tandoming is essentially the process whereby the second therapist invariably speaks after the first and before a member or members can respond to the first therapist. Put more simply, the sequence of interaction is T^1, T^2, M or M, T^1, T^2. This situation can be overtly rectified if each co-therapist agrees to allow at least one group member to respond to the therapist initiating the interaction before the other speaks. In other words, a more egalitarian sequence of interaction would be T^1, M, T^2 or T^1, M, M, T^2. Often tandoming occurs because the second therapist believes that the first therapist's initiative needs help to be effective. However, the assist may or may not be essential and the tandoming, regardless of how helpful, may undermine the authority, initiative, and expertise of the first therapist. This is not to say that when the second therapist really believes that the first therapist is going over the proverbial cliff, that he or she shouldn't help out. The question is: Is it indeed a cliff? Again, if the second therapist allows the members to react to the first therapist before trying to help out, it may obviate the need for assistance.

Another feature of the nonegalitarian co-therapy relationship is subject-changing—that is, one therapist initiates a subject and the other therapist changes the focus before the first therapist and members have a chance to complete their discussion of the subject. The phenomenon directly implies that competition or control issues, or perhaps both, exist between the co-therapists. An agreement between the co-therapists for each to allow the other to complete a discussion before changing the subject can help to build a more egalitarian relationship.

A final point: in the early stages of the co-therapy relationship, therapists must weigh the merits of pursuing a given subject at a particular time in a therapy group against the merits of developing egalitarian balance in the co-therapy relationship.

One of Us Is No Good
(Authority Crisis and Inclusion Phase)

As the co-therapy relationship develops, initial statuses and roles begin to erode. One of the first signs that the therapists may experience in this phase is the gnawing feeling that either they or the other therapist are inadequate as a group therapist. What ensues is a crisis of adequacy for each therapist. The crisis arises because each therapist progressively risks more in the therapeutic situation and begins to experience real differences in style, personality, and philosophies. If the relationship is to grow, these feelings of discontentment must be shared with the other co-therapist. Failure to either share or accept the other therapist's feelings on these matters will result in the perpetuation of the "It's nice to work with you" facade (McGee and Schuman, 1970). Also, conflicts between co-therapists will stay covert and possibly be acted out through the group members.

Depending on such factors as the therapists' personalities and expertise, the crisis takes various forms. One partner of the "separate but equal" co-therapy team may want himself (or herself) or the other therapist to function differently. In their own functioning, both may begin to realize that they are not feeling free to function as they would if they didn't have to contend with the other therapist. They may or may not express this to each other. The novice on the "expert-novice" co-therapy team often experiences "I'm not good, I'll never be able to be as good as. . ." feelings during this crisis or may feel that the expert "is not as good as he or she was reputed to be." If the expert is threatened by the novice's skill, the expert may have to preserve his or her self-esteem by not acknowledging the threat, covertly seeking to display his or her superior skills and possibly undermining the confidence of the novice. In the "dominant-submissive" co-therapy team, the submissive co-therapist often begins to feel like he or she wants more of the power in the relationship. Like the expert, the dominant therapist who is threatened by the potential increase in power and initiative of the submissive therapist may then try to undermine his or her co-therapist's initiative.

We Might Make It (Intimacy Crisis)

This phase is similar to the intimacy crisis in therapy group development, particularly as it relates to the sharing and accepting of each other's feelings about the relationship. If and as one co-therapist opts to share his or her hostile, aggressive, rejecting, rejected, adequate, or inadequate feelings during the "one of us is no good" crisis and if the other therapist not only accepts these feelings but identifies or empathizes from his or her own experience *in the co-therapy relationship,* then the therapists begin to establish the crucial affective bond that will serve as the foundation for growth in their relationship. This initial affective contact gives rise to the "we" feeling or bond in the co-therapy relationship. Co-therapists are more likely to refer to the group as "our" group rather than the "group we co-lead" or some other such reference after they have established this bond (Heifron, 1969). If the feelings are not shared, accepted, and empathized with, the relationship is in danger of reverting back to the "It's nice working with you" phase or one or both therapists resigning themselves to "It's a bad co-therapy situation, but what can you do" feelings. The danger in such a resolution is that an atmosphere may develop that inhibits the group members from freely expressing their feelings or one may develop that causes the members to act out the suppressed feelings of the co-therapists. In either event, intimacy among group members will be seriously hampered, if not prevented.

We're a Good Team (Mutuality Phase)

As both therapists become more accepting of their own and the other's feelings and ideas in the relationship, they are less concerned with power, status, and expertise issues and are freer to cope with the therapeutic issues (Heifron, 1969). The now mature co-therapy relationship makes it possible for the team to maximize the particular assets of each therapist and develop and coordinate the numerous techniques that only a well differentiated team can effectively employ.

Too Bad We Have To Give This Up
(Separation Crisis/Termination Phase)

This phase is the inevitable end of the co-therapy relationship. The relinquishment of a well-developed co-therapy relationship brings the same pain, hostility, depression, and regression that any separation may bring. Even if the co-therapists are leading or plan to lead another therapy group together, the relinquishment of the team effort with a particular group will still give rise to termination reactions. Sharing these feelings with each other not only helps the co-therapists end their relationship on a more positive note but also helps prevent their contaminating the therapy group with co-therapist issues. If the co-therapists must terminate their relationship before it reaches maturity—that is, before they are able to share and resolve feelings about the relationship—then one or both will be left with feelings of hostility toward the other, or feelings of inadequacy to co-lead another therapy group, or possibly feelings of inadequacy in being a group therapist.

CONFLICTS

The question is not if conflicts will arise in a co-therapy relationship but whether and how the therapists will resolve their mutual conflicts. With the aim of transparency and modeling, many co-therapists bring their conflicts to the therapy group meetings and overtly attempt to work on and resolve them during the meetings. Other co-therapists feel that their conflicts should never be unearthed or worked on in group meetings; these therapists reserve their conflict resolutions for private meetings or supervisory sessions. The authors hold a middle position. Exposure of their conflicts to the group can have a beneficial effect in allowing group members to experience two therapists disagreeing and still retaining mutual acceptance. However, two conditions are necessary to insure that the group will benefit and not be harmed by exposure to a co-therapist conflict. First, the co-therapists must have reached a point where they feel like a team. This insures that the co-therapy team presents a healthy model for conflict resolution to the therapy group and also insures that the group members will not have to become involved in treating the conflict of the co-therapy team. Second, the therapy group should have achieved some degree of intimacy in case members become upset by the conflict between the therapists. Then if members become upset by the conflict and cannot, at that moment, depend on the therapists for support, they can rely on other group members to sustain them until the conflict is resolved. Thus, until both the co-therapists and the group are ready to handle co-therapy conflicts in the group meetings, therapists should resolve their conflicts in private sessions or supervision. Even when the group and therapists are ready and can handle co-therapy conflict in the group meeting, the conflicts should be brought to group meetings only if both therapists agree on the possible therapeutic value to the group rather than the comfort of the co-therapists (Heifron, 1969).

CO-THERAPY TECHNIQUES

In addition to the many possible therapeutic interventions that an individual therapist can employ, the co-therapy situation provides a unique opportunity to develop techniques in which the co-therapists can take differential roles with individual group members or the group. Again, the authors caution that these differential roles are best created and performed after the co-therapists have achieved some degree of mutuality. Otherwise, there is a danger that these differential roles represent acting out of the co-therapists' conflicts rather than the intended therapeutic intervention. Although a well developed co-therapy team can develop an infinite number of special ways of working together, the following are a few that the authors use in therapy groups. Needless to say, any technique developed by a co-therapy team can only be helpful if used with empathy and sensitivity to its effect on the individual group member and the group.

Helping the Co-Therapist Connect

One therapist can help the other complete an intervention in two basic ways: First, when one therapist perceives that the group members do not fully comprehend what the second therapist is saying and the first therapist sees what the second therapist is driving at, the first therapist may reinterpret or attempt to express the same idea in a more comprehensible saying, for example: "I think she means. . . " "To say it in another way. . . ." "Do you mean. . . ."

Second, the other therapist can intervene when a group member is having trouble responding to the first therapist. Very often a group member has trouble responding to a therapist if what the therapist has said has angered the group member and the group member is uncomfortable with or unable to express the anger. If the other therapist feels that the group member is at a point where expressing the anger will be therapeutic, he or she can suggest things like, "You look very unhappy about what my co-therapist just said," or "If he had said that to me, I'd be angry." This type of intervention by the second therapist often frees the group member to respond to the first therapist.

Support-Confrontation

The co-therapists' splitting of roles—one being confrontative and one supportive—can insure a supportive confrontation when a group member is either resistive to confrontation or has demonstrated rigidity in response to past confrontations.

> A young woman in one of our therapy groups had a great deal of difficulty experiencing and expressing her angry feelings. She tended to rationalize away any anger. During one group meeting one of the members cut the young woman off from relating an incident to the group. One therapist then asked her how she felt about being cut off. When she hesitated for a few moments, the other therapist began to rationalize the other group member's actions for the young woman, saying, "He probably cut you off because he was more upset than you and needed to talk." The first therapist then said, jokingly, "You mean you're not angry about this?" To which the second therapist responded, "People don't get angry about a thing like that." At this point the young woman told both therapists to "Shut up," and she told off the group member who cut her off.

Splitting the Ambivalence

When a group member is highly ambivalent, each co-therapist supporting one side of the ambivalence can sometimes help a member to a resolution (Gottlieb, 1965).

> A young man in one of our groups was very ambivalent about breaking his strong ties with his mother. While intellectually recognizing his need to keep re-engaging his mother in his job-finding efforts and having her under-cut them, emotionally he could do little about breaking the tie. In a group meeting after he allowed his mother, once again, to undercut his job efforts by talking to her just after starting a new job, one therapist sup-ported his continuing to seek advice and support from his mother and the other therapist supported his wishes for self-dependence. The group member responded by getting angry at the co-therapists for playing games with his torment. However, in the next group session, the young man announced to the group that he decided not to talk with his mother just after starting a new job.

SUPERVISION

Co-therapy, like any other therapeutic endeavor, needs sound supervision for the professional development of the co-therapy team. Supervision should focus on both the development of the co-therapy relationship and the assessment of and help to the therapy group and its members. All too often co-therapy supervision focuses on one area with the exclusion of the other. Generally, the authors have found in supervising co-therapists that it is important for the team to have a meeting without the supervisor before coming to supervision. Such a meeting provides the co-therapists with the opporunity to work out some aspects of their relationship and, consequently, to be less dependent on supervisory intervention (Heifron, 1969). Issues the co-therapists cannot work out in their own sessions can then be appropriately brought to the supervisor for resolution.

As a training medium, co-therapy can be a very dynamic teaching device but one fraught with complexities and dangers (Anderson et al., 1972; Block, 1961: Maclennan, 1965). On the positive side, it gives the neophyte an opportunity to experience first hand the work of the experienced therapist. On the other hand, the neophyte is locked into a situation in which the supervisor is also the co-therapist. This confusion in roles can inhibit the trainee's struggles for equal partnership in the therapeutic process because the direct opponent in that struggle also serves as the "referee" after the meeting. Even when the trainer is well equipped to handle both roles, which isn't always the case, the trainee may not be able to cope with the situation and, consequently, may relegate himself to a junior partnership in the therapeutic situation.

When the trainee has a co-therapist relationship with his or her supervisor, it is particularly important that the trainee have other co-therapy experiences with peers and nonsupervisors and perhaps even that he or she have experiences as the only therapist in other groups. Even the trainees who are not co-leading with a supervisor, should have both co-therapist and sole leadership experiences in order to gain confidence and a fuller appreciation of their group therapeutic skills. Experience with only one co-leader can give the therapist a one-sided view of himself. However, there is nothing like the experience of a fully developed co-therapy relationship to help a therapist gain appreciation of his or her own therapeutic assets as well as a deeper appreciation and acceptance of how other therapists with perhaps different philosophies, styles, and personalities can achieve similar therapeutic ends in their own unique ways.

Bibliography

ANDERSON, B.N., I. PINE, and D. MEE-LEE 1972 "Resident Training in Co-therapy Groups." *International Journal of Group Psychotherapy* 22: 195.

ANDREWS, E.E. 1962 "Some Group Dynamics in Therapy Groups of Mothers." *"International Journal of Group Psychotherapy* 12: 476-91.

ARONOWITZ, E. 1968 "Ulterior Motives in Games: Implications for Group Work With Children." *Social Work* 13: 50-55.

ASTRACHAN, B.M., A.H. SCHWARTZ, R. BECKER, and M. HARROW 1967. "The Psychiatrist's Effect on the Behavior and Interaction of Therapy Groups." *American Journal of Psychiatry* 123: 1379-1387.

BANDURA, A. 1956 "Psychotherapist's Anxiety Level, Self-Insight, and Psycho-therapeutic Competence." *Journal of Abnormal Social Psychology* 52: 333-37.

BARDILL, D.R. 1973 "Group Therapy Techniques With Pre-adolescent Boys in a Residential Training Center." *Child Welfare* 52: 533-41

BASS, B. and F. NORTON 1951 "Group Size and Leaderless Discussions." *Journal of Applied Psychology* 35: 397-400.

BATTEGAY, R. 1966 "Geschwisterrelationen als Funktionsmuster der (Thera-peutischen) Gruppen" ("Sibling Relations as a Functional Pattern in a Therapeutic Group") *Psychotherapy and Psychosomatics* 14: 251-63.

BECK, D.F. 1958 "The Dynamics of Group Psychotherapy as Seen by a Sociol-ogist" Part 1. *Sociometry* 21: 98-128.

BENNIS, W.G. and H.A. SHEPARD 1974 "A Theory of Group Development," In G. Gibbard, J. Hartman, R. Mann (eds.) *Analysis of Groups.* San Fran-cisco: Jossey-Bass. Pp. 127-153.

BERELSON, B. and G. STEINER 1964 *Human Behavior.* New York: Harcourt Brace Javonovich, Inc.

BERGER, M. 1974 "The Impact of the Therapist's Personality on Group Pro-cess." *American Journal of Psychoanalysis* 34: 213-19.

BERNSTEIN, S. 1950 "There are Groups and Groups." *The Group* 13, 1: 3-10.

BION, W.R. 1961 *Experiences in Groups and Other Papers.* New York: Basic Books.

BLOCK, S. 1961 "Multi-Leadership as a Teaching and Therapeutic Tool in Group Practice." *Comprehensive Psychiatry* 2: 211-18.

BLOCK, S. 1966 "Some Notes on Transference in Group Psychotherapy." *Comprehensive Psychiatry* 7, 1: 31-38.

BOAS, C. 1962 "Intensive Group Psychotherapy With Married Couples." *International Journal of Group Psychotherapy* 12, 2: 142-53.

BORDIN, E.S. 1965 "The Ambivalent Quest for Independence." *Journal of Counseling Psychology* 12, 4: 339-45.

BOVARD, E.W., Jr. 1951 "The Experimental Production of Interpersonal Affect." *Journal of Abnormal Social Psychology* 46: 521-28.

BROSS, R.B. 1959 "Termination of Analytically Oriented Psychotherapy in Groups." *International Journal of Group Psychotherapy* 3: 326-37.

BRUCK, M. 1966 "An Evaluation of the Use of Group Treatment for Hard-to-Reach-Latency-Age Children in a Community Guidance Clinic." *Child Welfare* 45: 395-403.

BUSH, G. 1969 "Transference, Countertransference, and Identification in Supervision." *Contemporary Psychoanalysis* 5: 158-62.

BUXBAUM, E. 1945 "Transference and Group Formation in Children and Adolescents." *Psychoanalytic Study of the Child, Vol 1.* New York: International Universities Press.

CAPLAN, G. and S. LEBOVICI eds. 1969 *Adolescence: Psychosocial Perspectives.* New York: Basic Books.

CAPLAN, S.W. 1957 "The Effect of Group Counseling in Junior High School Boys' Concept of Themselves in School." *Journal of Counseling Psychology* 4: 124-28.

CARTWRIGHT, D. and F. HARARY 1956 "Structural Balance: A Generalization of Heider's Theory." *Psychological Review* 63: 277-93.

CARTWRIGHT, D. and ZANDER A. (eds. 1968) *Group Dyanamics Research and Theory.* Third ed. New York: Harper and Row.

CELIA, S.A. 1970 "Mileu Therapy in Brazil: 2. The Club as an Integrative Factor in a Therapeutic Community for Children." *American Journal of Orthopsychiatry* 40: 130-34.

CHAPIN, F.S. 1950 "Sociometric Stars as Isolates." *American Journal of Sociology* 56: 263-67.

CHESSICK, R.D. 1965 "Empathy and Love in Psychotherapy." *American Jornal of Psychotherapy* 19: 205-19.

CHURCHILL S. 1959 "Prestructuring Group Content." *Social Work* 4: 52-59.

COFFEY, H.S. and L.L. WIENER 1967 *Group Treatment of Autistic Children.* New Jersey: Prentice-Hall.

Committee on Adolescence, Group for the Advancement of Psychiatry. 1968 *Normal Adolescence: Its Dynamics and Impact.* New York: Schribner's.

COSER, L. 1964 *The Function of Social Conflict.* New York: Free Press of Glencoe.

COTTRELL, L.S., Jr. and R.F. DYMOND 1949 "The Empathic Responses: A Neglected Field of Research." *Psychiatry* 12: 355-59.

COWDEN, R.C. 1955 "Empathy or Projection?" *Journal of Clinical Psychology* 11: 188-90.

COYLE, G. 1930 *Social Process in Organized Groups.* New York: Smith.

CRISS, F.C. and R. C. GOODWIN 1970 "Short-Term Group Counseling for Parents of Children in Residential Treatment." *Child Welfare* 49: 45-48.

CROOK, J.H. 1961 "The Basis of Flock Organization in Birds," in W.H. Thorpe and D.C. Zangwill (eds.), *Current Problems in Animal Behavior.* Cambridge: Cambridge University Press. Pp. 125-49.

CROW, M.S. 1967 "Preventive Intervention Through Parent Group Education." *Social Casework* 48: 161-65.

DAVIS, F. and N. LOHR 1971 "Special Problems With the Use of Co-Therapists in Group Psychotherapy." *International Journal of Group Psychotherapy* 2: 143-57.

DURKIN, H.E. 1964 *The Group In Depth.* New York: International Universities Press.

DYMOND, R.F. 1948 "A Preliminary Investigation of the Relation of Insight and Empathy." *Journal of Consulting Psychology* 12: 228-33.

EBERSOLE, G.O., P.H. LEIDERMAN, and I.D. YALOM 1969 "Training the Non-Professional Group Therapist: A Controlled Study." *Journal of Nervous Mental Disorders* 149: 294-302.

EICKE, D. 1967 "Therapeutic Group Work With Schizophrenics." *Zeitschrift fur Psychotherapie und Medizinische Psychologie* 17: 100-111.

EISENMAN, R. 1965 "Usefulness of the Concepts of Interiority Feeling and Life Style With Schizophrenics." *Journal of Individual Psychology* 21: 171-77.

ERIKSON, E.H. 1968 *Identity Youth and Crisis.* New York: Norton.

FIDLER, J.W. 1965 "Group Psychotherapy of Psychotics." *American Journal of Orthopsychiatry* 35: 688-94.

FIEDLER, F.E. 1950 "The Concept of an Ideal Therapeutic Relationship." *Journal of Consulting Psychology* 14: 239-45.

FINGER, S. 1966 "The Group Method in Services to Unmarried Mothers and Their Parents." *Child Welfare* 45: 564-68.

FLESCHER, J. 1957 "The Economy of Agression and Anxiety in Group Formations." *International Journal of Group Psychotherapy* 7: 31-39.

FLINT, A.A., Jr. and B.W. MacLENNAN 1962 "Some Dyanamic Factors in Marital Group Psychotherapy." *International Journal of Group Psychotherapy* 12:355-61.

FOULKES, S.M. 1965 *Therapeutic Group Analysis.* New York: International Universities Press.

FRANK, J.D., J. MARGOLIN, H. T. NASH, A.R. STONE, E. VARON, and E. ASCHER 1952 "Two Behavior Patterns in Therapeutic Groups and Their Apparent Motivation." *Human Relations* 5: 289-317.

FRANK, J.D., E. ASCHER, J.B. MARGOLIN, H. NASH, A.R. STONE, and E.J. VARON 1952 "Behavioral Patterns in Early Meetings of Therapy Groups." *American Journal of Psychiatry* 108: 771-78.

FREEDMAN, M.B. and B.S. SWEET 1954 "Some Specific Features of Group Psychotherapy and Their Implications for Selection of Patients." *International Journal of Group Psychotherapy* 4: 355-68.

FREEMAN, D.R. 1965 "Counseling Engaged Couples in Small Groups." *Social Work* 10: 36-42.

FREEMAN, S.J., E.J. LEAVENS, and D.J. McCULLOCH 1969 "Factors Associated With Success or Failure in Marital Counseling." *Family Coordinator* 18: 125-28.

FRENCH, T.M., 1952 *The Integration of Behavior, Volumns I and II.* Chicago: University of Chicago Press.

FREUD, S. 1935 *A General Introduction to Psychoanalysis.* New York: Doubleday.

FREUD, S. 1960 *Group Psychology and the Analysis of the Ego.* New York: Bantam Books.

FREY, L.A. (ed.) 1967 *Use of Groups in the Health Field.* New York: National Association of Social Workers, 1967.

FREY, L.A. and R.L. KOLODNY 1966 "Group Treatment for the Alienated Child in the School." *International Journal of Group Psychotherapy* 16: 321-37.

FRIED, EDRITA 1956 "Ego Emancipation of Adolescents Through Group Psychotherapy." *International Journal of Group Psychotherapy* 6: 358-73.

FROMM, E. 1969 *Escape From Freedom.* New York: Avon.

GADPAILLE, W.J. 1959 "Observation on the Sequence of Resistances in Groups of Adolescent Delinquents." *International Journal of Group Psychotherapy* 9: 275-86.

GANS, R. 1962 "Group Co-therapists and the Therapeutic Situation: A Critical Evaluation." *International Journal of Group Psychotherapy* 12: 82-88.

GANTER, G., M. YEAKEL, and N.A. POLANSKY 1967 *Retrieval From Limbo: The Intermediary Group Treatment of Inaccessible Children.* New York: Child Welfare League of America.

GARLAND, J.A., H.E. JONES, and R.L. KOLODNY 1965 "A Model For Stages of Development in Social Work Groups," in Saul Bernstein, ed. *Explorations in Group Work.* Boston: Boston University School of Social Work. Pp 12-54.

GARRETT, A. 1970 *Interviewing: Its Principles and Methods.* New York: Family Service Association of America.

GELLER, J.J. 1963 "Concerning the Size of Therapy Groups," in M. Rosenbaum and M. Berger (ed.) *Group Psychotherapy and Group Function.* New York: Basic Books.

GERARD, H.B. 1956 "Some Factors Affecting an Individual's Estimate of His Probable Success in a Group Situation." *Journal of Abnormal and Social Psychology* 52: 235-39.

GETTY, C., and A.M. SHANNON 1969 "Cotherapy as an Egalitarian Relationship." *American Journal of Nursing* 69: 767.

GIBBARD, G.S., and J.J. HARTMAN 1973 "The Oedipal Paradigm in Group Development: A Clinical and Empirical Study." *Small Group Behavior* 4: 305-54.

GLATZER, H. 1956 "The Relative Effectiveness of Clinically Homogeneous and Heterogeneous Psychotherapy Groups." *International Journal of Group Psychotherapy* 6: 258-65.

GLATZER, H.T. 1965 "Aspects of Transference in Group Psychotherapy." *International Journal of Group Psychotherapy* 15: 167-76.

GOLDSTEIN, A. and W. SHIPMAN. 1961 "Patient Expectancies, Symptom Reduction and Aspects of the Initial Psychotherapeutic Interview." *Journal of Clinical Psychology* 17: 129-133.

GOLEMBIEWSKI, R. 1962 *The Small Group.* Chicago: University of Chicago Press.

GOODMAN, M., M. MARKS, and H. ROCKBERGER 1964 "Resistance in Group Psychotherapy Enhanced by the Countertransference Reactions of the Therapist." *The International Journal of Group Psychotherapy* 14: 332-43.

GOTTLIEB, A., and M. KRAMER 1965 "Alternate-Therapist Group Meetings: An Approach to the Severly Ambivalent Patient." *International Journal of Group Psychotherapy* 15: 187-97.

GOTTLIEB, A. and E.M. PATTISON 1966 "Married Couples Group Psychotherapy." *Archives of General Psychiatry* 14: 143-52.

GRUNEBAUM, H., and J. CHRIST 1968 "Interpretation and the Task of the Therapist with Couples and Families." *International Journal of Group Psychotherapy* 18: 495-503.

HACKER, A. 1956 "A Political Scientist Looks at Psychotherapy." *International Journal of Group Psychotherapy* 2: 23-33.

HACKMAN, J.R., and N. VIDMAR 1970 "Effects of Size and Task Type on Group Performance and Member Reactions 33: 37-54.

HADLEY, R.G., W.V. LEVY, and M.P. MANSON 1963 "Group Therapy in a Mental Hospital." *Geriatrics* 18: 910-15.

HALLOWITZ, E. 1951 "Activity Group Psychotherapy as Preparation for Individual Treatment." *International Journal of Group Psychotherapy* 1: 337-47.

HALLOWITZ, E. and B. STEPHENS 1959 "Group Therapy With Fathers." *Social Casework.* 40: 183-92.

HARDCASTLE, D.R. 1972 Measuring Effectiveness in Group Marital Counseling." *Family Coordinator* 21: 213-18.

HARE, A.P. 1952 "A Study of Interaction and Consensus in Different Sized Groups." *American Sociological Review* 17: 261-67.

HARE, A.P. 1962 *Handbook of Small Group Research.* New York: Free Press.

HARE, A.P. 1973 "Theories of Group Development and Categories for Interaction Analysis." *Small Group Behavior* 4: 259-303.

HARRISON, R. and B. LUBIN 1965 "Personal Style, Group Composition and Learning." *Journal of Applied Behavioral Science* 1: 286-301.

HARTFORD, M.E. 1971 *Groups in Social Work.* New York: Columbia University Press.

HASTINGS, P.R., and R.L. RUNKLE 1963 "An Experimental Group of Married Couples With Severe Problems." *International Journal of Group Psychotherapy* 13: 84-92.

HAYTHORN, W., A. COUCH, D. HAEFNER, P. LANGHORN, and C.F. CARTER 1956 "The Behavior of Authoritarian and Equalitarian Personalities in Groups." *Human Relations* 14: 57-74.

HEARN, G. 1957 "The Process of Group Development." *Autonomous Groups Bulletin* 13: 1-7.

HEFFRON, W.A., K. BOMMELAERE, and R. MASTERS 1973 "Group Discussion With the Parents of Leukemic Children" *Pediatrics* 52: 831-40.

HEIDER, F. 1958 *The Psychology of Interpersonal Relations.* New York: Wiley.

HEIFRON, M. 1969 "Cotherapy: The Relationship Between Therapists." *International Journal of Group Psychotherapy* 19: 366-81.

HEITLER, J.B. 1973 "Preparation of Lower-Class Patients for Expressive Group Psychotherapy." *Journal of Consulting and Clinical Psychology* 41: 251-60.

HIRSCH, S. 1969 "Group Program in a General Hospital: A Consideration of Differential Factors." *Journal of Jewish Communal Service* 45: 248-53.

HOLLIS, F. 1972 *Casework: A Psychosocial Therapy,* 2nd ed. New York: Random.

HOLLISTER, W.G. 1957 "The Risks of Freedom-Giving Group Leadership." *Mental Hygiene* 41: 238-44.

HOMANS, GEORGE C. 1950 *The Human Group.* New York: Harcourt, Brace and World.

HULSE, W.C. 1961 "Multiple Transference or Group Neurosis?" *ACTA Psychotherapeutica* 9: 348-57.

HULSE, W.C., W.V. LULOW, B.K. RINDSBERG, and N.B. EPSTEIN 1956 "Transference Reactions in a Group of Female Patients to Male and Female Coleaders." *International Journal of Group Psychotherapy* 6: 430-35.

ISAACS, S. 1933 *Social Development in Young Children,* pp. 247-72. New York: Harcourt Brace Jovanovich.

IZARD, C.E. 1960 "Personality Similarity, Positive Affect, and Interpersonal Attraction." *Journal of Abnormal and Social Psychology* 61: 484-85.

JESKE, J.O. 1973 "Identification and Therapeutic Effectiveness in Group Therapy." *Journal of Consulting Psychology* 20: 528-30.

JOSSELYN, I.M. 1971 *Adolescence.* New York: Harper & Row.

KADIS, A.L., J.D. KRASNER, C. WINICK, and S.H. FOULKES 1974 *A Practicum of Group Psychotherapy.* New York: Harper & Row.

KARSON, S. 1965 "Group Psychotherapy With Latency-Age Boys." *International Journal of Group Psychotherapy* 15: 81-89.

KASSOFF, A.I. 1958 "Advantages of Multiple Therapists in a Group of Severely Acting-Out Adolescent Boys." *International Journal of Group Psychotherapy* 8: 70-75.

KATZ, R.L. 1963 *Empathy, Its Nature and Uses.* New York: Free Press of Glencoe.

KELMAN, H.C. 1963 "The Role of the Group in the Induction of Therapeutic Change." *International Journal of Group Psychotherapy* 13: 399-451.

KLAF, F.S. 1961 "The Power of the Group Leader: A Contribution to the Understanding of Group Psychology." *Psychoanalysis Review* 48: 41-51.

KLAPMAN, J.W. 1951 "Clinical Practices of Group Psychotherapy With Psychotics." *International Journal of Group Psychotherapy* 1: 22-30.

KLUCKMANN, C., F. STREPPE, and H. BRUNNER 1967 "Erfahrungen einer Gruppentherapie mit Männlichem und Weiblichem Therapeuten" (Experience in Group Therapy with a Male and Female Therapist) *Praxis der Kinderpsychologie und Kinderpsychiatrie* 16: 67-74.

KONOPKA, G. 1963 *Social Group Work: A Helping Process*. Englewood Cliffs, N.J.: Prentice-Hall.

LAKIN, M., M.A. LIEBERMAN, and D.S. WHITAKER 1969 "Issues in the Training of Group Psychotherapists." *International Journal of Group Psychotherapy* 19: 307-25.

LEICHTER, E. 1962 "Group Psychotherapy of Married Couples' Groups: Some Characteristic Treatment Dynamics." *International Journal of Group Psychotherapy* 12: 154-63.

LEICHTER, E. 1973 "Treatment of Married Couples' Groups." *Family Coordinator* 22: 31-42.

LENNARD, H. and A. BERNSTEIN, with H.C. HENDIN and E.B. PALMORE 1967 *The Anatomy of Psychotherapy: Systems of Communication and Expectation*. New York: Columbia University Press.

LEVINE, B. 1965 "Principles for Developing An Ego-Supportive Group Treatment Service." *Social Services Review* 39: 422-32.

LEVINE, B. 1967 *Fundamentals of Group Treatment*. Northbrook, Ill.: Whitehall.

LEVINE, B. 1968 "Factors Related to Interpersonal Balance in Social Work Treatment Groups." Unpublished Doctoral Dissertation, School of Social Service Administration, University of Chicago.

LEVINE, B. and J. SCHILD 1969 "Group Treatment of Depression." *Social Work* 14: 46-52.

LEVINSON, H.M. 1973 "Use and Misuse of Groups." *Social Work* 18: 66-73.

LEWIN, K. 1951 *Field Theory in Social Science*. New York: Harper.

LEWIN, K., R. LIPPITT, and R.K. WHITE 1939 "Patterns of Aggressive Behavior in Experimentally Created 'Social Climates.'" *Journal of Social Psychology* 10: 271-99.

LIEBERMAN, F. 1964 "Transition From Latency to Prepuberty in Girls: An Activity Group Becomes an Interview Group." *International Journal of Group Psychotherapy* 14: 455-64.

LIEBERMAN, M.A., I.D. YALOM, and M.B. MILES 1973 *Encounter Groups: First Facts*. New York: Basic Books.

LIFTON, N. and E.M. SMOLEN 1966 "Group Psychotherapy With Schizophrenic Children." *International Journal of Group Psychotherapy* 16: 23-41.

LIGHT, N. 1974 "The Chronic Helper in Group Therapy." *Perspectives in Psychiatric Care* 12: 129-34.

LINDEN, M.E., M.M. GOODWIN, and M. RESNIK 1968 "Group Psychotherapy of Couples in Marriage Counseling." *International Journal of Group Psychotherapy* 18: 313-24.

LOW, M. and P. LOW 1975 "Treatment of Married Couples in a Group Run by a Husband and Wife." *International Journal of Group Psychotherapy* 25: 54-56.

LUNDIN, W.M. and B.M. ARONOV 1952 "Use of Co-therapists in Group Psychotherapy." *Journal of Consulting Psychology* 16: 77.

MacLENNAN, B.W. 1965 "Co-therapy". *International Journal of Group Psychotherapy* 15: 154.

MacLENNAN, B.W. and N. FELSENFELD 1968 *Group Counseling and Psychotherapy With Adolescents*. New York: Columbia University Press.

MANN, R.D. 1967 *Interpersonal Styles and Group Development.* New York: Wiley.

MASLER, E.G. 1969 "The Interpretation of Projective Identification in Group Psychotherapy." *International Journal of Group Psychotherapy* 19: 441-47.

McGEE, T.F., F.R. RACUSEN, and B.N. SCHUMAN 1972 "Termination in Group Psychotherapy." *American Journal of Psychotherapy* 26: 521-32.

McGEE, T.F. and B. SCHUMAN 1970 "The Nature of the Co-therapy Relationship." *International Journal of Group Psychotherapy* 20: 25-31.

McGee, T.F., M. WILLIAMS, F.R. RACUSEN, and J. COWEN 1968 "Further Evaluation of Small Group Living Program With Schizophrenics." *Archives of General Psychiatry* 19: 717-26.

McINTYRE, C.J. 1952 "Acceptance by Others and Its Relation to Acceptance of Self and Others." *Journal of Abnormal and Social Psychology* 47: 624-25.

McNEIL, J.N. and A. VERWOEROT 1972 "A Group Treatment Program Combined wih a Work Project on a Geriatric Unit of a State Hospital." *Journal of the American Geriatrics Society* 20: 259-64.

MILLER, P.R. and L. FERNONE "Group Psychotherapy With Depressed Women." American Journal of Psychiatry 123: 701-703.

MILLS, T.M. 1964 *Group Transformation: An Analysis of a Learning Group.* Englewood Cliffs, N.J.: Prentice-Hall.

MINTZ, E. 1963 "Special Values of Co-therapists in Group Psychotherapy." International Journal of Group Psychotherapy 13: 127-32.

MOWATT, M.H. 1972 "Group Psychotherapy for Stepfathers and Their Wives." *Psychotherapy: Theory, Research and Practices* 9:328-31.

MOXNES, P. 1974 "Verbal Communication Level and Anxiety in Psychotherapeutic Groups." *Journal of Counseling Psychology* 21: 399-403.

NACHT, S., M. BOUVET, M. BENASSY, and F. LECHAT 1954 "Criteria for Terminating Psychoanalytic Treatment," *Revue Francais Psychanalytique.* 18: 328-65.

NASH, E., J. FRANK, L. GLIDEMAN, S. IMBER, and A. STONE 1957 "Some Factors Related to Patients Remaining in Group Psychotherapy." *International Journal of Group Psychotherapy* 7: 264-75.

NEIGHBOR, J.E., M. BEACH, D. BROWN, D. KENIN, and J. VISHER 1963 "An Approach to the Selection of Patients for Group Psychotherapy. Pp. 413-23 in M. Rosenbaum and M. Berger (eds.), *Group Psychotherapy and Group Function.* New York: Basic Books.

NORTHEN, H. 1969 *Social Work With Groups.* New York: Columbia University Press.

ORANGE, A.J. 1955 "A Note on Brief Group Psychotherapy With Psychotic Patients." *International Journal of Group Psychotherapy* 5: 80-83.

ORMONT, L.R. 1957 "The Preparation of Patients for Group Psychoanalysis." *American Journal of Psychotherapy* 11: 841.

ORMONT, L.R. 1968 "Group Resistance and the Therapeutic Contract." *International Journal of Group Psychotherapy* 18: 147-154.

OSTERRIETH, P.A. 1969 "Adolescence: Some Psychological Aspects." Pp. 11-21 in G. Caplan and S. Lebovich (eds.), *Adolescence: Psychosocial Perspectives.* New York: Basic Books.

PARKS, C.M. 1964 "Recent Bereavement as a Cause of Mental Illness." *British Journal of Psychiatry* 110: 198-204.

PAYN, S.B. 1974 "Reaching Chronic Schizophrenic Patients With Group Pharmacotherapy." *International Journal of Group Psychotherapy* 24: 25-31.

PHILLIPS, G.M. 1966 *Communication and the Small Group.* Indianapolis: Babbs-Merrill.

PINE, I., W.E. TODD, and C. BOENHEIM 1963 "Special Problems of Resistance in Co-therapy Groups." *International Journal of Group Psychotherapy* 13: 355.

PINSKY, S. and E.S. LEVY 1964 "Social Group Work in a Private Hospital." *Mental Hospitals* 15: 516-24.

RABIN, H.M. 1967 "How Does Co-therapy Compare with Regular Group Therapy?" *American Journal of Psychotherapy* 21: 249-52.

RASKIN, N.J. 1954 "Play Therapy With Blind Children." *New Outlook for the Blind* 48: 290-92.

REDL, F. 1942 "Group Emotion and Leadership." *Psychiatry* 5: 573-96.

REDL, F. 1951 "The Art of Group Composition." Pp. 76-96 in Susanne Schulze (ed.), *Creative Group Living in a Children's Institution.* New York: Free Press.

REDL, F. 1966 *When We Deal With Children.* New York: Free Press.

REES, T.P. and M.M. GLATT 1955 "The Organization of a Mental Hospital on the Basis of Group Participation." *International Journal of Group Psychotherapy* 5: 157-61.

RHODES, S.L. 1973 "Short-Term Groups of Latency-Age Children in a School Setting." *International Journal of Group Psychotherapy* 23: 204-16.

RICHMOND, A.H. and S. SCHECTER 1964 "A Spontaneous Request for Treatment by a Group of Adolescents." *International Journal of Group Psychotherapy* 14: 97-106.

RIPPLE, L. 1964 "Motivation, Capacity, and Opportunity; Studies in Casework Theory and Practice." Chicago: School of Social Services Administration, University of Chicago.

ROBINSON, L.H. 1974 "Group Work With Parents of Retarded Adolescents." *American Journal of Psychotherapy* 18: 397-408.

ROSENTHAL, L. 1953 "Countertransference in Activity Group Therapy." *International Journal of Group Psychotherapy* 3: 431-40.

SAMUELS, A.S. 1964 "The Use of Group Balance as a Therapeutic Technique." *Archives of General Psychiatry* 11: 411-20.

SARRI, R.C. and M.J. GALINSKY 1967 "A Conceptual Framework for Group Development," in R. Vinter (ed.), *Readings in Group Work Practice.* Ann Arbor: Campus Publishers.

SCHAFER, R.A. 1959 "Generative Empathy in the Treatment Situation." *The Psychoanalytic Quarterly* 28: 342-73.

SCHEIDLINGER, S. 1960 "Experiential Group Treatment of Severely Deprived Latency-Age Children." *American Journal of Orthopsychiatry* 30: 356-68.

SCHEIDLINGER, S. 1964 "Identification: The Sense of Belonging and of Identity in Small Groups." *International Journal of Group Psychotherapy* 14: 291-306.

SCHEIDLINGER, S. 1966 "The Concept of Empathy in Group Psychotherapy." *International Journal of Group Psychotherapy* 16: 413-24.

SCHLESINGER, L., J.M. JACKSON, and J. BUTMAN 1960 "Leader-Member Interaction in Management Committees." *Journal of Abnormal Social Psychology* 61: 360-64.

SCHONBAR, R.A. 1973 "Group Co-therapists and Sex-Role Identification." *American Journal of Psychotherapy* 27: 540.

SCHREIBER, S.C. 1969 "Some Special Forms of Aggressiveness in Activity Group Therapy and Their Impact on the Therapist." *Smith College Studies in Social Work* 39: 138-46.

SCHRODER, H. and O.J. HARVEY 1963 "Conceptual Organization and Group Structure. In D.J. Harvey, (ed.), *Motivation and Social Interaction.* New York: Ronald Press.

SCHUAL, F., H. SALTER, and M.G. PALEY 1971 " 'Thematic' Group Therapy in the Treatment of Hospitalized Alcoholic Patients." *International Journal of Group Psychotherapy* 21: 226-33.

SCHUTZ, W.C. 1966 *The Interpersonal Underworld.* Palo Alto, Calif.: Science and Behavior Books.

SCHWARTZ, E.K. and A. WOLF 1964 "On Countertransference in Group Psychotherapy." *Journal of Psychology* 51: 131-42.

SHADER, R.I., and H.Y. MELTZER 1968 "The Breast Metaphor and the Group." *International Journal of Group Psychotherapy* 18: 110-113.

SHARPE, R., E. GRIFFIN, F. SACHS, and B. LEVINE 1969 *A Report on Group Work Services Among Pregnant Adolescents in the Inner City.* Chicago: Florence Crittenton Association of America.

SHATAN, C.F., B. BRODY, and E.R. GHENT 1962 "Countertransference: Its Reflection in the Process of Peer-Group Supervision." *International Journal of Group Psychotherapy* 12: 335-46.

SHELDON, W.D. and T. LANDSMAN 1950 "An Investigation of Non-Directive Group Therapy With Students in Academic Difficulty." *Journal of Consulting Psychology* 14: 210-15.

SHELLOW, R.S., J.L. WARD, and S. RUBENFELD 1958 "Group Therapy and the Institutionalized Delinquent." *International Journal of Group Psychotherapy* 8: 265-75.

SHEPHERD, C. 1954 *Small Groups.* San Francisco: Chandler.

SINGER, M., 1974 "Comments and Caveats Regarding Adolescent Groups in a Combined Approach." *International Journal of Group Psychotherapy* 24: 429-38.

SLATER, P.E. 1958 "Contrasting Correlates of Group Size." *Sociometry* 21: 129-39.

SLATER, P.E. 1966 *Microcosm: Structural, Psychological and Religious Evolution in Groups.* New York: Wiley.

SLAVSON, S.R. 1950 *Analytic Group Psychotherapy With Children, Adolescents and Adults.* New York: Columbia University Press.

SLAVSON, S.R. 1957 "Are There Group Dynamics in Therapy Groups?" *International Journal of Group Psychotherapy* 7: 131-54.

SLAVSON, S.R. 1964 *A Textbook in Analytic Group Psychotherapy.* New York: International Universities Press.

SMITH, P.B. 1974 "Group Composition As a Determinant of Kelman's Social Influence Modes." *European Journal of Social Psychology* 4: 261-77.

SNOEK, J.D. 1962 "Some Effects of Rejection Upon Attraction to a Group." *Journal of Abnormal Social Psychology* 64: 175-82.

SOLMS, H. and M. de MEURON 1969 "Group Therapy for Alcoholics in the Psychiatric Hospital Environment: Preliminary Results of a Practical Experience Under Difficult Conditions." *Toxicomanies* 2: 201-16.

SOLOMON, J.C. and G.F. SOLOMON 1963 "Group Psychotherapy with Father and Son as Co-therapists: Some Dyanamic Considerations." *International Journal of Group Psychotherapy* 13: 133-40.

SPEAR, F.G. 1960 "Deterioration in Schizophrenic Control Groups." *British Journal of Medical Psychology* 33: 143-48.

SPOTNITZ, H. 1952 "A Psychoanalytic View of Resistance in Groups." *International Journal of Group Psychotherapy* 2: 3-9.

STEINZOR, BERNARD 1950 "The Spatial Factor in Face-to-Face Discussion Groups." *Journal of Abnormal and Social Psychology* 45: 552-55.

STEWART, D.A. 1954 "The Psychogenesis of Empathy." *The Psychoanalytic Review* 41: 216-28.

STOCK, D. 1962 "Interpersonal Concerns During the Early Sessions of Therapy Groups." *International Journal of Group Psychotherapy* 12: 14-26.

STOTLAND, E., N.B. COTTRELL, and G. LAING 1960 "Group Interaction and Perceived Similarity of Members." *Journal of Abnormal and Social Psychology* 61: 335-40.

STRUNK, C. and L. WITKIN 1974 "The Transformation of a Latency-Age Girls' Group From Unstructured Play to Problem-Focused Discussion." *International Journal of Group Psychotherapy* 24: 460-70.

SUGAR, M. 1974 "Interpretive Group Psychotherapy With Latency Children." *Journal of Child Psychiatry* 13: 648-66.

SUGAR, M. 1975 "The Structure and Setting of Adolescent Therapy Groups." In M. Sugar (ed.) *Adolescent in Group and Family Therapy.* New York: Brunner Mazel.

TANAKA, H. 1962 "Group Living on a Psychiatric Ward." *Social Work* 7: 51-58.

THELEN, H.A. 1954 *Dynamics of Groups at Work.* Chicago: University of Chicago Press.

THEODORSON, G.A. 1962 "The Function of Hostility in Small Groups." *Journal of Social Psychology* 56: 57-66.

TOWEY, M.R., S.W. SEARS, J.A. WILLIAMS, N. KAUFMAN and M.K. CUNNINGHAM 1966 "Group Activities With Psychiatric Inpatients." *Social Work* 11: 50-56.

TUCKER, D.M. 1973 "Some Relationships Between Individual and Group Development." *Human Development* 16: 249-72.

TUCKMAN, B. 1965 "Developmental Sequence in Small Groups." *Psychological Bulletin* 63: 384-99.

VAN SCOY, M. 1972 "Activity Group Therapy: A Bridge Between Play and Work." *Child Welfare* 51: 528-34.

VINTER, R.D. (ed.) 1967 *Readings in Group Work Practice.* Michigan: Campus Publishers.

WAX, JOHN 1960 "Criteria for Grouping Hospitalized Mental Patients." *Use of Groups in the Psychiatric Setting.* New York: National Association of Social Workers.

WEIGERT, E. 1960 "Loneliness and Trust: Basic Factors of Human Existence." *Psychiatry* 23: 121-31.

WEINER, M. 1973 "Termination of Group Psychotherapy." *Group Process* 5: 85-96.

WERNER, H. 1948 *Comparative Psychology of Mental Development.* New York: Follett.

WHITAKER, D.S. and M.A. LIEBERMAN 1964 *Psychotherapy Through Group Process.* New York: Atherton Press.

WHITMAN, R.M., M.A. LIEBERMAN and D. STOCK 1960 "The Relation Between Individual and Group Conflicts in Psychotherapy." *International Journal of Group Psychotherapy* 10: 259-86.

WILLIAMS, M. 1966 "Limitations, Fantasies, and Security Operations of Beginning Group Psychotherapists." *International Journal of Group Psychotherapy* 16: 150-62.

WINDER, A.E., L. FERRINI, and G.E. GABY 1965 "Group Therapy With Parents of Children in a Residential Treatment Center." *Child Welfare* 44: 266-71.

WINDER, A.E. and S.A. TIERNEY 1963 "A Conjoint Use of Casework and Group Psychotherapy with the Parents of Emotionally Disturbed Children." *Child Welfare* 47: 7-16.

WINDER, C.L., F.Z. AHMAD, A. BANDURA, and L.C. RAU 1962 "Dependency of Patients, Psychotherapists' Responses, and Apsects of Psychotherapy." *Journal of Consulting Psychology* 26: 129-34.

WINICK, C. and H. HOLT 1961 "Some External Modalities of Group Psychotherapy and Their Dynamic Significance. *American Journal of Psychotherapy* 15: 56-62.

WINNICOTT, D.W. 1960 "Counter-Transference, Part III." *British Journal of Medical Psychology* 33: 17-21.

WODARSKI, J.S., R.A. FELDMAN, and N. FLAX 1973 "Social Learning Theory and Group Work Practice With Antisocial Children." *Clinical Social Work Journal* 1: 78-93.

WOLF, A. 1963 "Resistance to Joining a Group." Pp. 277-79 in M. Rosenbaum and M. Berger, (eds), *Group Psychotherapy and Group Function.* New York: Basic Books.

WOLMAN, B.B. 1969 "Interactional Group Psychotherapy With Schizophrenics." *Psychotherapy: Theory, Research and Practice* 6: 194:98.

YALOM, I.D. 1966 "A Study of Group Therapy Dropouts." *Archives of General Psychiatry* 14: 393-414.

YALOM, I.D. 1966 "Problems of Neophyte Group Therapists." *International Journal of Social Psychiatry* 12: 52-59.

YALOM, I.D., P.S. HOUTS, G. NEWELL, and K.H. RAND 1967 "Preparation of Patients for Group Psychotherapy: A Controlled Study." *Archives of General Psychiatry* 17: 416-27.

YALOM, I.D. 1975 *The Theory and Practice of Group Psychotherapy.* New York: Basic Books.

YALOM, I.D., and K. RAND 1966 "Compatibility and Cohesiveness in Therapy Groups." *Archives of General Psychiatry* 13: 267-76.

ZILLER, R.C., and R.V. EXLIN 1958 "Some Consequences of Age Heterogeneity in Decision Making Groups," *Sociometry* 21: 198-211.

ZIMMERMAN, D. 1968 "Notes on the Reactions of a Therapeutic Group to Termination of Treatment by One of its Members," *International Journal of Group Psychotherapy* 18: 86-94.

Index